The IDG Books *Creating Cool* Series Advantage

We at IDG Books Worldwide developed *Creating Cool Web Applets with Java* to meet your growing need for quick access to the most complete and accurate computer information available. Our books work the way you do: They focus on accomplishing specific tasks — not learning random functions. Our books are not long-winded manuals or dry reference tomes. In each book, expert authors tell you exactly what you can do with your new technology and software and how to evaluate its usefulness for your needs. Easy-to-follow, step-by-step sections; comprehensive coverage; and convenient access in language and design — it's all here.

The authors of IDG books are uniquely qualified to give you expert advice as well as to provide insightful tips and techniques not found anywhere else. Our authors maintain close contact with end users through feedback from articles, training sessions, e-mail exchanges, user group participation, and consulting work. Because our authors know the realities of daily computer use and are directly tied to the reader, our books have a strategic advantage.

Our authors have the experience to approach a topic in the most efficient manner, and we know that you, the reader, will benefit from a "one-on-one" relationship with the author. Our research shows that readers make computer book purchases because they want expert advice. Because readers want to benefit from the author's experience, the author's voice is always present in an IDG book.

In addition, the author is free to include or recommend useful software in an IDG book. The software that accompanies each book is not intended to be a casual filler but is linked to the content, theme, or procedures of the book. We know that you will benefit from the included software.

You will find what you need in this book whether you read it from cover to cover, section by section, or simply one topic at a time. As a computer user, you deserve a comprehensive resource of answers. We at IDG Books Worldwide are proud to deliver that resource with *Creating Cool Web Applets with Java*.

Brenda McLaughlin
Senior Vice President and Group Publisher

Internet: YouTellUs@idgbooks.com

CREATING COOL™ WEB APPLETS WITH JAVA®

Paul J. Perry

CREATING COOL™ WEB APPLETS WITH JAVA®

Paul J. Perry

IDG Books Worldwide, Inc.
An International Data Group Company

Foster City, CA ♦ Chicago, IL ♦ Indianapolis, IN ♦ Braintree, MA ♦ Southlake, TX

Creating Cool™ Web Applets with Java®

Published by
IDG Books Worldwide, Inc.
An International Data Group Company
919 E. Hillsdale Blvd.
Suite 400
Foster City, CA 94404

Library of Congress Catalog Card No.: 96-75746

ISBN: 1-56884-881-1

Printed in the United States of America

10 9 8 7 6 5 4 3 2 1

1A/SW/QU/ZW/IN

Distributed in the United States by IDG Books Worldwide, Inc.

Distributed by Macmillan Canada for Canada; by Computer and Technical Books for the Caribbean Basin; by Contemporanea de Ediciones for Venezuela; by Distribuidora Cuspide for Argentina; by CITEC for Brazil; by Ediciones ZETA S.C.R. Ltda. for Peru; by Editorial Limusa SA for Mexico; by Transworld Publishers Limited in the United Kingdom and Europe; by Al-Maiman Publishers & Distributors for Saudi Arabia; by Simron Pty. Ltd. for South Africa; by IDG Communications (HK) Ltd. for Hong Kong; by Toppan Company Ltd. for Japan; by Addison Wesley Publishing Company for Korea; by Longman Singapore Publishers Ltd. for Singapore, Malaysia, Thailand, and Indonesia; by Unalis Corporation for Taiwan; by WS Computer Publishing Company, Inc. for the Philippines; by WoodsLane Pty. Ltd. for Australia; by WoodsLane Enterprises Ltd. for New Zealand.

For general information on IDG Books Worldwide's books in the U.S., please call our Consumer Customer Service department at 800-762-2974. For reseller information, including discounts and premium sales, please call our Reseller Customer Service department at 800-434-3422.

For information on where to purchase IDG Books Worldwide's books outside the U.S., contact IDG Books Worldwide at 415-655-3021 or fax 415-655-3295.

For information on translations, contact Marc Jeffrey Mikulich, Director, Foreign & Subsidiary Rights, at IDG Books Worldwide, 415-655-3018 or fax 415-655-3295.

For sales inquiries and special prices for bulk quantities, write to the address above or call IDG Books Worldwide at 415-655-3200.

For information on using IDG Books Worldwide's books in the classroom, or ordering examination copies, contact the Education Office at 800-434-2086 or fax 817-251-8174.

For authorization to photocopy items for corporate, personal, or educational use, please contact Copyright Clearance Center, 222 Rosewood Drive, Danvers, MA 01923, or fax 508-750-4470.

About the Author

Paul J. Perry is a computer book author living in sunny California who specializes in writing books about programming, online communications, and multimedia electronic publishing. His previous book, *World Wide Web SECRETS,* was a featured selection for the Computer Book of the Month Club.

ABOUT IDG BOOKS WORLDWIDE

Welcome to the world of IDG Books Worldwide.

IDG Books Worldwide, Inc., is a subsidiary of International Data Group, the world's largest publisher of computer-related information and the leading global provider of information services on information technology. IDG was founded more than 25 years ago and now employs more than 7,700 people worldwide. IDG publishes more than 250 computer publications in 67 countries (see listing below). More than 70 million people read one or more IDG publications each month.

Launched in 1990, IDG Books Worldwide is today the #1 publisher of best-selling computer books in the United States. We are proud to have received 8 awards from the Computer Press Association in recognition of editorial excellence and three from Computer Currents' First Annual Readers' Choice Awards, and our best-selling *...For Dummies®* series has more than 19 million copies in print with translations in 28 languages. IDG Books Worldwide, through a joint venture with IDG's Hi-Tech Beijing, became the first U.S. publisher to publish a computer book in the People's Republic of China. In record time, IDG Books Worldwide has become the first choice for millions of readers around the world who want to learn how to better manage their businesses.

Our mission is simple: Every one of our books is designed to bring extra value and skill-building instructions to the reader. Our books are written by experts who understand and care about our readers. The knowledge base of our editorial staff comes from years of experience in publishing, education, and journalism — experience which we use to produce books for the '90s. In short, we care about books, so we attract the best people. We devote special attention to details such as audience, interior design, use of icons, and illustrations. And because we use an efficient process of authoring, editing, and desktop publishing our books electronically, we can spend more time ensuring superior content and spend less time on the technicalities of making books.

You can count on our commitment to deliver high-quality books at competitive prices on topics you want to read about. At IDG Books Worldwide, we continue in the IDG tradition of delivering quality for more than 25 years. You'll find no better book on a subject than one from IDG Books Worldwide.

John Kilcullen
President and CEO
IDG Books Worldwide, Inc.

IDG Books Worldwide, Inc., is a subsidiary of International Data Group, the world's largest publisher of computer-related information and the leading global provider of information services on information technology. International Data Group publishes over 250 computer publications in 67 countries. Seventy million people read one or more International Data Group publications each month. International Data Group's publications include: **ARGENTINA:** Computerworld Argentina, GamePro, Infoworld, PC World Argentina; **AUSTRALIA:** Australian Macworld, Client/Server Journal, Computer Living, Computerworld, Digital News, Network World, PC World, Publishing Essentials, Reseller; **AUSTRIA:** Computerwelt, PC TEST; **BELARUS:** PC World Belarus; **BELGIUM:** Data News; **BRAZIL:** Annuário de Informática, Computerworld Brazil, Connections, Super Game Power, Macworld, PC World Brazil, Publish Brazil, SUPERGAME; **BULGARIA:** Computerworld Bulgaria, Networkworld/Bulgaria, PC & MacWorld Bulgaria; **CANADA:** CIO Canada, ComputerWorld Canada, InfoCanada, Network World Canada, Reseller World; **CHILE:** Computerworld Chile, GamePro, PC World Chile; **COLUMBIA:** Computerworld Colombia, GamePro, PC World Colombia; **COSTA RICA:** PC World Costa Rica/Nicaragua; **THE CZECH AND SLOVAK REPUBLICS:** Computerworld Czechoslovakia, Elektronika Czechoslovakia, PC World Czechoslovakia; **DENMARK:** Communications World, Computerworld Danmark, Macworld Danmark, PC World Danmark, PC World Danmark Supplements, TECH World; **DOMINICAN REPUBLIC:** PC World Republica Dominicana; **ECUADOR:** PC World Ecuador, GamePro; **EGYPT:** Computerworld Middle East, PC World Middle East; **EL SALVADOR:** PC World Centro America; **FINLAND:** MikroPC, Tietoverkko, Tietoviikko; **FRANCE:** Distributique, Golden, Info PC, Le Guide du Monde Informatique, Le Monde Informatique, Reseaux & Telecoms; **GERMANY:** Computer Business, Computerwoche, Computerwoche Extra, Computerwoche Focus, Electronic Entertainment, GamePro, I/M Information Management, Macwelt, PC Welt; **GREECE:** GamePro, Macworld & Publish; **GUATEMALA:** PC World Centro America; **HONDURAS:** PC World Centro America; **HONG KONG:** Computerworld Hong Kong, PCWorld Hong Kong, Publish in Asia; **HUNGARY:** ABCD CD-ROM, Computerworld Szamitastechnika, PC & Mac World Hungary, PC-X Magazine; **INDIA:** Computerworld India, PC World India, Publish in Asia; **INDONESIA:** InfoKomputer PC World, Komputek Computerworld, Publish in Asia; **IRELAND:** ComputerScope, PC Live!; **ISRAEL:** PC World 32 BIT, People & Computers; **ITALY:** Computerworld Italia, Computerworld Italia Special Editions, Lotus Italia, Macworld Italia, Networking Italia, PC Shopping, PC World Italia, PC World/Walt Disney; **JAPAN:** Macworld Japan, Nikkei Personal Computing, SunWorld Japan, Windows World Japan; **KENYA:** East African Computer News; **KOREA:** Hi-Tech Information/Computerworld, Macworld Korea, PC World Korea; **MACEDONIA:** PC World Macedonia; **MALAYSIA:** Computerworld Malaysia, PC World Malaysia, Publish in Asia; **MEXICO:** Computerworld Mexico, GamePro, Macworld, PC World Mexico; **MYANMAR:** PC World Myanmar; **NETHERLANDS:** Computable, Computer! Totaal, LAN Magazine, Macworld, Net Magazine; **NEW ZEALAND:** Computer Buyer, Computerworld New Zealand, MTB, Network World, PC World New Zealand; **NICARAGUA:** PC World Costa Rica/Nicaragua; **NIGERIA:** PC World Africa; **NORWAY:** Computerworld Norge, Computerworld Privat, CW Rapport Klient/Tjener, CW Rapport Nettverk & Telecom, CW Rapport Offentlig Sektor, IDG's KURSGUIDE, Macworld Norge, Multimedia World, PC World Ekspress, PC World Nettverk, PC World Norge, PC World's Produktguide, Windows Spesial; **PAKISTAN:** Computerworld Pakistan, PC World Pakistan; **PANAMA:** GamePro, PC World Panama; **PARAGUAY:** PC World Paraguay; **P. R. OF CHINA:** China Computerworld, China Infoworld, Computer & Communication, Electronic Product World, Electronics Today, Game Camp, PC World China, Popular Computer Week, Software World, Telecom Product World; **PERU:** Computerworld Peru, GamePro, PC World Profesional Peru, PC World Peru; **POLAND:** Computerworld Poland, Computerworld Special Report, Macworld, Networld, PC World Komputer; **PHILIPPINES:** Computerworld Philippines, PC Digest, Publish in Asia; **PORTUGAL:** Cerebro/PC World, Correio Informático/Computerworld, Mac•In/PC•In Portugal; **PUERTO RICO:** PC World Puerto Rico; **ROMANIA:** Computerworld Romania, PC World Romania, Telecom Romania; **RUSSIA:** Computerworld Rossiya, Network World Russia, PC World Russia; **SINGAPORE:** Computerworld Singapore, PC World Singapore, Publish in Asia; **SLOVENIA:** MONITOR; **SOUTH AFRICA:** Computing S.A., Network World S.A., Software World; **SPAIN:** Computerworld España, COMUNICACIONES WORLD, Dealer World, Macworld España, PC World España; **SWEDEN:** CAP&Design, Computer Sweden, Corporate Computing, MacWorld, Maxi Data, MikroDatorn, Nätverk & Kommunikation, PC/Aktiv, PC World, Windows World; **SWITZERLAND:** Computerworld Schweiz, Macworld Schweiz, PCtip; **TAIWAN:** Computerworld Taiwan, Macworld Taiwan, PC World Taiwan, Publish Taiwan, Windows World; **THAILAND:** Thai Computerworld, Publish in Asia; **TURKEY:** Computerworld Monitör, MACWORLD Turkiye, PC WORLD Turkiye; **UKRAINE:** Computerworld Kiev, Computers & Software Magazine, PC World Ukraine; **UNITED KINGDOM:** Acorn User, Amiga Action, Amiga Computing, Amiga, Appletalk, CD Powerplay, CD-ROM Now, Computing, Connexion, GamePro, Lotus Magazine, Macaction, Macworld, Open Computing, Parents and Computers, PC Home, PC Works, The WEB; **UNITED STATES:** Cable in the Classroom, CD Review, CIO Magazine, Computerworld, Computerworld Client/Server Journal, Digital Video Magazine, DOS World, Electronic, InfoWorld, I-Way, Macworld, Maximize, MULTIMEDIA WORLD, Network World, PC World, PUBLISH, SWATPro Magazine, Video Event, WebMaster; **URUGUAY:** PC World Uruguay; **VENEZUELA:** Computerworld Venezuela, GamePro, PC World Venezuela; and **VIETNAM:** PC World Vietnam 10/17/95a

Dedication

This book is dedicated to my family and friends, who have shown terrific support for me ever since I started writing. Thank you!

Credits

Senior Vice President and Group Publisher
Brenda McLaughlin

Acquisitions Manager
Gregory Croy

Acquisitions Editor
Ellen L. Camm

Marketing Manager
Melisa M. Duffy

Managing Editor
Andy Cummings

Administrative Assistant
Laura J. Moss

Editorial Assistant
Timothy Borek

Production Director
Beth Jenkins

Production Assistant
Jacalyn L. Pennywell

Supervisor of Project Coordination
Cindy L. Phipps

Supervisor of Page Layout
Kathie S. Schnorr

Supervisor of Graphics and Design
Shelley Lea

Reprint Coordination
Tony Augsburger
Theresa Sánchez-Baker
Todd Klemme

Blueline Coordinator
Patricia R. Reynolds

Media Archive Coordination
Leslie Popplewell
Melissa Stauffer
Jason Marcuson

Senior Development Editor
Erik Dafforn

Editor
Hugh Vandivier

Technical Reviewer
Greg Guntle

Associate Project Coordinator
Regina Snyder

Graphics Coordination
Gina Scott
Angela F. Hunckler

Production Page Layout
E. Shawn Aylsworth
Elizabeth Cárdenas-Nelson
Dominique DeFelice
Mark Owens

Proofreaders
Henry Lazarek
Christine Meloy Beck
Dwight Ramsey
Carl Saff
Robert Springer

Indexer
Sharon Hilgenberg

Cover Design
three 8 creative group

Acknowledgments

The IDG Books teams in Indianapolis, Indiana and Foster City, California deserve acknowledgment for making the process of writing this book easier. Thanks to Erik Dafforn and Melisa Duffy for providing inspiration at just the right time. Thanks to Greg Croy for asking me to do the project in the first place. Thanks to Ellen Camm for getting some hot software for the book's CD-ROM. Thanks to Greg Guntle for a complete technical edit. Thanks to Hugh Vandivier for activating my passive voice. Thanks to the layout and proofreading staff, who turned raw electrons into the book you're holding now. Finally, special thanks to Michael O'Connel at *JavaWorld* for writing the Foreword.

(The publisher would like to give special thanks to Patrick J. McGovern, without whom this book would not have been possible.)

Foreword xxiii
Introduction 1
Chapter 1: Introducing Java 5
Chapter 2: Working with Netscape Navigator 37
Chapter 3: A Review of HTML 61
Chapter 4: Introduction to Java Programming 107
Chapter 5: Incorporating Text and Graphics 145
Chapter 6: Incorporating Images and Animation 163
Chapter 7: Working with Sound 175
Chapter 8: Adding Interactivity 187
Chapter 9: Enhancing Web Pages with Java 209
Chapter 10: Network Communications 245
Chapter 11: User Interface Controls 265
Chapter 12: Windows and Dialog Boxes 299
Appendix A: HTML Quick Reference 323
Appendix B: Java Language Reference 329
Appendix C: Java Resources 335
Index 337
IDG BOOKS WORLDWIDE, INC.
END-USER LICENSE AGREEMENT 356

Installation Instructions **359**
Reader Response Card .... **Back of Book**

Foreword .... **xxiii**

Introduction **1**

What This Book Is About 1
What You Should Know to Use This Book 1
How This Book Is Organized 2
Text Conventions Used in This Book 3
A Note about Working with Java 4

Chapter 1: Introducing Java **5**

Cyberspace Is Taking Over the World 5
What Is Java Anyway? 9
About the Internet 11
About the World Wide Web 11
A History of the Web 12
Java Technology in Action 14
A History of Java 15
What about HotJava? 18
What about Netscape Navigator? 19
Technical Details About the Internet 20
Understanding TCP/IP 21
Understanding URLs 21
Cross-Platform Compatibility 23
The Features of Java 24
Interactive multimedia 24
Platform independence 26
Security 27
Software distribution and installation 28
Features multiplied 28

Uses for Java ... 29
Developer tool kits ... 29
Educational applications ... 30
Enhancing Web pages ... 30
Games and entertainment ... 32
Internet and Web access agents ... 32
Productivity tools ... 33
The list goes on ... 33
The Future of Java ... 33
Quick Overview ... 34

Chapter 2: Working with Netscape Navigator ... 37

Getting Started with Netscape ... 37
Installation ... 39
Starting Netscape ... 40
The Main Window ... 40
The preview area ... 41
The menu bar ... 42
Netscape's top-line display ... 43
The status bar ... 46
Using Program Options ... 47
Loading and saving HTML files ... 47
Printing files ... 50
Working with the history list ... 50
Working with bookmarks ... 50
Setting Options ... 53
Modifying Preferences ... 54
The Online Help System ... 56
The Help menu ... 56
Directory ... 58
Keyboard Shortcuts ... 58
Quick Overview ... 60

Chapter 3: A Review of HTML ... 61

Developing Home Pages ... 61
About Hypertext Markup Language ... 62
Does anybody know SGML? ... 62
The purpose of HTML ... 63
Advantages of HTML ... 65
Disadvantages of HTML ... 66
Using HTML ... 66
HTML file overview ... 67
Working with tags ... 67

Structural Formatting 68
Specifying an HTML file 68
Specifying the header 69
Specifying the body of your document 70
Adding comments 71
Paragraph Formatting 73
Line breaks 74
Horizontal rules 75
Specifying headings 77
Specifying pre-formatted text 78
Logical text formatting 82
Character Formatting 83
Displaying special characters 84
Displaying extended characters 86
List Specification Formatting 87
Unordered lists 87
Ordered lists 89
Directory and menu lists 90
Glossary lists 91
Formatting Hyperlinks 93
HTML and Multimedia 95
Viewing images 96
Image maps 97
Accessing sound 98
Viewing digital video 99
HTML Authoring Tools 104
Quick Overview 105

Chapter 4: Introduction to Java Programming 107

Object-Oriented Programming Overview 107
Object-Oriented Programming with Java 108
Making Java Applets 109
The last HTML tag you'll ever need to know 110
A Minimum Java Application 113
Program comments 114
Specifying class imports 114
Creating a class 115
Methods in action 116
Compiling the code 118
Java Language Information 120
Numerical object types 120
Alphabetic object types 122
Defining classes 123
Defining methods 124
Arrays 125

Introduction to Applet Events 125
Control Flow Statements 128
The if. . .else statement 128
The for loop 130
The while statement 132
The do. . . while statement 132
The switch statement 133
Passing Parameters to an Applet 134
Using the Java Development Kit 138
The Java compiler 138
The Java interpreter 139
The applet viewer 140
The Java documentation tool 140
The Java disassembler 141
Future Java Development Tools 142
Quick Overview 143

Chapter 5: Incorporating Text and Graphics 145

Displaying Text with Java 145
Working with fonts 147
Working with Color 153
Displaying Graphics 155
Displaying lines 155
Displaying squares and rectangles 155
Displaying shapes 158
The Polygon class 159
Displaying circular shapes 160
Quick Overview 161

Chapter 6: Incorporating Images and Animation 163

Drawing Images in Java 163
Still Frames Come to Life 167
How to animate pictures 168
Multithreaded code 169
The Animator Applet 171
Quick Overview 173

Chapter 7: Working with Sound 175

What is Sound? 175
Working with Sound Objects 176
Controlling audio playback 179
Playing Sound 179
Playing Random Sounds 181
Quick Overview 185

Chapter 8: Adding Interactivity 187

What Is Interactivity? 187
Keyboard Input 188
Keyboard events 188
Modifier keys 189
Special keys 190
Checking Mouse Buttons 194
Mouse movement events 198
Mouse dragging 199
Tying It All Together 203
Quick Overview 208

Chapter 9: Enhancing Web Pages with Java 209

Overview 209
Animator 210
ArcTest 212
BarChart 214
BlinkingText 216
BouncingHeads 217
CardTest 218
DitherTest 220
DrawTest 221
Fractal 222
GraphicsTest 224
GraphLayout 225
ImageMap 227
ImageTest 229
JumpingBox 230
MoleculeViewer 232
NervousText 233
ScrollingImages 235
SimpleGraph 236
SpreadSheet 237
TicTacToe 239
See also 240
TumblingDuke 240
UnderConstruction 241
WireFrame 242
Quick Overview 244

Chapter 10: Network Communications 245

Error Handling 245
About error handling 246
About exception handling 247
Displaying a New Web Page 251
The uniform resource locator class 251
Getting the applet context 252
Sample code 253
Opening Files at Your Web Site 257
Communicating with Sockets 261
Client socket connections 262
Server socket connections 263
Quick Overview 264

Chapter 11: User Interface Controls 265

About User Interface Controls 265
Working with Controls 266
Creating controls 268
Understanding Layout Managers 268
Choosing control locations 269
Working with Standard Controls 276
Adding label controls 276
Using buttons 277
Using checkboxes 278
Using radio buttons 279
Using choice items 280
Using text fields 280
Handling Standard Control Actions 281
An applet sample 283
Working with Enhanced Controls 286
List items 287
Scrollbar controls 288
Text areas 289
Handling Enhanced Control Events 290
A sample applet 291
Controlling the Status Line 294
A sample applet 295
Quick Overview 298

Chapter 12: Windows and Dialog Boxes 299

Working with Frames 299
Creating the frames 300
Menus and Menu Bars 304
Creating menus 305
Creating menu items 305
Submenu items 306
Checkbox menu items 307
Detecting menu action 308
Sample code 309
Working with Dialog Boxes 312
Sample dialog box 315
A sample applet 318
Quick Overview 322

Appendix A: HTML Quick Reference 323

Structural tags 323
Paragraph formatting 323
Character formatting 324
Logical text formatting 324
Hypertext links 324
Lists 325
In-line images and sound 325
Extended characters 325
Escape sequences 326
Embedding a Java applet 326
Netscape enhanced tags 328
Netscape tables 328
Netscape font specification 328

Appendix B: Java Language Reference 329

General Applet Construction 329
Data types 330
Character formatting sequences 330
Relational operators 331
Unary operators 331
Mathematical operators 331
Conditional statements 331
Program control statements 333
Defining classes 333
Defining methods 334
Exception handling 334

Appendix C: Java Resources 335

The Java home page 335
The Java newsgroup 335
The Java Developer page 336
The Symantec home page 336
The Borland home page 336
The Netscape home page 336
The JavaWorld home page 336

Index 337

IDG BOOKS WORLDWIDE, INC.
END-USER LICENSE AGREEMENT 356

Installation Instructions 359

Reader Response Card .... Back of Book

Foreword

If you're reading this book, you no doubt concern yourself with the Web. And you're likely wondering exactly how Java can enhance your Web development efforts. Well, you've turned to the right place.

Many Web sites today lack richness and interactivity. The bare-bones HTML Web pages grapple with the inherent constraints of the hypertext markup language. Indeed, HTML by itself leaves much to be desired. CGI scripts and proprietary, platform-specific extensions to HTML have added some spice, but they lack the robustness and versatility of a full-fledged programming language or application development environment.

Enter Java. Thanks to this programming language from Sun Microsystems, Web developers now have unprecedented control over how their Web pages look and behave, and can more easily deliver exciting, interactive content. If you want to create cool Web content or Web-based applications, Java should play a key role in your efforts.

Creating Cool Web Applets with Java shows Web developers how to use Java to enhance their Web sites. After reviewing the fundamentals of HTML, veteran author and software engineer Paul Perry explains in this book the fundamentals of Java program development in a way that even non-programmers can understand. Once you've grasped the three steps to creating Java applets for the Web and learned to write a simple "Hello World" Java program, you'll be ready to glide through the book's chapters on text and graphics, animation, sound, and interactivity, and then explore in detail how to enhance your Web pages with the power of Java, drawing from the book's plentiful supply of examples.

Java already has attracted broad attention and an abundance of hype, and as of early 1996, more than 1,000 Java applets exist. Most of these applets strive to bring Web pages to life with interactive, multimedia features. As companies rush to provide Java tools for non-programmers, more and more Web developers will be able to enhance their Web sites with Java-based content and applications.

Java's versatility means it will be used outside of Web applets, too — in embedded systems for consumer electronics, as the user interface in PDAs and $500 network appliances that connect consumers to the Internet, and as a full-fledged alternative to C and C++ for development of general applications (such as Krakatoa, CADIS Inc.'s $100,000 "publishing search and retrieval" software, which was written in Java). This broad range of uses gives Java resilience that other Web enhancers (such as Macromedia's Shockwave for Director and Microsoft's OCX/ActiveX technologies) lack.

Perhaps the greatest strength of Java, however, is its platform independence. This means it no longer matters what hardware or operating system your computer (or Internet appliance) has. Developers no longer have to port their products to multiple platforms or maintain multiple hardware- or OS-specific versions. (If Sun and its partners can indeed deliver on this promise, the Web may someday surpass Microsoft Windows as the most popular software application platform.)

For Web developers, Java's platform independence and widespread acceptance make it an obvious solution. People viewing your Web site won't be turned off by a requirement to first download the latest plug-in for their browser, and won't need a specific computer or operating system to experience your content in its full glory.

Despite the hype, the Internet and the World Wide Web most likely won't impact humanity as profoundly as fire or the wheel. On the other hand, pet rocks and disco it ain't. The Web — whether on the public Internet or on private corporate intranets — has staying power. Increasingly, it plays a key role in businesses' administrative functions and even in their core missions. Thanks to innovations such as Java, which greatly enhances developers' abilities to create cool (and functional) Web sites, the Web is becoming increasingly potent. And thanks to this book, even Web developers who don't know C++ from Pascal can easily employ the power of Java.

Michael O'Connell
Editor-in-Chief
JavaWorld magazine (`www.javaworld.com`)

What This Book Is About

Creating Cool Web Applets with Java is a book about developing Web applets with the Java programming language. This book teaches you how to create enhanced home pages that make the most of what Java can provide. At the same time, you will have a good time learning about this great new technology.

The book is for the user who wants to get up and running quickly and does not want to be burdened with arcane programmer talk. It starts with a review of the hypertext markup language (HTML), including coverage of the Netscape enhancements. You then immediately move on to specific ways to enhance your home pages through Java applications that incorporate the standard elements of multimedia: text, graphics, sound, and video. It even follows up by taking a special look at adding fast-paced interactive features to your Web pages.

What You Should Know to Use This Book

This book assumes that you are familiar with using DOS commands. For example, you should be able to list directories and create, execute, copy, and erase files. You should be familiar with tree-structured directories and know how to move within them. You should also be familiar with using Windows. You don't have to be any kind of computer superuser. If you know how to move the mouse, make menu selections, and query dialog boxes, you are plenty far along in your computing journeys to enjoy this book.

Even if you aren't connected to the Internet, you can use this book and software to learn how to design Web pages and learn the techniques of creating cool Web applications. If you already have a Web browser hooked up, you can easily explore files on your local computer and then log on to explore the many fascinating examples of Web-page design on the Internet itself.

How This Book Is Organized

Chapter 1: "Introducing Java" covers the basics of Java. You will also gain an understanding of the Internet, the World Wide Web, and a basic understanding of HTML. You will learn about what you can do with Java and why Java is such a powerful language.

Chapter 2: "Working with Netscape Navigator" takes a look at the newest version of Netscape Navigator and gives you the information you need to know about running Java applications with Netscape.

Chapter 3: "A Review of HTML" discusses the basics of creating HTML documents, including head and body information, page titles, paragraph and section-head marks, and other layout elements. It then continues on to describe the HTML 3.0 specification, which is used with the Netscape browser. Finally, the chapter ends by explaining how to incorporate basic Java applications into your Web page.

Chapter 4: "Introduction to Java Programming" covers the basic concepts you need to know in order to use Java. You will learn how to use the Java Developers Kit (JDK) and find out how an object-oriented language like Java can help you create better applications.

Chapter 5: "Incorporating Text and Graphics" shows you how to use Java to add specialized text and graphics to your Web page. You will find out how compelling a Web page can be when you take advantage of the fonts and graphics available through a system like Java.

Chapter 6: "Incorporating Images and Animation" provides instruction on implementing snazzy animation techniques. You will find out how to implement "bubble-gum for the eyes" using specialized Java animation classes that work to your favor in creating cool Web pages.

Chapter 7: "Working with Sound" defines how to use Java features in order to add cool sound effects and impressive audio elements to your Web pages. You will also learn how to work with audio sound formats and discover ideas on creating your own audio sound.

Chapter 8: "Adding Interactivity" explores the idea of adding user input to your Java applications. The chapter specifically looks at obtaining input from the mouse and keyboard. This is the place where you will find out how to create real-time applications that require user input.

Chapter 9: "Enhancing Web Pages with Java" shows you how to use the Java features that you have already learned to enhance your Web pages. In this chapter, you will really learn how to integrate Java features into a single, cool-looking Web page.

Chapter 10: "Network Communications" teaches you how to program an applet that goes out over the Internet and retrieves data from your Web site.

Chapter 11: "User Interface Controls" examines using Java to create a graphical user interface within an applet.

Chapter 12: "Windows and Dialog Boxes" explores user interfaces in further detail by showing you how to open windows and dialog boxes separately from the Web browser.

Appendix A: "HTML Quick Reference" and **Appendix B: "Java Language Reference"** provide a nice summary of all the HTML tags and Java language elements explained throughout the book.

Appendix C: "Java Resources" provides you with sources for further information about Java.

Appendix D: "Glossary" defines most Web- and Java-related terms used in this book.

Text Conventions Used in This Book

To get the most out of this book, you need to know something about how it is designed. Each chapter contains bold text, italicized text, bulleted lists, numbered lists, figures, code listings, and tables of information. I think you'll agree that all these design features will help you understand the material being presented.

This book uses several margin icons to lead your eye to areas that reveal hidden and little-understood facts about Java and the World Wide Web.

The Tip icon separates tips and techniques from the rest of the text. You'll find information such as programming tips, tricks, and shortcuts in a tip box.

The Note icon holds convenient notes that help you learn to program and use Java. A note box includes a brief statement to remind you about important facts about using Java.

The Caution icon provides important cautions about problems or possibly unwanted side effects that might occur while using Java, as well as important cautions.

A Note about Working with Java

Most readers will already have experience working with computers and maybe even creating Web pages in HTML. For best results with this book, you should have basic computer knowledge and know some programming basics. If you have such experience, you probably need no further explanation about how to learn effectively.

If, however, you are approaching Java as your first programming experience, you need to know an important point about learning: You cannot learn without writing sample programs, running programs, and observing the way they work (or possibly don't work). It's just like getting in healthy physical shape. You wouldn't exercise once and assume you will be healthy for the rest of your life. It takes attention and continued practice. The same is true when learning computer concepts like working with Java.

Because practicing programming is essential to learning programming, this book includes many sample programs so that you can see how they work. However, I also urge you to try different things. Experimenting is important when trying to learn something really well.

Introducing Java

In This Chapter

What Java can do for the Internet and the World Wide Web.

Background information about the Internet, the World Wide Web, and Java.

How HotJava and Netscape Navigator fit into the Java picture.

Major features of Java, along with an example of applications you can create with Java.

This chapter covers the basics of what Java is. You will also gain a good background understanding of the Internet and the World Wide Web. You will learn what you can do with Java and why Java is such a powerful technology. Along the way, you will learn about the history, features, and uses for Java.

Cyberspace Is Taking Over the World

Question: What do CNN, NBC, CBS, *The Wall Street Journal*, *The San Francisco Chronicle*, BMW, Honda, Toyota, MGM, Sony Pictures, Warner Bros., and Disney all have in common? Answer: They all publish material on the Internet's World Wide Web.

You should notice something about these companies. None of them is a computer hardware manufacturer or a software developer. Most of us are not surprised to find companies like IBM, Microsoft, Sun, Borland, Symantec, Compaq, and HP publishing content on the Web. After all, these are computer companies, and we expect their participation in the Internet.

However, when network television stations (see Figure 1-1), newspaper publications (see Figure 1-2), automobile manufacturers (see Figure 1-3), and entertainment companies (see Figure 1-4) stand up and start creating a presence on the Internet, you know something important is happening.

Figure 1-1: The Cable News Network (CNN) home page.

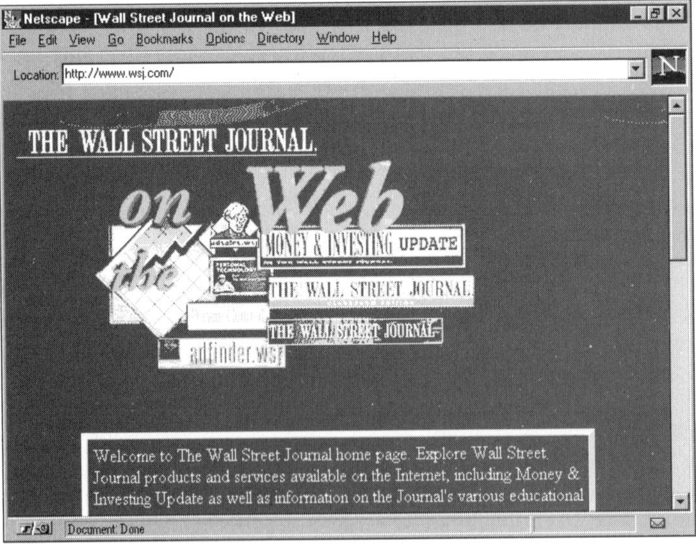

Figure 1-2: The *Wall Street Journal* home page.

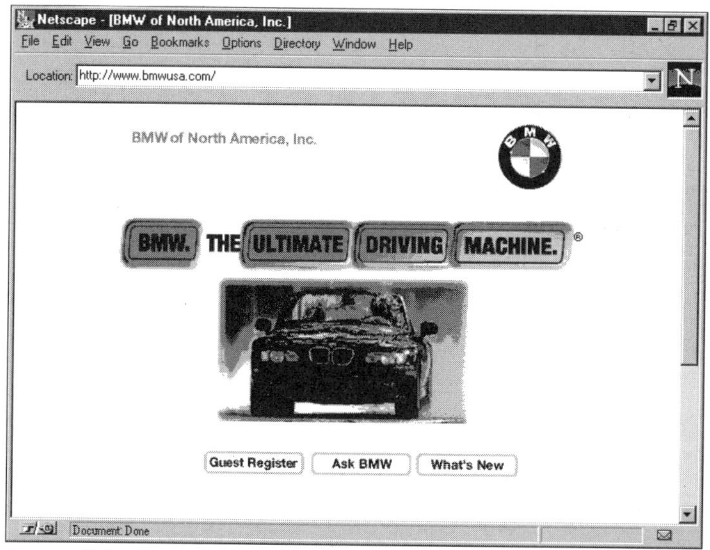

Figure 1-3: The BMW of North America home page.

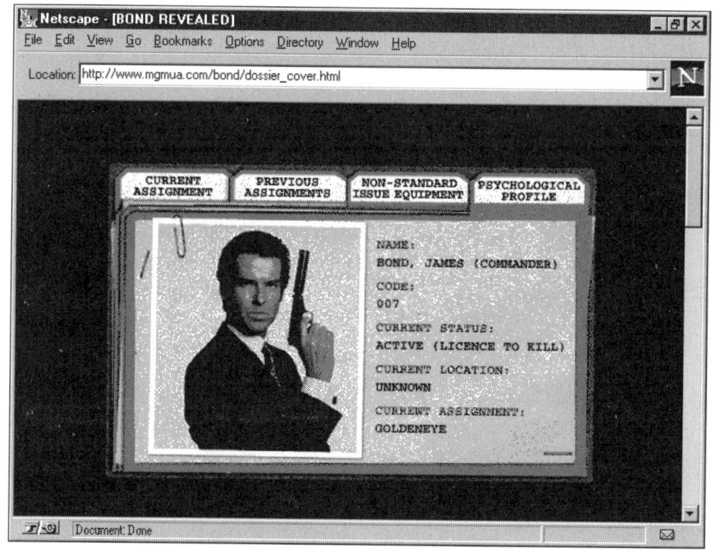

Figure 1-4: The MGM United Artists *GoldenEye* home page.

People are using the Web for everything from publishing the works of Shakespeare (see Figure 1-5) to marketing the latest music album from the Rolling Stones (see Figure 1-6). Companies are betting big on new strategies designed around the Web. People have become millionaires because of their involvement with the Web. Obviously, the Web is hitting the mainstream. However, the best is yet to come: in the form of Java. This will be an even more interesting and exciting time for Web users and will transform the way we communicate.

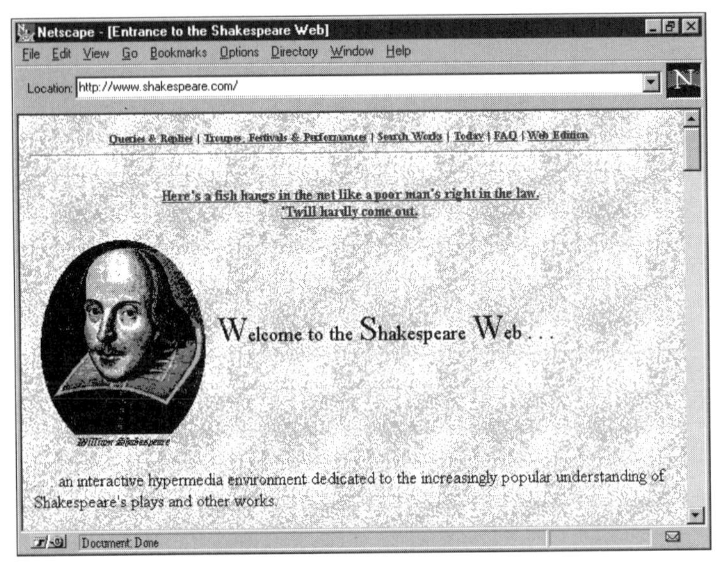

Figure 1-5: The Shakespeare Web home page.

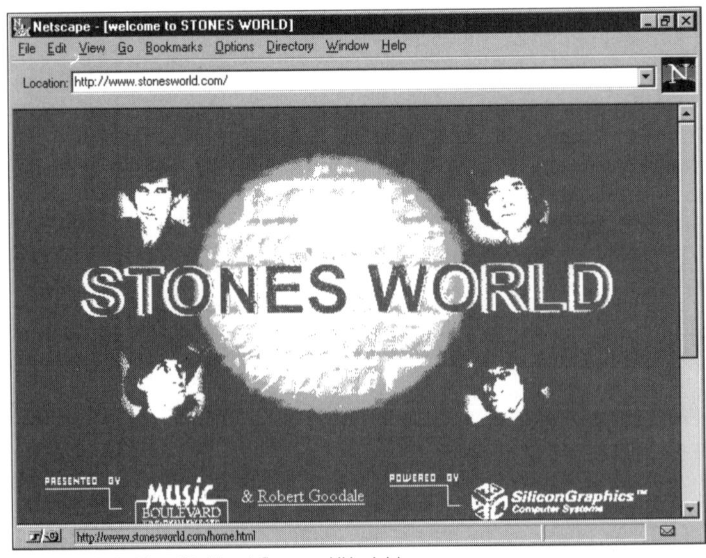

Figure 1-6: The (Rolling) Stones World home page.

Time will only tell how big the Internet becomes. Hopefully, it won't become just a fad, comparable to citizens band (CB) radio during the '70s. But, all signs indicate that there is no slowing down. A survey carried out by the CommerceNet/Nielsen Internet Demographics group highlights the exponential growth of the Web. The survey pointed out the following:

- Of the total persons age 16 and older in the United States and Canada, 17 percent (37 million) have access to the Internet.
- Of the same population, 11 percent (24 million) have used the Internet in the past three months.
- People use the Internet an average of 5.5 hours per week.
- Web users tend to have high incomes (25 percent over $80,000 per year), professional careers (50 percent professional or managerial), and advanced education (64 percent with at least college degrees).

These numbers show that only a fraction of the population has tapped into and is actually using the Web. Many others have not even had a chance to "get wired," and millions are still waiting to get connected.

According to *Newsweek* magazine, about 3 percent of the Internet population is addicted to the Net and spends every waking moment cruising the Information Superhighway. Could a market exist for a recovery and support program for Internet junkies? Maybe. More probably, these people will be featured on television talk shows like Oprah Winfrey or Ricki Lake.

What Is Java Anyway?

In the same way that a cup of coffee will jolt most people into action, the Java programming language (see Figure 1-7) moves the Internet's World Wide Web into action by jolting static Web pages into dynamic, multimedia-rich presentations. Java brings a new level of interactivity to the Web. You could say that Java is to the Web as a carpenter's tools are to building a house. Java provides the Web publisher with the tools necessary to control what a user experiences on the Web.

Now, don't get worried. Just as building a house can be hard work, programming can be difficult. However, just like a carpenter can go to the hardware store and purchase prefabricated doors, sinks, and bathtubs, the Java developer can use ready-made modules (known as *objects* or *classes*) to incorporate fancy multimedia effects into Web pages with minimal programming knowledge. This is the great advantage of being an object-oriented programming system, of which Java takes full advantage.

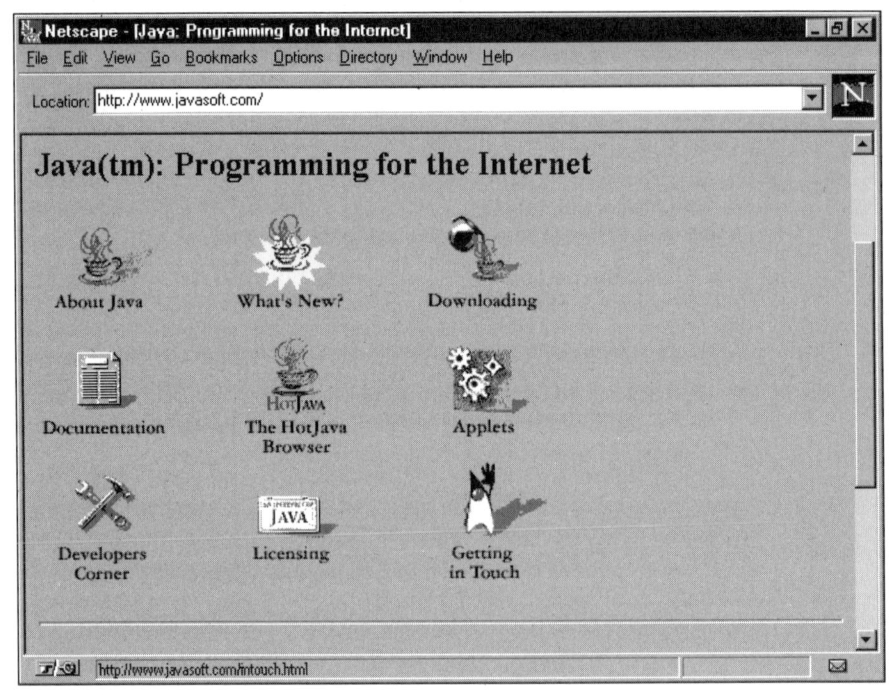

Figure 1-7: The Java home page.

Java lets you provide users with a way to actually *do something* at a Web site. Be it interact with the system, be impressed with animation, or have control over the playback of audio. Java gives you the capability to control what a Web page actually *looks like* in greater detail than ever before.

Java works in conjunction with the hypertext markup language (HTML) to allow the publication of information on the Web. HTML is actually a pretty limited method of controlling the display of information, but Java goes many miles beyond what plain HTML provides. Java provides more than a mere markup language, but an actual way to control Web sites.

The reason for the high level of control is that Java really *is* an actual high-level programming language that you can use to control what a Web browser is doing. When you think of programming language like C, C++, FORTRAN, COBOL, or Visual Basic, you should also think of Java. The big difference from the other languages is that Java is the first programming language developed for a network computer system, like the Internet.

About the Internet

You probably have heard about the Internet, upon which the World Wide Web is based. The *Internet* is a network of interconnected computer systems in 130 countries that uses special communication protocols. The Internet is now the largest network of computers in the world and provides many services, including electronic mail, file transfer, news information, remote computer login, and access to an almost unlimited number of databases.

The Internet, also known as the *Net*, is the world's largest computer network of networks, providing information access around the world. (There aren't any Internet computers in outer space yet.) You can think of the Internet as being two things: the computer systems that comprise it and the information that resides on those computers.

Every time somebody connects to the Internet, he or she adds to it because, unlike other systems, every computer connected to the Internet actually expands the network. Each computer is, in a sense, a network of its own.

About the World Wide Web

The *World Wide Web* — also known as *WWW, W3*, or simply *the Web* — is a networked information service, based on the Internet, that provides a hypertext multimedia information retrieval system. The Web provides a method of displaying information in different formats in a way that is fast, powerful, consistent, and easy to use.

As a means of accessing the Internet, the World Wide Web is one of the easiest systems available. The Web allows you to access Internet information services through an easy-to-use system. Beyond providing access to standard Internet services, the Web is a vast source of unique information.

The Web is a client-server network system. The computer that provides the information is called the *server*. The computer that displays the information is called the *browser*, or more frequently, the *Web browser*. You need special software for both the Web server and browser. Examples of browsers include Netscape Navigator, Microsoft Internet Explorer, and Spry Mosaic. Some online services, including Prodigy and America Online, have their own browsers that you can easily download if you subscribe to the service.

The Web uses something called *hypertext*, a system that enables you to access documents that have been linked with other documents in a nonlinear fashion. These Web documents don't use hierarchical menus or directory listings; rather, they contain links to other documents.

The Web gets its name because, like a spider's web, its hypertext links connect information from one point to another. The great thing is that you don't have to know the location of linked documents. By working in a single interface, the Web provides a user-friendly method of accessing data. One of the important features of the Web is that it provides a consistent interface for accessing a wide variety of information from a huge number of sources.

A History of the Web

The Web originated from a specification developed in 1989 at *CERN*, the European Laboratory for Particle Physics, based near Geneva across the French-Swiss border (see Figure 1-8). CERN is not a Swiss institute but is funded by 18 European member states. At the time, the tools used to navigate the Internet required considerable expertise. The HEP (High Energy Physics) researchers were looking for a better way to access each other's databases. They wanted to design a system that would allow physicists and other scientists to share information with others and to provide support for information such as physics event displays in the form of graphics.

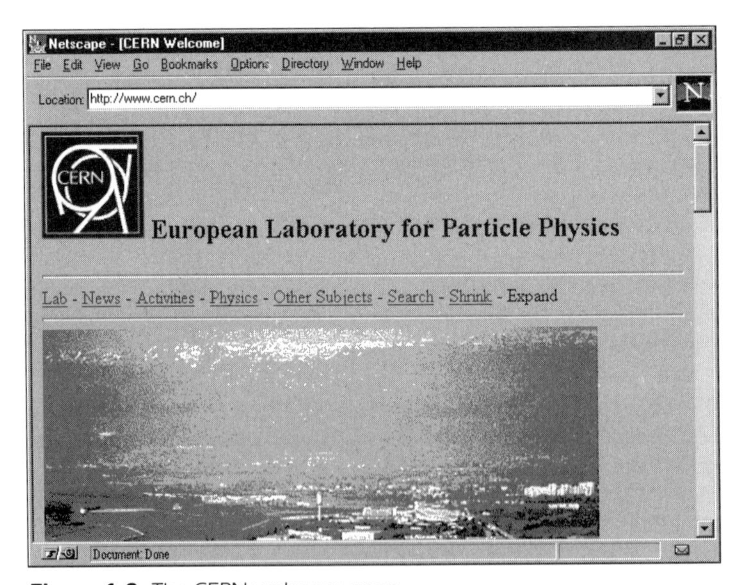

Figure 1-8: The CERN welcome page.

The specification that the CERN researchers developed is called the *hypertext transfer protocol* (HTTP). Once the researchers at CERN established the specification, people began writing Web client and server software, thereby making the Web a popular means of electronic navigation.

Early Web browsers were text-based. Instead of denoting hot spots in a hypertext format, each hot spot was numbered, similar to a menu. The user typed a number to navigate between home pages. Most of the early software was written on UNIX-based computers, and nobody gave much thought to the average computer user working on a PC-based machine running Windows. However, all that changed with the emergence of Mosaic and the NCSA.

In March 1993, several students at the National Center for Supercomputing Applications, also known as *NCSA* (see Figure 1-9), released the first version of a Web browser. This browser, called Mosaic, ran on UNIX-based computers and was available for downloading free of charge. This project was the result of a student research project designed to solve the problem of accessing Internet resources, especially the Web. Within months, Mosaic captured the attention of longtime Internet users as well as new users. The software provided an ideal method of Internet navigation.

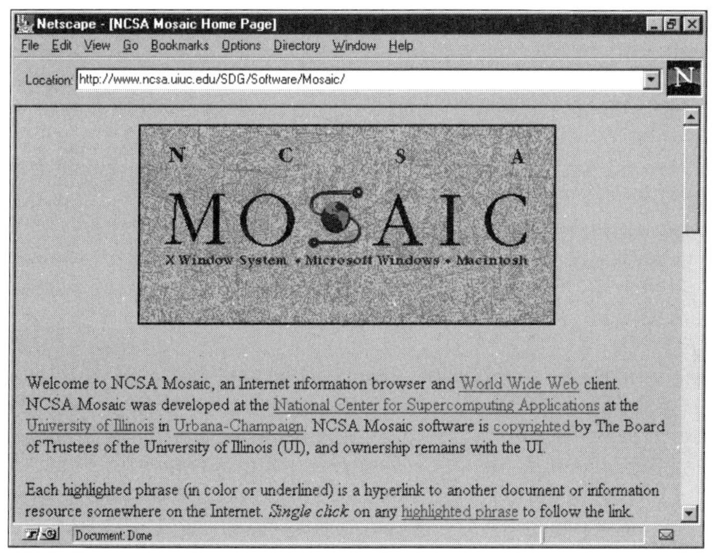

Figure 1-9: The NCSA home page.

The students at NCSA decided to create working versions of Mosaic for other computers. Soon, versions of Mosaic (eventually renamed NCSA Mosaic) arrived for UNIX, NeXT, Microsoft Windows, and Apple Macintosh. When these Web browsers became available, the rest of the world was starting to learn what the Web had to offer, and the popularity of the Web started to blossom.

By the end of 1991 (when it was developed), the Web boasted approximately 400 home pages, mostly in the areas of research and education. As the popularity of the system grew, the number of home pages grew. Today, an average 12 new Web pages are added daily, equivalent to 360 pages per month or about 4,320 new home pages per year.

Java Technology in Action

The Web is constantly evolving and changing. New technological innovations continue to make the Web so incredibly exciting, and Java is no exception.

While the students at NCSA were developing Mosaic, researchers at Sun Microsystems in Palo Alto, California, were developing a programming language that people could use to control access to information services, specifically cable television.

Although originally developed for purposes other than controlling the Internet, the researchers found that it would work well as a method of controlling the multimedia display of information that people were used to on the Web.

Anybody who has started surfing the Web will tell you that most people go through three levels of enthusiasm. First, they can't believe the amazing things they are seeing. They become excited about being able to connect to a computer in Jamaica, tracking the delivery of a FedEx package (see Figure 1-10), or checking out the weather in Germany. They just click on a hyperlink, and they are there.

The second level of enthusiasm occurs when the user realizes how chaotic the Web is and how easily someone can get lost in information overload. Finally, the user realizes how many poorly designed sites are on the Web, and worst, how frustratingly slow the system can be, especially when connected to the Internet with a modem. At this point, what the person originally thought of as interesting and exciting is no longer interesting enough. The user wants Web pages that do more than just integrate text, graphics, video, and audio. The user wishes he or she could actually *do* something on a Web page. This is where Java fits into the picture.

Java lets a Web page deliver, in addition to visual content, a tiny application program, called an *applet*, that, once loaded, can bring a Web page to life. Applets can create dancing advertising, updating scoreboards, moving stock ticker marquees, animated cartoons, and even games. In business, Java applets can add smarts to a statistical table so that the recipient can modify numbers and test assumptions, just as with a conventional spreadsheet.

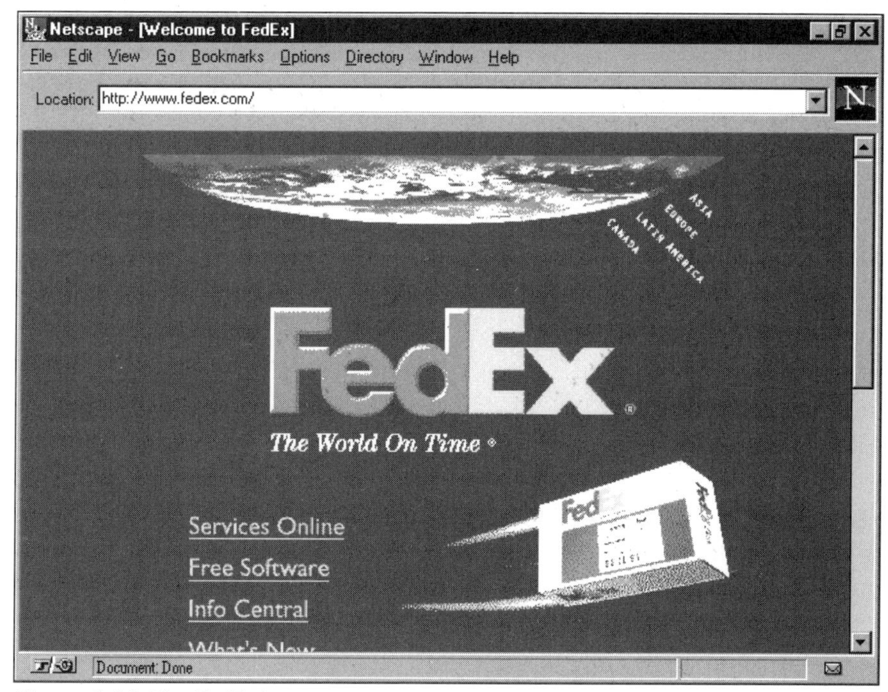

Figure 1-10: The FedEx home page.

Imagine yourself pointing to the Ford Motor Web site. Without Java, you will see words and pictures of the latest cars and trucks available from the company. You might also see an interactive form that you can fill out so that Ford will mail you printed material that you request. Enter Java. Now the Ford's Web server can transfer a Java applet to your computer. From there, you can customize options on a new Mustang while calculating the monthly tab on various loan rates offered by a financial institution or local bank. Because Java is so new, the possibilities seem almost endless.

A History of Java

Sun Microsystems originally developed Java as a language to control set-top television boxes. (Set-top boxes are similar to cable television boxes that sit on top of your television and help you control what you see on the TV. However, the set-top boxes provide much more interactivity and power than today's cable TV boxes.) Sun wanted to develop an operating environment for consumer devices that presents information via cable television. The original project began in 1991 and was referred to as the "Green" team. Headed by James Gosling, this small team of people designed and implemented Java outside of Sun's main headquarters near Stanford University in Palo Alto, California.

Java was recently awarded the *PC Magazine* Technical Excellence award for Internet tools (see Figure 1-11). The editors hit the nail on the head when they said that "[Java] will transform the way we use the Web for years to come."

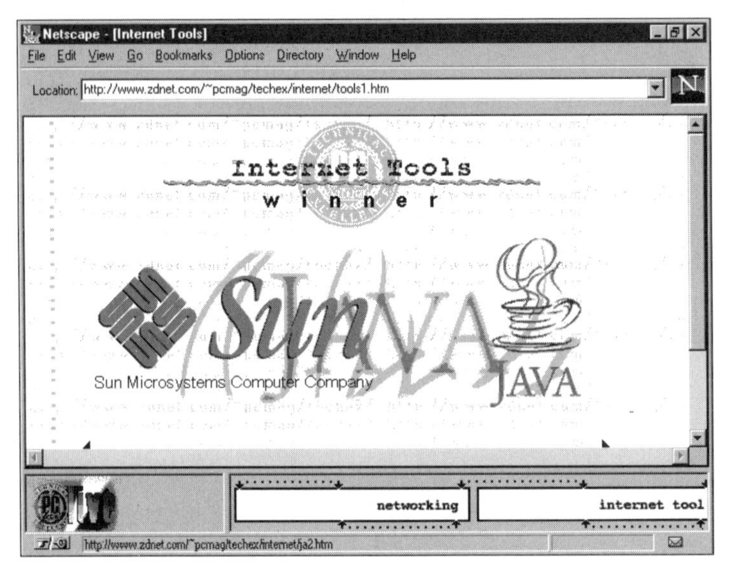

Figure 1-11: Technical Excellence Award for Java.

When members of the team first began planning the Green project, they realized that any system of controlling consumer electronic devices would have to be platform-independent: it could not rely on specific microprocessors or hardware. The developers wanted a system that could run just as well on a Sony VCR, an Apple Newton PDA (personal digital assistant), a wireless telephone, or maybe even a personal computer.

The team was successful in developing this project. The operating system was implemented in a proprietary PDA known as *7 (*Star Seven*). By the end of 1991, Gosling had a beta version of the operating system that he called *Oak* (named for the tree outside his office window). At the time, the company wanted to market the technology in a similar method to how Dolby Labs has successfully marketed its noise reduction system for stereo equipment. The team wanted to license Oak to a large number of different companies — even companies that might compete against one another.

Developing a software for consumer electronics devices turned out to be much more of a challenge than developing software for computers. When researching the differences between the consumer electronic market and the personal computer market, the Green team found that consumer devices generally have a much longer life than computer products. For example, there are working toasters that are 10, 20, maybe 50 years old. You can still plug this unit into an electrical socket and insert slices of bread. However, software generally improves every couple of years, if not every year. The team found that software for consumer electronic devices would have to be backward compatible in order to be commercially feasible.

Also, the team found that software used in consumer electronics must be extremely reliable, much more so than most computer software. If a consumer product fails, the manufacturer usually has to replace the entire machine. This is not something any manufacturer enjoys.

In the meantime, the Green team was now incorporated as a separate company from Sun, known as FirstPerson Inc. The team found out that Time-Warner was developing a video-on-demand service that required set-top boxes. Because the group had developed Oak in a device-independent manner, it saw this as the perfect opportunity. Although the team completed a working prototype, the folks at Time-Warner ultimately ended up going with another company's technology. Looking back, it was probably all the better because the Timer-Warner video-on-demand service turned out to be a disaster.

Around the same time, Sun almost cut a deal with 3DO, a company selling an expensive CD-ROM game machine. It took only ten days to get Oak running on one of the 3DO boxes, but the companies could never negotiate an agreement. Again, this probably turned out to be all the better because 3DO has still not made any large penetration into the game market.

As the Internet and the Web were becoming popular in 1993, the Green team realized that it could use a platform-neutral programming language, like Oak, for programming Web applications.

Bill Joy, the cofounder of Sun, finally got involved and wrote a new plan for the technology for interface into the Internet. In early 1995, the company discovered that someone had already filed a trademark for the name *Oak*, so the language was renamed to *Java*. Rumors have circulated that the letters stand for *Just Another Valueless Acronym*, but the company denies this. Instead, it says that the inspiration struck one day during a trip to the local coffee shop, which sounds likely enough.

As the plan went into action, the team created a new Web browser originally called WebRunner, later named as HotJava. The team then set out to license the Java language to other companies that create Web browsers.

What about HotJava?

So, HotJava (see Figure 1-12) is the Web browser from Sun Microsystems that enables the display of interactive content on the Web, using the Java language. HotJava is written entirely in Java and demonstrates the capabilities of the Java programming language.

When the Java language was first developed and ported to the Internet, no browsers were available that could run Java applets. Although you can view a Web page that includes Java applets with a regular browser, you will not gain any of Java's benefits. HotJava was developed to demonstrate Java's capabilities and is available free of charge from the Java Web site at `http://www.javasoft.com`.

HotJava is currently available for the SPARC/Solaris 2.x platform as well as Windows 95 and Windows NT. As far as a Web browser goes, it is nothing special and does not offer anything special that most other Web browsers don't offer. It's biggest draw is that it was the first Web browser to provide support for the Java language. Of course, the product is continually being expanded and enhanced and could become a major player.

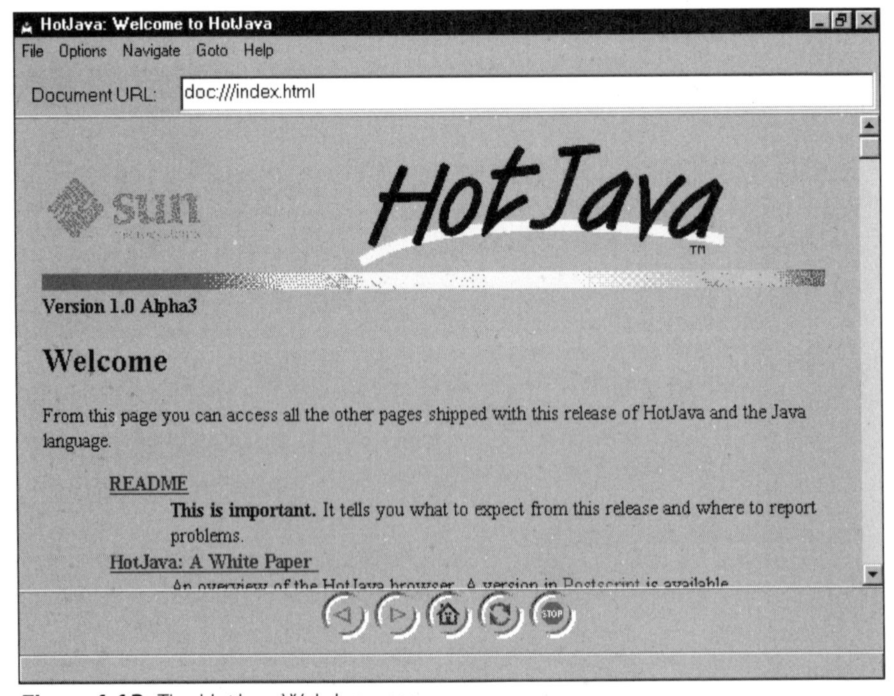

Figure 1-12: The HotJava Web browser.

What about Netscape Navigator?

The Netscape Navigator browser (see Figure 1-13) was designed by Marc Andreessen, who created the NCSA Mosaic prototype when he was a student at NCSA. Upon graduation, he and his fellow students were approached by ex-Silicon Graphics CEO Jim Clark, who asked whether they would like to start a new software company that would provide software for the Web. Netscape Communications was born.

Besides providing one of the best Web browsers, Netscape Communications was the first company to license the Java language from Sun. With versions available for Windows 3.*x*, Windows 95, NT, Solaris, and the Apple Macintosh, Netscape Navigator is one of the most widely used browsers available today. Roughly 80 percent of Web users have it.

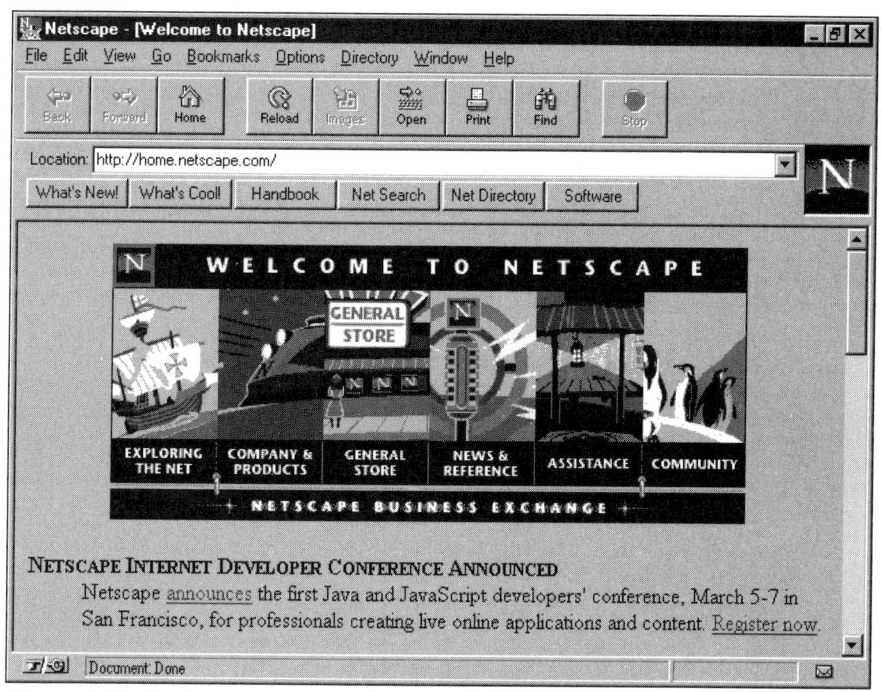

Figure 1-13: The Netscape Navigator Web browser.

Netscape Navigator has many useful features, including visual clues about the downloading process. The program signals when it connects to a site, displays the total number of bytes that will be downloaded, and keeps a running count of the number of bytes transferred.

The program also phases in any graphics on a home page. Instead of waiting for the entire image to appear, Netscape Navigator starts with a low-resolution version of the image and updates the image three or four times until you see the entire image. You can actually watch the graphics appear.

Besides being the first to provide support for the Java language, the newest version of Netscape Navigator adds many other features, such as:

- **Support for product *plug-ins*.** These are specialized programs that extend the way Netscape Navigator operates. They allow third-party companies to extend the way Netscape works and provide added functionality to a Web page. Some plug-ins currently in the works include ones to display three-dimensional graphics (also known as VRML) and the capability to integrate a Macromedia Director application (a tool used to author multimedia systems) into a Web page, called ShockWave.
- **Great extensions to the HTML page-description language.** These extend the presentation of Web pages to include new fonts, different background colors, new bullet styles, and even multiple windows or frames.
- **The addition of *JavaScript*.** This is a subset of Java, which is embedded into standard HTML files as commands to provide easy control of Web pages through script statements without all the complexities of Java code. The biggest difference between Java and JavaScript is that Java applets are a binary standard, whereas JavaScript statements are embedded directly into a Web page as standard ASCII text strings.
- **The addition of *LiveWire*.** This is a method of delivering interactive information to Web users and is a set of development tools for creating, deploying, and maintaining interactive online applications.

Maybe I shouldn't be taking sides (although this is my book), but Netscape is my all-around favorite Web browser. The feel and response of this program is better than that of all other Web browsers that I have used, and it includes many enhancements that place it head-and-shoulders above the competition.

Technical Details About the Internet

Although the technical details of the Internet and the World Wide Web could fill up many volumes in themselves, this section provides you with background information on some of the main buzzwords and concepts you will need to understand in order to work with the Web and Java.

Understanding TCP/IP

The TCP/IP system lets your PC (and many other types of computers) connect to the Internet. You don't have to know much about the TCP/IP protocol, other than the fact that it stands for *Transfer Control Protocol/Internet Protocol.* Mainly, it allows computers to talk together, or communicate, in a network. Although the technical details could fill up a whole book in themselves, the main idea behind the protocol is to break data up into small chunks, or packets, and send each packet individually. The receiving computer must repackage the data into the original mass of data.

With Windows 95 and Windows NT, most PCs now come with built-in TCP/IP support. As a result, Microsoft developed a specification for standard TCP/IP support under Windows. This system, named *Windows Sockets* (or simply *WinSock*), allows programmers to write network software for Windows that uses the TCP/IP system without having to support several TCP/IP implementations. All Web browsers rely on these functions in order to interact with the Internet.

Understanding URLs

A *uniform resource locator* (*URL*) is the means of locating another computer on the Web. A URL is usually pronounced *you-are-el* (but some people pronounce it *earl*). You need to know about URLs so that you can work with HTML and Java, and this section should set you straight on how URLs work and what they mean.

You can think of a URL as being like a post office box or mailing address. URLs are the only method of locating target Web home pages. Each URL allows your Web browser software to access any file on just about any Web server.

Besides providing a method of identifying a target home page, a URL expresses the address of a resource and the method by which you can access that resource. The URL naming system is extremely simple yet powerful.

A standard URL consists of three parts: the *transfer format,* the *host name* of the machine that holds the file that you want to access, and the *path* to the file. The general format of a URL is as follows:

```
format://host.name.com/path/filename.html
```

The standard format for the World Wide Web is http (hypertext transfer protocol). Several formats are available, however, including ftp (file transfer protocol) and news (Usenet newsgroups).

For http, a colon and two slashes (://) separate the transfer format from the host name. For the other standards, you use only a colon (no slashes). Standard Internet naming conventions are used for the host name part of the URL. The parts of the host name, which can contain several words, are separated by periods. The path name uses standard directory naming conventions and can end with a file extension.

What follows is a sample URL:

http://www.idgbooks.com/index.html

This URL is the home page for IDG Books (see Figure 1-14). The `http` part refers to the transfer protocol. The `www.idgbooks.com` part refers to the host name. Finally, the `index.html` part is the filename of the Web page to be accessed. If you do not specify a filename, the system accesses the default file returned by the server computer system. In many cases, you don't have to worry about a full path and filename.

Figure 1-14: The IDG Books home page.

Many times, a URL becomes extremely long, partly because the UNIX computer system (on which the Internet is based) allows filenames of virtually unlimited length. This UNIX characteristic is good, however, because it allows almost limitless names for home pages. Also, URLs are case-sensitive, due mainly to the fact that UNIX has a case-sensitive file structure.

Cross-Platform Compatibility

At this point, I need to discuss the topic of UNIX computers and also cross-platform compatibility on the Web. Remember that the Web is a network of computers that communicate with one another. As a result, the Web is a mixing ground for many brands of computers and any number of computer operating systems. One of the most important operating systems (as far as the Web is concerned) is UNIX.

The UNIX operating system has become the cornerstone of the Internet, and most other operating systems are customized to work with UNIX when they hook into the Internet (by emulating TCP/IP). To build a good understanding of the Web, a little knowledge of UNIX is helpful. To use the Web, however, you need to know only a tiny portion of UNIX. Luckily, most Web browsers shield users from the details of the UNIX operating system.

Although the Web was based on UNIX, many other types of computers are connected to it. Because of the Web's diversity, you will find that it encompasses just about every type of popular computer (and even computers that are not so popular), including Apple Macintosh, PCs running DOS and Windows, UNIX workstations, NeXT, Amiga, and Commodore computers.

One of the cool things about Java is that it shields the programmer from the details involved with platform-dependent programming. This book covers developing Java applets from the viewpoint of a Windows PC user. When necessary, however, this book covers other platforms. You certainly will be notified about different file types and told how to use them.

Interestingly enough, more companies are using Windows NT to host a Web site rather than any version of UNIX. With its inherent graphical user interface, Windows NT is much easier to set up and maintain than a UNIX machine, which is still based on command-line tools.

The Features of Java

Sun Microsystems describes Java as "a simple, object-oriented, distributed, interpreted, robust, secure, architecture-neutral, portable, high-performance, multithreaded, and dynamic language." Whew, that sure is a mouthful. Let's iron this down to the important features that we can make use of now.

Java allows a programmer to pack a good amount of functionality into a relatively small package that can run anywhere in a highly distributed network, such as the Internet. This is cool because it is a language designed to support networking — something that other computer languages don't even take into account.

The Java language supports the following major features:

- Interactive multimedia
- Platform independence
- Several layers of security
- Software distribution and installation

The following sections will take a closer look at each of these features.

Interactive multimedia

We have heard so much about multimedia and interactivity in the last couple of years that many of us are sick and tired of hearing about it and a bit confused as to what it really is. The term has been applied to everything from computer software to talking Coke machines.

Multimedia is simply the integration of software, text, static graphics images, audio, and digital video. The Web already has provisions for the integration of text, graphics, audio, and video. Java provides the missing key by providing the software to control the way the media types work together. Java applets can put animated figures on Web pages, such as that in Figure 1-15.

Multimedia special effects can include animated company logos or text that moves or scrolls across the screen. Graphics images don't necessarily have to come from a graphics file. Instead, they can be created based on data supplied by the network.

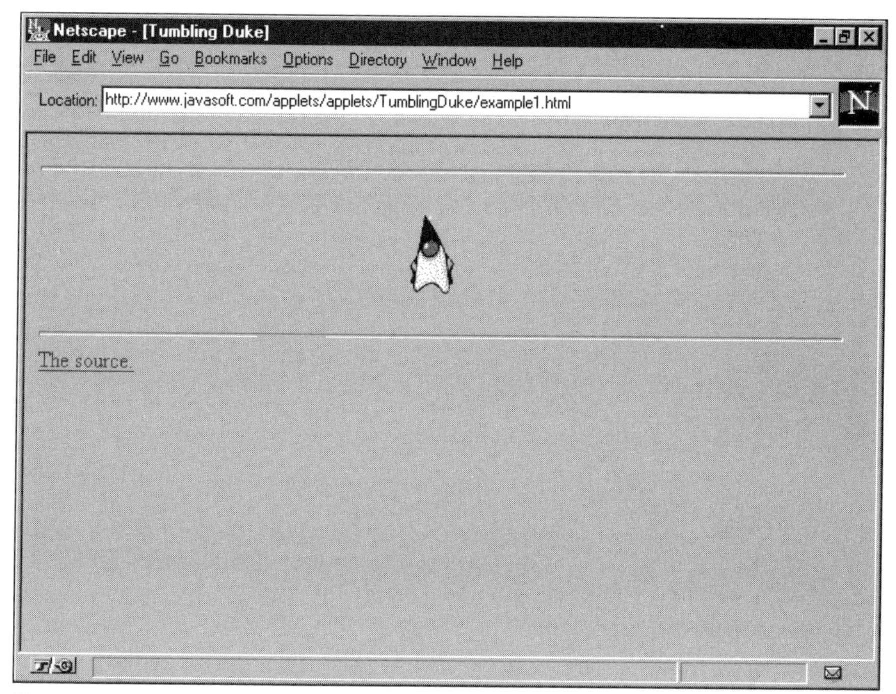

Figure 1-15: Duke, the Java Mascot, doing a dance. Of course, you can't tell that here because this is only a picture.

As far as playing audio and digital video data, the Web without Java provides one method for accessing them. You the user must click on a hot spot and wait for the data to transfer to your computer. Upon completion of the transfer (which could take many minutes with a slow connection), the Web browser accesses a *helper application* to play the audio or display the video information. A Java applet could be developed that would transfer the data in the background and then display it in the main Web browser window. Using Java, you have many ways to make audio and video playback better.

Interaction refers to the way that the user interacts with a system. Up to this point, the main method of interactivity on the Web has been through hypertext links (the move of a wrist along with the press of a mouse button) and interactive forms. Java provides interaction between the user, the computer, and the applet as well as between the applet and the network. This allows real-time interaction that provides some probabilities for interesting games and entertainment.

Platform independence

You already know that Java was designed to work on many different types of computer systems, but this is a lot easier to talk about than to implement. Here's why. For a program to run on a computer, it must first be translated from a language like Pascal or C++ into the machine's native tongue (this is done by something called a *compiler*). Because this translation process is time-consuming, most software comes already compiled. This means that different versions must be created for different computers. Java averts this problem by using an intermediate binary language.

The result is that small applets can move around the Internet without regard to the kind of hardware used. If you need to watch an animation that requires a particular program to run it, your machine will pick up the Java coded applet along with the animation files and run it. It doesn't matter what hardware your machine uses.

A Java applet must execute on many different platforms. The method chosen to realize this aim is an architecture-neutral binary representation. These architecture-neutral byte codes contain computer instructions that possess no allegiance to or dependence on a specific computer architecture.

You convert your Java programs into platform-independent binary byte codes, which a platform-specific Java run-time system then interprets. The developer must maintain only one source of a Java program for many different platforms. For example, you develop a Java applet and then compile it. You can then run the same program on a PC, Mac, or UNIX system, which contains the Java run-time environment (part of the Web browser). Thereby, developers can more quickly create applications for the Web that more users can access.

Java is platform-neutral, but it has been optimized to take advantage of multithreaded operating systems such as Windows NT, Windows 95, and UNIX Solaris systems. Interactive applications are much more impressive when the processor seems to act on multiple pieces of data at once. Users realize real-time behavior and superior interactive responsiveness. The implementation of multithreading in Java programs is straightforward and quite robust.

Another reason that several different platforms can use Java applets is because Java takes advantage of IEEE standards for data types on different computers. This is a standard, devised by the Institute of Electrical and Electronic Engineers, that stores numbers in a consistent manner. For instance, a character is stored in 8 bits, or one byte, under Windows 3.*x*. However, on Windows NT a character is 16 bits, or two bytes. These differences take place on two versions of an operating system from the same company. Imagine the complexities involved in storing numbers of different sizes between different computer types. These differences make it hard to store data uniformly across different systems.

Java also includes an extensive library of routines that provide access to underlying operating systems. When these libraries are used, applets will work on any platform where Java is supported.

So, the bottom line of device independence is that the applets will run on a PC, Macintosh, UNIX, or any machine for that matter, in an identical manner.

Java provides a couple of nice features that C++ programmers wish they had. In addition to consistent IEEE data types, Java has a built-in string type. Using consistent IEEE data types means that the way the numbers are stored in memory is standard, and backward-compatible, with any system that stores numbers in IEEE format. The built-in string type makes it easy to work with alphanumeric data. Unlike C++, Java strings are not arrays of characters and can be treated like BASIC-style strings. Another cool feature is that the programmer doesn't have to think about memory management and automatic garbage collection. C++ programmers are accustomed to managing memory explicitly (with the `malloc` function), but Java programmers don't have to think about this because the system takes care of it for you. *Garbage collection* is freeing up chunks of memory that have been previously allocated but are no longer used. The Java garbage collection system takes advantage of idle periods when the user is doing nothing and frees memory at these times.

Security

We generally think of security as something that happens at a bank or savings and loan. We walk in with our account book, request some of our hard-earned cash, and walk out of the bank with our pockets full. The security includes the uniform guards, the two-inch thick Plexiglas, and the bank vault — not to mention the video cameras at each door.

Security features with Java are somewhat the same. Because Java is designed for network applications, a user has to worry about any executable code that he or she receives from the network because the program could be infected with a computer virus. Java applications are guaranteed to be tamper-resistant and virus free because they cannot access system memory the way programs written in C or C++ can. Java also features several layers of security, including the following:

- **A byte code verification system.** This checks the Java applet for language compliance. Even though the compiler generates correct code, the code could have been intentionally (or unintentionally) changed between compile-time and run-time. Security safeguards prevent this from happening.
- **File access restrictions.** If a Java applet attempts to access a file that it doesn't have permission to, a dialog box appears that allows the user to stop or abort applet execution.

- **Run-time class verification.** This system checks Java applets for function names and access restrictions during applet loading. This is a good means of security.

Future versions of Java are supposed to include public key encryption routines to verify the source of the Java applet as well as its integrity after passing through a network. This encryption technology could be the key to secure financial transactions across the Internet.

Java is different from C++ is in its capability to check for bugs early and build more reliable programs. Java allows only single inheritance for an object class instead of multiple inheritance. Multiple inheritance gives C++ programmers the chance to complicate object-oriented programming by defining class behavior from multiple classes.

Software distribution and installation

Distribution of information for sharing is an essential characteristic of any client-server information system. Java contains a library of routines to interface to TCP/IP protocols. Through these routines, you can easily move messages and files around the Internet. You do this when a Java application opens a URL to request information from the Web. Specifically, Java includes support for access to information on the Web through transfer formats like HTTP (hypertext transfer protocol) and FTP (file transfer protocol).

Lately, folks have been talking about a new type of software distribution, which works something like this. Today, if you want the latest version of a software product, you go to the local software superstore and purchase it. You do this if the application is a word processor, which you use everyday, or a desktop publishing application, which you might use once a year.

Some proponents of Java envision a time when the Web will be the spot to download hundreds of different applications — most likely specialized applets that are not used on a regular basis but could be extremely useful. Users could connect to the computer with this specialized software and for a small fee use it as if they owned it. This would remove the need to buy ten pounds of software and upgrade it every time a new version comes out.

This is an interesting vision. If it does happen, it might happen through the software distribution and installation routines that are built into Java.

Features multiplied

Each one of these features is interesting in and of itself. However, imagine the effect if you used them in conjunction with each other. The use of the distribution routines along with interactive multimedia could create some really cool network games where thousands of players could play against each other. It might sound ridiculous now, but you never know. Some 20 years ago, a computer on your desktop would have been ridiculous to imagine.

Another combined effect would be the use of the platform dependence and interactive multimedia to provide Web information for television users. The idea would create a set-top computer that contains only the bare essentials, such as a microprocessor, minimal memory, and a mouse. This set-top computer would display its output on a standard television and would connect to the Internet through a cable modem. This would provide Internet access for the couch potato. It could also provide the answer to the so-called 500-channel interactive television system. In fact, considering each Web site as a different channel, this system would provide hundreds of thousands of channels to view. The concept might not be as far-fetched as it sounds. Again, you never know.

Uses for Java

So, with the all the hype and propaganda that Java has received recently, let's take a look at some actual uses for it. Java might be great as an object-oriented language that can turn computer programmers' heads, but Java, more importantly, has some solid uses. The following categories explain some of the largest application categories:

- Developer tool kits
- Educational applications
- Enhanced Web pages
- Games and entertainment
- Internet and Web access agents
- Productivity tools

Take a look at each category, and you'll see what types of applications are already available.

Developer tool kits

Developer tool kits are applets designed to help users create tools for the development and deployment of knowledge- and information-based systems. These could be something like a drag-and-drop development tool, an online knowledge base, or a Java development tool that provides a visual interface to applet development, much like Visual Basic. Figure 1-16 shows a sample Java applet built into the Netscape Navigator browser that displays a real-time status of Java applets.

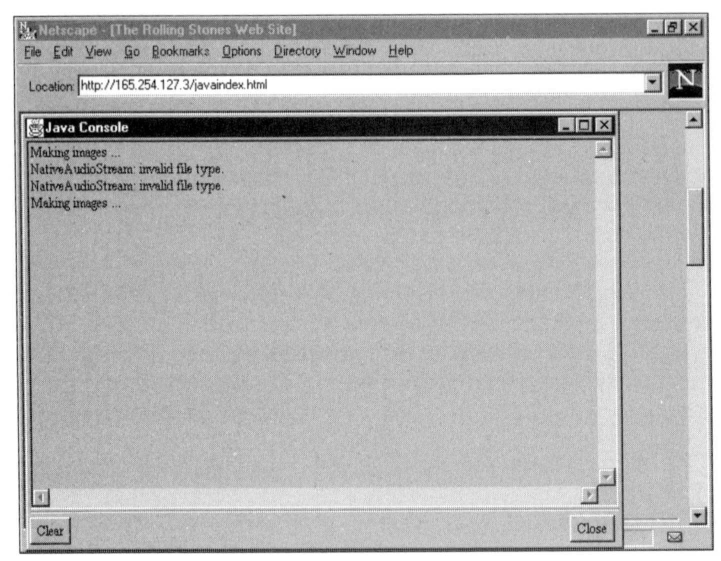

Figure 1-16: The Java Console in Netscape Navigator.

Educational applications

Education applets (see Figure 1-17) are designed to help users gain insight. An educational applet can behave like scientific instruments or interpret and display input data so that students can focus on the meaning of scientific principles. With the integration of audio and video, the resulting educational applet could be an effective means for learning. Imagine the possibilities if our educational system could grasp this technology.

Enhancing Web pages

The greatest use so far for Java is in adding flair to Web pages (see Figure 1-18). This means making use of all those great multimedia features to make Web pages come alive. At the very least, a Web designer can add animated words, like "What's New!" to draw attention to them and to make the new information really stand out on a page.

Right now, you can find multimedia applets that provide different types of animation, the playback of audio, and the display of fancy graphics. Some applets also provide tricks for displaying text, like blinking text and scrolling text.

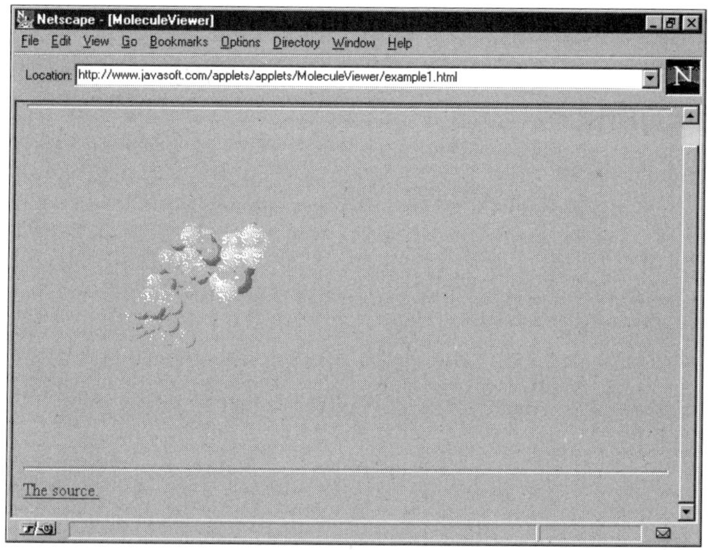

Figure 1-17: A three-dimensional chemical model for educational purposes.

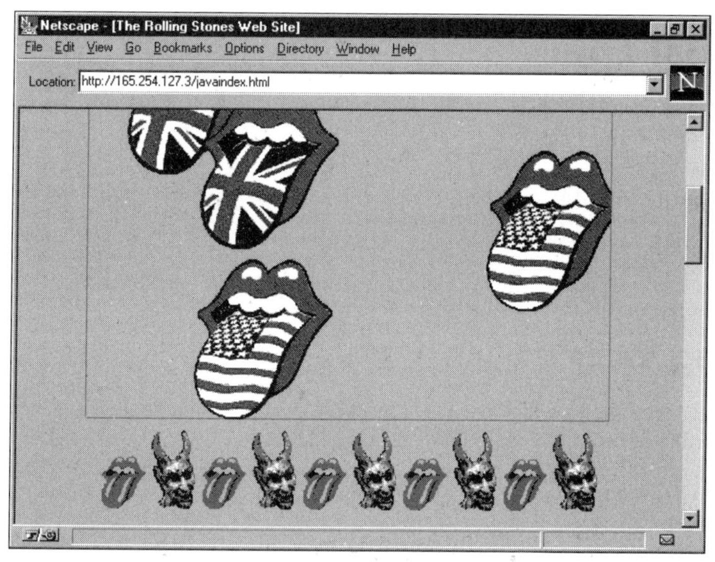

Figure 1-18: Animated bouncing tongues, courtesy of the Rolling Stones.

Games and entertainment

The developer can also create applets to provide an environment for entertainment purposes (see Figure 1-19), providing the user with an interactive experience. Tic-tac-toe and hangman probably seem like poor reasons to use an expensive computer, but these are only examples. More games will certainly become available. Multiple-player Internet-based games could become a reality. Of course, these applets would probably make use of the multimedia features that Java provides for enhancing Web pages. Hopefully, this category will overlap with educational applets because the best type of educational experience is an entertaining one.

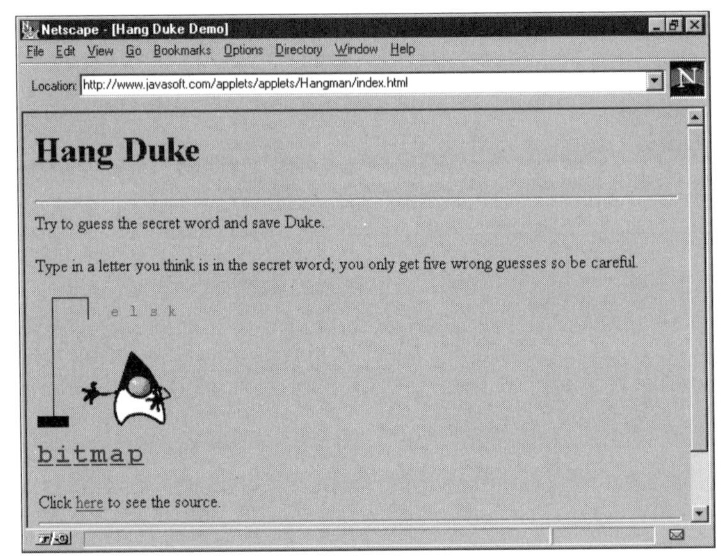

Figure 1-19: The Hang Duke game.

Internet and Web access agents

Another interesting type of Java applet is one that retrieves information from a network, making it possible to take over a user's display and exhibit a series of network resources (Figure 1-20). The big talk these days is about a type of Internet agent that would watch the types of home pages you view on a regular day-to-day basis and would then find others related to the ones that already interest you. As the system begins to learn about your interests, it can start fetching your favorite Web pages for you.

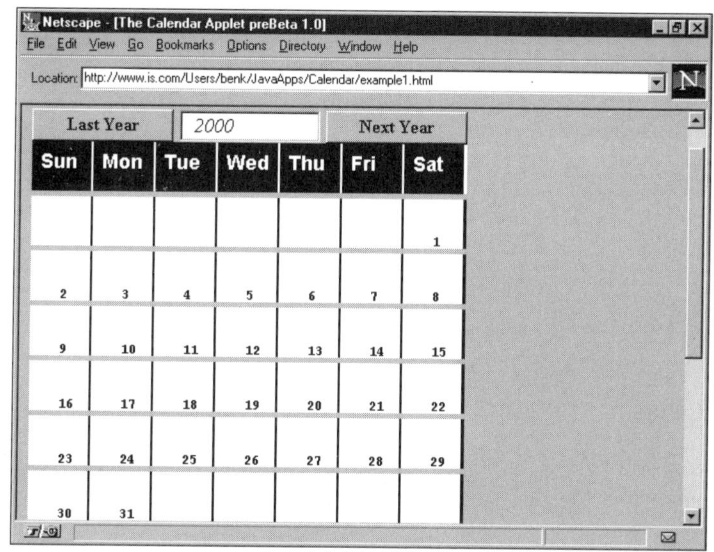

Figure 1-20: A Calendar Applet that allows network scheduling.

Productivity tools

Productivity tools are specialized home applets (see Figure 1-21) or business applications that provide an interface to programs for information processing. The biggest picture would be applets like specialized spreadsheets, word processing, and presentation packages. However, on a smaller basis, the applet could be something as simple as returning a customized database query.

The list goes on

Although I have tried to highlight the major categories here, this is by no means an all-inclusive list. Hopefully, you will find your own uses for Java. As Java extends to new platforms and gains added functionality, I hope you will find your own uses for Java.

The Future of Java

Because Java was developed in a platform-independent manner, it can be used in many different types of embedded systems for consumer electronics, such as hand-held devices, telephones, and VCRs. In fact, Mitsubishi Electronics has been working on ways to use Java in its newest consumer electronic devices.

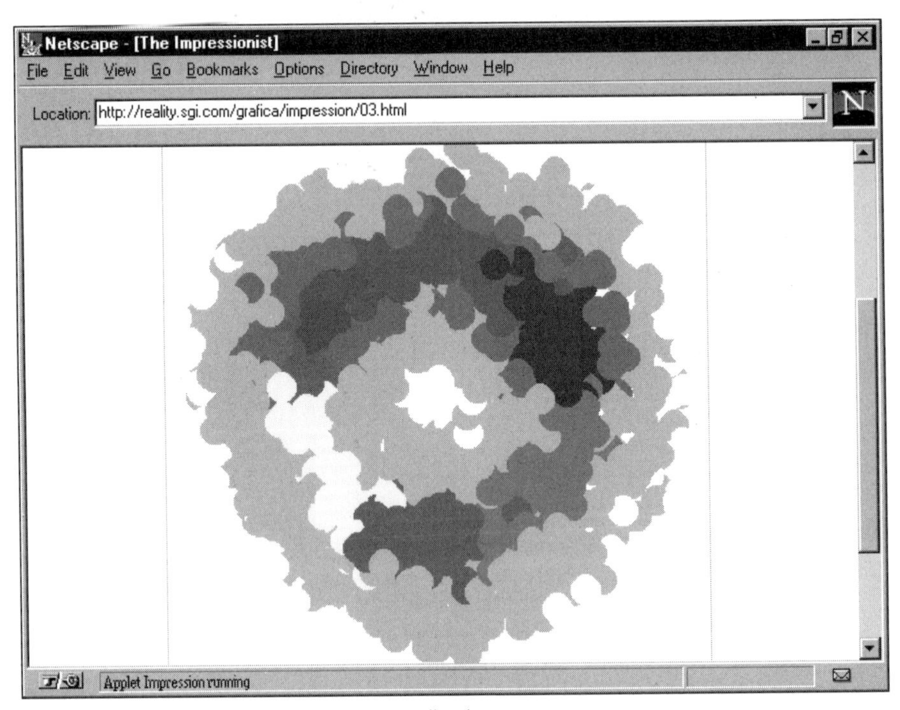

Figure 1-21: The Impressionist paint application.

However, as far as the Web goes, Sun has already signed agreements with Microsoft, IBM, America Online, Prodigy, and other Web browser developers to license the Java language. Furthermore, companies like Symantec and Borland have both announced plans to develop visual programming environments for the Java language. Symantec is said to be using technology from its Symantec C++ product to develop Java applications in a graphical environment, and Borland is using technology from its Delphi product to make developing Java applications easier. As these other companies add Java support to their products, Java just may become the best way to publish information on the Internet.

Quick Overview

From the depth of this chapter, you can see that Java offers quite a lot. You learned how Java was developed for platform-independent applications, like the Web. You also gained a lot of background knowledge about the Web, the Internet, and Java. In particular, this chapter covered the following topics:

- Java is a platform-independent programming language developed to control a broad variety of different microprocessor devices and has relatively recently been ported for use on the Web.
- The Web itself is a special service of the Internet that provides a hypertext multimedia information retrieval system.
- HotJava is the name of the first Web browser to support Java applets and was itself written in the Java language. Netscape Navigator also supports Java applets, is the most popular Web browser available, and was created by the original developers of NCSA Mosaic.
- The Java language (which was first named Oak) was developed by Sun Microsystems in 1991 for the control of consumer electronic devices. In 1995, it was ported to computer platforms and made available for inclusion into Web browsers.
- The most useful features of Java include support for interactive multimedia, platform-independence, several layers of security, and software distribution and installation support.
- Uses for Java include developer tool kits, educational applications, enhancements to Web pages, games and entertainment, Internet and Web access agents, productivity tools, and maybe more.

Here is a brief overview of what is to come...

- Skip ahead to Chapter 2, "Working with Netscape Navigator," to find out how to use Netscape and Java.
- Skip on to Chapter 3, "A Review of HTML," to find out how the hypertext markup language works.

Working with Netscape Navigator

In This Chapter

How to obtain, install, configure, and start Netscape.

What the graphical elements of the main window are used for and how to make the best use of them.

What each main-menu command is for and how to use these commands.

How to use bookmarks to make surfing the Web as easy as switching channels on your television set.

An overview of what options you can customize.

This chapter teaches you how to use the Netscape Navigator Web browser from Netscape Communications Corporation. You will learn how to use and operate Netscape and find out how to customize it.

You should find this chapter extremely useful because the documentation for Netscape is available on-line only and therefore is not accessible unless you are connected to the Web.

Getting Started with Netscape

Netscape Navigator, which allows you to view multimedia documents on the Web, is designed to provide optimum performance and ease of use for surfing the Web. Considering that the team that originally wrote NCSA Mosaic also designed Netscape, Netscape is completely compatible with the original Mosaic.

What does Netscape do so well that other browsers don't? Just this:

- It allows for the display and interaction of documents as they are loaded.

- It provides security features for communicating with certified Web servers. You can find out when you are communicating with these machines, as described later in this chapter ("The Security Bar").
- It allows for loading multiple images and text at the same time. This feature improves performance and speeds your Web surfing.
- It provides document and image caching to reduce network access. This results in more efficient memory usage and quicker program execution.
- It includes a configurable user interface, with status bars, toolbars, and directory bars.
- It provides bookmarks that make revisiting Web sites easy.
- It provides access to other parts of the Internet, including newsgroups and ftp.
- It is available for multiple platforms, including Macintosh, Windows, UNIX, and Windows 3.*x*/95/NT. This feature is nice if you use different computers because the interface will always be the same. The programs operate fairly consistently between platforms. This chapter focuses on the Windows version.
- It supports Java applets. This feature is almost transparent to the user, other than the experience of all kinds of new visual effects. Please note that Java support is only available in 32-bit versions of the product and therefore not included with the Windows 3 version of Netscape Navigator.

The first thing that you need to do to use Netscape is to acquire the software. This book contains a copy of Netscape with the CD-ROM. However, a newer version may be available, in which case you would want to obtain that version. Netscape is available by ftp from `ftp.netscape.com` in the `netscape` directory. The file is self-extracting, meaning that when you execute the file, it creates several other files. You will probably want to view the readme.txt file to find out any important last-minute information about installing the program before proceeding.

You may wonder how Netscape Communications Corporation makes money if it gives away its software. Actually, the company doesn't give software away. Besides the fact that the company sells Web server software (which costs more and probably is more lucrative), it requires users to register Netscape Navigator "at the time that the user feels he or she is going to use it permanently." Currently, the charge is $39, which does not include any documentation. You can receive printed documentation (which is simply the online manual in print form) for $20. You order the program directly from Netscape Communications, and the company will mail it to you on floppy disk.

Netscape recently released another version of Navigator, called Navigator Gold. This version has all the features of the regular Navigator, but it also contains authoring tools that allow the user to edit Web pages. It works much like a word processor for the Web. Although you don't need Navigator Gold to write Java applets, it can sure make creating Web pages easier.

Installation

The setup utility makes installing Netscape an easy task. You just need to tell the setup program which subdirectory on your hard drive should receive the program. The setup program then copies the files to the appropriate location on your hard drive.

If you have ever used the Microsoft Setup utility, this process will be easy for you. To begin the installation process, place the program disk in a floppy drive and choose the Run option from the File menu within Program Manager.

At the Run dialog box, type ***x*:setup**, where *x* is the drive letter where the files are located (usually C). This command loads the setup program and starts the automated setup procedure. When the setup program begins, it displays a dialog box that enables you to specify which directory location to use for storing files on your hard drive (see Figure 2-1).

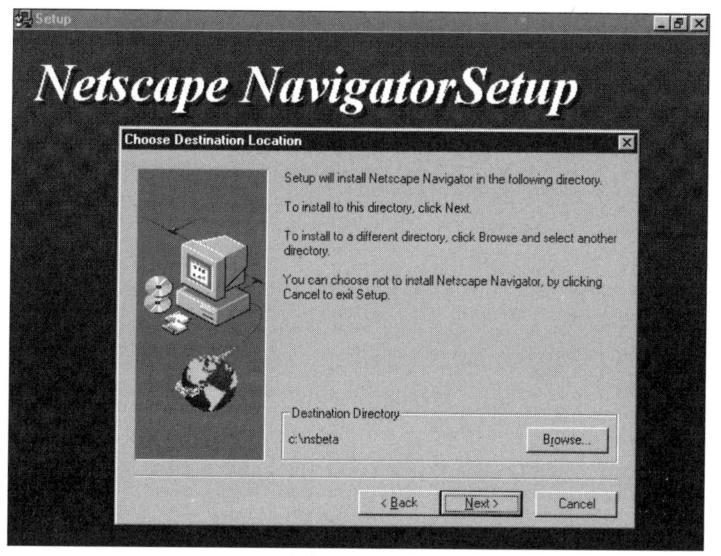

Figure 2-1: The Netscape Navigator installation program.

After you enter the appropriate hard drive location, tell the Setup program the name of the group where you want to add the Netscape program icon. The default group is *Netscape*, which should work in most situations.

When you answer these simple questions, the program files are copied to the location that you selected. A large progress bar appears, telling you how much longer it is going to take to copy the files. This process should take no more than a couple of minutes.

When the installation program finishes running, you will find the required files on your hard drive in the specified directory. If you are using Windows NT, you will find a new program group created in Program Manager. If you are using Windows 95, a new icon is created on your desktop.

Starting Netscape

Starting Netscape is easy. First, make sure any TCP/IP drivers that you may need are enabled (check the Control Panel). Then, from Program Manager (in Windows NT) or the desktop (in Windows 95), choose the Netscape program group and double-click the Netscape icon.

The first time you start Netscape, a copyright message will appear. After you click the OK button, the program loads. Before you start using the program, look at Netscape's menus and buttons. With an understanding of the main window, which the next section discusses, you will be able to surf the Web like a seasoned pro.

The Main Window

Netscape Navigator uses most of the features that have become known to denote a user-friendly program. These features are displayed in the program's main window, as follows:

- **Preview area.** This area is the part of the main window where you view Web pages.
- **Menu bar.** The menu bar contains the top-level menus for Netscape Navigator. As in most Windows programs, the menu bar is the means by which you access most of the features of the program.
- **Toolbar.** The toolbar, located directly below the menu bar, is a quick way to choose menu commands with the mouse. The toolbar contains commonly used commands that you can turn on and off. If you don't want the toolbar, you can remove it.
- **Location box.** The location box provides an area that displays the current URL you are browsing. This box also doubles as an area in which you can type a URL that you want to view. If you don't want the location box, you can remove it.
- **Directory bar.** The directory bar, located below the location box, mimics some of the options in the Directory menu. These options give you a quick means of surfing certain spots on the Web. If you don't want the directory buttons, you can remove them.

- **Status bar.** Located at the bottom of the window, the status bar displays information about a selected menu option's purpose. While you are browsing the Web, the status bar also displays the URL for a target hyperlink and the rate at which a home page is being downloaded.

Let's take a closer look at the elements of the Netscape main window. The next sections will give you an idea of what each feature is for and why it was designed into the program.

The preview area

When you surf the Web, you do your viewing in the main preview area, which makes up the majority of the program's window. You can open any number of preview windows at the same time, and you are limited only by your computer's memory (see Figure 2-2). To open another preview area (which really just launches additional copies of Netscape), choose New from the File menu (or press Ctrl+N). The new instances of Netscape are launched directly on top of the original, so don't become confused by which window you are viewing. As you open multiple windows, they will appear as options in the Window menu.

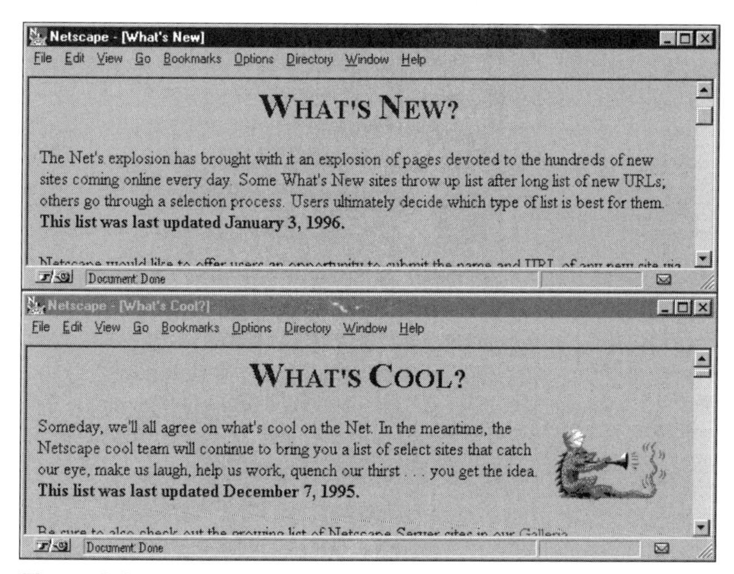

Figure 2-2: Multiple Netscape preview windows.

Netscape Navigator makes the best use of window real estate by displaying the name of a Web home page in the title bar of the main window. As you surf through home pages, you will notice that the Netscape title bar continuously displays the title of the current document or Web site.

Viewing the document with the vertical scroll bar

On the right side of the preview area is a vertical scroll bar. Like the vertical scroll bar in other Windows programs, this bar tells you that the information you are now viewing is larger than the window can hold. You can use the scroll bar to display the rest of the document.

Many Web home pages are extremely large and contain much more than a single window of information. The scroll bar is the tool that you use to view the entire home page. Click the buttons at either end of the scroll bar to move the image up or down a line at a time. If you click the area above or below the scroll bar thumb (the box that moves up and down the scroll bar), you move the image up or down a page at a time. You can drag the scroll bar thumb with the mouse to move between portions of the home page.

Viewing the document with the keyboard

If you don't like to rely on the mouse for Web surfing, keyboard-equivalent commands mimic most of the mouse functions. The up and down arrow keys move the image up or down a line at a time. The PgUp and PgDn keys move the image up or down a page at a time.

The menu bar

The menu system provides the features that you need to access the many features of Netscape. In the menu system, you'll find features for handling files, working with the clipboard, and accessing bookmarks.

Some menu commands are context-sensitive: depending on the state of your work, certain menu options are available, whereas others are not. Commands that are not available are displayed in gray.

Often, a command in the main level of the menus leads to another option. Each menu command that is followed by an ellipsis (...) displays a dialog box that enables you to make several choices about the command you selected. Here are the main menus:

- **File.** This menu enables you to open Web pages, open text files, save files, and print pages. Choose Exit to end your Netscape Navigator session.
- **Edit.** Use the options in this menu to cut, copy, and paste text to the Windows clipboard and to find text in the preview window.

- **View.** With the options in this menu, you can reload or refresh the home page that you are viewing, inspect the source HTML listing of the current home page, or find out information about the currently displayed document.
- **Go.** Using this menu, you can navigate forward and backward through Web pages. The menu also keeps a history list of items that correlate with the Web pages you have visited during the current session. You can choose items from that list to return to Web pages that you want to visit again.
- **Bookmarks.** This menu allows you to bring up a window in which you can create, manage, and access hot links to a private list of Web home pages.
- **Options.** This menu enables you to set options related to the way that Netscape Navigator operates. You set communication information with this menu and control what screen elements appear while you use the program.
- **Directory.** This menu allows you to access helpful and interesting locations on the Web Netscape Communications maintains. Options such as What's New! and What's Cool! allow you to find fun and interesting Web home pages quickly.
- **Window.** This menu gives you a way to select other Internet services, like newsgroups or e-mail, and to display an address book, a bookmark, and a history list. It also provides a method of accessing multiple instances of Navigator windows, in case you are viewing more than one Web site at a time.
- **Help.** This menu provides access to the Netscape online help system. Except for the About option, you must be connected to the Web to use the options in this menu.

Netscape's top-line display

The top-line display (see Figure 2-3) has three parts: the toolbar, the location box, and the directory buttons. The display appears at the top of the screen, directly below the menu bar.

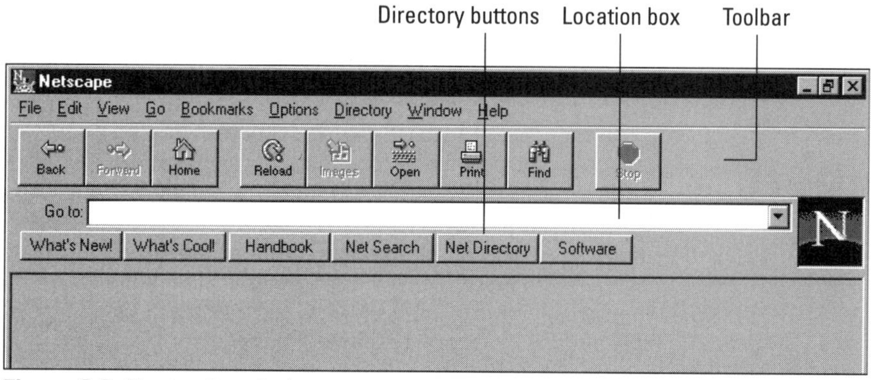

Figure 2-3: The top-line display.

Toolbar

The toolbar (see Figure 2-3) contains nine buttons: Back, Forward, Home, Reload, Images, Open, Print, Find, and Stop. These buttons mimic menu commands. Because you will use these functions routinely in your Web surfing, having the toolbar available at all times is valuable. From the Options menu, General Preferences menu item, you can choose how the toolbar is displayed. You can choose between text only, picture only, or both text and pictures.

The Back and Forward buttons take you through the trail of locations that you have visited. You can think of each home page that you view on the Web as being added to a list of locations where you have been. Netscape keeps the URL for each location that you visit during the current session. If you click the Back button, Netscape checks the list and takes you to the preceding location. If you want to move farther back, you can click the button a second time and move back another page.

Likewise, if you decide that you want to return to the location from which you clicked the Back button, you can click the Forward button. Netscape takes you to the appropriate location. The procedure may sound a bit confusing, but it really isn't.

The Back and Forward buttons are invaluable when you move through documents on the Web through hyperlinks. The buttons in the toolbar hide much of the complexity involved with moving through hyperlinks.

The Home button takes you back to the page where you started during the current session.

The Reload button simply accesses and reloads the current home page. This feature is useful when a connection has *timed out* (your computer is waiting for a reply from another computer, but it never responds) and you want to try loading it again.

The Images button allows you to turn on or off the display of graphic images. You may wonder why somebody would want to do this. Although browsing the Web is much more fun with graphic images, these images can take a long time to download — so long, in fact, that you may get tired of waiting. In such a case, you can turn the images off. The display may not be quite as exciting, but at least you won't be waiting for an image to download. You can turn the option on and off as you work through your current session.

The Open button (which emulates the Open Location option in the File menu) allows you to enter a new URL, which Netscape will access (see Figure 2-4). Type the name of the target URL in the Open Location dialog box and then click the OK button. Netscape takes you to the appropriate home page.

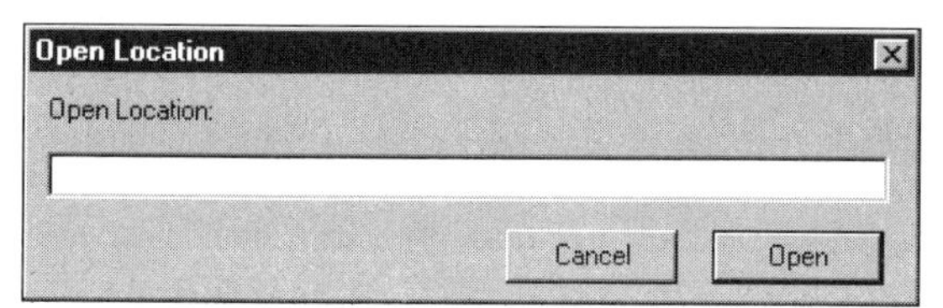

Figure 2-4: The Open Location dialog box.

The Print button will send the currently displayed Web page to a printer. It uses the current print configuration. You can also select a menu option to view how the current Web page would appear on paper (choose File menu and select Print Preview).

The Find button allows you to search the currently displayed home page for a word or phrase (see Figure 2-5). By clicking the Up or Down radio button in the Find dialog box, you can control the direction of the search.

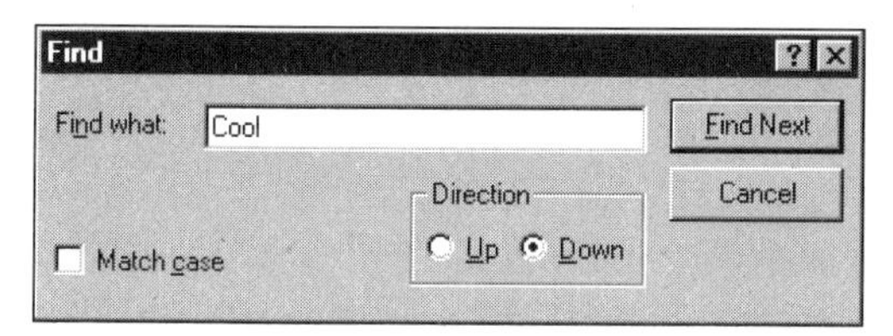

Figure 2-5: The Find dialog box.

Finally, the Stop button aborts the current attempt to download a home page. This command works on text files as well as graphic images.

Location box

At the top of the preview window, below the toolbar, is the location box (see Figure 2-3). This box displays the current address, or URL, of the home page that you are accessing. The location box reminds you exactly which document you have transferred to your computer. This feature is useful for reminder purposes, as well as for entering a new URL.

The location box has another purpose. You can click inside the location box, type a new URL, and press Enter to load the home page related to the URL that you typed. This feature is useful for moving to a desired address without having to access the Open Location dialog box.

You can turn off the location box, although I doubt that you will want to do so. I think you'll quickly find that the location box is a very useful feature.

The directory bar

The last row of buttons in the top-line display is called the directory bar (see Figure 2-3). Its buttons mimic items in the Directory and Help menus. Click these buttons to jump to home pages on the Web that are maintained by Netscape Communications.

The What's New! button, which displays information about Netscape Communications, is the same as the What's New! item in the Directory menu. The What's Cool! button displays information about interesting places to surf and is the same as the What's Cool! item in the Directory menu.

The Handbook button is a news and reference page providing support information about Netscape Navigator. It is the same as the Handbook option on the Help menu.

The Net Search button, which connects to the Netscape Web site and allows you to search for Web sites related to a particular topic, is the same as the Internet Search item on the Directory menu.

The Net Directory button displays a document listing a directory of interesting places to view on the Web. It allows you to choose by typing in a keyword or by selecting options from a list.

Finally, the Software button provides information about updating your version of Netscape Navigator.

The status bar

The status bar at the bottom of the window (see Figure 2-6) shows the status of your Web surfing session in several important pieces of information.

Figure 2-6: The status bar.

The first purpose of the status bar is to show the progress of a download. As you access home pages, the status bar shows a running count of the number of bytes being transferred to your computer. This feature is helpful because when traffic on the Internet is heavy, the progress bar moves slowly, making you aware of what is happening. Although the program's logo (in the top-right corner, next to the location box) informs you that the program is accessing information, it doesn't give you any indication of the progress. Used in conjunction, the status bar at the bottom of the screen along with the program logo tell you exactly what is happening to your data connection.

The status bar serves another purpose. When you place the cursor on a hypertext link, the status bar displays the link's target address. This feature enables you to check the URL before clicking a hyperlink so that you can determine whether you want to make the jump. If the link is one that you have already visited or if the link is to a computer that is down, you will know in advance that you shouldn't waste time by clicking it.

You will notice a small picture of a paper envelope on the right side of the status bar. If you double-click on this image with the mouse, a dialog box displays that allows you to send electronic mail. You need to tell the system your e-mail address and the target address. The dialog box then provides space for you to type the text of your message. Another feature of Netscape Navigator is the image of a broken key displayed at the far left end of the status bar. When you are working with secure transactions (those in which the data is encrypted), this image is a full key. When you are communicating with a server that is not secure, the key is cracked. This display is a clever way to notify the user of the current status of security. At this time, the only Web servers that support security features are those from Netscape Communications.

Using Program Options

You have learned how to use the window elements to navigate the Internet, access specified URLs, and view the status of program operations. This section describes other program operations that you access through the main-menu options, including loading and saving HTML files, printing home pages, and working with bookmarks.

Loading and saving HTML files

When Netscape accesses a home page on the Web, it is actually accessing a disk file that is transferred from the host computer in the hypertext markup language (HTML). A great feature of Netscape is that it allows you to load HTML files directly from disk, treating them just as though they were accessed over the Internet.

To display an HTML file in Netscape, choose Open File... from the File menu (or press Ctrl+O). A dialog box appears, in which you can enter the name of the file (see Figure 2-7).

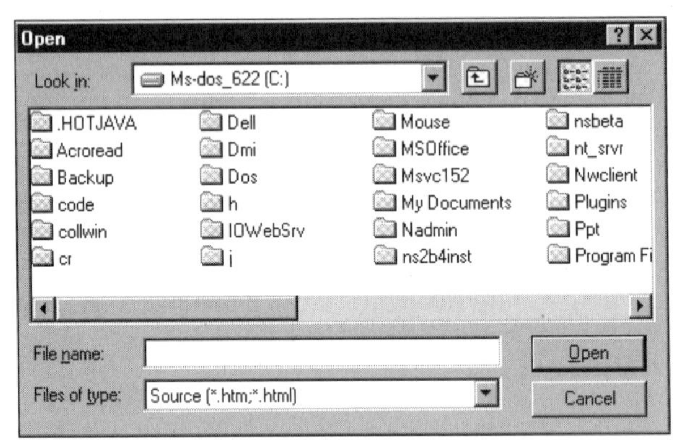

Figure 2-7: The Open dialog box.

You can always access a Web home page by choosing Open Location from the File menu (or pressing Ctrl+L). Netscape enables you to save this file, which you obtain from the Internet, to a local disk file by choosing Save As from the File menu (or pressing Ctrl+S). Using this feature is a great way to learn about authoring HTML documents because you can examine the statements that describe home pages you like and then use those elements in your own home pages.

If you are not sure whether you want to save a home page to a disk file, you can view the HTML source first by choosing Document Source from the View menu. A new window opens, displaying the HTML source code (see Figure 2-8) for the current Web page.

Another option on the View menu is Document Info (see Figure 2-9), which provides a graphical view of the layout of image and hyperlink files that are part of the Web page. It provides additional information like the size (in bytes) of the document, the security level, and the transfer protocol. The Document Info window is actually split into two parts: the top part displaying the links inside the current file, and the bottom part displaying file date, size, and security information about each file. You can resize the window to make more information come into view.

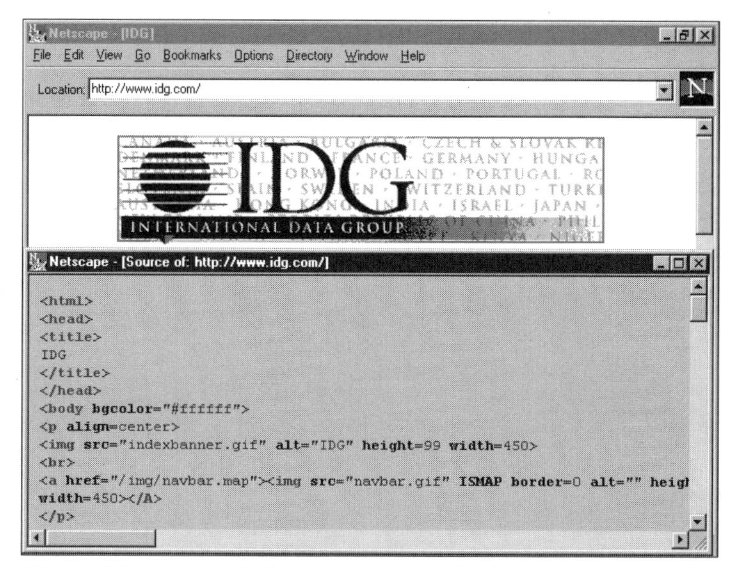

Figure 2-8: The View⇨Document Source window.

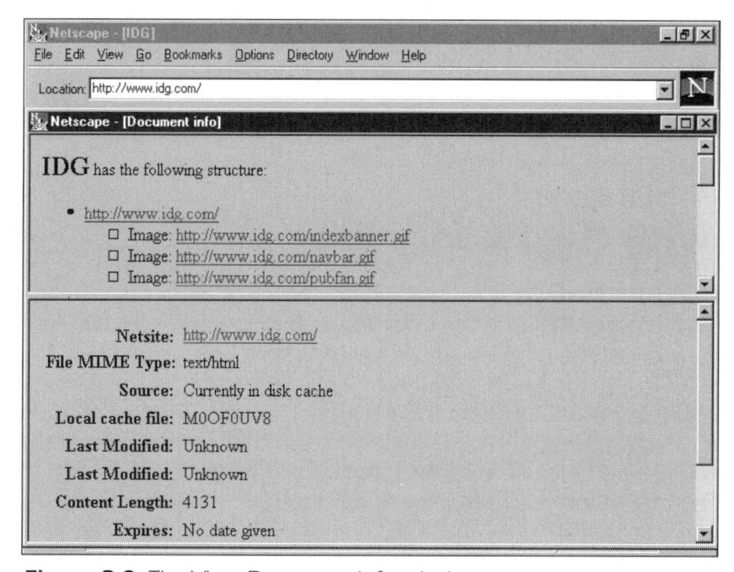

Figure 2-9: The View Document Info window.

Printing files

As you find interesting home pages, you can print them to your printer by choosing the Print option from the File menu. The first time you choose this menu item, a standard Windows Print dialog box appears (see Figure 2-10). If you want to modify your printer setup, click the Setup button; otherwise, click the OK button to send the current document to your printer.

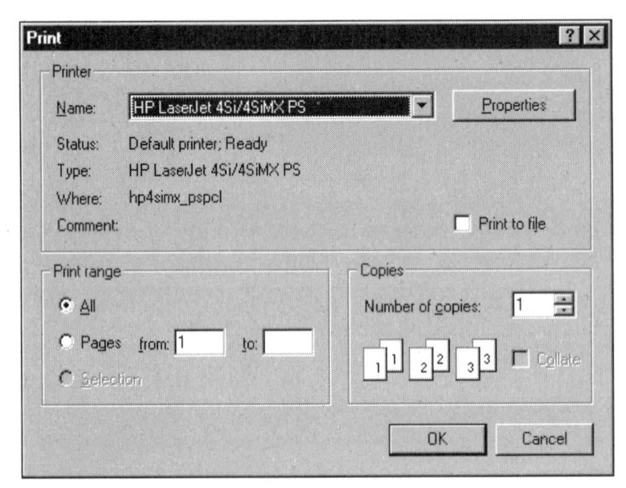

Figure 2-10: The Print dialog box.

Working with the history list

The history list works in conjunction with the Back and Forward buttons in the toolbar. It lets you return to any document that you have visited during the current session and keeps track of where you've been.

Display the history list by choosing History from the Window menu (or pressing Ctrl+H). A dialog box appears, displaying the URL for every page that you have visited. Select a URL in the list box and then click the Go to button. Netscape instantly transports you to the specified location.

Working with bookmarks

Bookmarks are one of the greatest features of using Netscape to surf the Web. They keep track of your favorite Web spots so that you can easily return to them later. You create a bookmark by giving Netscape the URL of a home page that you want to save. Later, you can choose the home page title for that URL from the Bookmarks menu, and Netscape Navigator displays the appropriate home page. You no longer have to remember long and confusing URL names.

Access bookmark functions from the Bookmarks menu. Choose the Add Bookmark item (or press Ctrl+D) to store the URL of the currently displayed home page in the bookmark list (see Figure 2-11).

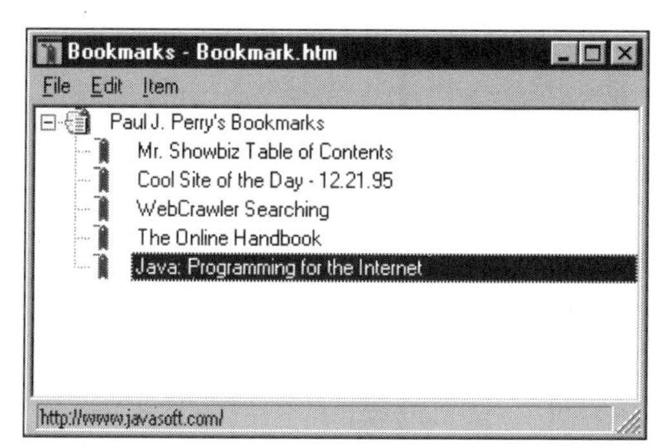

Figure 2-11: The Bookmark Window.

After you mark a page as a bookmark, the title of that page is added to the bottom of the Bookmarks list. As you continue to add bookmarks, this menu grows. There probably is a limit to the number of bookmarks you can store, but I haven't run into it. Usually, you put only the most important home pages in your bookmark list. By listing bookmarks as menu items, Netscape makes viewing saved Web addresses easy. You don't have to select items from a list in a dialog box.

Each time you add a bookmark, the new title is added to the bottom of the Bookmarks menu. You have a high degree of control of bookmarks through the Bookmark List context menu (see Figure 2-12), which you display by right-clicking the mouse over the bookmark you wish to modify. The Goto Bookmark option will force Netscape Navigator to display the highlighted bookmark. The Internet Shortcut item works in conjunction with Windows 95 to add an icon to the desktop. If you double-click on that icon, it will start Netscape Navigator and connect you to the specified location. The Properties... option displays the Properties dialog box that enables you to change the URL of the Web page, as well as add a description about the site.

To gain even more control of your bookmarks, select the Item option in the Bookmark Window (see Figure 2-13). There are options for sorting bookmarks, adding bookmark folders (for organizing many bookmarks), creating aliases, and managing the bookmark list.

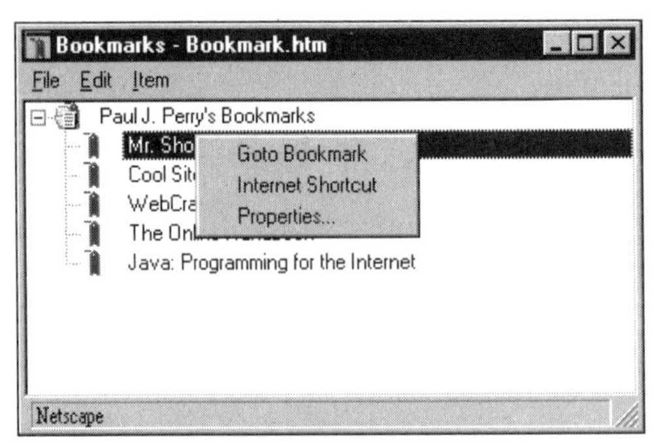

Figure 2-12: The Bookmark List context Menu.

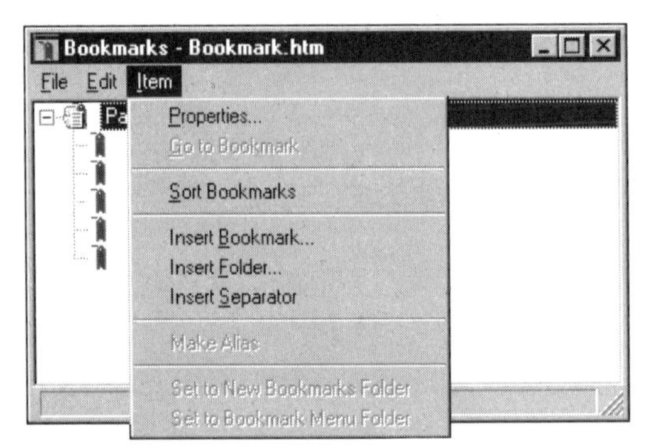

Figure 2-13: The Bookmark Item Menu.

Another useful feature is the capability to delete a bookmark. Use the arrow keys to highlight the bookmark URL in the Window and then click the Del key. Netscape removes the bookmark.

As you make your rounds surfing the Web, you will find many interesting places that you will want to add to your Bookmarks menu. I have heard of people who started swapping bookmark data files with friends to learn about new places to surf.

If you have used NCSA Mosaic to browse the Web and have created your own set of bookmarks in that program, you can save yourself some time by copying any hot list from Mosaic to Netscape bookmarks. To transfer the bookmarks, click the Import Bookmarks button in the extended Bookmark List dialog box. Netscape prompts you for the file. Enter the name, and all your bookmarks are transferred.

Setting Options

You set Netscape preferences through the Options menu (see Figure 2-14). The menu contains many items for customizing Netscape Navigator. The first section of items includes the following: General Preferences..., Mail and News Preferences..., Network Preferences..., and Security Preferences... .

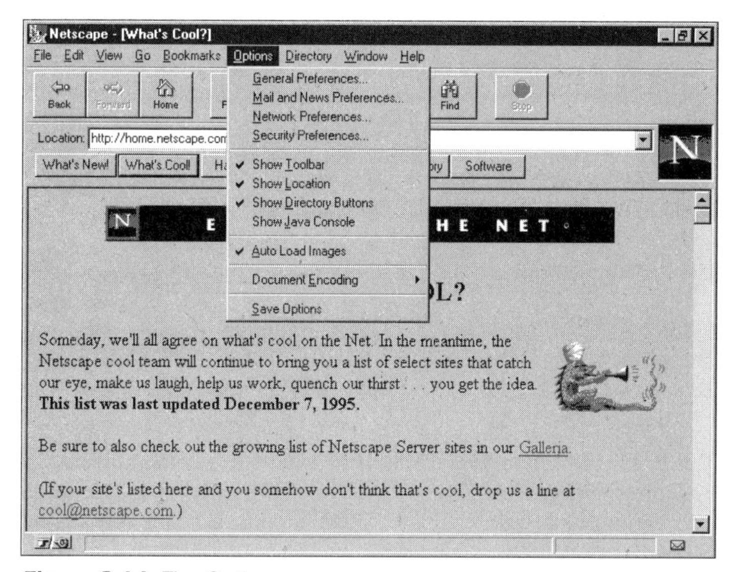

Figure 2-14: The Options menu.

The next several options (Show Toolbar, Show Location, Show Directory Buttons, Show Java Console, and Auto Load Images) are self-explanatory and can be toggled on and off. A checkmark next to an item signifies that the item is on. The Show Java Console option is a nice status display for the execution of Java applets. If any errors occur during execution, information is displayed in this window, as well as status information about the execution of the applet. The Document Encoding option allows you to set the language character set you would like Netscape to display. Most North American users will set this option to Western.

The last option in the menu, Save Options, saves all the current settings to disk, ready for future surfing sessions.

Modifying Preferences

You modify Netscape preferences through tab-style dialog boxes. Netscape presents you with four of these dialog boxes, which you select with the first four preference items on the Options menu (General, Mail and News, Network, and Security). Each dialog box has tabs at the top, much like file folder tabs. You click on the tab to display new options in the dialog box relating to the tab name. The following list describes the purpose of each preference dialog box:

- **The General Preferences dialog box** (see Figure 2-15) allows you to choose how toolbars will appear, what font to use for proportional or fixed-pitch fonts, and how long to keep track of hyperlinks that you've visited. It also lets you enter information about the directories that Netscape should use for various operations, as well as some of the supporting applications that Netscape should access when you access other parts of the Internet.
- **The Mail and News Preferences dialog box** (see Figure 2-16) lets you configure Netscape to work with your e-mail name and set information related to what newsgroups you would like to access.
- **The Network Preferences dialog box** (see Figure 2-17) allows you to provide information about your current network and how you are connected to the Internet.
- **The Security Preferences dialog box** (see Figure 2-18) allows you to set options related to Internet security, including giving you a reminder message every time you access a secure Web site. You can also disable the execution of Java applets in this dialog box.

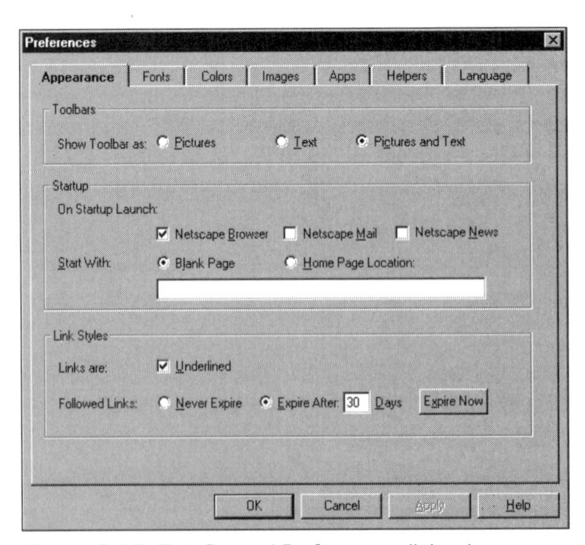

Figure 2-15: The General Preferences dialog box.

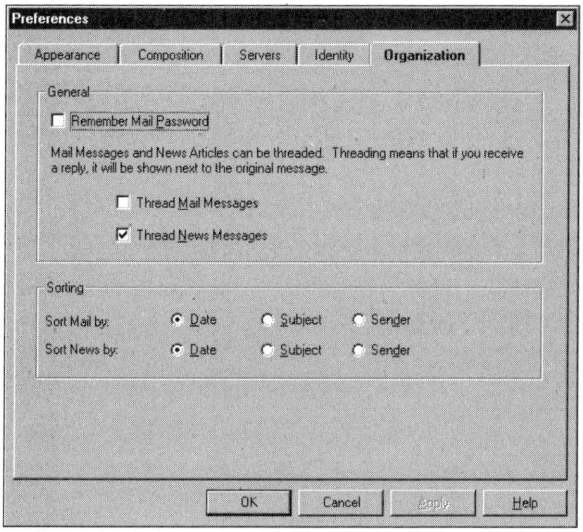

Figure 2-16: The Mail and News Preferences dialog box.

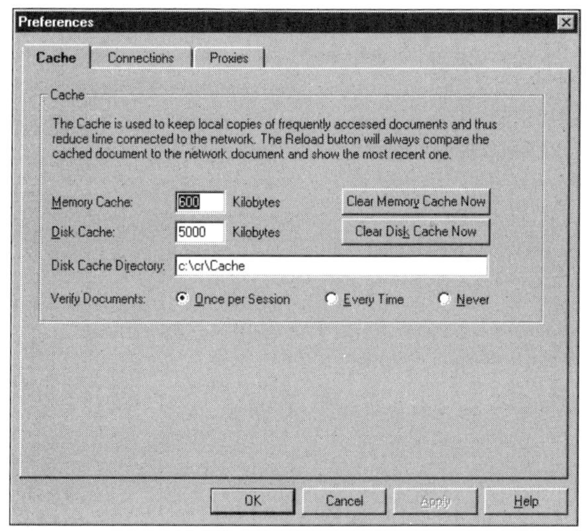

Figure 2-17: The Network Preferences dialog box.

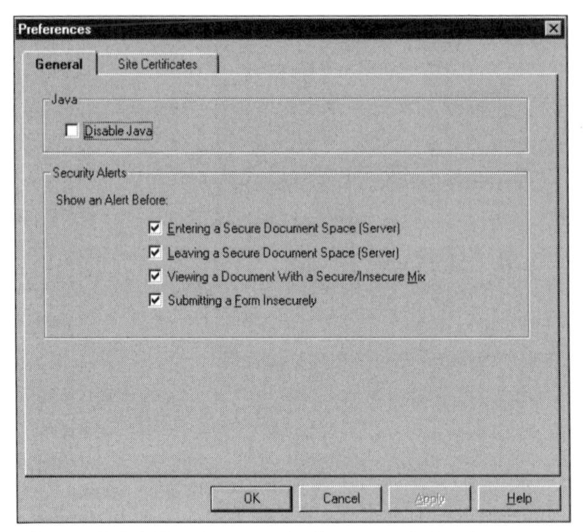

Figure 2-18: The Security Preferences dialog box.

The Online Help System

Maybe as an incentive to coax users into surfing the Web, the Netscape developers decided not to include any documentation with the software. Rather, they chose to make this information available as a home page on the Web. As a result, you must be up and running to access the help system. In most cases, this requirement is probably not much of a problem, except for being a contradiction in terms. (Why, yes, I know that help is available online, but I need help *getting* online!)

The Help menu

The Help menu contains eleven items: About Netscape..., About Plug-ins, Registration Information, Software, Handbook, Release Notes, Frequently Asked Questions, On Security, How to Give Feedback, How to Get Support, and How to Create Web Services.

The About Netscape... option displays information about the company. (Hint: Click the company logo to view hidden information about the developers.) The About plug-ins option displays information about any add-in (a.k.a. plug-in) software that has been added to the browser. The Registration Information option tells you about registering your version of Netscape Navigator. The

Software option provides information about upgrading your version of Netscape Navigator. The Handbook option (see Figure 2-19) is the main source of information about the program. The Release Notes option displays what has been fixed and added in the version of the program that you are using. The Frequently Asked Questions option displays a document, in question-and-answer format, that provides insight on standard areas of confusion in using Netscape.

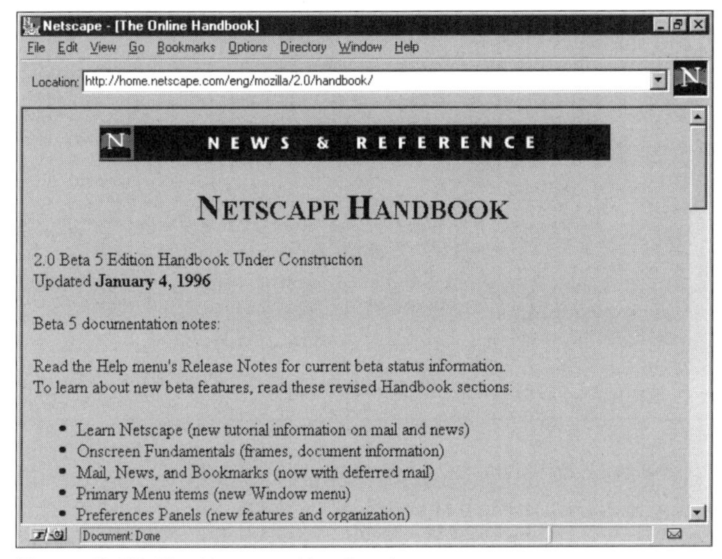

Figure 2-19: The Netscape Handbook.

The On Security option tells you how to make sure that you are making secure transactions when you send proprietary data (such as credit card numbers) over the Web. In order for security to work, the computer at the other end *must* be running the Netscape server software, and at the same time you *must* be running the Netscape browser. When both of these occur, the graphic image of a key on the Netscape browser status bar will be full, and secure transactions can occur. The problem is that most server sites do not use the Netscape server software. As a result, the user can't be guaranteed of secure transactions.

The last three options allow you to send information to Netscape. The How to Give Feedback option tells you how to contact the company. The How to Get Support option points you in the direction of technical support (one of the requirements is to have a registered copy of the program). Finally, the How to Create Web Services option gives you information about setting up your own Web site.

Directory

The Directory menu (see Figure 2-20) enables you to access the Netscape Communications Web site. The menu has nine options that provide information about the Internet in general (compared with the Netscape program, in which the Help menu gives you program information).

The Netscape's Home option displays the Netscape Communications Welcome home page. The What's New! option gives you information about the latest happenings on the Internet. The What's Cool! option displays a home page that has links to many cool and interesting locations on the Web.

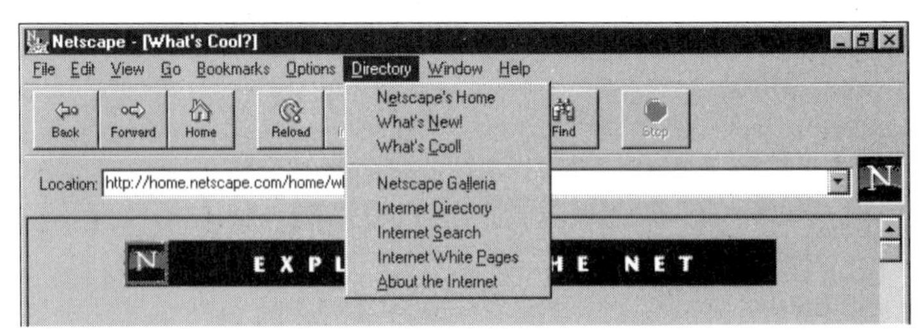

Figure 2-20: The Directory menu.

Netscape Galleria is a page with links to companies that use the Netscape server applications. The last section of options provides ways to search the Internet. The first option, Internet Directory, displays a directory of places that you can search on the Internet. The Internet Search option displays a list of ways to search the Web for specific topics. The Internet White Pages option allows you to access users on the Internet in a fashion similar to accessing people's names in the white pages of the phone book. The About the Internet option displays information about the Internet.

Keyboard Shortcuts

This chapter has covered a great deal of ground. As you have learned, you can carry out almost every command in Netscape by using the mouse. The program does, however, provide keyboard shortcuts for choosing common commands from the keyboard. Table 2-1 summarizes these keyboard commands.

Table 2-1 Netscape Navigator Accelerator Keys

Key	Command
Ctrl+A	Select All
Ctrl+B	View Bookmarks
Ctrl+C	Copy (to Clipboard)
Ctrl+D	Add Bookmark
Ctrl+F	Find Character String
Ctrl+H	View History List
Ctrl+I	Load Images
Ctrl+L	Open Location (URL)
Ctrl+M	New Mail Message
Ctrl+N	New Web Browser
Ctrl+O	Open File...
Ctrl+R	Reload
Ctrl+S	Save As...
Ctrl+V	Paste (from Clipboard)
Ctrl+W	Close Window
Ctrl+X	Cut (to Clipboard)
Ctrl+Z	Undo
up arrow	View Previous Line
down arrow	View Next Line
PgUp	View Previous Page
PgDn	View Next Page
Ctrl+>	Go Forward (to next item in history list)
Ctrl+<	Go Back (to previous item in history list)
Esc	Abort (loading home page)
Alt+F4	Exit
F3	Find Again

Quick Overview

This chapter uncovered the secrets of using Netscape Navigator. You learned how to use Netscape as your interface to the Web and Java. You also learned about how each window element and menu item functions. Finally, you learned how to access features such as bookmarks and online help.

In particular, this chapter covered the following topics:

- You install Netscape Navigator with the Setup program. This program automatically copies the appropriate files to a subdirectory on your hard disk and creates the necessary Program Manager group.
- The main window contains six elements: preview area, menu bar, toolbar, location box, directory buttons, and status bar.
- Netscape's top-line display has three parts: toolbar, location box, and directory buttons. The toolbar contains eight buttons that make navigating the Web easier. The location box contains the URL for the current home page. The directory buttons provide a way to surf commonly accessed areas of the Web.
- Bookmarks are a great feature that allow you to store the URLs of commonly accessed home pages and then revisit those home pages by selecting their names from a menu.

Here is a brief overview of what is to come...

- Move on to Chapter 3, "A Review of HTML," to learn how to create your own Web documents.
- If you already know HTML, skip to Chapter 4, "Introduction to Java Programming," where you will get up to speed with how to program Java.

A Review of HTML

In This Chapter

What HTML is, how it is used, and the basis for its use on the Web.

The advantages and disadvantages of HTML.

How to format paragraphs and characters using HTML commands.

What types of lists are supported by HTML and how to implement them in your documents.

How to add hypertext capability to your HTML documents.

Special HTML commands that are available with Netscape Navigator.

How to display multimedia elements, such as graphical images, audio sound, and digital video in your HTML documents.

This chapter provides a thorough review of the hypertext markup language (HTML), the system that the Web uses for marking up text documents. This is the first step in creating cool web applications because when you create Java applets, you must already be familiar with HTML. HTML is a fairly easy skill to master, and by the time you complete this chapter, you should have an excellent grasp of how it works.

Developing Home Pages

As a Web information provider, you prepare documents in a markup language known as HTML, which is short for hypertext markup language. HTML is not a page description language (like Postscript), nor is it a language that you can easily generate from your favorite desktop publishing program (like PageMaker). With HTML, you can describe the structure of your Web documents, including related information such as the integration of multimedia and the use of hyperlinks. It also links Java applets to your Web site.

Originally, there was no standard definition for HTML. In other words, no particular organization took charge and produced the definitive standards for the format. This led to a situation where different organizations added extensions that caused confusion among users. As a result, a move evolved to standardize HTML. The original version of HTML has now been named version 1.0. Version 2.0 is the current definition and the one I cover in this book. Discussions are already taking place about the next version of HTML, known as version 3.0 (and sometimes called HTML+). At the same time, Netscape Navigator has added special commands to the specification. At first, the folks at Netscape added HTML 3.0 capability. They soon started adding specialized tags that other Web browser developers hadn't even thought about.

Some Web browsers provide a superset of HTML. In particular, Netscape Navigator provides support for many unique tags. Some say that when you author Web pages, you should not target any particular browser. Unfortunately, when you do this, you lose out on some specialized commands. As a cool feature of HTML, if a Web browser does not recognize a tag, it will be ignored. Therefore, you can use extended tags and won't cause any negative effects to users who are not using Netscape Navigator (about 30 percent of the population). This chapter presents some of those extended tags. If you think that they could be helpful for your Web page creation, please make use of them. Otherwise, you can ignore them. If you do decide to use them, let your users know that you've enhanced the site for Netscape.

About Hypertext Markup Language

HTML is a method for representing the appearance and content of a document using a standard ASCII text file. HTML consists of reserved markup directives, or tags, mixed with plain text to compose a document. A document is what makes up a Web page.

Does anybody know SGML?

HTML is actually a subset of an internationally known standard called *SGML* (ISO 8879), which stands for the *Standard Generalized Markup Language*. SGML processes text information and is most often used on mainframe computers. IBM was one of SGML's original developers.

Where SGML was defined as being extensible and customizable, HTML is defined as being rigid and well-defined. The advantage of HTML is that you can create its documents with a simple ASCII text editor, which is not always true for documents based on SGML.

The purpose of HTML

HTML, similar to a computer programming language or a script language, requires you to express your thoughts in a specific structure. Its purpose is to transmit the structure of documents between users.

Although HTML is not complicated, using it requires that you think in terms of rules (and nobody likes rules). This sets HTML apart from standard word processors where you concentrate on a document's *appearance*. When using HTML, you concentrate on the document's *structure* (see Figure 3-1).

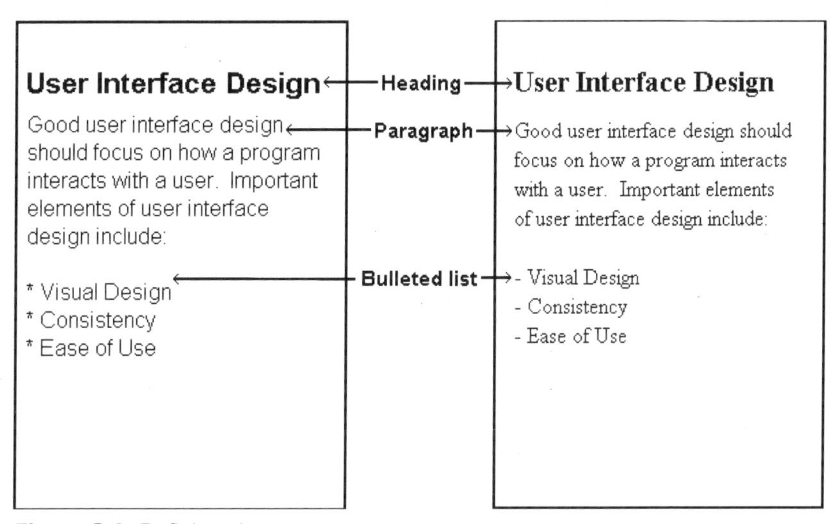

Figure 3-1: Defining document structure.

HTML was developed to force you to think about document structure rather than document appearance because of the Web's focus on being a cross-platform information service. HTML defines documents so that any browser running on any computer can read and display them.

This means that you can develop documents in HTML and not have to create separate versions for Netscape (see Figure 3-2), Microsoft Internet Explorer (see Figure 3-3), and America Online (see Figure 3-4). This is a nice change of pace from using word processors such as WordPerfect or Word for Windows that require documents to be stored in their native file format.

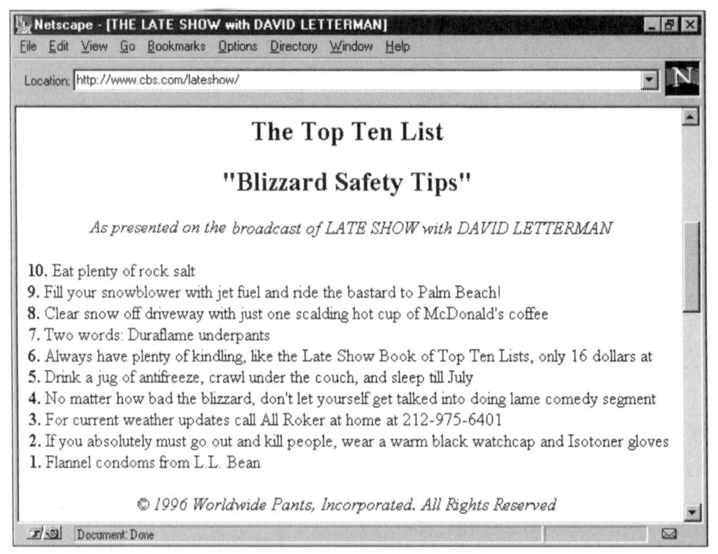

Figure 3-2: An HTML document displayed in Netscape Navigator, running under Windows 95.

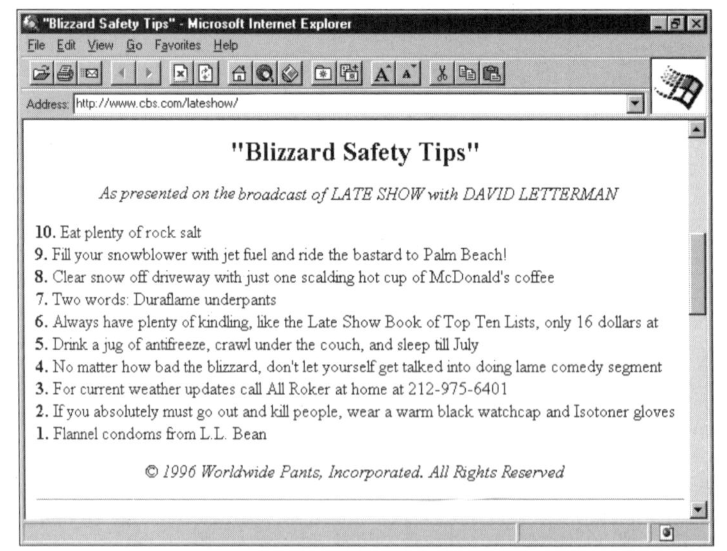

Figure 3-3: The same HTML document displayed in Microsoft Internet Explorer, running under Windows 95.

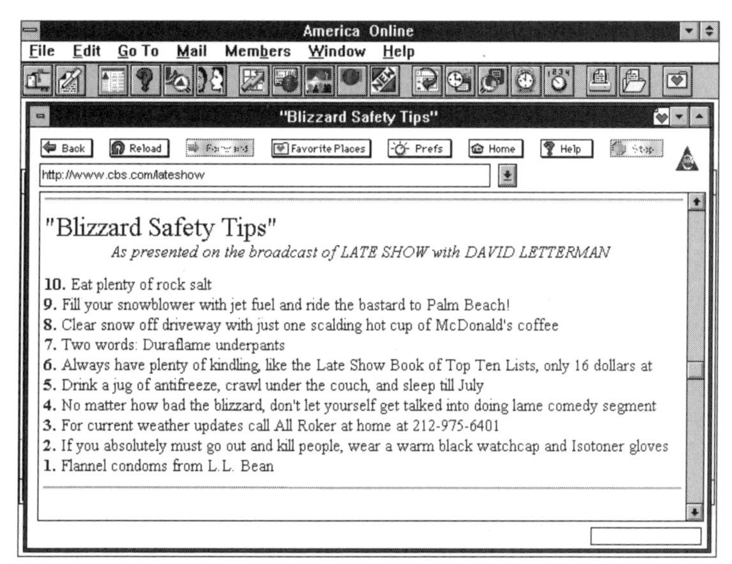

Figure 3-4: The same HTML document, this time displayed in America Online, running under Windows 3.1.

Also, HTML was developed as a language for describing structured documents: documents with elements in common, such as titles, headings, paragraphs, and lists.

If you have ever used a word processing program's style sheet feature, you have worked in a similar manner. Each style conforms to one of a set of styles that are pre-defined. What style sheets provide (in contrast to HTML) is the actual appearance of each part of a document on the page. For example, styles in Word for Windows not only have a name ("Heading 1" for a heading), but they also describe the font, the size, and the indentation of the style.

Thus, HTML serves as a format for expressing information in its raw form, without having to consider formatting. Instead of thinking about formatting, you focus on content.

Advantages of HTML

The designers of the Web had many different choices in how to communicate documents over the Internet. Although HTML may sound somewhat limited, it provides several advantages:

- Your HTML files are compatible with any Web browser. In effect, this is saying that the HTML documents are *system-independent,* and they can be displayed on any computer that supports HTML.

- Because HTML is based on structure rather than on appearance, an HTML author can define a numbered list, and the users can specify whether they wish to view that list with Roman or Arabic numerals. This provides users with more flexibility in how a document is viewed.
- HTML files are small. The tags used to describe an HTML file have little overhead. Although HTML does not use any type of compression (such as that used in bitmap files), the language really doesn't need it.
- HTML is easy to learn. You don't need to find out about many tags, and editors are also available to make authoring HTML documents easier. (See "HTML Authoring Tools" later in this chapter for more information.)

As you learn how to write in HTML, you will find that you really can communicate easily without having to learn a lot of complicated commands.

Disadvantages of HTML

As is always the case, using HTML poses some disadvantages:

- HTML is limited. The choices you have for the elements in your documents are rather limited.
- You cannot create new tags. Therefore, you are limited to the set of tags that are currently available.
- Because HTML focuses on the structure of documents, you don't know *exactly* how a target document will appear.

However, the good news is that as HTML matures and progresses to new levels, its formatting features will also improve. For now, you can only work with what you have. Most certainly as the Web becomes more important, people will find new ways to work around some of HTML's limitations.

Using HTML

The basic HTML commands you need to familiarize yourself with to create Web pages fall into the following categories:

- **Structural commands.** These identify a file as an HTML document and provide information about the data in the HTML file.
- **Paragraph formatting commands.** These specify paragraph endpoints and heading levels.
- **Character formatting commands.** These allow you to apply various styles (such as boldface or italic) to the characters in your documents.

- **List specification commands.** HTML supports several list formats including numbered, bulleted, and definition lists.
- **Hyperlinking commands.** These allow you to provide information about moving from one document to another.
- **Asset integration commands.** These allow you access to multimedia information. Through these commands, you can display graphical images, access sound, and provide digital movies for your users.

In the following sections, we will examine the exact commands used for these categories. We start out by learning how HTML files are arranged.

HTML file overview

As mentioned, HTML files are standard ASCII text files that have the MS-DOS file extension .HTM. (UNIX computers, which allow longer file extensions, use the file extension .HTML.) Windows 95 and Windows NT also allow long filenames, and you can use either the .HTM or .HTML.

Working with tags

Tags are instructions to the browser software that tell how to display text. They are represented by enclosing string with the less-than (<) and greater-than (>) symbols to separate the tags from the rest of the text. For example, `<TagName>` would be a valid tag.

Tags are not case-sensitive, therefore the tag `<HTML>` is the same as the tag `<HtMl>` and the tag `<html>`. In this book, I use all uppercase because I want to be consistent and because it forces the tags to stand out when you are scanning text quickly.

Tags have two types. The first type is the single-element tag that stands by itself.

The second type affects the page from where the tags are inserted down until the command ends. These tags are symmetric, meaning that you use them in pairs. You close a command by issuing the same command with a forward slash before it, as in `</HTML>`. Many tags also accept parameters, which we will look at later.

Before you start learning how to write your own HTML documents, you can get a feel for what an HTML document looks like by looking at HTML documents that have already been written. Most Web browsers let you look at the source HTML that is downloaded from each Web home page. Usually, you only see the formatted version, but viewing the raw source code can be helpful while learning to use HTML.

To view HTML source code in Netscape Navigator, use the Document Source command from the View menu. A window will appear with the appropriate commands (see Figure 3-5). The actual screen you will see may be different. If the browser that you are using does not have a view source menu command, it will usually allow you to save the currently displayed web page to an HTML file and then view the saved file from an editor. Either way, both provides a method for examining HTML source.

Netscape - [Source of: http://www.cbs.com/lateshow/]

```
<html>
<head><title>THE LATE SHOW with DAVID LETTERMAN</title></head>
<body BGCOLOR=FFFFFF>
<CENTER>
<img src="http://www.cbs.com/graphics/ban_dave.gif">
<p>
<img src="http://www.cbs.com/graphics/bar_tour.gif">
</center>
<br clear=all>

<b>
<img src="/graphics/i_dave3.gif">

Here's your source for Daily Top Ten lists,
Dave's lines of the week, upcoming guests, cast bios,
and our complete
<a href="/lateshow/ttlist.html">archive</a> of LATE SHOW Top Tens
and <a href="/eyeware/mm_late.html">photos</a> from LATE SHOW. You can orde
 t-shirts, sweatshirts etc. from our online <a href="/blackrock/store.html"
catalog</a>.  And don't miss our other late night show <a
href="/snyder">THE LATE LATE SHOW with TOM SNYDER</a> and the new homepage
for the LATE SHOW's <a href="http://www.calvertdeforest.com">Calvert
DeForest</a>.Also, to save you the trouble of us sending us email, find out
answers first (How do I get LATE SHOW tickets or merchandise?) in the new C
(Frequently Asked Questions)</a>.<p>
```

Figure 3-5: The Netscape view source window.

Structural Formatting

HTML has three tags that describe a document's overall structure. These document structure tags don't affect what the document looks like when it's formatted. They are included only to help browsers and search tools learn about the basic structure of a document.

Specifying an HTML file

The first document structure tag that every HTML document contains is the `<HTML>...</HTML>` set of tags which indicates that the content of the file is indeed HTML. Everything in your document should go inside the beginning and ending HTML tags, which look like this:

```
<HTML>
...
document text
...
</HTML>
```

Once you have marked the entire document as an HTML file using the <HTML> tag, you need to break the document down into two other parts: the header and the body.

Specifying the header

The first part is the prologue to the file, and it is marked with the <HEAD>... </HEAD> set of tags. Generally, only a few tags go into the heading portion of a document. At this point, the file looks like this:

```
<HTML>
<HEAD>
...
header information
...
</HEAD>
...
document text
...
</HTML>
```

Each HTML document needs a title. To give a document a title, use the *<TITLE>...</TITLE>* set of tags, which you must locate inside the header tags. When your browser interprets the *<TITLE>...</TITLE>* tag, it displays this as the title. Netscape Navigator displays this information in the title bar of the window. Other browsers, like Mosaic, display the title in the toolbar below the main menu items. Here's a typical example of how you would use the title tag:

```
<HTML>
<HEAD>
<TITLE>This is the document title</TITLE>
</HEAD>
...
document text
...
</HTML>
```

You should choose a document title that properly describes the information being displayed. Remember, somebody might jump to this page from a completely different location on the Web, so it makes sense to have a title that describes the current page, without relying on previous pages from where the user might have jumped.

Although the HTTP specification requires the use of the <HTML>...</HTML> and <HEAD>...</HEAD> tags, many Web browsers don't. As a result, you will see documents that don't contain these tags. You should choose whether to use them. My personal suggestion is that because it is in the specification, you should go ahead and use them. It doesn't take much extra effort and results in a more complete document. However, if you decide not to, don't worry, because no Web police will come and arrest you.

Specifying the body of your document

The remainder of your HTML document, including all the document text is stored inside a <BODY>...</BODY> set of tags. The document now looks something like this:

```
<HTML>
<HEAD>
<TITLE>This is the document title</TITLE>
</HEAD>
<BODY>
...
This is the document text
...
</BODY>
</HTML>
```

Although an HTML document should always contain these three tags, most browsers will still read the file even if they are not present. However, you should get in the habit of including them in your documents, and you won't have to worry about updating your files later if the tags become necessary.

Recent versions to Netscape Navigator have added tags to specify the background and foreground color of a Web page. You change the background color by specifying a color code to the <BODY> tag. This works when you pass parameters to the tag, which looks something like this:

```
<HTML>
<HEAD>
<TITLE>Document with Cool background color</TITLE>
</HEAD>
<BODY BGCOLOR="FFFFFF" TEXT="000000">
...
```

```
Black text on White background.  Pretty Cool!
...
</BODY>
</HTML>
```

Notice the addition of the BGCOLOR and TEXT parameters to the opening <BODY> tag. The BGCOLOR parameter specifies the background color, and the TEXT parameter allows you to specify the text color. With these tags, you specify a hexadecimal (base 16) RGB (red, green, blue) color value, which is used as the color of your Web page.

Humans don't usually speak in hexadecimal (unless they have been around computers too long), but computers do. Table 3-1 provides an example of hexadecimal color values that you might want to use. If you have some extra time, you can also try other values because you can numerically set up to 65K different colors with this tag. Of course, if your display can view only 16 colors, that is all you get.

Table 3-1 Color Values for the <BODY> Tag

Color	Hexadecimal Color Value
White	FFFFFF
Black	000000
Red	FF0000
Green	00FF00
Blue	0000FF
Violet	FF00FF
Olive green	505000
Yellow	FFFF00
Turquoise	00FFFF
Dark gray	808080
Light gray	C0C0C0

Because you use the <BODY>...</BODY> tag only once at the beginning of your document, you can only set the color values once, and they apply to the entire document. You cannot change coloring when you're partially through a document.

Adding comments

Anyone who has written computer programs knows the power of adding useful information to a program's source code that the person executing the program does not see.

In a similar way, you can add comments to an HTML document to provide some useful information about the file. A browser ignores text inside a comment. Comments don't show up on the screen. Their only use is to provide extra information about a document, such as a revision number or reminders for updating the document in the future.

You must provide a comment tag for every comment line, which is separated by <! and -> characters. Here's an example of a single-line comment:

```
<!- This is a comment ->
```

Comments can appear anywhere in an HTML document, except within a tag. You may not nest comments. For example, to use multiple comments, you use the following:

```
<!- This is an HTML document. ->
<!- I was feeling especially good when I finished it. ->
<!- It is modified from the original document MYDOC.TXT. ->
```

Unlike comments in program source code, which is never displayed in the final program, comments in an HTML file will be transmitted to the user. Therefore, if you put a large amount of comments in an HTML file, it could slow down the perceived transmission of a file. However, the comments would have to go on for several pages in order for the user to notice lower performance.

Skeleton crew

Because you will have certain tags in all your HTML documents, it is a good idea to create a template for yourself (you can call it MINIMAL.HTM) that contains the basics, including:

```
<HTML>
<!- Comment line.  MINIMAL.HTM ->
<HEAD>
<TITLE>This is the document title</TITLE>
</HEAD>
<BODY>
...
This is the document text.
...
</BODY>
</HTML>
```

You can use this file whenever you start a new home page, thus making the process of creating the basic HTML document easier.

Paragraph Formatting

The most basic element of an HTML document is the paragraph. The text you type into an HTML file outside of any of the elements marked by the <HTML>, <HEAD>, <TITLE>, and <BODY> tags (as well as their counterparts) will be displayed as paragraphs.

A Web browser flows all the contents of a paragraph together from left to right and from top to bottom using the current window size. This is referred to as *autoflowing*. Therefore, as the user resizes the browser window, the locations where the text breaks will change. As a result, how you break lines in the HTML source file is irrelevant to how it finally displays.

You can have as many returns in your file as you like. However, only the <P> tag marks the end of a paragraph, and hence a paragraph break. Most browsers also remove any extra space between words, so you won't be able to format your text using spaces. (You can, however, use pre-formatted text that is described later.)

For example, an HTML file (see Figure 3-6) might look like this:

```
<HTML>
<!- Conference Description.  CONF.HTM ->
<HEAD>
<TITLE>WinDev Conference Description</TITLE>
</HEAD>
<BODY>
Join us for a gathering of the leading Windows programming talent
in the country! <P>
With 80 information packed seminars to choose from, you'll leave
this week-long Windows conference with valuable new programming
skills, tips and techniques for problem solving, and new insight
into upcoming Windows technologies gained from the experts! <P>
WinDev is a great opportunity for you to experience what's
happening in the world of Windows program development.  <P>
</BODY>
</HTML>
```

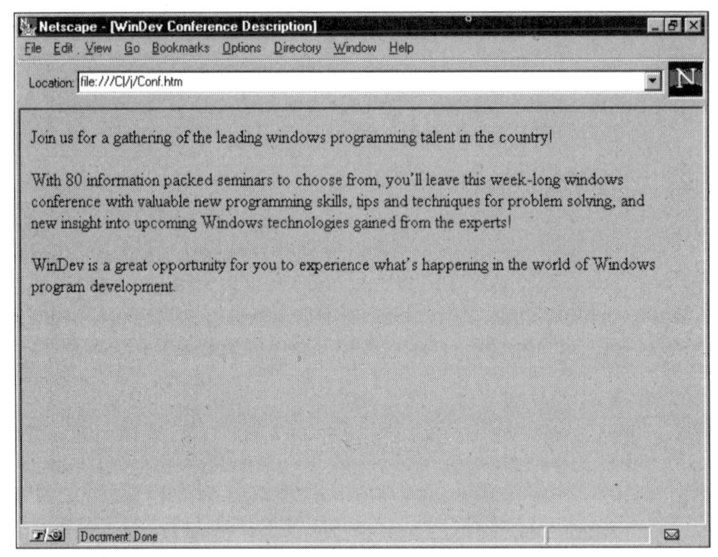

Figure 3-6: The Conference Description file displayed in Netscape Navigator.

Notice that the <P> tag is used only to break paragraphs. For readability in the HTML source file, I've added line breaks, but they don't make any difference in how the browser displays the text. The browser breaks lines and wraps lines of text based on how wide the browser window is, not based on the HTML source code.

As you start adding text to your HTML documents, you will want to see how the document appears in your favorite Web browser. The best way to do this is to use the Open File⇨File in Browser . . . feature provided with most Web browsers. The document will display just as if you were viewing it over the Internet.

Also, remember that several different graphical and character-based Web browsers will read your document. As a result, just because one browser breaks a line at one spot doesn't mean that others will do the same.

Line breaks

To indicate the start of a new line, use the line break tag, <BR>. Without this tag, all text, even text you leave blank in the HTML file will run together into a single paragraph. You should use the <BR> tag when you want to add a line break.

A couple of special tags that are built into Netscape Navigator allow you more control over line breaks. The <NOBR>...</NOBR> set of tags, (short for NO BReak) will force the Web browser to ignore all line breaks for text between the start and end of this tag. Be careful with this tag. Long text strings can look rather odd.

The <WBR> tag (short for Word BReak) is for the very rare case where you have used the <NOBR> tag but you wish to break the line. This does not force a line break (
 does that), but it tells Netscape Navigator where a line break should occur if one is needed.

Horizontal rules

A single tag, <HR>, indicates that the browser should create a line, which goes across the width of the display window. For example, you might modify the previous file to look like this (see Figure 3-7):

```
<HTML>
<!- Conference Description.  HREX.HTM ->
<HEAD>
<TITLE>WinDev Conference Description</TITLE>
</HEAD>
<BODY>
Join us for a gathering of the leading Windows programming talent
in the country! <P>
<HR>
With 80 information packed seminars to choose from, you'll leave
this week-long Windows conference with valuable new programming
skills, tips and techniques for problem solving, and new insight
into upcoming Windows technologies gained from the experts! <P>
<HR>
WinDev is a great opportunity for you to experience what's
happening in the world of Windows program development.  <P>
<HR>
</BODY>
</HTML>
```

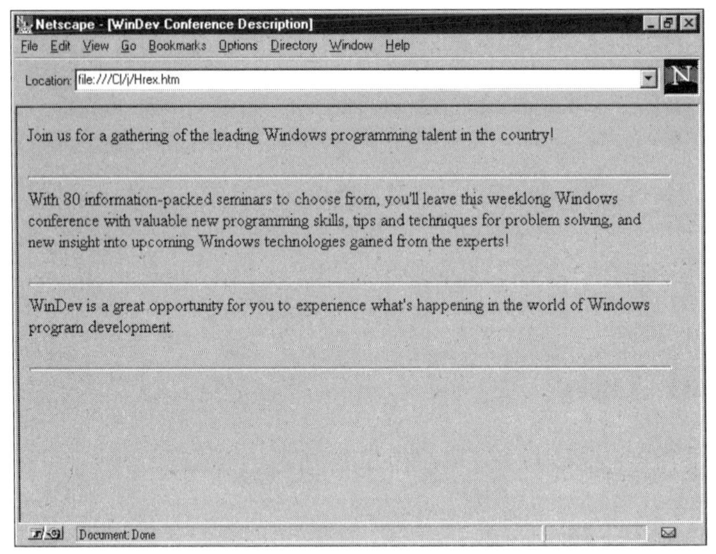

Figure 3-7: An example showing the effects of the horizontal rule tag.

Netscape adds some cool extensions to the horizontal rule tag. They provide some flexibility in how the horizontal rule should appear. The new functionality comes in the form of parameters passed to the `<HR>` tag, including `SIZE`, `WIDTH`, `ALIGN`, and `NOSHADE`. The `SIZE` parameter lets you choose the thickness of the horizontal rule and has the following structure:

```
<HR SIZE=x>
```

The *x* value is the desired thickness of the tag. This parameter appears to have no limits as to the size of the value that you can pass with it.

A horizontal rule is usually as wide as the page. The next extension allows you to specify the exact width of the rule, in pixels or as a relative width measured in percent of document width. It looks like this:

```
<HR WIDTH=x>
```

The *x* value is the number of pixels wide, or if you include the percent (%) sign, you can specify a relative width of the document. For example, using `<HR WIDTH=50%>` will display the rule as one-half (50 percent) of the width of the current page.

Now that the horizontal rule is not the entire width of the page, the system also provides some way to let you specify the alignment of the rule. That is, should the rule be displayed all the way to the left, to the right, or centered in the document? The default is centered, but with another extension, you can change it to either left- or right-justified. The syntax is as follows:

```
<HR ALIGN="LEFT"|"RIGHT"|"CENTER">
```

where you choose only one of the keywords, "LEFT", "RIGHT", or "CENTER". Remember, you can also combine these parameters, so you could use a tag like this:

```
<HR SIZE=15 WIDTH=50% ALIGN="RIGHT">
```

This would display a horizontal rule that is 15 pixels thick, has a width of 50 percent of the final page, and is aligned to the right side of the browser window.

Specifying headings

Headings mark divisions of a document and divide sections of a book into parts. You can have up to six levels of headings when using HTML. Heading tags look like this:

```
<H1>Course Description</H1>
```

The number indicates the heading level, which can be `<H1>...</H1>` through `<H6>...</H6>`. The headings themselves are not displayed, but they are usually displayed in larger text that is often displayed in boldface. However, you don't have any control over this, and in some cases users can specify whatever text style they want to use for each heading. The main idea is to use a style that forces the heading to stand out from the other text. Headings can be any length you wish them to be.

You will usually want to use a first-level heading at the top of your document that either duplicates the title (which is displayed somewhere else) or provides a shorter form of the title. For example:

```
<HTML>
<!- Conference Description ->
<HEAD>
<TITLE>WinDev Conference Description</TITLE>
</HEAD>
<BODY>
<H1>Conference Description</H1>
Join us for a gathering of the leading Windows programming talent
```

```
in the country! <P>
WinDev is a great opportunity for you to experience what's
happening in the world of Windows program development.  <P>
</BODY>
</HTML>
```

The levels of headings in your document provide you with the opportunity to create an information hierarchy in your document. In some ways, you can think of each heading level as an item in an outline. You are probably beginning to see how HTML lends itself well to structured documents.

Specifying pre-formatted text

Usually all text displayed in a Web browser strips any whitespace found in the HTML file. The one exception to the rule is with pre-formatted text. *Pre-formatted* text refers to text that you want to have displayed in a fixed-width monospace font (usually Courier), with all spacing information preserved.

Any whitespace that you put into text surrounded by the `<PRE>...</PRE>` tags is displayed in the final output. This has the advantage of allowing you to format the text the way you want it to appear. Pre-formatted text is ideal for such things as program source code, but you can employ it for such things as tables and graphs or for displaying diagrams created with the standard character set. An example would be as follows:

```
<HTML>
<!- Conference Attendance Info.  CONFINF.HTM ->
<HEAD>
<TITLE>Conference Attendance Information </TITLE>
</HEAD>
<BODY>
<H1>Conference Attendance Information</H1>
<PRE>

              Conference Attendance Chart


               Day 1           Day 2            Day 3
               -----           -----            -----
Marketing      1234            863              97
Engineering    564             859              424
Sales          982             895              87


</PRE>
</BODY>
</HTML>
```

Figure 3-8 shows how the file appears using the Netscape browser.

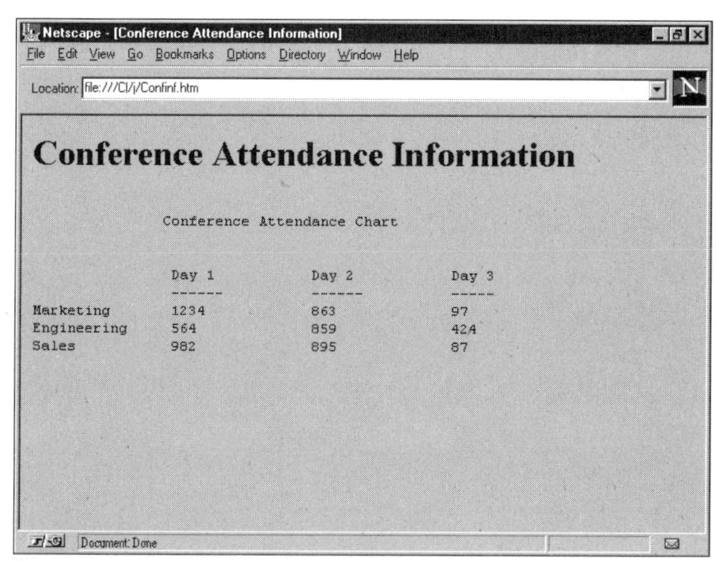

Figure 3-8: Pre-formatted text displayed in Netscape.

You can also specify a width argument to the pre-formatted text tag that tells the browser how wide the lines should be, and therefore the browser won't try to wrap the text onto the line below it. The format is as follows:

```
...
<PRE WIDTH="80">
Preformatted text
</PRE>
...
```

One of the most requested features in the HTML 3.0 specification is the capability to create tables inside a document. Although you can use the tags related to pre-formatted text (as previously illustrated), you are stuck with boring, unattractive text, and you are responsible for making sure the columns line up correctly.

Netscape Navigator is ahead of the proposed specification by providing early support for table definitions.

A combination of five tags helps achieve the goal of specifying document structure. With these tags, you are responsible for defining the data that belongs in the table, rather than how the table visually appears to the user. The browser is responsible for displaying data in a pleasing manner. The following is an example of creating an HTML table:

```
<HTML>
<!- Attendance Info., Table Version  TABLE.HTM ->
<HEAD>
<TITLE>Conference Information </TITLE>
</HEAD>
<BODY>
<H1>Netscape Navigator Table Example</H1>

<TABLE BORDER=1 CELLSPACING=5 CELLPADDING=5>
<CAPTION ALIGN=TOP>Conference Attendance Chart</CAPTION>

<TR>
 <TD> </TD>
 <TH>Day 1</TH>
 <TH>Day 2</TH>
 <TH>Day 3</TH>
</TR>

<TR>
 <TH>Marketing</TH>
 <TD>1234</TD>
 <TD>863</TD>
 <TD>97</TD>
</TR>

<TR>
 <TH>Engineering</TH>
 <TD>564</TD>
 <TD>859</TD>
 <TD>424</TD>
</TR>

<TR>
 <TH>Sales</TH>
 <TD>982</TD>
 <TD>895</TD>
 <TD>87</TD>
</TR>

</TABLE>

</BODY>
</HTML>
```

Figure 3-9 illustrates how the data looks. You will see that this is noticeably longer than the earlier example of a table using pre-formatted text. The only reason for this is the decision (by me) to add plenty of whitespace, resulting in easier readability and therefore better understanding of the table definition tags.

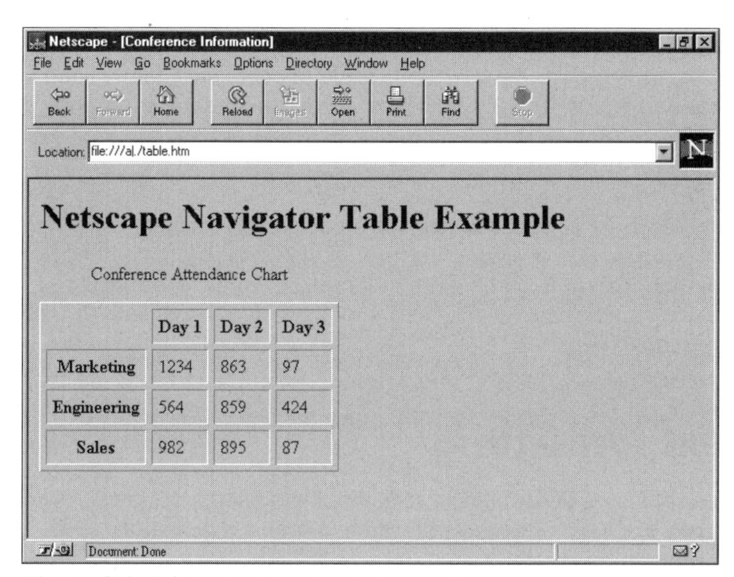

Figure 3-9: A formatted table in Netscape Navigator.

You begin a table definition with the `<TABLE>` tag. You can specify several parameters to customize how the table appears to the user. The `BORDER` parameter specifies the width (in pixels) of the border to be drawn around the table cells. If the `Border` parameter is absent, no border will appear.

The `CELLSPACING` and `CELLPADDING` parameters are also optional, but they allow you more control over the display of cells. `CELLSPACING` lets you specify the amount of space inserted between individual cells, and `CELLPADDING` sets the amount of space between the border of the cell and the contents of the cell. To create the most compact table possible, set both to zero.

Inside the table, you optionally use the `<CAPTION>...<CAPTION>` tags to specify caption text, which will be displayed in a different font in relation to the table. You can set the `ALIGN` parameter to either `TOP` or `BOTTOM`, depending on where you want the caption to appear in relation to the table.

The data in the table is defined by row and item. That is, you specify the beginning of a row, the beginning and end of each data item, and then the end of the row. You may define as many rows as you like.

Row definitions begin and end with the <TR>. . . </TR> set of tags (which stands for table row). Each data item in the row is set off with the <TD>. . . </TD> tag (which stands for table data). You can use the <TH>. . . </TH> pair of tags to mark table headers instead. Table headers are mainly used for column and heading labels. The only difference from table data is that they are displayed in boldface type. To end the table definition, use the </TABLE> tag.

Although creating a table like this may seem like a lot of work, the result is visually nicer. Also, you can display complex spreadsheet-style data. The previous example may seem like a lot of work, but try formatting something like the periodic table of the elements using plain old pre-formatted tags. I guarantee you that it won't come out looking as good as with the table layout tags described here.

Logical text formatting

Logical style tags describe how text should be used, not how it should be displayed. Logical text styles indicate text that is a definition, code, address, or many other things.

The browser always determines the way text is displayed for logical tags. You cannot guarantee that text will appear in any specific way when using logical text formatting. Each logical text formatting tag has both beginning and ending tags, and they affect the text within those tags. Table 3-2 provides an overview of the logical text formatting tags provided in HTML.

Table 3-2 Logical Text Formatting Tags

HTML Tag	Description
<ADDRESS>...</ADDRESS>	Displays address information. Usually in italics.
<BLOCKQUOTE>...</BLOCKQUOTE>	Indents text to separate from surrounding text. Used for quotations.
<CITE>...</CITE>	For citations (titles of books, films, and so on). Usually italics.
<CODE>...</CODE>	For snippets of computer code. Usually a fixed-width font.

HTML Tag	Description
<DFN>...</DFN>	Used for words being defined. Usually italics.
<EM>...</EM>	Used for emphasis. Usually italics.
<KDB>...</KDB>	User keyboard entry. Usually bold fixed-width font.
<SAMP>...</SAMP>	For computer status messages. Usually a fixed-width (proportional) font.
<STRONG>...</STRONG>	For strong emphasis. Usually displayed in boldface.
<VAR>...</VAR>	For variable information that might change. Usually in italics.

Character Formatting

With character formatting tags, you can make certain characters (and words) stand out. There are really only two character formatting commands: <B>...</B> for boldface and <I>...</I> for italics. You use them around the characters where you want to apply the corresponding attribute. For example, take a look at the following list:

```
<HTML>
<!- Character formatting example.  CHAR.HTM ->
<HEAD>
<TITLE>This is the document title</TITLE>
</HEAD>
<BODY>
<B>This is boldface text</B><BR>
<I>This is italic text</I><BR>
<B><I>This is boldface italic text</B></I><BR>
</BODY>
</HTML>
```

This results in Figure 3-10, as displayed in Netscape.

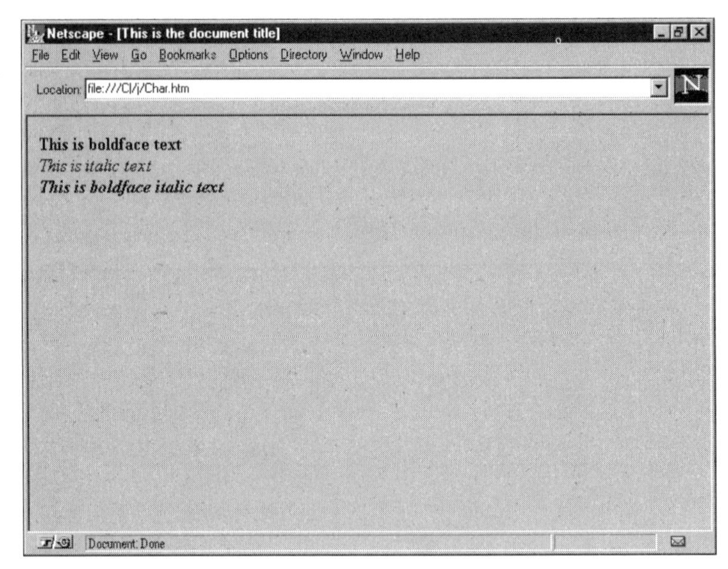

Figure 3-10: A character formatting example.

Do you remember the old IBM monochrome monitors, which were used frequently in the earlier days of the PC? Besides boldface and underlining (they didn't have italics), those monitors also had blinking text. Well guess what? Those days are back. You can do that with your Web pages that rely on Netscape Navigator. The format is simple, as follows:

```
<BLINK>This text blinks!</BLINK>
```

All text between the `<BLINK>...</BLINK>` tags will blink approximately once a second. All I can say is be careful with this tag. Too much blinking text can become a little painful on the eyes. Take it from someone who has seen this tag overused.

Displaying special characters

HTML uses the < character to start a tag, so you cannot use this character inside your documents because the browser will interpret it as the beginning of a command. To represent the character in your HTML documents, you must use a special command. Table 3-3 shows the commands you must use for reserved characters like < and >.

Table 3-3	HTML Escape Sequences	
Command	Description	Character
<	Less than	<
>	Greater than	>
&	Ampersand	&
"	Double quote	"
	Non-breaking space	' '

A couple of specialized tags actually let you change the size of the font that is being used to display text in a browser window. You start with the <BASEFONT> tag, which allows you to set the base size of the font with which text is currently being displayed. The easiest form is as follows:

```
<BASEFONT>
```

This has a default value of 3. To set a specific size, use the following format:

```
<BASEFONT SIZE=x>
```

The *x* value is the size of the font you wish to use. The value you specify can range from 1 through 7. To change the font size in relation to the current basefont, use the following tag:

```
<FONT SIZE=x>
```

The *x* value is again a number between 1 and 7. You can optionally use a plus (+) or minus (-) sign to indicate differences in size compared to the currently displayed font, for example:

```
<FONT SIZE=+2>
```

This will increase the current font size by two.

Another very cool Netscape Navigator formatting attribute allows you to center text. It has the following format:

```
<CENTER>This is text I want centered on the page </CENTER>
```

All of the text between the tags is centered between the margins. This tag is effective for making an announcement or for specialized formatting.

Displaying extended characters

You might wish many different characters for use in your documents that you cannot even enter on a standard U.S. keyboard. For the most part, these characters include foreign language characters. Similar to the way you enter special characters in HTML, you can use a set of commands to display extended characters. Table 3-4 summarizes this set.

Table 3-4 Extended Characters

Command	Description	Character
`Á`	Uppercase *A* with acute accent	Á
`Â`	Uppercase *A* with circumflex	Â
`Æ`	Uppercase *AE* diphthong	Æ
`À`	Uppercase *A* with grave accent	À
`Ã`	Uppercase *A* with tilde	Ã
`Ä`	Uppercase *A* with umlaut	Ä
`Ç`	Uppercase *C* with cedilla	Ç
`É`	Uppercase *E* with acute accent	É
`Ê`	Uppercase *E* with circumflex	Ê
`È`	Uppercase *E* with grave accent	È
`Ë`	Uppercase *E* with umlaut	Ë
`í`	Uppercase *I* with acute accent	Í
`î`	Uppercase *I* with circumflex	Î
`ì`	Uppercase *I* with grave accent	Ì
`ï`	Uppercase *I* with umlaut	Ï
`Ñ`	Uppercase *N* with tilde	Ñ
`Ó`	Uppercase *O* with acute accent	Ó
`Ô`	Uppercase *O* with circumflex	Ô
`Ò`	Uppercase *O* with grave accent	Ò
`Õ`	Uppercase *O* with a tilde	Õ
`Ö`	Uppercase *O* with umlaut	Ö
`Ú`	Uppercase *U* with acute accent	Ú
`Û`	Uppercase *U* with circumflex	Û
`Ù`	Uppercase *U* with grave accent	Ù
`Ü`	Uppercase *U* with umlaut	Ü
`Ý`	Uppercase *Y* with acute accent	Ý

List Specification Formatting

HTML allows for formatting of lists and supports several kinds of lists, including:

- Unordered (or bulleted) lists
- Ordered (or numbered) lists
- Directory lists, for very short items
- Menu lists, with each item one line in length
- Glossary lists (also called definition lists), where each item has a term and a definition

You can nest lists and different types of lists within each other. Table 3-5 provides an overview of the tags for each type of list.

Table 3-5 Overview of HTML List Tags

Description	Start tag	End tag
Unordered	<UL>	</UL>
Ordered	<OL>	</OL>
Directory	<DIR>	</DIR>
Menu	<MENU>	</MENU>
Glossary	<DL>	</DL>

To create a list, start the section with the appropriate tag from Table 3-5. You then use the <LI> tag (for *list item*) before each item in the list. After you have typed all the items in the list, end the list with the end tag. The following sections take a closer look at each type of list and how you implement them.

Unordered lists

Unordered lists are displayed as lists of bulleted items. The items in the unordered lists can appear in any order. Individual items inside the list can be quite large and may even include other formatting tags (such as boldface, images, and hypertext). An example of specifying an unordered list follows:

```
<HTML>
<!- Unordered list example.  UL.HTM ->
<HEAD>
<TITLE>Example of unordered lists</TITLE>
</HEAD>
```

```
<BODY>
<P>Using unordered lists in HTML.<P>
The basic food groups, according to computer users include:<P>
<UL>
<LI>Sugar
<LI>Salt
<LI>White flour
</UL>
<P>Sad, but true!
</BODY>
</HTML>
```

Figure 3-11 shows how this file appears in Netscape. As you can see, you start the table with the <UL> tag. The <LI> tag precedes each list item, and the list is terminated with the </UL> tag.

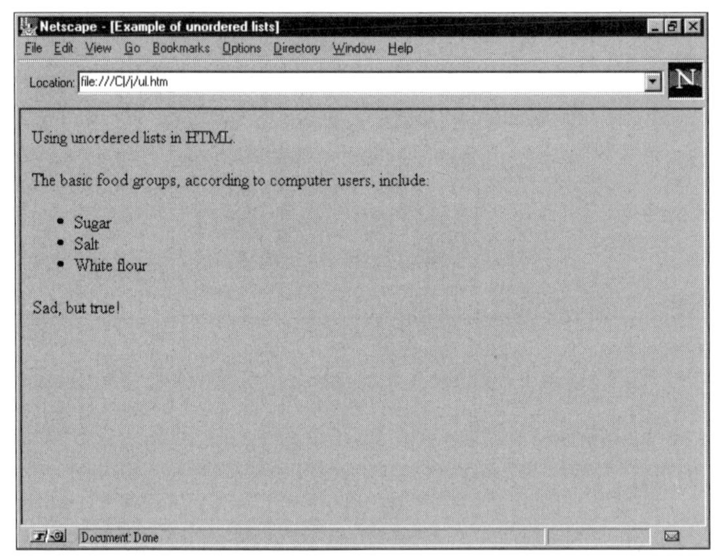

Figure 3-11: An unordered list in Netscape.

Those folks at Netscape are at it again. They have extended the unordered list. A basic list has a default progression of bullet types that changes as you move through indention levels. They've added a parameter to the <UL> tag so that no matter what your indention level, you can specify which bullet type to use. The parameter affects the opening tag, such as the following example:

```
<UL TYPE="DISC">
<UL TYPE="CIRCLE">
<UL TYPE="SQUARE">
```

The standard use of <LI> along with </UL> remains the same.

Ordered lists

In ordered lists, each list item occurs in a particular order. The text is displayed with consecutive numbers for each list item. Ordered lists are surrounded by the <OL>...</OL> tags, and each item is marked with the <LI> tag. When a browser displays an ordered list, it numbers and often indents each of the elements. You don't want to do the numbering yourself; otherwise, you would start seeing double. An example of an ordered list follows:

```
<HTML>
<!- Ordered list example.  OL.HTM ->
<HEAD>
<TITLE>Example of an ordered list in HTML</TITLE>
</HEAD>
<BODY>
<P>Cooking with Paul:
<OL>
<LI>Buy food.
<LI>Microwave food.
<LI>Eat food.
</OL>
</BODY>
</HTML>
```

Figure 3-12 shows how the file appears in Netscape.

The Netscape Navigator extensions to the ordered list tag let you specify how a list should be marked. The parameter name is TYPE. Here are some examples of how it works:

```
<OL TYPE="A">
<OL TYPE="a">
<OL TYPE="I">
<OL TYPE="i">
<OL TYPE="1">
```

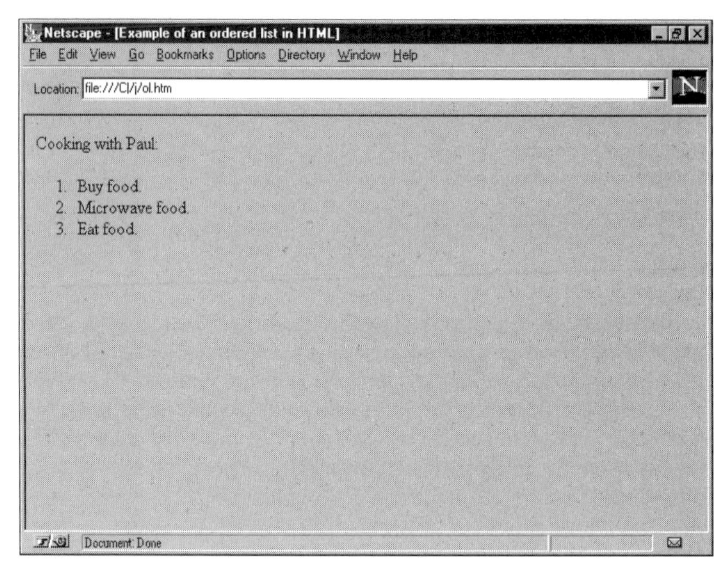

Figure 3-12: An Ordered (numbered) list in Netscape.

You can choose between uppercase and lowercase letters, large and small Roman numerals, or the default numbering, which uses numbers starting from 1. The rest of the ordered list tag remains the same. Unlike other tags, the case of the parameter is important.

Directory and menu lists

Directory and menu lists are variants of unordered lists. They are intended for lists of short items that can be displayed in a compact style. The items on a menu list are frequently set up as hypertext links to create the functionality of a menu. Each menu item is usually a single line.

Menu lists are lists of items (or even short paragraphs) with no bullets, numbers, or other labels. They are similar to simple lists of paragraphs, except that some browsers display them differently from normal paragraphs. Browsers display menu or directory lists with or without the bullets that are characteristic of unordered lists. It seems that some browsers display items tagged this way differently. Sample directory and menu lists follow:

```
<HTML>
<!- Directory and menu lists example.  DL&ML.HTM ->
<HEAD>
<TITLE>Example of directory and menu lists</TITLE>
</HEAD>
<BODY>
<P>Example menu lists.<P>
```

```
<P>Types of HTML commands:<P>
<MENU>
<LI>Structural tags.
<LI>Paragraph formatting tags.
<LI>Character formatting tags.
<LI>List Specification tags.
<LI>Hyperlinking tags.
<LI>Asset integration tags.
</MENU>
<P><P>Example directory list.<P>
<P>Types of HTML List:<P>
<DIR>
<LI>Unordered
<LI>Ordered
<LI>Menu
<LI>Directory
<LI>Glossary
</DIR>
</BODY>
</HTML>
```

From the example, you can see that both of these forms of lists use the same format as the previous lists.

Glossary lists

Glossary lists, also called definition lists, are slightly different from other lists. They are intended for lists of terms and their definitions. Each list element has two parts: the term and the term's definition.

The term is preceded by a `<DT>` tag and the definition by a `<DD>` tag. The two tags usually appear in pairs. The entire glossary list is indicated by the tags `<DL>...</DL>` in the same way as other types of lists.

As the name implies, glossary lists are most commonly used for glossaries, where you have a word, along with a word description. Obviously, you don't have to use glossary lists for this. You can use them anywhere that an indented list is required. Here is an example of a glossary list:

```
<HTML>
<!- Example glossary list.  GL.HTM ->
<HEAD>
<TITLE>Example glossary list</TITLE>
</HEAD>
<BODY>
```

(continued)

```
<P>Important definitions:<P>
<DL>
<DT>Bandwidth
<DD>The amount of data that can travel through a circuit, mea-
sured in bits per second.
<DT>Browser
<DD>A type of software program which allows a Web user to gain
access to documents.  Examples of browser software include
Mosaic, Netscape, and NetCruiser.
<DT>ARPANET
<DD>Advanced Research Projects Agency Network.  An early experi-
mental network which was the forerunner of the Internet.
<DT>CERN
<DD>The name of the particle physics laboratory in Geneva Swit-
zerland where the World Wide Web was created in 1989.
</DL>
</BODY>
</HTML>
```

Figure 3-13 shows how the file appears in the Netscape Navigator browser.

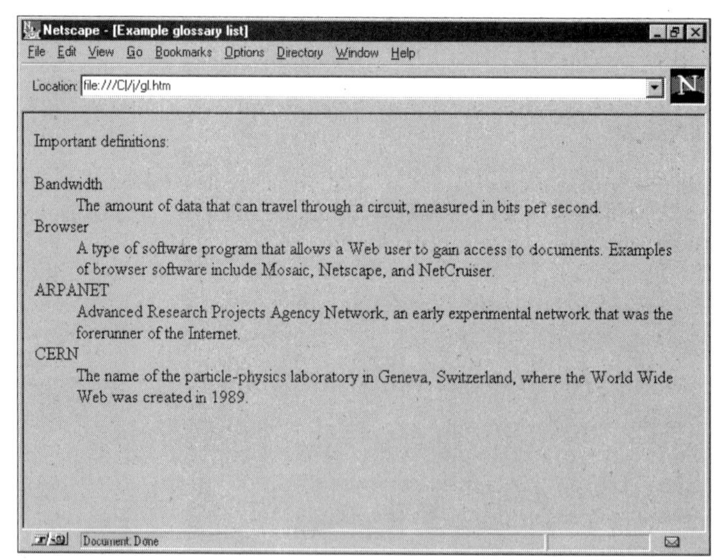

Figure 3-13: A sample glossary list in Netscape.

Formatting Hyperlinks

Up to now, you have seen HTML formatting tags that provide information as to how a document should appear. The hyperlink formatting tags allow you to specify how your document relates to itself and other documents on the Web. Through hyperlinks, you make your documents nonlinear.

A *hypertext link* is a pointer from a place in your document to a place in another document. At its simplest, the destination is a location inside your own document. However, you can also hyperlink to different documents as well as external graphical images, digital video clips, and audio sound.

Through the formatting hyperlinks, you put the *hyper* into hyperlink. Both the starting point and the destination of a hypertext link are referred to as *anchors* and are marked with the `<A>` tag.

To create a hyperlink in your document, you need to know about two pieces of information:

- The name of the file (or URL) where you wish to link.
- The text that will be highlighted in your document and therefore will serve as the hotspot.

The first kind of hyperlink is one that links a hotspot in your text to another location inside the same file. This type of link allows the user to jump quickly to another section in the same document. It uses the following format:

```
<HTML>
<!- Example hyperlink jump inside file.  ->
<HEAD>
<TITLE>Example Hyperlink jump</TITLE>
</HEAD>
<BODY>
Click <A HREF="#TargetName">here</A> to find out more about this
topic.
...
other document data
...
<A NAME="TargetName"></A>
This is the target location.
</BODY>
</HTML>
```

You see two forms of the <A> tag in the previous example. The first one specifies the name of the target location ("TargetName") along with the text to use as the hotspot (here). Notice the use of the # symbol inside the hyperlink target to refer to a location inside the current file. The second instance of the <A> tag specifies the location to jump to.

Another form of hypertext is to jump to a completely new document. This has the following format:

```
<HTML>
<!- Hyperlink to another file. ->
<HEAD>
<TITLE>Hyperlinking to another document </TITLE>
</HEAD>
<BODY>
To find out more about Sony,
click <A HREF="http://www.sony.com">here</A>.
</BODY>
</HTML>
```

This format only requires a single line. The reference inside the document specifies a Web address, which is the home page the system switches to when the user clicks on the hyperlink text *here*. You must make sure the target address is correct, or the Web browser will report an error.

A variation on these two methods is jumping to a specific location inside a different file. It takes the following format:

```
<HTML>
<!- Jumping to a named location in another file. ->
<HEAD>
<TITLE>Hypertext example </TITLE>
</HEAD>
<BODY>
To view more information,
click <A HREF="http://www.domain.name/name.html#TargetName">here.

</BODY>
</HTML>
```

This method requires that the target document file contains a location with the appropriate name, but it provides you more control over where users will end up in their hyperlink travels.

Earlier in the chapter ("Specifying the body of your document"), you saw how the Netscape Navigator provides extensions to HTML so that you can specify the background and foreground color of your Web page. At the same time, you can also specify the color of your hyperlinks. In fact, the system is extremely flexible because it lets you specify the color of all the hyperlinks on a page. You can specify a different color for hyperlinks that have been visited and those that are active. You set these colors with parameters to the `<BODY>` tag, which have the following structure:

```
<HTML>
<HEAD>
<TITLE>Colorful hyperlinks</TITLE>
</HEAD>
<BODY LINK="rrggbb" VLINK="rrggbb" ALINK="rrggbb">
...
Custom hyperlink colors has been activated.
...
</BODY>
</HTML>
```

As before, the numbers (`"rrggbb"`) are RGB values (see Table 3-1). You would probably combine these parameters along with `BGCOLOR` and `TEXT`, which you learned about earlier, to specify colors for the Web document.

Netscape Navigator, along with several other Web browsers, provides an enhanced version of the hyperlink tag for sending electronic mail. When the user clicks on the hyperlink, a dialog box appears that lets the user type a message and send it via Internet e-mail. The syntax for the command is as follows:

```
<A HREF="mailto:name@company.com">text to highlight</A>
```

You must specify your e-mail address along with the text to highlight. Oftentimes, you will use the same text for both, and users will see the e-mail address, while at the same time they can click on it and send you e-mail. Using this tag provides a great method for users to send you feedback about your Web site.

HTML and Multimedia

HTML provides built-in support for every element of multimedia. This section looks at displaying graphical images in a Web page and accessing audio sound and digital video using external viewers.

Not all Web browsers support the use of multimedia tags. However, one of the advantages of the HTTP specification is that if a Web browser does not understand a given tag, the browser is supposed to ignore the tag. Therefore, tags don't cause any harm if a Web browser fails to understand them.

Viewing images

Graphical images can convey a great deal of information very well. Graphical images can break up dry text into more interesting chunks and, when carefully selected, can make a page exciting.

On the down side, graphical images within Web documents can slow down the response time considerably because the extra data must be transmitted to the Web browser. Therefore, you should use graphical images with care.

HTML provides the <IMG> tag to embed in-line graphics into Web pages. The syntax is as follows:

```
<IMG SRC="name.ext">
```

You must specify the URL of the image file with the SRC element. Graphics on the Web are usually provided in the graphics interchange format (.GIF) or the Joint Photographic Experts Group, also known as JPEG (.JPG), graphics file formats. You can specify several alternate forms for specifying graphics files. The first one follows:

```
<IMG SRC="name.ext" ALT="[Text Description of Image]">
```

This allows you to provide a textual description of the image that is displayed in text-only browsers as well as between the time when the Web page is first displayed and when the graphics file is finished downloading. Some browsers display also the textual information when in-line images are turned off.

By default, when images are included on a line combined with text, the bottom edge of the image is aligned with the baseline of the text. You can override this alignment option with the ALIGN element. For example:

```
<IMG SRC="name.ext" ALIGN="TOP">
```

The alignment options can also be "MIDDLE" or "BOTTOM". Using these options allows you to select how images will be aligned with text.

The image element does not require an end tag. The </IMG> tag is illegal and should not be used.

Finally, you can use a graphical image inside a hyperlink anchor by combining the <IMG> and <A> tags. For example:

```
<A HREF="TargetName"><IMG SRC="name.ext"></A>
```

Any time someone clicks on any part of the image, he or she will automatically be brought to the appropriate hyperlink target.

If you are using Netscape Navigator, you can speed up the display of a document by specifying the width and height of a graphics image. The format looks like this:

```
<IMG SRC="name.ext" WIDTH=x HEIGHT=y>
```

The *x* and *y* values are the size of the image. This speeds up the display of information in the browser because the user will not have to wait for the image to load from the network in order for the browser to calculate the appropriate size.

Another extended parameter for the image tag allows you to control the thickness of the area around an image. It has the following prototype:

```
<IMG SRC="name.ext" BORDER=x>
```

Here, the *x* value is the thickness of the border. If you set the size to 0 and the image is a hyperlink, be careful because it could confuse your users. Usually when an image is a hyperlink, the browser displays a colored border indicating a hyperlink. Setting the size to zero removes that border, and thus the visual clue to the user that the bitmap contains a hyperlink.

Image maps

An extended type of graphics image is something known as an *image map.* The image map is a system in which you can designate certain areas of your graphical image to create hyperlinks to different locations. In theory, image maps are easy to implement. In practice, image maps have no standard method for implementation, and they are difficult to use. As a result, you must consult the documentation for your Web server for detailed information on using them.

For Netscape Navigator users, you can really spice up a Web page by using a new tag to specify a bitmap image as the background wallpaper of a Web page. It works by specifying the filename of a bitmap with a new parameter in the <BODY> tag. If the bitmap is too small to fill up the entire background window, it is tiled in order to fill the entire space. An example follows:

```
<HTML>
<HEAD>
<TITLE>This is the Title </TITLE>
</HEAD>
<BODY BACKGROUND="name.gif">
...
Text to appear on top of bitmap image.
...
</BODY>
</HTML>
```

The image is loaded once when your Web page first downloads and then used while the user is viewing the entire page. Setting the background image requires fetching a graphics file, so it will slow down the perceived speed of your document because users must download the graphics before any text on the page can be displayed. A good rule of thumb is to keep background images small.

Also, depending on what colors are used in the bitmap, you might choose to change the color of your text with the `TEXT` parameter, as described earlier (see "Specifying the Body of your Document").

Accessing sound

A Web browser does not directly support sound. Instead, you must use an external application to play the sound (while at the same time configuring your browser appropriately).

To specify an external sound file, use the `<A>` hyperlink tag with the following syntax:

```
<A HREF="file://audio.WAV">Click here<A> for audio sound.
```

When the user clicks on the words *Click here*, the browser retrieves the file AUDIO.WAV from the Web server computer and displays it in the viewer application that is configured for accessing files with the .WAV extension. The browser knows how to handle this data file by the file's extension.

The Web uses many different audio file formats, including Apple AIFF, Sun Workstation AU, SND, and Windows WAV files (see Table 3-6).

Table 3-6 Audio File Support for the Web

Format	Description
AIFF	Macintosh audio information file format
SND, AU	Audio file format on UNIX machines (Sun Workstations, NextStep)
WAV	Microsoft Windows WAVE audio sound

Viewing digital video

Digital video files are treated the same way as audio sound. To display digital video, a user must first have a computer capable of displaying the video images (translation, a fast computer). At that time, the user should configure his or her Web browser to launch an external application to view the video file. An example HTML statement for accessing digital video follows:

```
<A HREF="file://video.AVI">Click here<A> for digital video.
```

When the user clicks on the text *Click here*, the system downloads the VIDEO.AVI file from the Web server and launches an external application for viewing the movie file (most likely Windows Media Player). The standard formats for digital video include Video for Windows (or VfW), QuickTime (originally only on the Macintosh), QuickTime for Windows (or QTW), and Motion Picture Experts Group (MPEG). Table 3-7 provides an overview of these formats.

Table 3-7 Full-Motion Digital Video File Formats

Format	Description
AVI	Video for Windows (also known as Audio Video Interleaf)
MOV	QuickTime for Windows
MPG	Motion picture experts group

Netscape Navigator 2 provides a great new feature called *frames*. A frame is a rectangular area of the Web browser window. Each frame contains a separate HTML document. A frame can contain fixed rectangular areas such as banners or footers, or a frame can be refreshed with new content, sometimes as the result of a hyperlink. Although it doesn't have to, a frame can be related to others so that a hyperlink in one frame will result in a new document displayed in another frame.

You can implement frames without throwing away any HTML files that you already have. A Web browser that does not support frame functionality will ignore the new tag information. Some of the uses for frames include:

- **Creation of a table of contents.** The contents can remain visible in one frame while the information appears in another frame.
- **The reduction of user interface elements.** If you have control bars or copyright notices that are duplicated on multiple pages, you can use a frame at the bottom of the window to display the information just once and have it available for all your Web documents.
- **Making Web navigation easier.** Navigating the Web is less confusing when you don't have to link through many Web documents.

To understand the implementation of frames, you need to remember the levels of reference used in a standard Web page. Most HTML files contain two levels of reference. The first is the HTML file itself, and the other is the set of files that are referenced by hyperlinks, or in graphics files.

In a document using frames, you have three levels of reference: the main HTML file containing the frame (sometimes referred to as the *frameholder*), the HTML files that comprise each frame, and the images and hyperlink targets used within all the frames.

Two main requirements accompany the use of the frame tags. First, you must tell the system the size of each frame, and second, you need to tell the system what document should be displayed in each frame. A document that makes use of frames does not use the <BODY>...</BODY> set of tags. Instead, it uses the <FRAMESET>...</FRAMESET> combination of tags along with the <FRAME> tag to specify the names of the documents to display. Let's take a look at an example that creates three horizontal frames. (Figure 3-14 shows how the example appears.) Of the four files, this is the main file (which is the one you specify to the Web browser):

```
<HTML>
<!- Sample frame creation.  FRAME.HTM->
<HEAD>
<TITLE>Sample Frames</TITLE>
</HEAD>
<FRAMESET ROWS="15%, 70%, 15%">

 <FRAME SRC="top.htm" NAME="top" SCROLLING="YES">
 <FRAME SRC="middle.htm" NAME="MIDDLE">
 <FRAME SRC="bott.htm" NAME="BOTT">

<! The following is for browsers which don't understand frames ->
<NOFRAMES>To display this document, you need to
<A HREF="http://home.netscape.com/comprod/mirror/
```

```
index.html>download</A> Netscape Navigator 2.0.
</NOFRAMES>

</FRAMESET>
</HTML>
```

The following file is for the top frame. The middle and bottom frame files are functionally the same, so I won't show them. The only difference is that they contain modified text.

```
<HTML>
<!- TOP.HTM ->
<HEAD>
<TITLE>This is the document title</TITLE>
</HEAD>
<BODY>
This is displayed in the top frame.
<P>Let's add some text so the frame will be scroll-able.
<P>How about a little more text.
<P>And finally even some more.
</BODY>
</HTML>
```

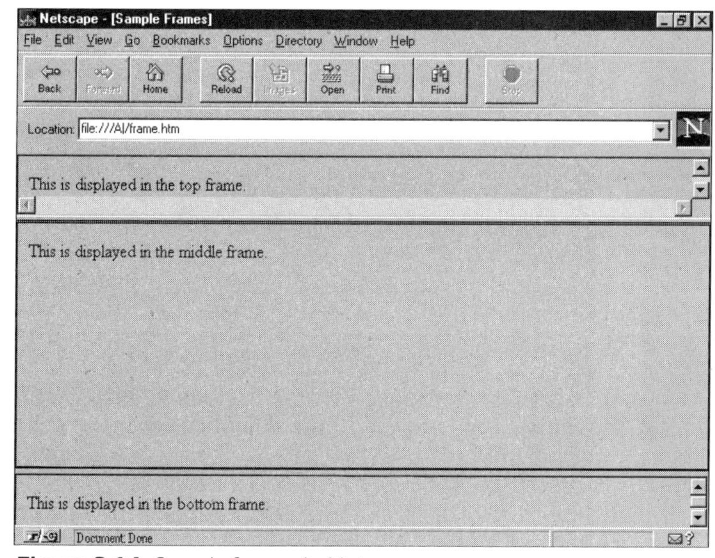

Figure 3-14: Sample frames in Netscape.

When creating Web pages with frames, you should start with an idea of how you want the user to view your information. A nontechnical way to begin is using a rough sketch (on paper, no less!) of each frame you want the user to see. You need to decide how much space you should use for each frame. This can be an absolute pixel amount or a percentage of the size of the window.

With the sizes of your frames determined, you need to inform the Web browser about them with the `<FRAMESET>` tag using either the `ROWS` or `COLS` parameter. A powerful feature is the capability to nest multiple frames, resulting in some pretty sophisticated layout schemes (see Figure 3-15). This capability displays multiple rows and columns in the same window. Each tag allows you to set up the location of frames in the window. Here is an example:

```
<FRAMESET ROWS="15%, 70%, 15%">
```

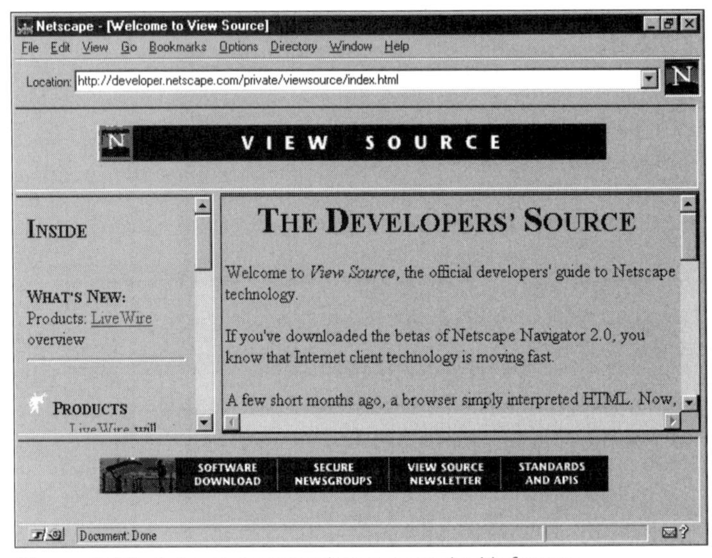

Figure 3-15: A developer newsletter created with frames.

This defines three horizontal frames, with the top frame being 15 percent of the window, the middle frame being 70 percent of the window, and the remaining frame being 15 percent of the window. If you pass percentage points as parameter, they must add up to 100. As an alternative, instead of setting values as percentages, you can use absolute pixel values, or even the asterisk (*) to specify a relative amount. For example:

```
<FRAMESET ROWS="100,*,100">
```

This will cause the top and bottom frames to be 100 pixels tall, while the middle frame will be all the remaining space. If you use absolute pixel references, you should try to use the asterisk in order to make sure the space is filled correctly. However, if your window size is actually larger than the total values you specify, the system will override your values to fill the window.

Once you have defined each frame, you have to tell the Web browser what information to display in them. Use the `<FRAME>` tag to specify a standard URL address. For example:

```
<FRAME SRC="name.htm">
```

`SRC` is the name of the target document. The order of the `<FRAME>` tag inside the document is important. Netscape Navigator fills horizontal frames from top to bottom, and vertical frames from left to right. The `SRC` parameter is not the only one you can use. The others include: `SCROLLING`, `NORESIZE`, `MARGINHEIGHT`, `MARGINWIDTH`, and `NAME`.

The `SCROLLING` parameter determines the behavior of scroll bars in the frame. You can set it to `YES`, `NO`, or `AUTO`. By default, the `AUTO` value is used, which automatically displays scroll bars only if they are needed. Setting `SCROLLING="NO"` results in a cleaner screen, but some of your data might not be visible if the user changes the size of the window. Setting `SCROLLING="YES"` always creates the scroll bars. If they are not needed, they are grayed out.

The `NORESIZE` attribute forces the current size of the frame to remain the same. If this attribute is not used, the user can freely resize the frame borders using the mouse. The `MARGINHEIGHT` and `MARGINWIDTH` parameters are passed numerical values that let you control the margins inside each frame. The value passed is in pixel units.

To allow the hyperlinks from one frame to affect the information in another frame, you must name the frame. The `NAME` parameter lets you set a name to a frame. The syntax looks like this:

```
<FRAME SRC="name.htm" NAME="frame_name.htm">
```

To point to a frame from within a hyperlink, specify the target name inside the link parameter. The hyperlink will look like this:

```
<A HREF="anothername.htm" TARGET="frame_name.htm">highlighted
text</A>
```

When the user clicks on this link, the frame named `frame_name.htm` will fill with data from the anothername.htm file.

You can see that the frame definitions provide a great amount of flexibility while being fairly easy to use. The unfortunate circumstance is that if you don't have the Netscape Navigator browser, and the user displays your Web site, it will appear as if nothing has happened. When I said that other browsers will ignore the frame tags, this is exactly what I meant. They display nothing. As a result, you may want to at least tell users with other Web browsers this fact. The `<NOFRAMES>` set of tags allows you to set text that will appear to other browsers. Here's an example:

```
<NOFRAMES>To display this document, you need to
<A HREF="http://home.netscape.com/comprod/mirror/
index.html>download </A> Netscape Navigator 2.0.
</NOFRAMES>
```

When a user comes along with another browser, a message appears "To display this document, you need to download Netscape Navigator 2.0." The highlighted word *download* will contain a hyperlink to the spot where users can download the browser. If you don't like the idea of requiring your users to use Netscape Navigator, you can include the information from all the frames together in one document as an alternative. However, this will force your Netscape Navigator users to download the information twice: once which they don't see (it is being used by non-Netscape Navigator users) and then once within frames. A better idea might be to add hyperlinks to the documents displayed in each frame.

HTML Authoring Tools

Throughout this chapter, you have been working with the raw codes that compose an HTML file. Looking at a screen full of greater-than and less-than symbols can strain the eye somewhat. At these times, mismatching an opening or closing tag becomes extremely easy.

As a result, many vendors have been working on HTML authoring tools. These tools make the creation of HTML files easier by allowing you to work in a visual environment. Literally, they provide word processing — or maybe I should say desktop publishing — power for the Internet. Some of these products are available free of charge; whereas others are available on a trial basis.

If you like Word for Windows, Microsoft has a support product called Internet Assistant (available free of charge from the Microsoft Web site at `http://www.microsoft.com`). It is a set of macros, templates, and plug-in DLLs for saving standard WinWord documents as HTML files. When you create a document based on the HTML style sheet, the system creates styles that correlate to standard HTML formatting tags. When you are done with the document, you save it as an HTML file. Of course, you need Word for Windows to use this tool.

A separate standalone application that has been gaining a lot of attention is a tool called HotDog, available from Sausage Systems (this company definitely has some personality). It is a standalone product that provides on-screen formatting of HTML documents. It provides keyword highlighting, a spell checker, and many other features for authoring Web documents. This tool is available from the Sausage Systems Web site at `http://www.sausage.com`. You can try the product for 60 days, and if you decide you like it, you must register your copy.

The HoTMetaL editor from Softquad Systems was probably the first HTML editor ever available. In fact, the company has provided SGML editors for some time and only recently, with the popularization of the Web, has made an HTML-specific editor. Two editions are available. The standard edition is available free of charge from the company's Web site (`http://www.sq.com`). The Pro edition, which is available directly from the company, adds features like spell checking and enhanced functionality. Both make it easier to work with HTML tags by taking away the task of having to think of the makeup of individual tags.

If you are thinking about any one of these editors, you can't go wrong by at least trying them out. They have all been highly rated (if not by others, at least by me). If you already have Word for Windows, it won't hurt to download Internet Assistant and give it a try. At the same time, you could download HotDog and HoTMetaL and see how you like the way they work. If you don't like them at all, the only thing you have lost is the time spent downloading and exploring them. If you do like them, you have found a great way to author Web home pages.

Quick Overview

This chapter covered a lot of ground. You started out by learning simple HTML statements for controlling the structure of a Web document. You then went all the way to including multimedia elements like audio sound and digital video in your Web presentation.

In particular, this chapter covered the following topics:

- How to specify the structure of your HTML document using the <HTML>... </HTML>, <HEAD>...</HEAD>, and <TITLE>...</TITLE> tags.
- How to specify headings using the <Hx>...</Hx> (where *x* is a number between 1 and 6) set of tags.
- How to display ordered (or numbered), unordered (or bulleted), directory, menu, and glossary lists.
- How to format hypertext links using the <A> tag.
- How to display graphical images using the <IMG> tag.
- How to access external files that are related to multimedia images like digital video and audio sound.

Here is a brief overview of what is to come...

- Move on to Chapter 4, "Introduction to Java Programming," where you will get up to speed with how to program Java.

Introduction to Java Programming

In This Chapter

How Java takes advantage of object-oriented programming techniques.

The three steps required for creating a web application with Java.

What the <APPLET> tag is used for and how it relates to Java.

How to say "Hello, World" in the Java programming language.

The numeric and alphabetic data objects supported by Java.

The basic constructs available for controlling program flow in the Java language.

How to use the Java Development Kit (JDK).

Now that you have a good understanding of the hypertext markup language, you are ready to dig into the fundamentals of writing Java applets. This chapter teaches you about program development in Java and gets you started with integrating Java applets into Web pages. At the end of the chapter, you will be able to tie Java applets into your HTML documents.

Object-Oriented Programming Overview

Everything in the universe is an object. This book is an object. This book consists of pages, which are objects. Ink was used to print text, and ink is an object. No matter where you look, everything is an object. Most objects are created from other objects.

So it is with computers and programming. Java applets are objects. Variables are objects. User interface elements, like buttons and scroll bars, are objects. When working with computers, using an object as a metaphor makes it easier to visualize the relationship of a program.

Unfortunately, object-oriented programming has become one of the most hyped computer technologies ever. If we were talking politics, it would be equivalent to talk of lowering taxes. The politicians always come up with great promises for lowering taxes, but in the end, they never seem to lower them. The same is true of programming: programmers always talk about new object-oriented programming concepts, but programming never seems to become easier.

The problem surrounding the hype is not in the concept of how object-oriented programming works because it is a good concept. Rather, the problem lies in the fact that most programming languages don't come with object building blocks.

For example, if you were building cars, your task would be so much easier if you already had the basic building blocks of a car, such as wheels, an engine, seats, and whatever else goes into a car. But we aren't building cars, we're building programs. We need a library of parts from which to borrow. For Windows programmers using C++, the Microsoft Foundation Classes (MFC) have become a standard set of objects. Java also provides a library of built-in objects, but these come with the basic implementation of the language and apply to any platform under which you are running the Web page.

In the earlier days of computers, when programs were entered via a stack of cards, there was no such thing as object-oriented programming. As computers have become more complex, software engineers have continued to research better methods of programming. Object-oriented programming methodologies are on the forefront of this research. Programming languages like Java, C++, Smalltalk, and Object Pascal provide the framework required to define computer objects. Traditional languages like C, BASIC, FORTRAN, and COBOL are not object-oriented and don't have any mechanism for defining objects. None of these languages has any object building blocks as part of the language.

Object-Oriented Programming with Java

An *object* combines (or encapsulates) program code and data into one self-contained unit. *Classes* are the program statements that act as a template to define the data and code in an object. Once you have created a class definition, you can reuse it to create as many objects as you need. Every Java applet is a class. When you access a Java applet from a Web page, the browser creates an instance of that class.

All classes inherit from a class named `Object` (see Figure 4-1). When a class is inherited from another class, the original class is called the *superclass*, and the class inheriting the functionality is called the *subclass*. The subclass inherits the properties of the superclass above it. The `Object` class is the only one that does not have a superclass. If a class does not specify which class it inherits from, Java assumes that it inherits from `Object`.

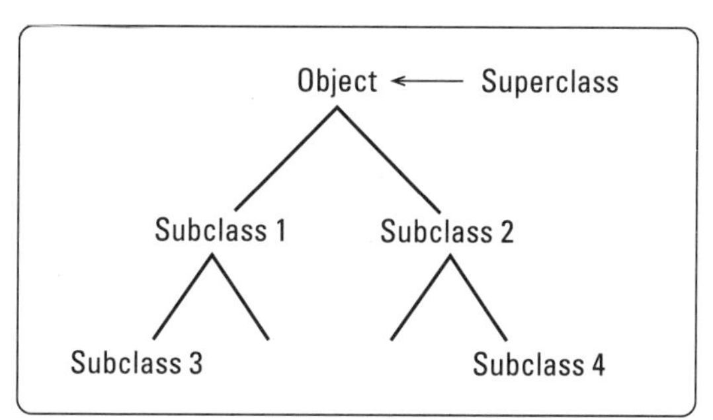

Figure 4-1: Inheritance from the Object class.

The Java development system allows the creation of two different types of programs. *Java applets* are programs that you integrate into a Web home page. *Standalone Java applications* are programs that do not integrate into a Web page (hence, they stand alone). Theoretically you can use them on any of the different platforms that support Java, such as set-top boxes, microwave ovens, personal digital assistants, and even personal computers.

Making Java Applets

To create cool Web applets with Java, you'll need to take three steps (see Figure 4-2):

1. **Lay out the structure of the Web page.** Most Java applets display information to the user. Just like you would set aside space for a picture, set aside space for the applet.
2. **Write the source code for the applet.** Use a text editor, such as Windows Notepad, for this task. If you have a favorite coding editor (I use Codewright from Premia systems), you can use it instead. Use anything that can edit plain text files. You could even use a word processor like Word for Windows, but you want to make sure that you save the file as a text file.
3. **Compile the applet with the Java compiler and test the entire Web page.** Make sure you are pleased with the final result.

The rest of this section provides a self-guided tour of the process. While creating Web applets with Java, you will find yourself working with several different file types, which are described in Table 4-1. Notice that Java requires a file system, such as Windows 95 or Windows NT, which supports long filenames. All the Java file extensions use four characters, which breaks the three-character file extension limit of Windows 3.

Table 4-1 File Types Used While Creating Java Applets

File Extension	Description
`.html`	Hypertext markup language source file
`.class`	Java binary file
`.java`	Java source code

You already know how to lay out Web pages with HTML, but you need to know one more thing. This is how to combine a Java applet into your Web page document.

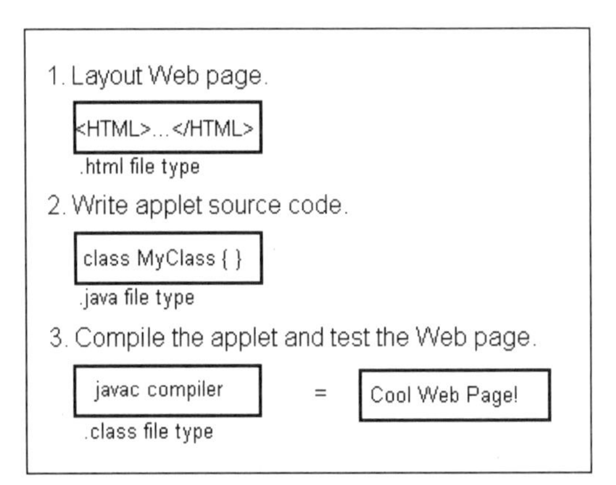

Figure 4-2: Steps to create a Java Web application.

The last HTML tag you'll ever need to know

. . . for now at least. This HTML tag is important because it brings the power of Java to your Web page. It allows you to add a Java applet to an HTML file.

To integrate the Java applet into your Web page, use the `<APPLET>` tag. When a Java-enabled Web browser (like HotJava or Netscape 2) encounters the `<APPLET>` tag, it downloads the applet from the Web server and executes it.

The tag lets you pass information to the applet, including the applet name and the amount of physical space to allocate for the applet. The tag has the following basic syntax:

```
<APPLET CODE="ClassName.class" WIDTH="x" HEIGHT="y">
<PARAM NAME="parameter name" VALUE="parameter value">
This text is displayed on non Java-enabled browsers.
</APPLET>
```

You can almost think of the `<APPLET>` tag as a function call from an HTML file to a Java applet. The first parameter to the `<APPLET>` tag is `CODE`, which allows you to specify the name of the Java class you wish to execute. You must specify the class name with the same case as its filename. Java is case-sensitive, so the system won't find the class if you use the wrong case. The class file extension will always be `.class`.

The `WIDTH` and `HEIGHT` parameters let you specify the size of the area where the applet has access. You specify the area in pixels. Be forewarned though: an applet can actually resize itself, so this number doesn't always mean much. Whether an applet resizes itself depends entirely on the implementation of the applet itself.

In the `<APPLET>` tag, you can use any number of `<PARAM>` tags to pass information (or parameters) to the applet. Some applets require these parameters, but others do not. Information that you might pass to an applet includes filenames, color values, or text strings or numbers. As with a function call inside a programming language, the type of information you can pass is unlimited.

Any text that appears between the beginning and ending `<APPLET>` tags is not displayed by Java-enabled browsers. However, it is displayed by any browser that is enabled by something other than Java. This creates an opportunity to let Web users who don't have a Java-enabled browser know that they are missing out on some fun.

The only parameters required by the `<APPLET>` tag are `CODE=`, `WIDTH=`, and `HEIGHT=`. However, the tag has several optional parameters that you might need to use, if not now, maybe sometime in the future:

- `ALT="Text"` — lets you specify alternate text for text-only Web browsers to display.
- `CODEBASE="http://www.myurl.com/directory"` — lets you provide a path to a directory containing class files.
- `NAME="Text"` — lets you assign a symbolic name to an applet. Other applets on the same page can use the name.

- `ALIGN="Position"` — you can position a Java applet just like you position an image in a Web page. You can choose one of the following: `LEFT`, `RIGHT`, `TOP`, `MIDDLE`, `BOTTOM`, `TEXTTOP`, `BASELINE`, or `ABSBOTTOM`. If you use the `LEFT` or `RIGHT` alignment options, the text in the Web page will flow around the space assigned to the applet.
- `VSPACE="size"` — used only with `ALIGN="LEFT"` or `ALIGN="RIGHT"` and allows you to specify the vertical space around the applet. With this parameter, you can specify the amount of whitespace around the applet.
- `HSPACE="size"` — used only with `ALIGN="LEFT"` or `ALIGN="RIGHT"` to specify the horizontal space around the applet. With this parameter, you can specify the amount of whitespace around the applet.

Here is an example:

```
<APPLET CODE="ClassName.class"  WIDTH="100"  HEIGHT="100"
        CODEBASE="http://www.myurl.com/directory"
        ALT="Msg"  NAME="MyName" ALIGN="LEFT"
        VSPACE="size" HSPACE="SIZE">
</APPLET>
```

In most instances, you don't need to use all these parameters. As you gain more experience with using the `<APPLET>` tag, you will see when you need to use the optional parameters.

Listing 4-1 provides a sample of an entire HTML file that includes a Java applet. Don't try to view the Web page just yet because you won't see anything. Although you won't receive any warnings, the file relies on a Java class that is not yet available. Shortly, you will see the Java source code for this class and learn how to compile it.

Listing 4-1 Hypertext Markup Language for Java MinimalApplet

```
<HTML>
<!- MinimalApplet.html ->
<!- To test the inclusion of a Java applet.  ->
<HEAD>
   <TITLE>Welcome to Java</TITLE>
</HEAD>
<BODY>
Hello, Java:<P><P>
<APPLET CODE="MinimalApplet.class" WIDTH="2000" HEIGHT="1000">
This Web page requires a <B>Java</B>-enabled Web Browser.
</APPLET>
</BODY>
</HTML>
```

You now know the first step in creating a cool Web page using Java. Pick up your hard hat because the next step is to write the Java source code that composes the applet.

As you snoop around the Web for pages that include Java applets, you might come across sites that use the `<APP>` tag. This outdated tag was used with the alpha release of HotJava but is no longer supported. If you see the old tag, just smile to yourself, knowing that you are a step ahead of the competition.

A Minimum Java Application

Listing 4-2 contains the source code for a minimal Java application with the name MimimalApplet.java. Some C programmers might recognize this as a "Hello, World"-style application. The term originated with Brian Kernighan and Dennis Ritchie, who were the creators of the C programming language. They believed that the first program one writes is the biggest hurdle because you have to create the program, compile it successfully, load it, run it, and find out where your output went. Although the program only displays a message on the screen, it provides a good start on your way to Java programming.

Listing 4-2 MinimalApplet.java Class Listing

```
/*
 *  MinimalApplet.java - Minimal Java Applet
 *
 *  Creating Cool Web Applets with Java
 *  By: Paul J. Perry,  Publisher: IDG Books
 *
 */

// Superclass and language definitions.
import java.lang.*;
import java.applet.*;
import java.awt.Graphics;

// Class definition and implementation.
public class MinimalApplet extends java.applet.Applet
{
   // This is where the graphics display is done.
   public void paint(Graphics g)
   {
      g.drawString("Java is Cool!", 10, 10);
   }
}
```

Before trying to compile and execute this example, let's discuss how it works.

Program comments

The first thing you will notice is the section of comments at the top of the listing. You can easily add comments to your Java source code that provide additional text for clarification of what the program is or how it does something. Programmers frequently use comments to jog their memory when they have been away from their code for a while and return to perform maintenance on it. The Java compiler ignores all comments, and they don't affect the execution time of the final program in any way.

Java actually provides two types of comment styles: single-line and multiple-line. Single-line comments start with a double slash (//) and terminate at the end of the line, as follows:

```
// This is a Java single-line comment
```

Multiple-line comments begin with the slash and asterisk character combination (/*) and end with the asterisk and slash characters (*/).

```
/* These are
   multiple
   comment lines.
*/
```

The single-line comment style is nice for creating a quick comment. For longer comments, multiple-line comments work just fine.

Specifying class imports

The `import` keyword allows an applet to use the functionality of classes already provided by Java and provides the capability to reuse existing classes and interfaces. You can also write your own class definitions and import their definition into projects. The sample code includes three import statements:

```
import java.lang.*;
import java.applet.*;
import java.awt.Graphics;
```

These make direct use of the paradigm of object-oriented computing by employing objects that are already created. The first import command (`java.lang.*`) imports the classes that define the Java language. Because the language definition is required for any program, the Java compiler automatically imports this command, and you don't need to specify it. In future programs, you will not see this line appear.

The next import statement (`java.applet.*`) imports the class definition for Web-based Java applets.

The last import (`java.awt.Graphics`) imports information about the abstract window toolkit, which provides classes for graphical environments, like Windows.

You will notice the use of the asterisk (*) in some of the lines. With it, you can specify multiple classes. You can import only certain classes, like `java.awt.Graphics`, or you can tell the system to import all classes within a category, such as `java.awt.*` or `java.lang.*`. The following list summarizes the classes that come with Java, which you might find used in this book:

- `java.applet` — provides classes that let you create Web-based applets.
- `java.awt` — includes classes for creating graphics- and window-based applets.
- `java.io` — contains classes used for input and output of disk files as well as standard I/O devices, like the keyboard or terminal.
- `java.lang` — provides the foundation classes for the entire Java language.
- `java.net` — includes classes for accessing networks, like the Internet.
- `java.util` — provides utility functions such as access to the current date, bit twiddling, string tokenization, and random number creation.

You can see that the standard Java classes provide plenty of functionality in and of themselves.

If you have programmed in C or C++, you are familiar with the `#include` preprocessor directive, which allows you to access function prototypes or class definitions from your program. Java's use of the `import` command is similar, but the class definitions being imported refer to the binary code (that is, the actual `.class` file) rather than the original source code.

Creating a class

All programs are based on classes. You create a new class with the `class` keyword. Here is the basic format:

```
Scope class ClassName
{
   // Class implementation
}
```

You provide a name for the class and the implementation of that class inside the curly braces. You will not find yourself using this syntax too much because you provide extra information in most situations. Here is the class definition used in the previous sample code:

```
public class MinimalApplet extends java.applet.Applet
{
   // Code and data go here.
}
```

The `public` keyword tells the compiler that code may use the class definition outside of this file. Only one public class is allowed per file, and the class must be named the same as the root name of the file. In the example, the name of the disk file is `MinimalApplet.java`, and the name of the class is `MinimalApplet`.

The `extends` keyword lets you make use of inheritance to use some of the classes that come standard with Java. By specifying a class name, you borrow from the effort of somebody else's — in this case, the Java designer's — work.

Methods in action

A *method* is a function that belongs to a class. The MinimalApplet has only one method, as follows:

```
public void paint(Graphics g)
{
   g.drawString("Java is Cool!", 10, 10);
}
```

The `paint()` method displays information in the Web browser window. It returns no value (`void`) and takes a graphics object (of type `Graphics`) as its only parameter. It is a *public* function: it is accessible by methods outside of the class.

The `paint()`method is special because the Web browser calls it every time the Java applet needs to be displayed. This will include the first time the applet executes, as well as every time the browser window has been covered up.

The `drawString()` method of the `Graphics` object is called to display a line of text on the screen. It takes three parameters: the string, along with the x and y position of where to display the string. You can pass a literal string (like that used here) or an object of type `String`.

A special type of method is called a *constructor*, which has the same name as the class and is called immediately when the class is first instantiated. Programmers often use constructors to initialize an object before other code can use data within the object. Here's an example of creating a class called `Square`, which contains a constructor:

```
class Square
{
   public Square()
   {
      // Constructor implementation
   }

   // Other methods and data
}
```

A constructor can take no parameters, as in the previous example, or it can take any number of parameters, which must be passed to the class when you first instantiate the class. For example, suppose the constructor required four parameters, the integer values for the top-left and lower-right coordinates of the square. The new class would appear as follows:

```
public void class Square
{
   public Square(int x1, int y1, int x2, int y2)
   {
      //   . . . implementation . . .
   }
}
```

To create an instance of this class, you would need to pass in the values for `x1`, `y1`, `x2`, and `y2`, as follows:

```
Square s = new Square(10, 10, 100, 100);
```

This ensures that parameters that may be required for a class will be passed when the class is first created. Suppose you wish to create the class by passing four parameters, but you would also like to have an option so that the new class can specify the coordinates later, after the class is already instantiated. You can have both:

```
public void class Square
{
   public Square(int x1, int y1, int x2, int y2)
   {
      //   . . . first implementation . . .
```

```
    }
    public Square()
    {
       //   . . . second implementation . . .
    }
}
```

Creating multiple methods with identical names that take different types of parameters is referred to as *operator overloading*. This is a complex sounding term, but as you can see, the concept is actually very simple.

Compiling the code

Now that I've gone over the source code for the example, you should try to compile it into a binary class file. The compiler is part of the Java Development Kit (JDK). The JDK also includes other tools, like an applet viewer, documentation tool, and sample program source code.

You can obtain the JDK free of charge from the Java home page (see http://www.javasoft.com). Just download the file, and when you execute the main file, it automatically decompresses into a directory named java.

Inside the directory, you will find a subdirectory called `bin`, which contains the Java development tools. You will also find a subdirectory containing sample source code. All the tools are based on the command-line and run from a DOS prompt. To make access to the tools easy, you should add **c:\java\bin** (or wherever you installed the JDK) to your path. This ensures that the system can find the compiler no matter what the current directory is.

To compile your code, use the program called `javac`, which is short for Java compiler. For example:

```
javac MinimalApplet.java
```

will compile the source file named MinimalApplet.java and create a binary file with the same root name and the .class extension.

The compiler is sensitive to the case of the filename that you enter. If you use mixed case in the source code, you need to use the same mixed case on the command line when you call the compiler. If the compiler does not understand any statements, it will display an error message on the screen.

With the Java applet compiled, you need to test it. Make sure that the HTML file and the class file are in the same subdirectory, start your Java-enabled browser (such as Netscape) and select Open File . . . from the File menu. Now, specify the name of the Web page file (MinimalApplet.html). The Web browser will load the document, along with the applet. (See Figure 4-3.)

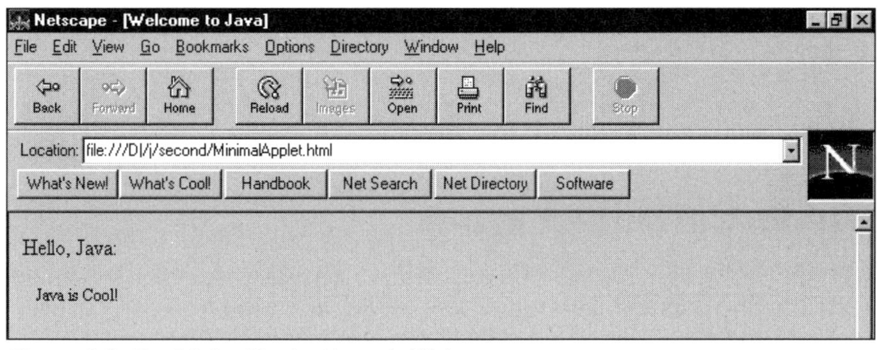

Figure 4-3: The MinimalApplet Example Web page.

You might wonder why we went through all this trouble of creating a separate Java program in order to display a line of text that we could have carried out by specifying the text directly in the HTML file. Well, as you will see in upcoming chapters, we can do a lot more than just display text. We can also work with graphical windows and implement in-page animation along with other multimedia effects.

At this point, the most important thing is that you compiled the program and were able to view it. Kernighan and Ritchie would be proud because you have "passed the greatest hurdle" to Java programming. Let's take a further look at some information about the Java language.

Java Language Information

All computer languages have data types for different types of information. This section takes a look at many of these types as they are implemented in Java. You will also learn more about declaring classes.

All programs consist of data and code. A Java class or variable name must start with an alphabetical letter (a–z, A–Z), an underscore (_), or a dollar sign ($). Characters following the initial character can also contain digits (0–9). Examples of valid identifiers include the following:

```
test
TestMe
SevenIs7
x_x
```

Numerical object types

All numerical data types are defined identically across all implementations of the language. This means that a byte will always be 8 bits, no matter if you are running on a UNIX Workstation or a Windows 95 personal computer. Table 4-2 provides an overview of the numerical data types.

Table 4-2 Java Numerical Data Types

Type	Description
boolean	True or false
byte	Eight-bit integer
short	16-bit integer
int	32-bit integer
long	64-bit integer
float	32-bit single precision floating point
double	64-bit double precision floating point

The boolean type has two states: true or false. These states are represented by the keywords `true` or `false`. You cannot convert between booleans and any of the other numerical data types. Therefore, unlike other languages, when an expression is expecting a `boolean` value, you cannot insert an integer value. Here is an example of using a boolean value:

```
boolean x;
x = true;
```

In Java, you can declare a variable at the same time you assign it a value. For example:

```
boolean x = true;
boolean Status = false;
```

Java provides four integer data types: `byte`, `short`, `int`, and `long`. Integers consist of any valid combination of digits along with a plus or minus sign. An *integer* is a number that does not contain a decimal point. For example:

```
int I;
byte b;
long l;

I = 255;
b = 35;
l = 75L;
```

As you can see, if you want to force an integer to be stored as a `long` data type, you can append an `l` or `L` to the end of the numerical assignment. You can display integers using decimal, octal, or hexadecimal notation. Decimal (base 10) is the standard notation used by Java. To specify octal (base 8), append a zero (`0`) in front of the digit. To specify hexadecimal (base 16), precede the number with `x0`. Table 4-3 provides an overview for using different counting systems to specify numerical values.

Table 4-3 An Overview of Specifying Numbers in Decimal, Octal, and Hexadecimal

Decimal	Octal	Hexadecimal
0	0	0x0
255	0377	0xff
65025	0177001	0xfe01

The floating point numerical types include `float` and `double`. Floating point numbers represent decimal numbers with fractional parts. Java uses the IEEE standard for representing floating point values, so you can be guaranteed that the representation will be the same on different computer platforms.

Alphabetic object types

Java provides two objects for working with alphabetic information: characters and strings.

Internally, Java represented each character using the Unicode character set. This is an international standard developed by Apple and Xerox in 1988. In 1991, some companies (namely, Adobe, Aldus, Apple, Borland, Digital, Go, IBM, Lotus, Metaphor, Microsoft, NeXT, Novell, the Research Libraries Group, Sun, Taligent, Unisys, WordPerfect, and Xerox) formed a consortium to develop and promote Unicode. Today, you'll find the full description of Unicode in the book *The Unicode Standard: Worldwide Character Encoding, Version 1.0*, from Addison-Wesley.

Unicode uses 16 bits (2 bytes) to store a character and offers a simple and consistent way of representing strings on an international basis. Because Unicode represents each character with a 16-bit value, more than 65,000 characters are available, making it possible to encode all the characters that make up written languages throughout the world. Currently, Unicode includes characters defined for the Arabic, Chinese bopomofo, Cyrillic (Russian), Greek, Hebrew, Japanese kana, Korean hangul, Latin (English) alphabets, and others. A large number of punctuation marks, mathematical symbols, technical symbols, arrows, dingbats, diacritical marks, and other characters are also included in the character set. Talk about internationalization! When you add all these alphabets and symbols together, they total about 34,000 different characters. Approximately 29,000 characters are currently unassigned but are reserved for future use. Furthermore, approximately 6,000 characters are reserved for your own personal use.

When you specify a character, you define it of type `char` and use the single quotation marks to assign it a value, as follows:

```
char c;
c = 'P';


char x = 'I';
```

You can also specify other important codes, such as line continuation, tabs, and returns, as described in Table 4-4.

Table 4-4 Special Character Representations

Description	Sequence
Line feed	\n
Horizontal tab	\t
Backspace	\b
Return	\r
Form feed	\f
Backslash	\\
Single quotation mark	\'
Double quotation mark	\"
Unicode character	\uxxxx

Strings are any number of characters enclosed in double quotation marks and are implemented by the `String` class. Here is an example of using a string type:

```
String  name = "Paul";

String p;
p = "This is a test of the emergency broadcast system.";
```

Java represents strings very differently from the way C++ does. In C++, a string is an array of characters. In Java, a string is its own object, implemented as a class.

Defining classes

You have already seen how to define a standard class:

```
Scope class ClassName [extends class]
{
   // Class implementation
}
```

When declaring the scope of the class, you have several options to control how other classes can access this class:

- `public` — can be used by code outside of the file. Only one class in a file may have this scope. File must be named class name followed by the four letter .java extension.
- `private` — can only be used within a file.
- `abstract` — cannot be used by itself. Must be subclassed.
- `final` — cannot be used by a subclass.
- `synchronizable` — instances of this class can be made arguments.

If you don't use a scope modifier, the class is only accessible within the current file.

Defining methods

As I discussed earlier, a *method* is a code that acts on data inside a class and is always declared inside the class declaration. A method has the following syntax:

```
Scope ReturnType MethodName(arguments)
{
   // Method implementation
}
```

The scope allows the programmer to control access to methods and can be one of the following:

- `public` — method is accessible by any system object.
- `protected` — method is only accessible by subclasses and the class in which it is declared.
- `private` — method is accessible only within the current class.
- `final` — method cannot be overridden by any subclass.
- `static` — method is shared by all instances of the class.

If a method does not receive a scope, it is only accessible within the scope of the current file. You can also use these scope operators when declaring variables. This allows you increased flexibility in declaring what parts of your program can access this method.

Arrays

An *array* is a list (or table) of objects of a related type. The variables in an array have a common name. Each individual element is accessed using an integer number called an index. What follows is a couple of examples of array declaration:

```
int list[] = new int[10];                    // Single dimensional.
int numbs[5] = {0, 1, 2, 3, 4,};             // Initializing an
array.
int matrix[][] = new int[10][20];            // Two-dimensional
array.
int matrix[][] = {{0, 0}, {1, 1}, {2, 2}}; // Initializing.
```

Notice how I used the `new` keyword to create instances of arrays. The `new` keyword allocates the memory required for the array. Unlike conventional languages that would allocate the array from the stack, Java allocates the array from the heap. As with C, array indexes start with zero (0).

Also, Java does provide bounds checking, so there is no way of overwriting memory by accessing an out of bounds array element.

Introduction to Applet Events

Now that you have learned more about the language, let's take a look at another example. Listing 4-3 provides the source code for an applet that shows you how to take advantage of applet events. Listing 4-4 contains the HTML source code that you use to view the applet in your Web browser.

Listing 4-3 MinimalApplet2.java Source Code

```
/*
 *  MinimalApplet2.java - Second Java Applet
 *
 *  Creating Cool Web Applets with Java
 *  By: Paul J. Perry,  Publisher: IDG Books
 *
 */

import java.applet.*;
import java.awt.Graphics;

public class MinimalApplet2 extends java.applet.Applet
{
```

(continued)

Listing 4-3 ***(continued)***

```
    // Always called first time applet is executed.
    public void init()
    {
       System.out.println("Hello.  Initializing applet...\n");
       resize(150,25);
    }

    // Called after init() and also whenever Web page is revis-
ited.
    public void start()
    {
       System.out.println("Starting applet...\n");
    }

    // Called when Web page that contains this applet disappears.
    public void stop()
    {
       System.out.println("Stopping applet...\n");
    }

    // Called when applet is being purged from memory.
    public void destroy()
    {
       System.out.println("Good bye.  Destroying applet...\n");
    }

    // This is where the graphics processing is done.
    public void paint(Graphics g)
    {
       g.drawString("Java is Cool!", 10, 10);
    }
}
```

Listing 4-4 **MinimalApplet2.html File**

```
<HTML>
<!- MinimalApplet2.html  ->
<HEAD>
   <TITLE>Welcome to Java</TITLE>
</HEAD>
<BODY>
Hello again, Java:<P><P>
```

```
<APPLET CODE="MinimalApplet2.class" WIDTH="200" HEIGHT="100">
This Web page requires a <B>Java</B>-enabled Web Browser.
</APPLET>
</BODY>
</HTML>
```

This sample code introduces four new methods. The `init()` method is called once after the applet has been loaded into the system and is the best place to initialize the applet. Called immediately afterward, the `start()` method informs the applet that it should take any action to start running. This occurs the first time the program is loaded and any time a Web page is revisited that contains an applet. The `stop()` method informs an applet that it should stop execution. This usually occurs when the user moves to a Web page that does not contain the applet. Finally, the `destroy()` method is called once to tell the applet that it's being purged from memory and that any resources it has allocated should be destroyed. Adding code to these methods provides great control over how an applet responds to the user.

The reason for these methods is that in order to provide better performance, Web browsers load an applet just once and cache the applet in memory. If the user revisits the same page or goes to another page that uses the same applet, that code is still in memory and the time required to download it from the Internet is saved for other purposes. The `start()` and `stop()` methods are called when moving between pages, whereas the `init()` and `destroy()` methods are called when the applet is first loaded and when it is finally purged from memory.

Looking at the `init()` method of the sample code, you will see a call to the `resize()` method. This method provides a way to let an applet change its own size. When an applet calls `resize()`, the values specified to the `<APPLET>` tag are ignored, and the applet communicates with the Web browser about its new size.

Using this technique allows you more control over the amount of the Web page that you can use.

Looking at the code, you'll also see several statements that look like this:

```
System.out.println("This is a message.\n");
```

This statement sends text to the standard output device. On a standalone Java applet, the message would most likely be displayed on the system terminal. Using Netscape as a browser, the output is forwarded to the Java console (choose the Options menu item and select Show Java Console). When you work with the sample program, you will see the output appear in the Java console window (see Figure 4-4). If you open the Java console window and move through several Web pages, including the previous example, you will see how the system makes use of the applet event methods.

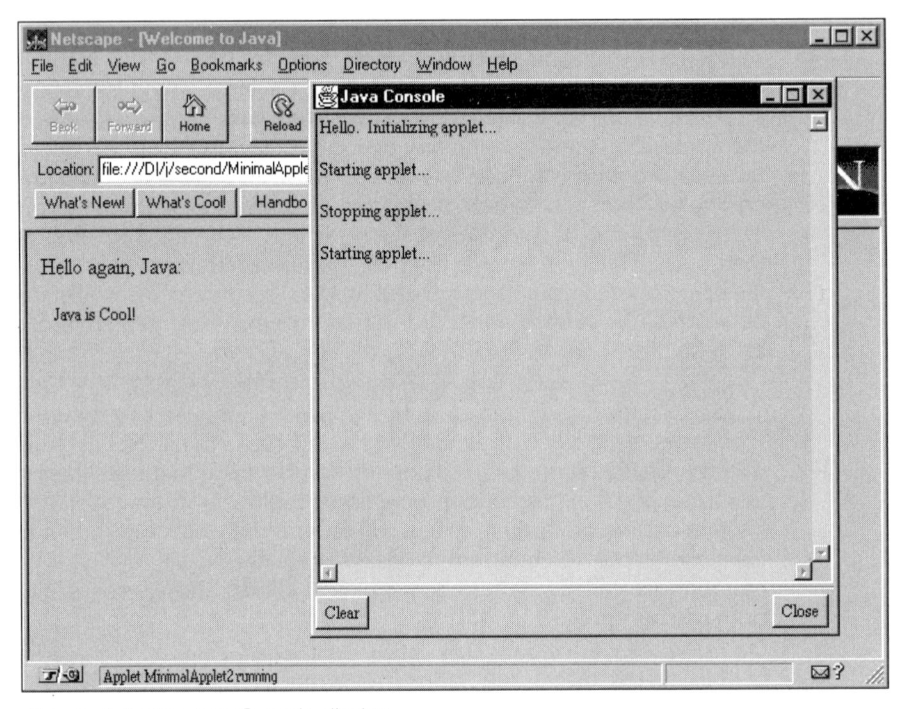

Figure 4-4: The Java Console display.

Control Flow Statements

Control flow statements are an important part of any programming language. In fact, the essence of any computer program is making decisions and acting upon them. The program makes comparisons and sets responses into motion depending on the results. The control flow statements that we examine allow a program to make a decision and act on it.

The `if...else` statement

The `if...else` statement enables your code to test an expression and a branch according to how it evaluates the expression. If the boolean expression evaluates to true, the computer will execute the statement that follows; if the condition evaluates to false, the computer does not execute the statement.

The simplest `if` statement follows:

```
if (booleanTest)
   callfunction();
```

The types of tests that you can carry out include testing for values or results from function calls. For example:

```
int p = 27;
if (p==45)
   g.drawString("p does not equal 45", 10, 10);
```

compares the variable `p` with the number 45. Because they don't equal one another, the `drawString()` method will always be called. Table 4-5 provides an overview of the relational operators available in Java.

Table 4-5 Relational Operators

Operator	Description
<	Less than
>	Greater than
<=	Less than or equal to
>=	Greater than or equal to
==	Equal to
!=	Not equal to

You can execute more than one function with curly braces, as follows:

```
if (booleanTest)
{
   callFunction();
   callAnotherFunction();
   // etc.
}
```

In Java, the test value *must* be a boolean variable. You cannot test an integer (`int`) object. For example:

```
boolean x = true;
if (x)
 g.drawString("Always displayed", 10, 10);
```

will always display the message. If you wish to take some action if the test is false, you can use the `else` clause. The syntax is as follows:

```
if (booleanTest)
{
   // Value is true.
}
else
{
    //  Value is false.
}
```

Finally, you can extend the `if...else` conditional statement to make additional comparisons. The format follows:

```
if (booleanTest)
{
   // do something
}
else if (booleanTest2)
{
   /// do something else
}
else
{
   // do something different
}
```

In this case, the computer starts with one test (`booleanTest`). If the statement is not true, it performs another test (`booleanTest2`). You can use the `else` clause in a program as much as you like. At the end, if the test expression is not true, the program executes the `else` clause.

The `for` loop

The `for` loop is the fundamental looping statement in Java. Often in programming, you will want to carry out a task a specific number of times. The `for` loop lets you do the job. Although found in almost every programming language, Java follows the C++ syntax very closely, therefore providing much power and flexibility. The general form of the `for` loop follows:

```
for (initialization; condition; increment)
   statement;
```

The `initialization` section initializes and optionally declares an index variable that controls looping. The `condition` section represents a condition that must be satisfied for the loop to continue. Finally, the `increment` clause is a value representing how to increment the index variable. The body of the `for` loop is located in the `statement` section. You can use braces to enclose multiple statements.

An example of a `for` loop follows:

```
for (int i = 0; i <10; i++)
{
   // do something
}
```

This loop will execute ten times, with the index variable counting from zero (0) to nine. The variable is declared inside the initialization section at the same time it is assigned to zero (0). Please notice that unlike C++, the scope of the variable declared in the initialization section is available only in the body of the `for` loop and does not extend beyond that. You will produce an error if you reference the variable outside the `for` loop.

The condition checks to see if the variable is less than 10. Finally, the increment section increments the variable by one, using the *unary increment operator*, which works on only a single variable or object. Java has three unary operators, as shown in Table 4-6.

Table 4-6 Integer Unary Operators

Operator	Description
~	Unary negation
++	Increment by one
--	Decrement by one

While you can use both the increment (++) and decrement (--) operators in the `for` statement, you cannot use the negation operator. If you prefer to count by two, you would use the standard mathematical addition operator, as follows:

```
for (int i = 0; i <10; I=I+2)
```

Table 4-7 provides an overview of the mathematical operators available in Java.

Table 4-7	Mathematical Operators
Operator	**Description**
+	Addition
-	Subtraction
*	Multiplication
/	Division

A common error occurs when you place a semicolon after the `for` loop parenthesis, like this:

```
for (int I = 0; I < 10; I++);
   statement;
```

Don't do it. Your program will still compile correctly, but it will not run right. The code will appear not to have any effect because your statement will execute just once. Instead, that semicolon at the end of the first line will execute multiple times. This is not exactly what you had in mind when writing the code.

The `while` statement

Another type of loop available in Java is the `while` statement, which takes this form:

```
while (booleanTest)
   statement;
```

The `while` keyword precedes an expression surrounded by parentheses. The statement can be a single statement followed by a semicolon or a block of statements surrounded by braces.

In the `while` loop, the body of the loop executes as long as the expression is true. When the expression becomes false, program control passes to the line that follows the loop.

The `do...while` statement

A famous television commercial tells you that you can "Have it your way." In Java, the `while` keyword provides just about the same number of choices as Burger King. The `do...while` loop is similar to the `while` loop. Unlike the `for` and `while` loops, which test the loop condition at the top of the loop, the

do...while loop checks its condition at the end of the loop. This means that the statements in a do...while loop will always execute at least once. The general form is as follows:

```
do
{
   // do something
}
while (booleanTest);
```

The do...while loop, unlike the other loop statements we have examined, has two keywords: do and while. The do keyword marks the beginning of the loop. The while keyword marks the end of the loop and contains the loop expression. Notice that the do...while loop expression terminates with a semicolon.

The statement(s) enclosed in braces will execute repeatedly, as long as the value of booleanTest is true. Although the braces are not necessary when a single statement is present, they are usually used to improve the overall readability of the statement. They are required when you are working with a block of statements, and most of the time, you'll use the do...while loop with a block of statements.

For most programmers, testing for loop continuation at the beginning is more natural than at the end of the loop. For this reason, programmers use the do...while statement less frequently than the other looping statements we have covered.

The switch statement

You can make some pretty advanced decisions using the if...else, while, or do...while branching statements. However, sometimes the resulting code can be difficult to follow and can confuse even advanced programmers. The Java programming language has a built-in, multiple-branch decision statement, called switch. The switch statement causes a particular group of statements to be chosen from several available groups. The general form of the switch statement follows:

```
switch(expression)
{
   case FirstCase :
      // First set of statements
      break;

   case SecondCase :
      // Second set of statements
```

(continued)

```
        break;

    case ThirdCase :
        // Third set of statements
        break;
    .
    .
    .

    default :
        // Default statement
        break;
}
```

In the switch statement, Java tests a variable consecutively against a list of integer constants. After finding a match, the computer executes the statement or block of statements that are associated with the specified case. Following each of the case keywords is an integer or character constant. This constant is finished with a colon. More statements can follow each case keyword. You do not need to enclose the statements in braces, but the entire body of the switch statement is enclosed in braces.

The default statement executes if the compiler does not find a match in the list of constants. The default statement is optional. If it is not present, no action takes place if all matches fail. When the computer finds a match, it executes the statements associated with the specified case until it reaches the break statement or the end of the switch clause.

Notice the use of the break statement at the end of each case. If you do not use the break statement, program flow continues to the next case. Most of the time, this is not what you want. Sometimes cases that run together when no break statement is present let you write efficient code by avoiding duplication: this is something that many Windows programmers have enjoyed.

As you can tell, the control statements are very important to writing Java programs because they allow you to control program flow. You will use a couple of these statements on a regular basis when you work in Java. Some others you won't use very regularly at all.

Passing Parameters to an Applet

One of the nice features of Java is the capability to pass data between an applet and an HTML file. The next example, Listing 4-6, shows you how to do this. The program creates the beginning of an applet that will display a signature within a Web page (somewhat like the signature that is always added to the end of an e-mail message).

For now, the applet takes only a single string. You could pass it your name or any phrase you like. Listing 4-5 is the supporting HTML file that passes parameters to the applet. Figure 4-5 shows how the example appears on the screen.

Listing 4-5 MiniSig.html File

```
<HTML>
<!- MiniSig.html    ->
<HEAD>
   <TITLE>This is a sample signature applet</TITLE>
</HEAD>
<BODY>
First instance of applet on page:<P><P>
<APPLET CODE="MiniSig.class" WIDTH="200" HEIGHT="100">
<PARAM NAME="text" VALUE="Hello from Java!">
</APPLET>
<P>
Second instance of applet on page:<P><P>
<APPLET CODE="MiniSig.class" WIDTH="200" HEIGHT="100">
<PARAM NAME="text" VALUE="Another Big Hello!">
</APPLET>
</BODY>
</HTML>
```

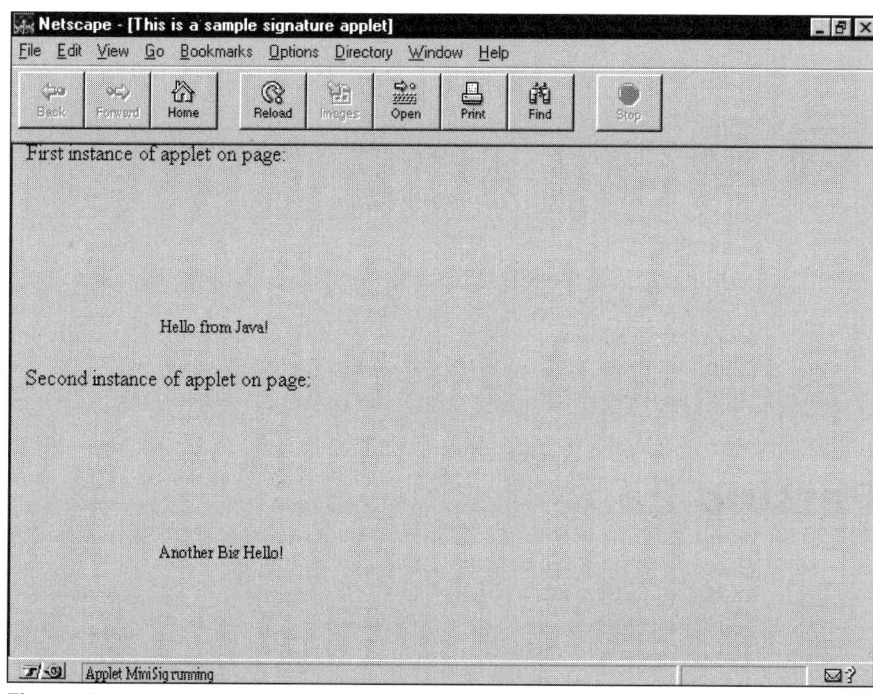

Figure 4-5: The MiniSig example.

Listing 4-6 **MiniSig.java Source Code**

```
/*
 *  MiniSig.java - Mini signature applet.
 *
 *  Creating Cool Web Applets with Java
 *  By: Paul J. Perry,  Publisher: IDG Books
 *
 */

import java.applet.*;
import java.awt.Graphics;

public class MiniSig extends java.applet.Applet
{
   // Data member
   String txt;

   // Initialization method
   public void init()
   {
     // Get parameters passed from HTML file
      txt = getParameter ("TEXT");
      resize(600, 500);
   }

   // Graphics processing.
   public void paint(Graphics g)
   {
      g.drawString(txt, 100, 100);
   }
}
```

Skimming over the HTML file, the first piece of code you will notice is the `<PARAM>` tag. The line looks like this:

```
<PARAM NAME="text" VALUE="Hello from Java!">
```

You specify the parameter name and the value to assign to the parameter. Notice the use of quotes. This is also standard with other HTML tags. Throughout the examples, I try to use quotes always, but you can sometimes get along without them. Any time you pass a continuous stream of characters (without spaces), you can omit the quotes. For example:

```
<PARAM NAME=text VALUE="Hello from Java!">
```

Notice that you can skip the quotes on the first item (`NAME`), but you must use them on the second (`VALUE`) because you are passing more than one word. This makes sense.

Now that the information has passed from the HTML file, you need a corresponding way of accessing the parameter inside the Java applet. You can do this with the `getParameter()` method, which takes one value that is the name of the parameter you wish to access. The `getParameter()` method returns the value of the specified parameter from the HTML file. The source code looks like this:

```
txt = getParameter ("TEXT");
```

As you can see from the program listing, the `txt` variable was previously declared as a string. The program obtains the parameter inside the `init()` function, which is called the first time the program runs (remember that?). If the user does not pass a parameter of the specified type, the `getParameter()` method returns the `null` value. Notice the use of the `resize()` function to set the area of space used by the applet. If the applet does not do this, it does not know how much space it has to use.

Although not used in the example, you might sometime wish to find the length of a string. You can do this with the `length()` method, as follows:

```
int x = txt.length();
```

Java also has functionality to convert the string into other data types. For example, suppose you are passing numeric values. The `getParameter()` method always returns a string. Therefore, you need some way to convert that string into an integer number. The functionality actually comes with the `Integer` object type because it contains a function that takes a string and returns a numeric value. Here's how:

```
String r = "99";
int x = Integer.parseInt(r);
```

Afterwards, the `x` variable equals the numeric value 99.

Two other methods fall in the same category as the `getParameter()` method, and you should know about them even though they are not used here. They are similar to `getParameter()` because they provide information about an applet. The first is `getDocumentBase()`. This method returns the URL address of a Web page that contains the applet. It has the following syntax:

```
URL u;
u = getDocumentBase();
```

`URL` is a special class that holds a uniform resource locator (see Chapter 1) that is used to access a Web site. Some methods require a URL to fetch data (audio, images, and so forth) from a Web site. The URL class contains methods that let you manipulate the address. By using the `getDocumentBase()` method, your applet will know exactly where the URL is executing.

The other method is called `getCodeBase()`, and it returns the URL of the applet itself, which may differ from the URL of the document where it is embedded. As before, this method returns an object of type `URL`. Remember that these functions are valuable for providing information about the applet.

Now that you have written a couple of programs in Java and you have an idea of the mechanism used to pass parameters between an applet and a Web page, let's take a break. But, before we do that, let's see an overview of what the JDK provides in the way of tools.

Using the Java Development Kit

The Java Development Kit (JDK) creates Java applets and includes several command-line tools that allow you to compile and test your Java code. Table 4-8 provides a summary of these tools.

Table 4-8 Java Development Kit Tools

Name	Description
javac.exe	The Java compiler.
java.exe	The Java interpreter. Executes standalone applications.
appletviewer.exe	The Java applet viewer. Executes Web page applets.
javadoc.exe	The Java documentation tool. Generates documentation from Java source code.
javap.exe	Java disassembler.

The Java compiler

The tool that you will use the most is `javac`, or the Java compiler. It converts Java source code contained in files with the .java extension into binary class files containing Java byte codes ending with the .class extension. You pass the filename of the source class you wish to compile on the command line. For example:

```
javac MyClass.java
```

The capitalization of the class is important because the compiler makes sure that the filename matches that of the class declared in the file. You can pass a couple of command line switches to the compiler, including:

- `-classpath` *`path`*, which specifies the path the compiler uses to look up classes. You should separate directories with semicolons.
- `-d` *`directory`*, which allows you to specify the root directory of a class hierarchy.
- `-g`, which enables debugging information for use by the Java debugger. This option will embed information about line numbers and local variables inside the applet. By default, this option is on.
- `-ng`, which turns off debugging information.
- `-nowarn`, which turns off warning messages.
- `-O`, which optimizes compiled code. Using this option can increase the size of your resulting files.
- `-verbose`, which causes the compiler and linker to print out messages about which source files are being compiled.

You should really know about one environment variable used by the compiler: `CLASSPATH`, which provides the compiler with a path to user-defined classes. Directories are separated by semicolons. You can specify this in your autoexec.bat batch file, as follows:

```
SET CLASSPATH=c:\java\classes;c:\java\proj;
```

Some of the other tools use this option as well.

The Java interpreter

The Java interpreter is the run-time tool that will execute Java classes. In essence, any Web browser that understands Java has this interpreter built in. If you target your applets for use in Web pages, the Java interpreter is not very useful because it does not implement any of the graphical windowing commands. You pass the filename of the compiled binary on the command line. For example:

```
java Myclass
```

Notice that you don't need to specify the file extension.

The applet viewer

The appletviewer tool takes an HTML filename and acts as a method to test Web pages without having to use a browser. You specify the HTML file on the command line, and the applet viewer loads the Web page, displays it, and executes any applets found on that page. You can also pass a URL on the command line in order to view applets at remote Web sites. Examples include

```
appletviewer MyClass
appletviewer http://www.javasoft.com
```

Although appletviewer is a good idea, I found using my favorite Web browser easier when testing my Web pages that contain Java classes.

The Java documentation tool

The javadoc utility takes a Java source code file (.java extension) and creates program documentation in HTML format. It even provides hyperlinks that let you work your way around the documentation easily. You must use special comment notation inside your program, which looks like this:

```
/** This is only a TestApp.
  * However it could be extremely useful.
  * Decide for yourself.
  */

public class TestApp extends java.applet.Applet
{
. . .
}
```

Notice the comment style that uses a single slash followed by two asterisks (/**). When you write programs that you wish to document with this tool, use this notation before a class declaration. In the comments, provide complete documentation for the class (or as much as you can). The idea is that programmers will write the best documentation for code while they are writing that code.

Later, when you are ready to create your documentation, specify your Java source file to the java documentation tool, as follows:

```
javadoc ClassName.java
```

The tool will create an HTML file that contains a class hierarchy for the class (see Figure 4-6). Be careful because if a file already exists with this name, it will be overwritten. (I learned this the hard way!)

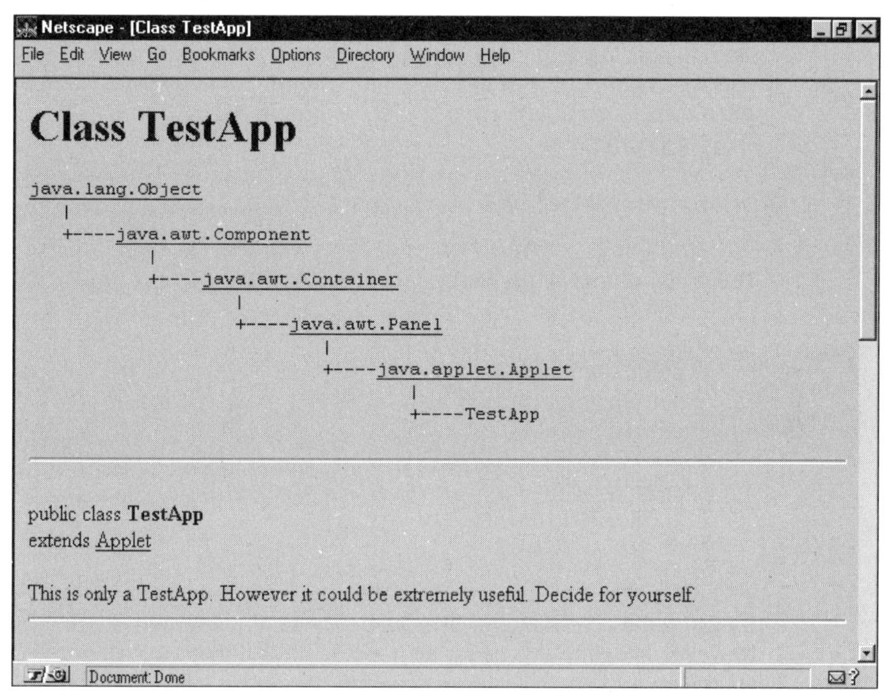

Figure 4-6: Program Documentation for TestApp class.

Although not the fanciest method to create documentation, it is a lot better than not having any method at all.

The Java disassembler

The Java disassembler (`javap`) converts Java class files into source code. The program has the following command line parameters:

- `-c` — disassembles the code for each function.
- `-classpathdirectory` — allows you to specify directories where you can look for classes and which should be separated by colons.
- `-h` — creates information that you can use in a C header file.
- `-p` — includes private fields and methods in the disassembly.

- `-v` — provides verbose information about disassembled files.
- `-verify` — runs the verifier that will print out debugging information.
- `-version` — displays the Java disassembler (`javap`) version string.

If you don't pass any parameters, the program will display the methods and data objects inside a class. For the most part, when you use the program, all you pass is the name of the class file, without the extension. For example, when using it on the MinimalApplet2 example (from Listing 4-3), use the following command:

```
javap MinimalApplet2
```

This is the output of the tool:

```
public class MinimalApplet2 extends java.applet.Applet {
    public void init();
    public void start();
    public void stop();
    public void destroy();
    public void paint(java.awt.Graphics);
    public MinimalApplet2();
}
```

By using the `-c` parameter, the utility will display more in-depth information. However, the output is never as good as having the original, documented source code. This tool is very powerful because it lets you learn the internal operations of applets that are already created.

Future Java Development Tools

The Java development tools are still in their infancy. For now, you won't see any of the fancy visual programming interfaces that many of us are used to seeing. But, don't fret. Almost assuredly, better development tools will come along soon. As an example, Symantec Corporation has a patch for its C++ compiler that allows it to act as a front-end to the Java compiler tools (see Figure 4-7). If you are interested, you must own the Symantec ++ compiler. Then, check out Symantec's Web page (http://www.symantec.com) for the path file to download. Other tools manufacturers have also promised development products for Java. None are available yet.

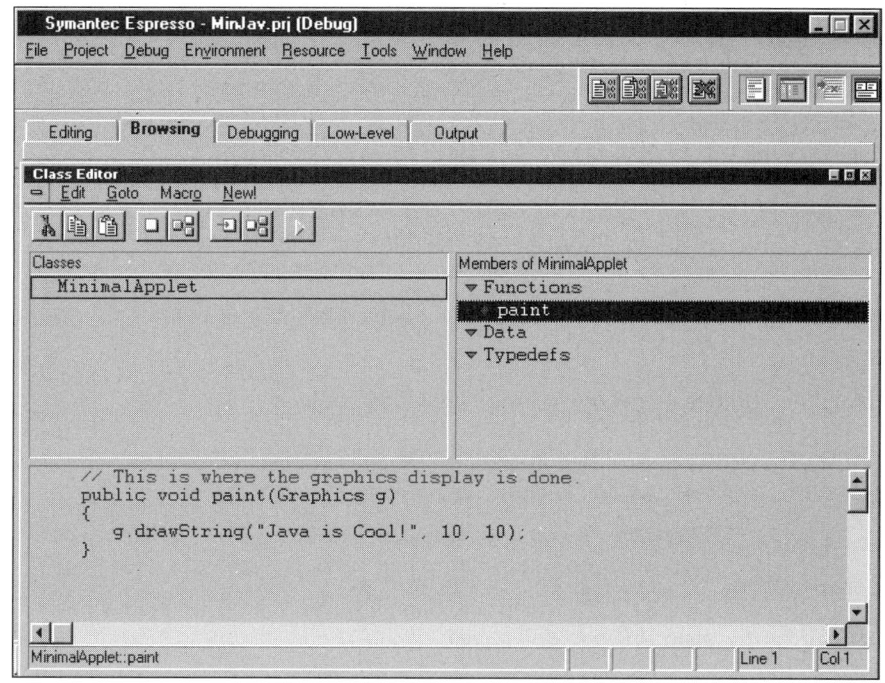

Figure 4-7: The Symantec Java development tool, called Espresso.

Quick Overview

This chapter has covered a lot of ground. You learned the basic structure of a Java applet. You learned about some of the primary functions that are called during initialization and shutdown. You deserve a break today.

In particular, this chapter covered the following topics:

- Java applets are based on objects. An object combines program code and data into one self-contained unit. Classes are the program statements that act as a template to defining objects.
- All Java classes inherit from `Object`.
- To create a Web page using a Java applet, you work with three types of files: the HTML source code (.html), the Java binary code (.class), and the Java source code (.java).
- The `<APPLET>` tag is used inside an HTML file to access a Java applet.
- You pass parameters from an HTML file to an applet using the `<PARAM>` tag. You access the parameters from the Java applet using the `getParameter()` method.

- A method is a function that belongs to a class.
- Java numeric types include: `boolean`, `byte`, `short`, `int`, `long`, `float`, and `double`.
- Java alphabetic types include `char` and `String`.
- Several methods inside a Java applet have special meaning. The `init()` and `destroy()` methods are called when the applet is first loaded and later called when the applet is removed from memory. The `start()` and `stop()` methods are called when the user moves to the specified page.
- The Java Development Kit (JDK) provides tools for compiling and viewing applets.

Here is a brief overview of what is to come . . .

- Chapter 5, “Incorporating Text and Graphics,” describes how to use multiple fonts, colors, and graphics objects in a Java applet.
- Chapter 6, “Incorporating Images and Animation,” describes how to use Java to incorporate fancy images and animation into your Web page.
- Chapter 7, “Working with Sound,” gives you information about using audio sound in your Web pages.

Incorporating Text and Graphics

In This Chapter

How to display text using multiple fonts.

How to work with different colors in your Java applets.

How to display graphics primitives such as lines, squares, rectangles, and circles.

In some ways, implementing the user interface of an applet (or any program for that matter) is the most important part of programming. You could have the best internal algorithms, but if a user cannot interact with a program, he or she will never use it. So it is with Java applets. This chapter examines the classes and methods available for displaying text and all kinds of basic graphical objects such as lines, rectangles, polygons, and circles.

Displaying Text with Java

Although the maxim says that a picture is worth a thousand words, text is probably the most important technique a computer program has for communicating with the user. This is also the reason why early computers displayed only text and lacked graphical capabilities.

Today we are lucky because many computers can display more than just the plain text that early computers did. This is especially true of a graphical environment such as Windows. Java applets can display text using multiple fonts and can display them in many different colors supported by the monitor used to display the applet. You have seen the basic technique used to display text in Java, which is the `drawString()` method:

```
public void paint(Graphics g)
{
   g.drawString("Java can display text", 10, 10);
}
```

This displays the string in the current font and color. The `Graphics` class is usually passed to the `paint()` method by the `Applet` class. The `drawString()` method of the `Graphics` class is responsible for displaying the string at the specified coordinates. The x and y values passed to the method are the coordinates of the baseline of the text. If you wish to display a numeric value, you must first convert it to a `String`. Although you cannot pass an integer value directly as the first parameter, you can trick the system into first converting it into an integer value, as follows:

```
public void paint(Graphics g)
{
   g.drawString(""+x+"", 10, 10);
}
```

By appending quotes around the integer variable, the compiler first converts the number into a string, thereby allowing your programs to display numbers easily.

The `drawString()` method has the following declaration:

```
void drawString(String s, int x, int y);
```

The `Graphics` class really provides the functionality for displaying text and graphics in Java applets. You cannot create `Graphics` objects directly. They must be obtained from another graphics context or provided by the `paint()` method, as shown. This makes sense because you can only display information at certain times, and the system lets you know when these times occur by providing a `Graphics` object. If a `Graphics` object is not available, you are probably trying to display information at the wrong time.

The `drawString()` method is not the only way to display information. The `Graphics` class provides a couple of other methods for displaying textual information. The first allows you to display characters and is declared as follows:

```
void drawChars(char array[], int offset,
               int length, int x, int y);
```

The first parameter is an array of characters. The second and third integer values let you specify the starting offset within the data, along with several characters to be displayed. Finally, the last two parameters specify the x and y coordinates of where you wish the characters to appear.

If you have your data stored as byte values, you can use a similar function, as follows:

```
void drawBytes(byte array[], int offset,
               int length, int x, int y);
```

This method uses an array of bytes rather than an array of characters. Here is a sample usage:

```
public void paint(Graphics g)
{
   byte bytearray[] = {74, 65, 86, 65};
   g.drawBytes(bytearray, 0, 4, 10, 10);
}
```

Interestingly enough, when the Graphics object displays the bytes (or characters) in the array, it interprets them as ASCII characters (rather than the Unicode characters on which Strings are based). Therefore, the previous code sample displays the text "*JAVA*".

With the fundamentals understood for displaying text, let's find out how to work with multiple fonts.

Working with fonts

If you don't specify another font, Java uses a default font named `"Dialog"` to display your text string. You can modify font attributes, such as boldface or italic, and you can also change the size of the font. You can choose from six standard fonts to display your text. Although not a huge variety (desktop publishing packages like PageMaker might provide hundreds of different fonts), the choices you have provide some flexibility in choosing how text will appear.

To display text in a different font, you must create a `Font` object. When you create a new font, you specify the font name, the style, and the point size. For example, the following statement

```
Font f = new Font("TimesRoman", Font.PLAIN, 12);
```

creates a regular 12-point Times Roman font. Table 5-1 provides an overview of the font names from which you can choose. As for the size of your text, you can select from point sizes of 8, 10, 12, 14, 24, and 36. The current attributes available are PLAIN, BOLD, and ITALIC, which are already defined in the Font class.

Table 5-1 Standard Java Fonts

Name	Description
Courier	Fixed spacing
Dialog	Fixed spacing
DialogInput	Fixed spacing
Helvetica	Proportional font
TimesRoman	Proportional font
ZapfDingBats	Special characters

Once you have created the font, you must set it as the default font, using the setFont() method of the Graphics class. Assuming you had created a font named "f," the following code would select it as the new font:

```
public void paint(Graphics g)
{
   Font f = new Font("TimesRoman", Font.PLAIN, 12);
   FontMetrics fm = new FontMetrics(f);
}
```

Any time you want to create a new font, you must create a font and then set it as the default in the Graphics object. You can create several font objects at once and then select them into the Graphics object as you need them.

The Graphics class has a counterpart function to setFont(), called getFont(), which will return the name of the current font. This can be helpful in finding out which font is currently selected.

When designing a user interface, you might need to find out information about the size of the font, such as the width and height of that font. For this, you must use a FontMetric object. You can obtain the font metric information either from the graphics object (in which case it applies to the current font), or you can pass a font object to the function directly. For example:

```
public void paint(Graphics g)
{
   FontMetrics fm = g.getFontMetrics();
}
```

or, if you have a `Font` object already hanging around, you can obtain the same information like this:

```
public void paint(Graphics g)
{
   Font f = g.getFont();
   FontMetrics fm = getFontMetrics(f);
}
```

Either way you go at it, the `FontMetric` object has a plethora of methods that provide basic information about the size of the font (see Table 5-2).

Table 5-2 Methods Available in the `FontMetric` Object

Method	Description
`int bytesWidth(byte arr[], int off, int len)`	Width of an array of bytes
`int charWidth(char ch);`	Width of a single character
`int charsWidth(char arr[], int off, int len);`	Width of a character array
`int stringWidth(String s);`	Width of string
`int getAscent();`	Distance from the baseline to the top of the character
`getDescent();`	Distance from the baseline to the bottom of the character
`Font getFont();`	Font name
`getHeight();`	Total height of font
`getLeading();`	Line spacing of font
`getMaxAdvance();`	Maximum advance width of any character
`getMaxAscent();`	Maximum ascent of characters
`getMaxDescent();`	Maximum descent of characters
`getWidths();`	Width of the first 256 characters in the font
`StringtoString();`	String representation of the font's metric values

Probably the most useful font metric information is returned by the stringWidth() and getHeight() methods. Using the information returned, you will know the exact size of a string of text. Several standard fonts are proportional fonts, however, in which each character has a different width. With proportional fonts, you cannot reliably know the exact size of the string from the width of a single character. Instead, you pass an entire string (which can also be a single character), and the system will return the width of the entire string. Knowing that information, you can position text at specific locations on the screen. An example of centering text follows:

```
public void paint(Graphics g)
{
   String str = "This is a test.";
   FontMetrics fm = g.getFontMetrics();
   int w = fm.stringWidth(str);
   int h = fm.getHeight();
   Dimension r = size();
   g.drawString(str, (r.width-w)/2,
                     (r.height-h)/2);
}
```

The only thing new here is the Dimension object. It contains width and height data members for the current applet. The size() method returns the size (or dimensions) of the applet. With that information, you can pass the drawString() method the exact location to display a string. As a result, the string is centered in the display area.

Listing 5-1 (TestFont.java) provides an example of using fonts in your program, as shown in Figure 5-1. Listing 5-2 provides the complimentary TestFont.html Web page to use when viewing the applet from a Web browser.

Listing 5-1 TestFont.java Sample Listing

```
/*
 *  TestFont - Display different fonts available.
 *
 *  Creating Cool Web Applets with Java
 *  By: Paul J. Perry,  Publisher: IDG Books
 *
 */

import java.applet.*;
import java.awt.*;

public class TestFont extends java.applet.Applet
```

```
{
   public void init()
   {
      resize(600, 400);
   }
   public void paint(Graphics g)
   {
      Font f1 = g.getFont();
      String s = f1.getName() + " " + f1.getSize() + " (De-
fault)";
      g.drawString(s, 10, 10);

      Font f2 = new Font("TimesRoman", Font.PLAIN, 10);
      s = f2.getName() + " " + f2.getSize();
      g.setFont(f2);
      g.drawString(s, 10, 50);

      Font f3 = new Font("Helvetica", Font.PLAIN, 12);
      s = f3.getName() + " " + f3.getSize();
      g.setFont(f3);
      g.drawString(s, 10, 150);

      Font f4 = new Font("ZapfDingbats", Font.PLAIN, 14);
      s = f4.getName() + " " + f4.getSize();
      g.setFont(f4);
      g.drawString(s, 10, 200);

      Font f5 = new Font("Courier", Font.PLAIN, 24);
      s = f5.getName() + " " + f5.getSize();
      g.setFont(f5);
      g.drawString(s, 10, 250);

      Font f6 = new Font("DialogInput", Font.PLAIN, 36);
      s = f6.getName() + " " + f6.getSize();
      g.setFont(f6);
      g.drawString(s, 10, 300);

   }
}
```

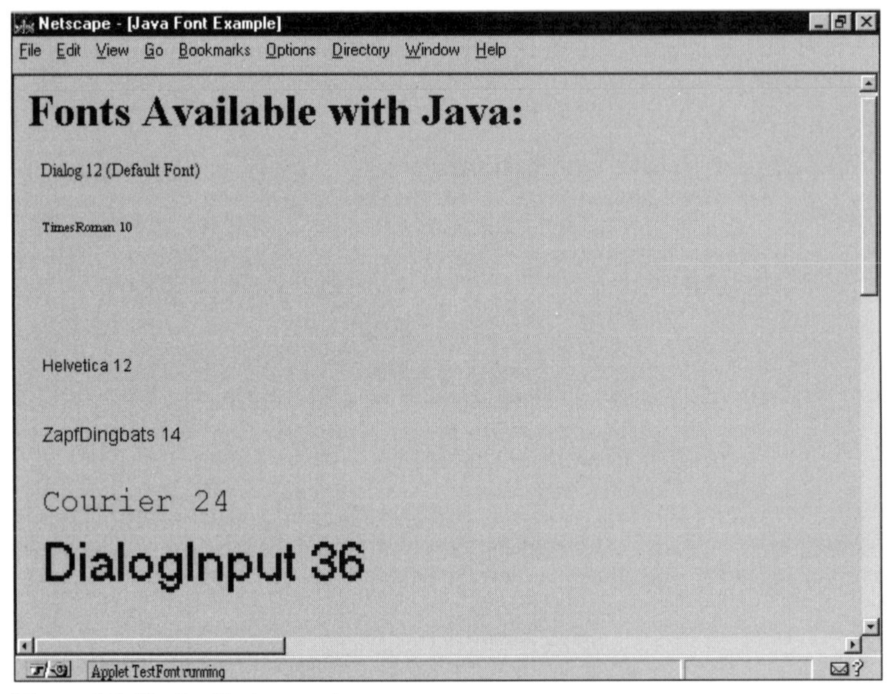

Figure 5-1: The TestFont example.

Listing 5-2 **TestFont.html Source File**

```
<HTML>
<!- TestFont.html ->
<HEAD>
   <TITLE>Java Font Example</TITLE>
</HEAD>
<BODY>
<H1>Fonts Available with Java:</H1><P>
<APPLET CODE="TestFont.class" WIDTH="2000" HEIGHT="1000">
This Web page requires a <B>Java</B>-enabled Web Browser.
</APPLET>
</BODY>
</HTML>
```

Working with Color

After working with the Font and FontMetric objects, you might already guess that the way to work with multiple colors in a Java applet is with a Color object. If that was what you were thinking, you hit the nail directly on the head. If that is not what you were thinking, well just follow along.

The Color object has 13 predefined colors that you can use without much effort. You just need to select them in the current Graphics object, using the setColor() method. For example:

```
public void paint(Graphics g)
{
    g.setColor(Color.orange);
    g.drawString("I'm Orange", 10, 10);
}
```

would display the text in orange. The default color is black. Table 5-3 shows all the predefined color values that you can use. They are always guaranteed to be available for you.

Table 5-3 Standard Colors

Color Identifier	Description
black	Black
blue	Dark blue
cyan	Light blue
darkGray	Dark gray
gray	Gray
green	Green
lightGray	Light gray
magenta	Light purple
orange	Orange
pink	Pink
red	Red
white	White
yellow	Yellow

If 13 colors is not enough for you and the user's hardware supports the display of more colors, you can create as many colors as you like by specifying the three values (red, green, and blue) that compose a color. It works like this:

```
public void paint(Graphics g)
{
   Color c = new Color(255, 0, 0);
   g.setColor(c);
   g.drawString("I'm Red.", 10, 10);
}
```

The three values you pass to the Color object are integers and should be in the range of 1 to 255. If the color value you choose is not available on the target system, Java will choose the closest available color that that system will display.

Besides setting the color, you can return the current color by calling the `getColor()` method of the `Graphics` class. If you would like to convert a `Color` object to its component parts, you can call the `getRed()`, `getGreen()`, or `getBlue()` functions to return each component value.

If you are used to working with the HSB (hue, saturation, and brightness) color scheme, the `Color` object provides methods that will benefit you. The computer prefers RGB values because each component value is an integer. On the other hand, HSB values are floating point, which requires more computing power to process. However, this doesn't mean you shouldn't use HSB values.

Instead of creating a new color based on an RGB value, you can use the `getHSBColor()` method to create a new color based on an HSB value. The `HSBtoRGB()` function takes three float values and returns an equivalent number in RGB format that you can then use to create the `Color` object. The `RGBtoHSB()` method takes three `int` values and a floating point array (`float[]`) and converts the RGB value to an HSB value.

Finally, two nifty functions change the brightness of a color value. The `brighter()` method takes no parameters and returns a brighter version of the current color. Correspondingly, the `darker()` method returns a darker version of the current color. Don't forget how to work with colors in Java because you use the same functions not just for text but for displaying graphics. In fact, this introduces our next topic very nicely.

Displaying Graphics

Any geometric shape that a computer displays consists of points, or pixels, on the screen. Interestingly enough, Java does not yet provide any means to display a single point. The simplest shape you can display is a line. Although you can easily create a rectangle or polygon with a few calls to the line drawing routine, Java also provides methods for displaying these shapes, circles, and arcs. All of these graphics primitives are part of the `Graphics` object. Let's start simple and move up in complexity.

Displaying lines

A line is actually a set of connected points, which is drawn with the `drawLine()` method in the `Graphics` object. You pass the method to both endpoints of the line, and Java draws the line in the current color. The method has the following prototype:

```
drawLine(int x1, int y1, int x2, int y2);
```

You would use it in the following manner:

```
public void paint(Graphics g)
{
   g.drawline(5, 100, 100, 200);
}
```

The coordinates correspond to the two endpoints of the line.

Displaying squares and rectangles

The Java system really only has routines for displaying rectangles. But that is all right because squares are just rectangles with identical width and heights. The basic rectangle drawing method is called `drawRect()`. It takes four parameters: the anchor point of the rectangle (that is, the bottom-left corner), along with the width and height, as follows:

```
drawRect(int x, int y, int width, int height);
```

The `drawRect()` method displays the rectangle in the current color. You have to be careful with this routine because if text or graphics already appears at the point where you are drawing the rectangle, the rectangle will not clear it. In order to do that, you must use the `clearRect()` function. The `clearRect()` function fills in the rectangular area with the current background color. It is declared as follows:

```
clearRect(int x, int y, int width, int height);
```

Suppose you want to choose the color you wish to display inside the rectangle. No problem. Just use the `fillRect()` method. The `fillRect()` method fills a rectangle with the current color.

```
fillRect(int x, int y, int width, int height);
```

If standard rectangles are not enough for you, Java provides a set of routines for drawing rectangles with rounded corners. You must still pass the starting point along with the width and height of the rectangle, but you must also specify the width and height of the arc that composes the rounded rectangle. Here are the prototypes:

```
drawRoundRect(int x, int y, int width, int height,
              int arcWidth, int arcHeight);
fillRoundRect(int x, int y, int width, int height,
              int arcWidth, int arcHeight);
```

The `arcWidth` is the horizontal diameter of the arc at the four corners, and the `arcHeight` is the vertical diameter of the arc at the four corners.

So, you say you are not impressed. Well, Java includes another set of rectangle routines. If rounded rectangles are just not enough, maybe these three-dimensional rectangles will impress you. The 3-D rectangle routines differ in that they take an extra `boolean` parameter, which if set to true will cause the rectangle to take on the appearance of depth (therefore, you can also use them to draw regular rectangles, too). The other parameters passed to these methods are the `x` and `y` point along with the `width` and `height`. This is how the functions are declared:

```
draw3DRect(int x, int y, int width, int height, boolean raised);
fill3DRect(int x, int y, int width, int height, boolean raised);
```

Notice that for each set of rectangle drawing routines, one routine displays the rectangle without drawing inside it. The other routine fills the rectangle with a specified color. Listing 5-3 provides an example of working with color and rectangles (see Figure 5-2). The applet creates a color bar that displays a rainbow of different colors. Listing 5-4 is the Web page that accesses the Java applet.

Listing 5-3 Sample DisplayColor.java Source Code

```
/*
 *  DisplayColor.java - Display rectangles using multiple
 *                      colors.
 *
 *  Creating Cool Web Applets with Java
 *  By: Paul J. Perry,  Publisher: IDG Books
 *
 */

import java.applet.*;
import java.awt.*;

public class DisplayColor extends java.applet.Applet
{
   public void init()
   {
      resize(600,400);
   }

   public void paint(Graphics gr)
   {
      int sqWidth=25, sqHeight=25, Border=5;
      int r=0, g=0, b=0;
      Color clr;

      // Draw six rows of colors
      for (int y=1; y<=600; y=y+sqHeight)
      {
         // Draw each row of colors
         for(int x=1; x<=4; x++)
         {
            System.out.print("c: ");

            // Create and select a color.
            clr = new Color(r, g, b);
            g = r;
            r = r + 64;
            gr.setColor(clr);

            // Display the shape.
            gr.fillRect((Border*x)+(sqWidth*x),
                        y+Border, sqWidth, sqHeight);
         }
         b=b+64;
      }
   }
}
```

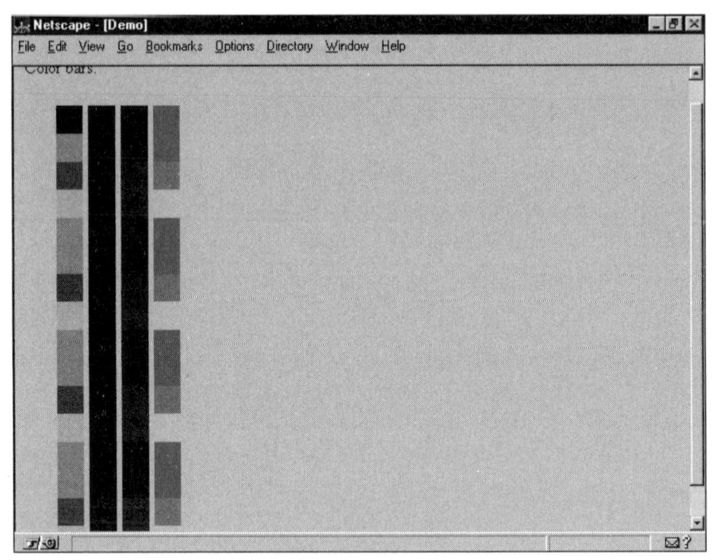

Figure 5-2: The sample color display applet.

Listing 5-4 **Sample DisplayColor.html File**

```
<HTML>
<!- DisplayColor.html ->
<HEAD>
   <TITLE>Demo</TITLE>
</HEAD>
<BODY>
Color bars:<P><P>
<APPLET CODE="DisplayColor.class" WIDTH="600" HEIGHT="400">
This Web page requires a <B>Java</B>-enabled Web Browser.
</APPLET>
</BODY>
</HTML>
```

Displaying shapes

Java provides support for drawing polygon figures. A *polygon* is a closed figure, usually with more than four sides. Although both squares and rectangles are technically polygons, we don't usually refer to them that way. The polygon drawing method in Java is called (appropriately enough) `drawPolygon()` and has the following prototype:

```
drawPolygon(int xPoints[], int yPoints[], int NumbPoints);
```

To use the routine, you must pass two arrays. The first array contains the x coordinates of the points in the polygon, and the second array contains the y coordinates of the points in the polygon. The last parameter, `NumbPoints`, tells the system how many points are in the array. If you wish to close the shape, remember to duplicate the starting point as the endpoint. However, despite the name, you don't have to close the shapes you draw with this method.

Just like the rectangle drawing routines contain counterpoint methods to fill in their interior, the same is true with the polygon drawing routine. The method takes the same parameters and is declared like this:

```
fillPolygon(int xPoints[], int yPoints[], int NumbPoints);
```

Both routines are easy to use. Here is an example of using the `drawPolygon()` method to display a triangle:

```
public void paint(Graphics g)
{
   int x[] = {5, 25, 5, 5};
   int y[] = {5, 5, 25, 5};
   g.drawPolygon(x, y, 4);
}
```

It draws a triangle within the area reserved for the applet. Because a triangle is a closed shape, notice how the routine uses identical points (5,5) for both the starting point and the endpoint.

The `Polygon` class

If you don't like working with integer arrays to declare your polygon values, guess what? Java has a predefined `Polygon` class designed just for you. To see why the `Polygon` class is so nice, first let me show you the `drawPolygon()` and `fillPolygon()` methods that have been overloaded to take a single parameter, an object of type `Polygon`. Here is the syntax:

```
drawPolygon(Polygon p);
fillPolygon(Polygon p);
```

To create a Polygon object, you must create a new instance of it, using the new operator. Once the object has been created, you can use the addPoint() method to add individual points to the array. Finally, you call the polygon drawing routine passing it the instance of the Polygon object you have created. Here is an example:

```
public void paint(Graphics g)
{
    Polygon p = new Polygon();
    p.addPoint(5,5);
    p.addPoint(25,5);
    p.addPoint(5,25);
    p.addPoint(5,5);

    g.drawPolygon(p);
}
```

Obviously, this method of drawing a polygon is easier to understand, but it also takes more time to type. Luckily, with Java you have the choice of which way to display the polygon.

As a bonus to using the Polygon class, a couple of methods help you in working with points. Beyond the addPoint() method, the inside() method takes an x and a y value that correspond to a point and returns a boolean value that specifies whether that point is inside the polygon. Finally, the getBoundingBox() method returns an object of type Rectangle that contains the bounding area of the polygon.

Displaying circular shapes

Polygons are great, but circles may be the most difficult shape to display for a computer — let alone for human beings. After all, creating a square is pretty easy by drawing a few straight lines. Try drawing a perfectly round circle. The reason circles are so hard to draw is because they contain no flat surfaces. Therefore, the system must do extra processing to figure out exactly how to plot the circle. Java provides a routine to draw the outline and fill in an oval shape (it doesn't have to be a perfect circle). The following methods are the ones provided by Java to display an oval:

```
drawOval(int x, int y, int width, int height);
fillOval(int x, int y, int width, int height);
```

You specify the coordinates of the bounding rectangular area. If the width is equal to the height, the figure will be drawn as a perfect circle. Again, we have our choice of just drawing the outside border (and not affecting the inside of the oval) and drawing a filled oval shape.

The last shape drawing methods available let us draw arcs. You can think of an arc as a piece of pie. The entire pie is the whole circle, and a piece of that pie is an arc. When calling these routines, you must specify the rectangular bounding region and the beginning and end angle. The prototypes are as follows:

```
drawArc(int x, int y, int width, int height,
        int StartAngle, int arcAngle);
fillArc(int x, int y, int width, int height,
        int StartAngle, int arcAngle);
```

Zero degrees is at the 3 o'clock position. Positive arc angles indicate counter-clockwise rotations, and negative arc angles are drawn clockwise. The `drawArc()` method draws the outline of the arc, whereas the `fillArc()` method displays a piece of pie, filled in with the current color.

Quick Overview

This chapter provided information on working with text, fonts, colors, and graphics primitives. With a good understanding of these topics, you are ready to move on in the steaming hot world of Java images and animation.

You learned about several different classes for working with graphics. The most important methods were discussed. However, by no means did the chapter cover every single method in every single graphics related class. This book is meant as a tutorial, not a reference. Because of that, it can't hurt to keep an eye on your Java documentation and take a look at the classes and related methods. In fact, that is your homework — gee, you thought you were almost done with this chapter. Anyway, you might find a method that fits the bill for what you need to do.

In particular, this chapter covered the following topics:

- You display textual information in Java with the `drawString()`, `drawChars()`, and `drawBytes()` methods.
- Six standard fonts are available in Java for displaying text. You select them with the `Font` object. You use the `FontMetric` object to return information like the `width` and `height` of the font.
- The `Color` object allows you to work with different colors in your Java applets.
- The `drawLine()` method draws a line between two points.
- The `drawRect()` method draws a rectangle, without filling it in. The `fillRect()` method draws a rectangle and fills it in with the current color.

- The `drawRoundRect()` method allow you to draw rectangles with rounded corners. The `draw3DRect()` method draws a rectangle that appears to contain depth.
- The `drawPolygon()` and `fillPolygon()` methods let you draw shapes with many sides.
- Circular shapes are drawn with the `drawOval()` and `fillOval()` methods.

Here is a brief overview of what is to come...

- Chapter 6, "Incorporating Images and Animation," describes how to use Java to bring fancy animation and images into your Web page.
- Chapter 7, "Working with Sound," gives you information about using audio sound in your Web pages.
- Chapter 8, "Adding Interactivity," provides valuable information on interacting with the user. This includes the movement of the mouse as well as keyboard input.

Incorporating Images and Animation

In This Chapter

How to display images inside a Java applet.

How to use animation in a Java applet.

How to use the built-in Java animation applets.

Although you already know how to imbed images into your HTML Web pages, the Java language also provides support for displaying graphics images. If you just want to display an image inside your Web page, you can do just fine with HTML. But, if you would like to build animation into a Web page or superimpose text and graphic objects over an image, you will want the functionality provided by Java. One of the main ways that Java-enabled Web pages come to life is through images and animation.

Drawing Images in Java

Unlike standard programming languages like C++ or Pascal, Java includes built-in functionality for several Internet graphics formats. Additionally, because they are implemented as classes, you don't have to know a single thing about complex file formats.

Image support is provided in the `Image` class, which inherits from the `awt` class. To use Java images in your applet, you will want to import the appropriate class. For example:

```
import java.awt.Image;
```

will allow you to create instances of the Image type in your program. It is as simple as this:

```
Image img;
```

Now, you have an instance of the Image class. You must load a graphics file from your Web site. The getImage() method will do just that. It works like this:

```
img = getImage(getDocumentBase(), "img.gif");
```

You must specify the URL to your Web site as the first parameter and the filename of the image as the second parameter. As you can see, you use the getDocumentBase() method to pass the URL from which the Web page is executing. Using the getDocumentBase() method to return the current URL is easier than using the hard code string.

The getImage() method will return immediately whether the image exists or not. The image file is not actually retrieved until an applet makes an attempt to display the image. This is meant as a way to optimize programs.

To display an image in your Web page, use the drawImage() method in the Graphic object. Here is how it works:

```
public void paint(Graphics g)
{
   g.drawImage(img, 0, 0, this);
}
```

The first parameter is the image object. The second and third parameters are the coordinates of the top-left corner of the image. The last parameter is that of an ImageObserver object. Most often, you can just pass the this pointer (as previously), but at specialized times you might want to pass an instance of an ImageObserver object. With it, your program will be notified when an image is loaded. This will also take care of loading the image into the system in chunks. You'll notice an obvious delay between when an applet requests an image over the Internet and when the image is ready for display on the screen. The ImageObserver class lets you build a notification system. For most cases, you won't need to use ImageObserver objects because standard functionality for loading the image in chunks is built into the system.

For added functionality, the drawImage() method is overloaded. Other variations of the method let you specify a background color that is displayed before the image is drawn (see Table 5-3 in Chapter 5). It looks like this:

```
public void paint(Graphics g)
{
   Color bgcolor = new Color(255, 0, 0);
   g.drawImage(img, 0, 0, bgcolor, this);
}
```

You can also use a version of the method to specify the width and height of the graphics image. The syntax looks like this:

```
public void paint(Graphics g)
{
   g.drawImage(img, 0, 0, ImageWidth, ImageHeight, this);
}
```

With this, you can control how much of the image should be displayed. You might want to display only a small portion of the entire image.

Java only works with a limited number of graphics file types. Table 6-1 provides an overview of the types that Java currently supports. If your image is in a different format, you will want to use a conversion tool to convert it to an appropriate format. The gif format is better for most images. However, the jpeg format is better for photographic-style images.

Table 6-1 **Java Image File Types**

Format	Description
gif	Graphics interchange format
jpeg	Joint pictures experts group

You might wonder why somebody would retrieve an image and display it with `getImage()` and `drawImage()` when he or she can do it directly in the HTML file with the `<IMG>` tag. The reason (besides learning how to program in Java) is that with a Java applet you can also display text and graphics on top of the image. You already saw in Chapter 5 how to display standard graphic shapes. Listing 6-1 provides sample code for displaying an image and drawing text on top of it (see Figure 6-1). Listing 6-2 provides the HTML file required by the Web browser. You will also need the img.gif graphics file in order for the program to work right.

Listing 6-1 ImageApplet.java Sample Source Code

```
/*
 *  ImageApplet.java - Displays Java Images
 *
 *  Creating Cool Web Applets with Java
 *  By: Paul J. Perry,  Publisher: IDG Books
 *
 */

import java.applet.*;
import java.awt.*;

public class ImageApplet extends java.applet.Applet
{
   // Class data member
   Image img = null;

   // Initialization method
   public void init()
   {
      img = getImage(getDocumentBase(), "img.gif");
   }

   // Display image
   public void paint(Graphics g)
   {
      g.drawImage(img, 0, 0, this);
      g.drawString("J a v a  C l o u d s", 10, 10);
   }
}
```

Listing 6-2 ImageApplet.html Sample Source Code

```
<HTML>
<!- ImageApplet.html ->
<HEAD>
   <TITLE>Demo</TITLE>
</HEAD>
<BODY>
Java Image:<P><P>
<APPLET CODE="ImageApplet.class" WIDTH="400" HEIGHT="400">
This Web page requires a <B>Java</B>-enabled Web Browser.
</APPLET>
</BODY>
</HTML>
```

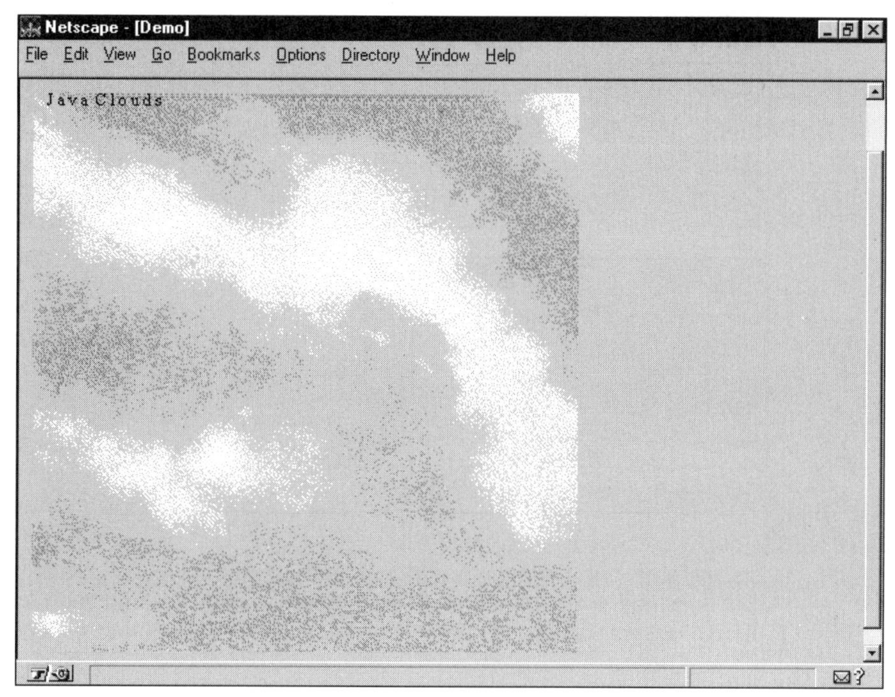

Figure 6-1: The ImageApplet sample code produces Java Clouds.

Still Frames Come to Life

Animation uses the passage of time as a means of creating motion and can be considered the process of converting static images into dynamic presentations. Animation is based on a technique known as *persistence of vision* (POV). This is the human eye's inability to notice two different pictures that are displayed in rapid succession. When you view a series of images in fast succession, the eye tends to perceive the changes in the picture as motion. Without POV, television, cartoons, and motion pictures (as well as animation within a Java applet) would be nonexistent.

Any type of animation that is created in a Java applet requires a series of images (see Figure 6-2). Each image is a single frame in a series of related events. The pace at which each image is displayed is referred to as the *frame rate*. Television in the United States uses a frame rate of approximately 30 frames per second (fps). However, a Java applet does not need to use this high rate, and in fact the eye becomes fooled at about 16 fps. Setting an appropriate frame rate is important because if the frame rate is too slow, the animation appears jumpy and crude. If the frame rate is too fast, the user will not see each individual frame.

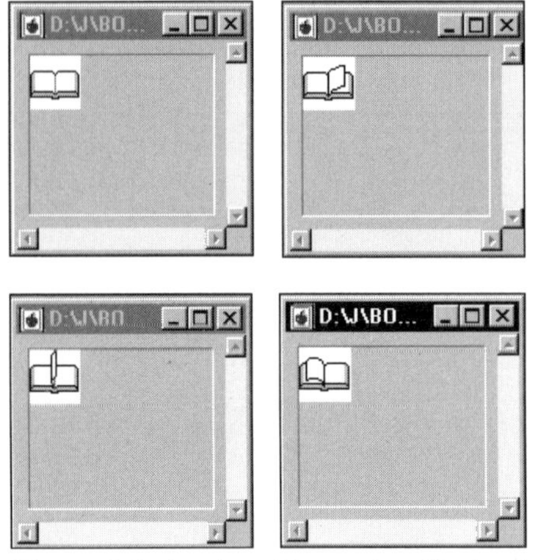

Figure 6-2: *A series of frames in a flipping book.*

So, there are two parts to creating an animation. First is the creation of content: that is, each frame of the animation. Once you have created each frame of an animation, you need code that will display each frame in succession.

How to animate pictures

Considering that each frame of an animation is just an image, the best way to store the frames is using an array of `Image` classes, as follows:

```
Image img[];
```

Notice that Java does not need the number of array elements specified within the declaration. The square brackets are enough for the system to know that you wish to create a number of objects. You specify each element when you load the images from the Web site. For example:

```
public void init()
{
   int MaxImgs = 5;

   // Load images
   for (int i=0; i<MaxImgs; i++)
      img[i] = getImage(getDocumentBase(), "book"+i+".gif");
}
```

will go through a loop to load each frame in the animation. This method assumes that a consistent naming convention has been used for storing the images. The example here uses a filename that begins with the phrase `"book"` followed by the image number and ending with the file extension `".gif"`. By modifying the code, you could use any naming convention you choose. The advantage of using a common root name (like `"book"`) is that you can easily load the entire image in a loop. If each frame of the animation had a different name, you would need a unique call to the `getImage()` method for each frame. This can really take a lot of time considering that animation consists of many frames.

You can implement animation in Java in several different ways. The key idea is that you need to paint a frame, wait for some amount of time, advance to the next frame, and repeat the process until each frame has been displayed. If you wish for the animation to continue on forever, you must keep track of when you have displayed the final frame and reset the count to the first frame in the series.

Probably the best method to use is creating a second thread. This second thread keeps track of the frame number and also provides a means to wait the specified amount of time before displaying the next image.

Multithreaded code

Threads can be a complex subject, but in this context I will make them easy. Every Java applet already contains a thread. The *thread* is the path of execution of the program. In many programs, only one thing is happening at any one time. However, with animation, the applet must wait a specified amount of time while the image is displayed. You don't want to hold up the entire applet for that amount of time. Therefore, by creating a second thread, you can create another path of execution.

In Java, you create another thread with a class. You create a thread by extending the `Thread` class and overriding the `run()` method, like so:

```
class MyThread extends Thread
{
   public void run()
   {
      // Body of thread execution
   }
}
```

If you had this class and wanted to use it in your applet, you would create an instance of it, just like any class:

```
MyThread mt = new MyThread();
```

When the thread is first instantiated, it will do nothing. You must go ahead and start it in the same way you must start your automobile or microwave oven. You do this with the `start()` method, as follows:

```
mt.start();
```

The `start()` method executes the thread's `run()` method. After the thread has begun, the method returns immediately, and the main thread of a program can continue execution. You can stop the thread with the `stop()` method, as follows:

```
mt.stop();
```

The `run()` method is where you repaint the frame of the animation. You cannot call the `paint()` method directly (remember all graphics must be carried out in the `paint()` method). You can, however, call the `repaint()` method, which causes the system to call the `paint()` method. Finally, to wait the specified amount of time, you can use the `sleep()` method of the `Thread` class, which takes a single parameter that is the number of milliseconds to delay. Your code will look something like this:

```
class MyThread extends Thread
{
   public void run()
   {
      repaint();
      sleep(500);
   }
}
```

So now you have some background information on threads and an idea about how to implement animation. Having gone over the material, you can actually do this an easier way. You don't even need to write a single line of Java code to display animation. Because of object-oriented programming, an applet will do all this (and more) for you. Let's check it out.

The Animator Applet

The good news is that the folks who developed the Java language figured that one of the hot uses for Java would be to create animation. As a result, they developed a standalone class in which you can embed in your Web page just for this purpose. The applet has been generalized and takes all its parameters from the HTML file.

You can find the Animator applet in the demo subdirectory of the Java development kit. Besides letting you specify each frame in an animation, the class will also play an audio sound at the same time. Other options allow you to specify if the animation should repeat and if the user can stop the animation by clicking on it. The following is a description of the parameters you may use:

- `IMAGESOURCE` — contains the URL of the directory containing the frames or images of the animation. The naming convention is simply `T1.GIF`, `T2.GIF`,...`T`*x*`.GIF`, where *x* is the last frame of the animation.
- `STARTUP` — contains the URL of an image that is displayed while loading the frames of the animation. Using this parameter allows the user to view something while the individual animation frames are being loaded.
- `BACKGROUND` — the URL of an image, which is displayed in the background of the animation.
- `STARTIMAGE` — the index of the first frame in the animation. Although this will usually be 1, you can tell the applet to start animation at a different frame.
- `ENDIMAGE` — provides the numerical number for the index of the last frame in the animation.
- `PAUSE` — the time (in milliseconds) to pause between each frame. You'll use this for every frame in the animation. If you wish to use a variable length of time between each frame, use the `PAUSES` parameter, described next.
- `PAUSES` — a list of pauses in milliseconds. This allows you to specify a different pause for each frame in the animation. Each number is separated by the | character. For example: `100|50|300...`
- `REPEAT` — set to either `TRUE` or `FALSE`, this parameter indicates if the animation should repeat. The default value is `TRUE`.
- `POSITIONS` — lets you to specify the coordinates to display each frame. This lets you move the animation around a Web page. Each pair of coordinates is separated by the | character.

- IMAGES — provides the indexes of each image in the animation sequence. This allows you to repeat frames of the animation. Each number is separated by a | character. For example: 1|2|3|4|2|1 will cause the first four frames to be displayed, followed by the second frame and the first frame.
- SOUNDSOURCE — the URL of a directory containing an audio file. This is only the directory. The next parameter provides the actual filename.
- SOUNDTRACK — the URL of an audio clip that is played repeatedly in the background.
- SOUNDS — a list of URLs for audio clips that are played for each individual frame. As usual, the list is separated by the | character.

You can see that the Animator applet is rather robust and provides much functionality. Listing 6-3 provides an example of using the Animator class in your own HTML Web page (see Figure 6-3):

Listing 6-3 AnimateDemo.html Web Page

```
<HTML>
<!- AnimateDemo.html ->
<HEAD>
   <TITLE>Animation Demo</TITLE>
</HEAD>
<BODY>
Animate Me:<P><P>
<APPLET CODE=Animator.class WIDTH=200 HEIGHT=200>
<PARAM NAME=imagesource VALUE="images/SimpleAnimation">
<PARAM NAME=endimage VALUE=2>
<PARAM NAME=soundsource VALUE="audio">
<PARAM NAME=soundtrack VALUE=spacemusic.au>
<PARAM NAME=sounds
       VALUE="1.au|2.au|3.au|4.au|5.au|6.au|7.au|8.au|9.au|0.au">
<PARAM NAME=pause VALUE=200>
This Web page requires a <B>Java</B>-enabled Web Browser.
</APPLET>
</BODY>
</HTML>
```

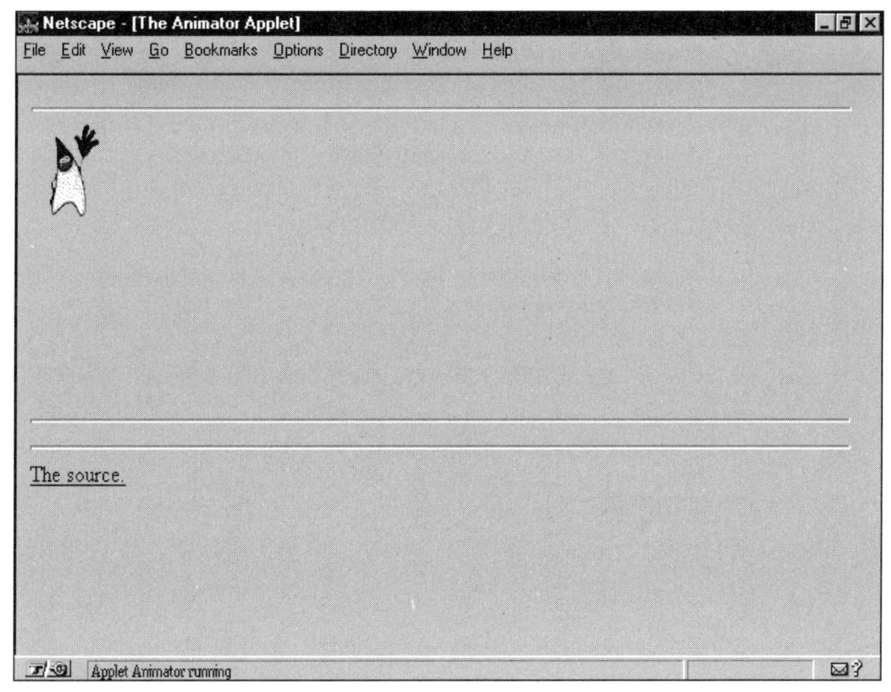

Figure 6-3: *Use of the Animator applet.*

Quick Overview

This chapter showed you how to display graphics within a Java applet and provided information on creating motion in your Web pages through the use of animation. Although text is an important part of any information system, part of what has made the Web so popular is its use of multimedia. By adding graphics and animation as described in this chapter, you are well on your way to creating cool Web applets.

In particular, this chapter covered the following topics:

- You worked with graphical images using the `Image` class, you loaded an image file with the `getImage()` method, and you displayed an image with the `drawImage()` method.
- Java applets can display two types of graphic images, graphic interchange format (gif) and joint pictures experts group (jpeg).

- Animation is created by the human eye's inability to notice the difference between frames of pictures displayed in succession. By displaying similar images in a sequence, a Java applet can create dynamic Web pages.
- The Animator applet provides a fast and easy way to display animation within your Web page without having to write any custom code.

Here is a brief overview of what is to come...

- Chapter 7, "Working with Sound," gives you information about using audio sound in your Web pages.
- Chapter 8, "Adding Interactivity," provides valuable information on interacting with the user. This includes the movement of the mouse as well as keyboard input.
- Chapter 9, "Enhancing Web Pages with Java," shows you how to create the coolest Web pages around by using all the features of Java to extend your Web page.

Working with Sound

In This Chapter

- How to play sound files from your Java applets.
- How to control when audio sound is played.
- How to use the audio file format in Java applets.

This chapter covers the integration of sound in your Java applets. You will learn how to add the playback of audio files to your Java applets and control how the sound is played. You will also find out about audio file formats and learn just how audio sound works.

What Is Sound?

An audio file stores the data needed to reconstruct a given sound. Each sound is recorded digitally in the form of numbers. Computer sound like that used in Java is sometimes referred to as *pulse code modulation* (PCM), after the technique used to convert sound into computer format (which is the same method used to store data on commercial compact discs). The process of recording digital sounds and storing them in a computer is called *sampling*. You can think of the process of sampling as breaking sound into small pieces of information and then representing each small piece as a number. For example, a second's worth of sound breaks down into thousands of individual units. The computer assigns a number to each unit, and that number is stored in the computer. To play back the sound, the computer must recreate the original one second of audio by combining each small unit back into one.

A computer must have the proper hardware and software to play sound files. Well-known manufacturers include Creative Labs (the Sound Blaster series of cards) and Turtle Beach. All sound cards come with appropriate software drivers needed to make them work in Windows. Luckily, most well-known computer manufacturers have started pre-installing sound cards on their new computers. This saves you a lot of the headache once associated with installing a sound card.

Although sound on the Web is available in several different formats, Java currently only supports one of these: the .AU file format. This is the standard format used by Sun workstations running the UNIX operating system, from which Java was originally developed. Unfortunately for Windows users, it is not a common format. The solution is to use a sound conversion utility that will convert the file from a standard Windows .WAV file into an .AU file. One example is a commercial product called Sound Forge (see Figure 7-1). This great tool will convert between most digital audio formats available, including .AU and .WAV. Sound Forge is available from Sonic Foundry, Inc.; 100 South Baldwin, Suite 204; Madison, WI 53703; (608) 256-3133.

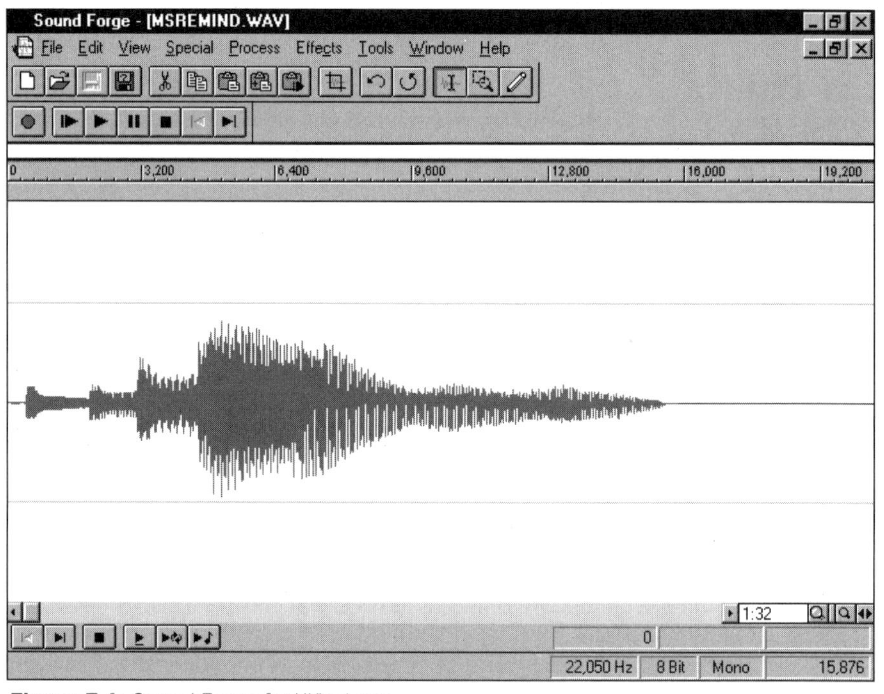

Figure 7-1: Sound Forge for Windows.

Working with Sound Objects

The audio support found in Java provides more control over the playback of sound than that provided by a standard HTML file. Remember that in HTML audio data is treated as a hyperlink. The user must click on highlighted text, which triggers the transfer of the audio information over the Internet, to the Web browser, and then to a helper application for playback to the user's enjoyment.

Although the audio data is still transferred over the Internet, using Java on your Web page can control when the sound is played back and even loop the sound so that it plays back repeatedly.

Hopefully, you have a good understanding of how the `Image` object works from Chapter 6 because you play back audio in a similar manner. First, to play any sound, you must import the `AudioClip` class at the beginning of your applet, as follows:

```
import java.applet.AudioClip;
```

All sound information is stored in an `AudioClip` object, which you declare as follows:

```
AudioClip audio;
```

This creates an instance of `AudioClip` called `audio`. Although each instance of the `AudioClip` object can stand on its own, you must first obtain the data that composes the audio sound (which is of course, transferred over the Internet). You do this with the `getAudioClip()` method of the applet class. This method has several different forms, but the most useful is probably:

```
AudioClip getAudioClip(URL url, String name);
```

This method takes two parameters: the URL address of the Web site containing the audio file to be downloaded and the file that contains the actual audio information. You can use our old friend, the `getDocumentBase()` method, to return the URL from which the current Web page is executing. A sample call might look something like this:

```
audio = getAudioClip(getDocumentBase(), "filename.au");
```

This would obtain the file named "filename.au" from the current Web site. Remember that the audio file must be in the .AU format. Java does not recognize other formats and will not be able to play them.

I mentioned other versions of the `getAudioClip()` method. If you have the filename of the string combined into a URL address of the site (of object type `URL`), you can use this overloaded version of the method:

```
AudioClip getAudioClip(URL url);
```

Either way, the end result transfers the audio information over the Internet. With the audio data loaded, you can begin to play the sound file. Three methods in the `AudioClip` object allow you to do this. The `play()` method does what it says. It takes no parameters and is very simple to use. Here is an example:

```
audio.play();
```

This starts playing the audio file. Each time this method is called, the playback of the audio clip restarts from the beginning. If playback is not interrupted, the audio data will play once. If you have an audio file that you would like to play repeatedly, you can use the `loop()` method to playback the audio clip. It looks like this:

```
audio.loop();
```

As long as the data was transferred correctly, the audio will play forever. Which of course brings us to the last thing you might want to do with audio data, which is stop it. You do this with the `stop()` method, as follows:

```
audio.stop();
```

Now that I have shown you all this, I want to present you with two other methods in the Applet class that allow you to work with audio information. The methods do the same thing: play an audio file. However, instead of returning an `AudioClip` object, these methods work on the audio files directly. They provide a little less control over playback of the audio, but they also require a little less work. The first one is the `play()` method, as follows:

```
void play(URL url);
```

This plays an audio clip directly, given a complete URL address (specified as an object of type URL). The other method is as follows:

```
void play(URL url, String name);
```

This takes a URL address (feel free to use the `getDocumentBase()` method) along with a string that contains the filename of the audio file. As soon as the audio information has been transferred, the applet will immediately begin playing the file.

Controlling audio playback

Remember how all Java applets have several methods that, if declared, will be called at times while the user is moving through the Web pages? As a review, the `init()` method is called when the Java applet is first loaded into memory. The `start()` method is called when the user begins to view a Web page that includes the applet. The `stop()` method is called when the user navigates to a different page. Finally, the `destroy()` method is called when the applet is removed from memory.

By using these methods in conjunction with those in the `AudioClip` object, you can provide complete control over the playback of audio information on your Web page. You might begin by playing an audio clip repeatedly, as with background music on some television commercials. You might then decide to start and stop the playback of the audio as the user moves through your group of Web pages.

Furthermore, (a peek to what is coming) in Chapter 8 when we discuss the keyboard and mouse, you will find ways to allow even more control over playing audio information.

Playing Sound

Listing 7-1 provides an example of playing audio files from a Java applet. Listing 7-2 is the Web page document that uses the PlaySound applet. Figure 7-2 shows what the Web page looks like when displayed in Netscape.

Listing 7-1 PlaySound.java Source Code

```
/*
 *  PlaySound.java - Sample applet to play audio
 *
 *  Creating Cool Web Applets with Java
 *  By: Paul J. Perry,  Publisher: IDG Books
 *
 */

import java.applet.*;
import java.awt.Graphics;
import java.applet.AudioClip;

public class PlaySound extends java.applet.Applet
{
   // Audio object
   AudioClip audio;
```

(continued)

Listing 7-1 *(continued)*

```
    public void init()
    {
        audio = getAudioClip(getDocumentBase(), "gong.au");
    }

    public void start()
    {
      audio.loop();
    }

    public void stop()
    {
        audio.stop();
    }

    public void destroy()
    {
        audio.stop();
    }

    public void paint(Graphics g)
    {
      g.drawString("Playing the GONG sound...", 10, 10);
    }
}
```

Listing 7-2 PlaySound.html Web Page

```
<HTML>
<!- PlaySound.html ->
<HEAD>
   <TITLE>Play Some Sounds</TITLE>
</HEAD>
<BODY>
<P>
<APPLET CODE="PlaySound.class" WIDTH="400" HEIGHT="400">
This Web page requires a <B>Java</B>-enabled Web Browser.
</APPLET>
</BODY>
</HTML>
```

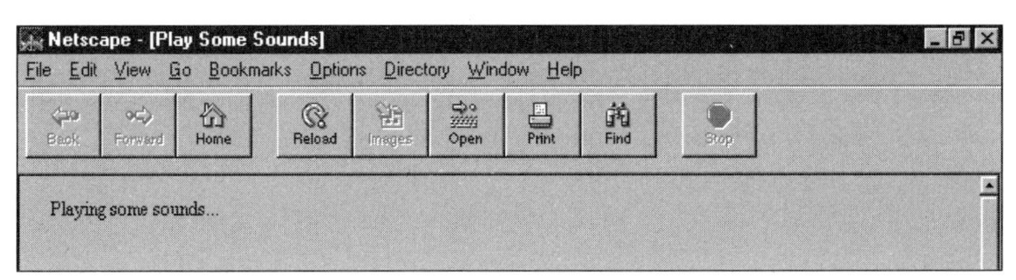

Figure 7-2: The PlaySound example.

After our discussion of the audio object, program operation should be more of a review than a new topic. The applet starts by creating an instance of the `AudioClip` object. When the `init()` method is called on applet startup, transfer of the audio file named gong.au begins with the `getAudioClip()` method. Later, in the `start()` method, playback of the audio clip begins. If the user leaves the Web page, the `stop()` method is called, which suspends audio playback. When the applet is removed from memory, the applet halts playback of the audio file with a call to the same method.

Playing Random Sounds

Besides allowing you to control when sounds are played from your Web page, Java applets can also help you control exactly what sounds will play. Because Java is a programming language, you can add a certain amount of variety to your Web page by playing a random sound. Maybe beforehand you can choose five or six different sound files that you would like your users to hear. You don't care which one. You can write a Java applet to choose at random which of these sounds to play each time a new user views your Web page. Regular Web pages based on HTML don't allow you to do this type of thing.

Here is one way to implement this. You create an array of string objects where each element contains the filename for the audio file. You then use the random number generation class of Java to return a number. You make sure it is within the bounds of the number of audio files you have available. You then fetch the audio file and play it back for the user.

You have already seen how to retrieve and play sounds. What you need to discover is generating random numbers in Java. Unfortunately, the numbers are not as random as we would like. In fact, the science of creating a truly random number in a computer program is extremely difficult.

Instead, what most programming languages (including Java) return is a *pseudo-random number*. A pseudo-random number is one that must first be reset (or seeded) with a number. If you seed the random number generator with the same number, you will see the same results every time. However, by using a unique seed number (such as the system date), you can obtain a fairly random number or what appears to be a random number. Here is the code we use for generating a random number object in Java:

```
Random r;
r = new Random();
```

You can see we first create an object of type `Random` and then create an instance of it using the `new()` operator. This requires that we import the `java.util.Random` class, as follows:

```
import java.util.Random;
```

The next thing we do is to set the seed value. However, we want to use the system date for this, so we must also create an object of type `Date`, as follows:

```
Date d = new Date();
```

We can then use this date value to return the current seconds of the time and send that to the `setSeed()` method of the `Random` class, as follows:

```
r.setSeed(d.getSeconds());
```

Finally, we are ready to return the random number. We do this with the `nestInt()` method, as follows:

```
index = r.nextInt();
```

Methods are also available for obtaining other types of numbers. The name of the method lets you know that you are not obtaining a truly random number. However, because we are not conducting the state lottery here, this should be good enough for our purposes.

Listing 7-3 contains the source code for the RandomSound applet (see Figure 7-3). Listing 7-4 contains the RandomSound.html Web document source, which plays one of five audio files: 0.AU, 1.AU, 2.AU, 3.AU, 4.AU, or 5.AU. It also displays the filename of the audio file being played. As the user moves back and forth between Web pages, a different audio file will play.

Listing 7-3 RandomSound.java Source Code

```
/*
 *  RandomSound.java - Sample applet to play audio
 *
 *  Creating Cool Web Applets with Java
 *  By: Paul J. Perry,  Publisher: IDG Books
 *
 */

import java.applet.*;
import java.awt.Graphics;
import java.applet.AudioClip;
import java.util.Random;
import java.util.Date;

public class RandomSound extends java.applet.Applet
{
   // ====== Data objects =================
   AudioClip audio;
   int index = 0;
   Random r;
   // String array containing filenames of audio files
   String fNames[] = { "0.AU", "1.AU", "2.AU", "3.AU", "4.AU" };
   // Integer specifying how many strings are in above array
   int NumNames = 5;

   // ======= Methods =====================

   // absolute value of a number
   int abs(int a)
   {
      return (a < 0) ? -a : a;
   }

   // Create the random number object and seed it
   public void init()
   {
       r = new Random();
       Date d = new Date();
       r.setSeed(d.getSeconds());
   }

   // Each time user enters Web page, get new random number, and
   //  begin playing new sound.
   public void start()
```

(continued)

Listing 7-3 *(continued)*

```
    {
       // Get a random number.  We need one which is within
       //  array bounds.
      index = r.nextInt();

       // Make the number positive
       index = abs(index);

       // Make sure the number is within array bounds
       while (index>=NumNames)
       {
          index = index/2;
       }

       // Load new file each time Web page gets displayed
       audio = getAudioClip(getDocumentBase(), fNames[index]);

       // Play audio in a loop
      audio.loop();
    }

    public void stop()
    {
       audio.stop();
    }

    public void destroy()
    {
       audio.stop();
    }

    public void paint(Graphics g)
    {
      g.drawString("Playing sound: "+fNames[index], 10, 10);
    }
}
```

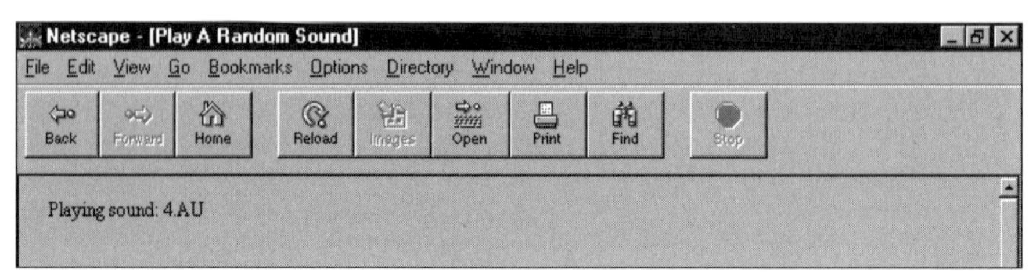

Figure 7-3: The RandomSound demonstration Web page.

Listing 7-4 RandomSound.html Web Page

```
<HTML>
<!- RandomSound.html ->
<HEAD>
   <TITLE>Play A Random Sound</TITLE>
</HEAD>
<BODY>
<P>
<APPLET CODE="RandomSound.class" WIDTH="400" HEIGHT="400">
This Web page requires a <B>Java</B>-enabled Web Browser.
</APPLET>
</BODY>
</HTML>
```

Quick Overview

Well, from the length of this Chapter, you have seen that adding audio support to your Java applet is pretty easy. By using the methods available for controlling program execution and audio file playback, you can provide complete control over the playback of audio data.

In particular, this chapter covered the following topics:

- What is required to playback audio on a Windows computer.
- How to use the AudioClip object for storing information about an audio file and then playing it back.
- How to control the playback of audio information using the `init()`, `start()`, `stop()`, and `destroy()` methods available in the Applet class.

Here is a brief overview of what is to come...

- Chapter 8, "Adding Interactivity," provides valuable information on interacting with the user. This includes the movement of mouse and keyboard input.
- Chapter 9, "Enhancing Web Pages with Java," shows you how to create the coolest Web pages around by using some of the already created Java applets in your Web pages.
- Chapter 10, "Network Communications," shows you how to transfer data over the Internet using your Java applet.
- Chapter 11, "User Interface Controls," shows you how to work with Java user interface objects and find out how to use all those fancy controls, like buttons and list boxes that are associated with modern operating systems, such as the Macintosh, X-Windows (UNIX), and (of course) Microsoft Windows.

Adding Interactivity

In This Chapter

What interactivity is and how to add it to your Java applets.

How to respond to the mouse in your Java applets.

What is necessary to acquire keyboard input from your Java applets.

On most computers, the user primarily uses the keyboard and the mouse as the methods of input. Java has built-in functionality for obtaining access to these system devices. In this chapter, you'll gain a fundamental understanding for acquiring user input from both the keyboard and mouse.

What Is Interactivity?

Although Web pages provide limited interactivity through the use of hyperlinks, using a Java applet inside your Web page provides a key advantage by responding to system input devices in an intelligent manner. A Java applet can take factors into consideration related to what the user is doing and provide more than just a jump to a new Web page. Being able to decide what action to take based on keyboard or mouse input will provide depth and provide a more interesting journey for users of your Web site. The two main methods of interactivity provided by Java include the keyboard and the mouse.

With *interactive multimedia*, your Web site can offer all the incredible advantages of text, audio, graphic images, and video and then tie them all together with Java. You have the advantages of electronic publishing, and at the same time, you reap the rewards of responding to each individual user. For example, if you were to put a training program on your Web site, you could actually provide a quiz that would tailor the tutorial to the user depending on his or her skill level.

Real-time interactivity refers to the fast-action response that a video game usually provides. For example, if you are driving a Formula 1 car around a virtual race track, the program should update the display to make you feel like you're actually sitting in the driver's seat. Dedicated game machines, such as the Sony PlayStation or Sega Saturn, provide this type of fast-paced action. Because of the slow connection to the Internet, however, the Web does not yet provide this type of experience, but this functionality is already built into Java. Once the speed issue is resolved, we might see this type of adventure on the Internet itself.

In the meantime, you have plenty to learn in how to trap mouse movements. So let's take a look at how to do this.

Actually, the Abstract Window Toolkit (AWT) set of classes (and not Java itself) implements and manages the keyboard and mouse input that we discuss in this chapter.

Keyboard Input

Most serious computer users could not make it through the day without using the keyboard. If you are a touch typist, you probably prefer to use the keyboard as your primary input device over any other method. Java defines keyboard input as being a type of event. To receive input from the user, your applet must gain focus. Not only can you have multiple applications running on your computer at once, but you can also have multiple applets running in a Web page at once. You only have one keyboard, and the events (key presses and key releases) that occur must be directed towards a specific applet. With Netscape, you must click on the Applet to give it focus. Once the Java applet has focus, it will receive information about keyboard input.

Keyboard events

The Advanced Window Toolkit Event provides keyboard event support. You must import the appropriate package at the beginning of your code, as follows:

```
import java.awt.Event;
```

You provide access to keyboard events through the `KeyDown()` method. The simplest version looks like this:

```
public void keyDown(int key)
{
   // Keyboard processing done here

   return;
}
```

The integer value passed to the KeyDown() method contains a special code (that appears to be an ASCII code) relating to the key that the user has pressed. A related method is KeyUp(), which is called when the key has been released. It looks like this:

```
public void keyUp(int key)
{
   // Key has been released

   return;
}
```

Through the keyDown() and KeyUp() methods, you can decide when to process the event. However, most keyboards provide for more advanced input than the press or release of a single key. We will look at these next.

Modifier keys

Keyboards also employ another type of a key, called a *modifier key*. Computers have been working with uppercase and lowercase characters for many years. To type information in mixed case, computer users must use the Shift key. The Shift key, in itself, does nothing. However, when used in combination with an alphabetical key, it decides if the character typed is uppercase or lowercase. If the key is a numeric key, the Shift keyboard modifier decides if the key should display a number or another special character. Other examples of modifier keys include Ctrl and Alt.

In order for your Java applet to detect modifier keys, we must use a more advanced version of the keyboard access method. These methods provide the extra information you need to know about system events and have the following syntax:

```
public boolean keyDown(Event evt, int key)
{
   // Keyboard processing done here

   return true;
}
```

and

```
public boolean keyUp(Event evt, int key)
    {
      // Keyboard processing

      return true;
    }
```

Both of these methods return a boolean value. Most often you will return `true`, but if you return `false`, the keyboard character that was entered will be ignored. The other difference with this pair of functions is that an object of type `Event` is passed into the method. By calling methods associated with the `Event` class, you can test for keyboard modifier keys. For example:

```
if ( evt.controlDown() )
{
   // Ctrl key is pressed
}
if ( evt.shiftDown() )
{
   // Shift key is pressed
}
if ( evt.metaDown() )
{
   // Meta key is pressed
}
```

The first functions are self-explanatory. The third, which deals with a *Meta key*, is a special type defined within the Java event class. The Meta key is prevalent on UNIX-based computers. Windows machines usually use the Alt key instead.

Special keys

The `Event` class also provides a set of constants that refer to several standard computer keyboard keys, such as cursor movement and function keys. If your interface uses these keys, you can provide more readable code by testing for the named constants rather than testing for esoteric keyboard codes. Table 8-1 provides an overview of the standard keyboard keys defined in the `Event` class.

A sample program shows how to work with keyboard input and events. Listing 8-1 is the source code for KeyboardYacker.java. Listing 8-2 contains the source code for the KeyboardYacker.html Web page. The code displays the keyboard character, along with the ASCII code for the character. It will also notify you if a keyboard modifier key has been pressed.

Table 8-1 Special Keys

Constant Name	Description
Event.UP	Up arrow
Event.DOWN	Down arrow
Event.LEFT	Left arrow
Event.RIGHT	Right arrow
Event.PGUP	Page up
Event.PGDN	Page down
Event.HOME	Home key
Event.END	End key
Event.F1 - Event.F12	Function keys F1 through F12

Listing 8-1 KeyboardYacker.java Source Code

```
/*
 *  KeyboardYacker.java - Get keyboard input
 *
 *  Creating Cool Web Applets with Java
 *  By: Paul J. Perry,  Publisher: IDG Books
 *
 */

import java.applet.*;
import java.awt.Graphics;
import java.awt.Event;

public class KeyboardYacker extends java.applet.Applet
{
   // Data members
   String lastKey;
   String lastModifier;

   // Initialization
   public void init()
   {
      lastKey = "";
       lastModifier = "";
}
```

(continued)

Listing 8-1 ***(continued)***

```
public boolean keyDown(Event evt, int key)
{
    // Check for special keys
    switch (key)
    {
       case Event.DOWN :
           lastKey = "Down Arrow";
           break;

        case Event.UP :
           lastKey = "Up Arrow";
            break;
        case Event.LEFT :
            lastKey = "Left Arrow";
            break;

        case Event.RIGHT :
           lastKey = "Right Arrow";
            break;

        case Event.PGUP :
           lastKey = "Page Up";
            break;

        case Event.PGDN :
           lastKey = "Page Down";
            break;

        case Event.HOME :
           lastKey = "Home";
            break;

        case Event.END :
           lastKey = "End";
            break;

        default :
            char c;
            c = (char)key;
           lastKey = "Code: " + Integer.toString(key);
            lastKey = lastKey + ",  Key = " + c;
     }
```

```
        // Check for modifier keys
        if (evt.controlDown())
           lastModifier = "Ctrl Key";
       if (evt.shiftDown())
           lastModifier = "Shift key";
        if (evt.metaDown())
           lastModifier = "Meta key";

       // Display the information
       repaint();
       return true;
    }

    public boolean keyUp(Event evt, int key)
    {
        lastKey = " ";
        lastModifier = " ";

       repaint();
       return true;
    }

    public void paint(Graphics g)
    {
       g.drawString("Current key pressed: "+lastKey, 10, 10);
        g.drawString("Modifier key: "+lastModifier, 10, 25);
    }
}
```

Listing 8-2 KeyboardYacker.html Web Page

```
<HTML>
<!- KeyboardYacker.html ->
<HEAD>
   <TITLE>Keyboard Input demo</TITLE>
</HEAD>
<BODY>
Keyboard status:<P><P>
<APPLET CODE="KeyboardYacker.class" WIDTH="400" HEIGHT="400">
This Web page requires a <B>Java</B>-enabled Web Browser.
</APPLET>
</BODY>
</HTML>
```

Remember that when you run the program, you must first click the applet so that it can receive keyboard event information. One of the interesting things you will notice (see Figure 8-1) as you use the program is that all the keys on a PC keyboard don't necessarily map to the Java keyboard set. Also, some of the special keys (such as up arrow and down arrow) are actually converted from old WordStar keyboard commands (for example, Ctrl+D is the down arrow).

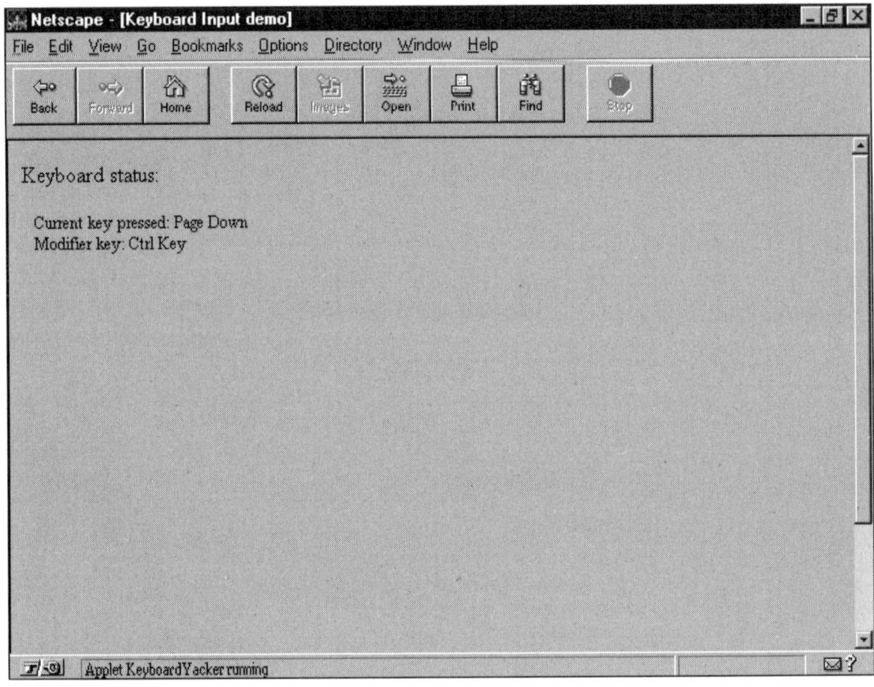

Figure 8-1: The KeyboardYacker applet.

Checking Mouse Buttons

The mouse input device first gained popularity with the Apple Macintosh computer in the mid-1980s. However, the mouse really didn't take long to catch on and become a standard on almost any personal computer: just about all computers sold today come with one of these devices. Just as Java's Abstract Windowing Toolkit provides support for the keyboard, it also provides support for the mouse in the form of methods that are called in response to mouse activity.

Because mouse events are part of the same `Event` class that the keyboard uses, you must remember to import the appropriate class file, as follows:

```
import java.awt.Event;
```

Java programs can detect the press or release of a mouse button. Mouse click events occur when your user clicks the mouse somewhere in the body of the applet. You can trap the mouse buttons to do very simple things, such as toggling sound on and off, or moving to the next image in a set of images. This results in more control over the applet by the user.

In the PC world, you'll usually see two kinds of mice. The first, such as those from Microsoft, has two buttons. The other, like the ones from Logitech, has three buttons. However, don't worry about a thing. You don't need to think about mouse buttons. Java does not differentiate which mouse button the user presses, no matter how many mouse buttons the mouse may have. Your applet will only know that a mouse button has been pressed.

In order for Java to read a mouse click, you must add the `mouseDown()` event to your applet. It looks like this:

```
public boolean mouseDown(Event evt, int x, int y)
{
   // Mouse down processing goes here

   return true;
}
```

The method receives three parameters. The first is an instance of object type `Event`. Any system event that occurs will receive an object of this type. You saw how we used the `Event` object with keyboard input. With the `mouseDown()` method, you don't need to query the `Event` object for any additional information. The two integer values passed to the method are the x- and y-coordinates of where the mouse button was pressed. The method returns a boolean value that indicates if the event is handled. For most cases, you will want to return a `true` value.

The companion method to `mouseDown()` is `mouseUp()`, which takes and returns the same parameters.

```
public boolean mouseUp(Event evt, int x, int y)
{
   // Mouse up processing goes here

   return true;
}
```

The only difference between the two functions is when they are called. Listing 8-3, MouseDroppings.java, is a sample program that shows you how to work with mouse button events. Listing 8-4 contains the MouseDroppings.html file, which you should use for your Web page.

The program (see Figure 8-2) displays a filled circle at the point where the mouse button is pressed. It then draws that circle twice as large when the mouse button is released. The code also makes use of the Java `Point` class. This is a handy data object that you can use to store the x- and y-coordinates of a point. Although the program does not make use of them, several methods in the `Point` class compare and modify points (these could come handy in your future programming projects). Studying the program listing should give you an idea for how to use mouse button events in your program.

Listing 8-3 MouseDroppings.java

```
/*
 *  MouseDroppings.java - Get mouse key up/down information
 *
 *  Creating Cool Web Applets with Java
 *  By: Paul J. Perry,  Publisher: IDG Books
 *
 */

import java.applet.*;
import java.awt.Graphics;
import java.awt.Event;
import java.awt.Point;

public class MouseDroppings extends java.applet.Applet
{
   // Data members
   Point p;
   int width;
   int height;

   public boolean mouseDown(Event evt, int x, int y)
   {
      p = new Point(x, y);

      // Draw smaller circles when user presses mouse button
      width = 5;
      height = 5;

      repaint();
```

```
        return true;
    }

    public boolean mouseUp(Event evt, int x, int y)
    {
        // Draw larger circles when user lets up on mouse button
        width = 10;
        height = 10;

        repaint();
        return true;
    }

    public void paint(Graphics g)
    {
        // Simple instructions for user
        g.drawString("Click Mouse Button", 10, 10);

        // Draw the circle, at point P with specified width &
height
        g.fillOval(p.x, p.y, width, height);
    }
}
```

Listing 8-4 MouseDroppings.html Web Page

```
<HTML>
<!- MouseDroppings.html ->
<HEAD>
   <TITLE>Mouse keypress demo</TITLE>
</HEAD>
<BODY>
Mouse button press<P><P>
<APPLET CODE="MouseDroppings.class" WIDTH="400" HEIGHT="400">
This Web page requires a <B>Java</B>-enabled Web Browser.
</APPLET>
</BODY>
</HTML>
```

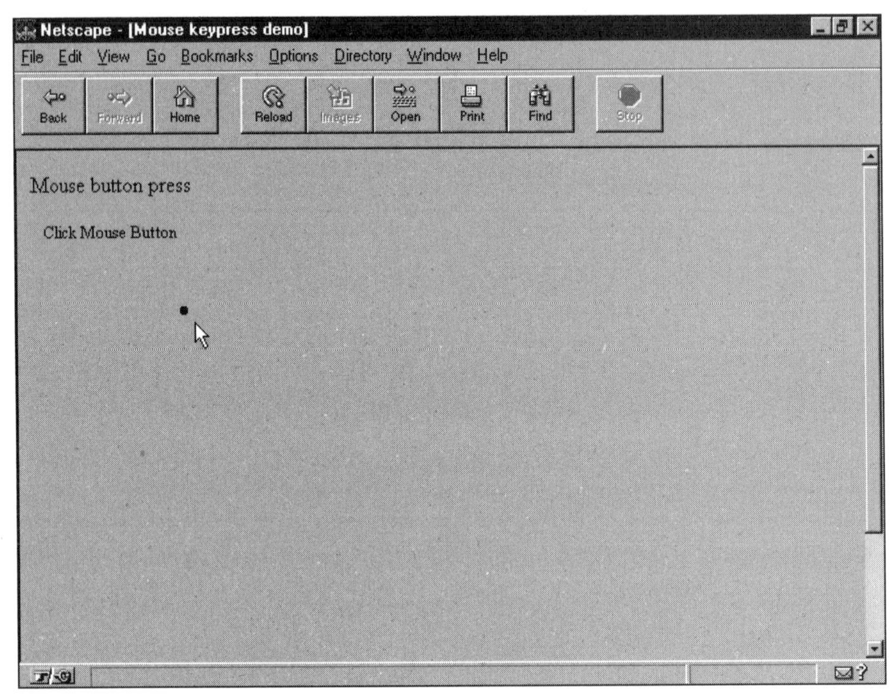

Figure 8-2: The MouseDroppings sample applet.

Mouse movement events

Besides pressing mouse buttons to make use of the mouse, you must be able to detect mouse movement. You can easily add functionality to Java programs for detecting mouse movement. As you probably suspect, this is just a matter of adding an appropriate method to the applet class.

The very basic system of trapping these mouse movement events occurs through the `mouseMove()` method, as follows:

```
public boolean mouseMove(Event evt, int x, int y)
{
   // Mouse has been moved

   return true;
}
```

Every time the user moves the mouse over a single pixel in any direction, a mouse move is generated, and the method described previously is called. The first parameter is of object type `Event`. The other two parameters are integer values that are the current x- and y-coordinates — in other words, where the mouse movement was detected.

Interestingly enough, the Java system includes two methods in which an applet can detect that the user moves the mouse over the area that makes up the applet. They are the `mouseEnter()` and `mouseExit()` methods, as follows:

```
public boolean mouseEnter(Event evt, int x, int y)
{
   // Mouse has entered applet window area

   return true;
}
```

and

```
public boolean mouseExit(Event evt, int x, int y)
{
   // Mouse has left the bounds of the applet

   return true;
}
```

Both of these functions pass the standard parameters you are now used to seeing: the `Event` object along with the coordinates where the mouse entered or exited the applet region. Both methods also return a boolean value that determines if the mouse event has been handled. In almost all cases, you will want to return a `true` value. If you return a `false` value, the event is passed up in the hierarchy of the window manager and dealt with in an appropriate manner (usually no action is taken).

Mouse dragging

If the user presses the mouse button and moves the mouse at the same time, Java refers to it as a *mouse drag*. If you wish to respond to mouse drags in a Java applet, you will want to add the `mouseDrag()` method to your applet, as follows:

```
public boolean mouseDrag(Event evt, int x, int y)
{
   return true;
}
```

This method has the same parameters as several of the previous mouse-related methods that we have already discussed. The `mouseDrag()` method simplifies mouse event processing because without this method, an applet would have to detect all of the `mouseDown()`, `mouseMove()`, and `mouseUp()` events and take an action based on mouse dragging. Luckily, this has been done for you.

The sample program, called MouseYacker.java in Listing 8-5, provides status information about the mouse (see Figure 8-3). It tells the user all mouse events that occur including mouse moves, mouse button presses, and mouse dragging. Listing 8-6 contains the MouseYacker.html Web page.

Listing 8-5 MouseYacker.java

```
/*
 *  MouseYacker.java - Get keyboard input
 *
 *  Creating Cool Web Applets with Java
 *  By: Paul J. Perry,  Publisher: IDG Books
 *
 */

import java.applet.*;
import java.awt.Graphics;
import java.awt.Event;
import java.awt.Point;

public class MouseYacker extends java.applet.Applet
{
   // Data members
   Point p = new Point(1,1);   // Location
   boolean mInApp;                 // Mouse inside applet?
   boolean mMove;                  // Mouse movement occuring?
   boolean mDrag;                  // Mouse dragging occuring?
   boolean mDown;                  // Mouse button down?

   // Initialization
   public void init()
   {
       mInApp = false;
       mMove = false;
       mDrag = false;
       mDown = false;
   }
```

```
public boolean mouseEnter(Event evt, int x, int y)
{
    p.x = x;
    p.y = y;
    mInApp = true;
    repaint();

    return true;
}

public boolean mouseExit(Event evt, int x, int y)
{
    p.x = x;
    p.y = y;
    mInApp = false;
    repaint();

    return true;
}

public boolean mouseMove(Event evt, int x, int y)
{
    p.x = x;
    p.y = y;
    mMove = true;
    mDrag = false;
    repaint();

    return true;
}

public boolean mouseDrag(Event evt, int x, int y)
{
    p.x = x;
    p.y = y;
    mDrag = true;
    mMove = false;
    repaint();

    return true;
}

public boolean mouseDown(Event evt, int x, int y)
{
    p.x = x;
    p.y = y;
    mDown = true;
```

(continued)

Listing 8-5 *(continued)*

```
        repaint();
        return true;
    }

    public boolean mouseUp(Event evt, int x, int y)
    {
        p.x = x;
        p.y - y;
        mDown = false;

        repaint();
        return true;
    }


    public void paint(Graphics g)
    {
        if (mInApp)
           g.drawString("Cursor inside applet at", 10, 10);
        if (mMove)
           g.drawString("Mouse movement event", 10, 25);
        if (mDrag)
           g.drawString("Mouse drag event", 10, 40);
        if (mDown)
           g.drawString("Mouse button is pressed", 10, 55);

        // Always display mouse location
       g.drawString("Mouse Coordinates: "+p.x+";"+p.y, 10, 70);

    }
}
```

Listing 8-6 MouseYacker.html Web page

```
<HTML>
<!- MouseYacker.html ->
<HEAD>
   <TITLE>Mouse status information demo</TITLE>
</HEAD>
<BODY>
Mouse Information<P><P>
<APPLET CODE="MouseYacker.class" WIDTH="400" HEIGHT="400">
This Web page requires a <B>Java</B>-enabled Web Browser.
</APPLET>
</BODY>
</HTML>
```

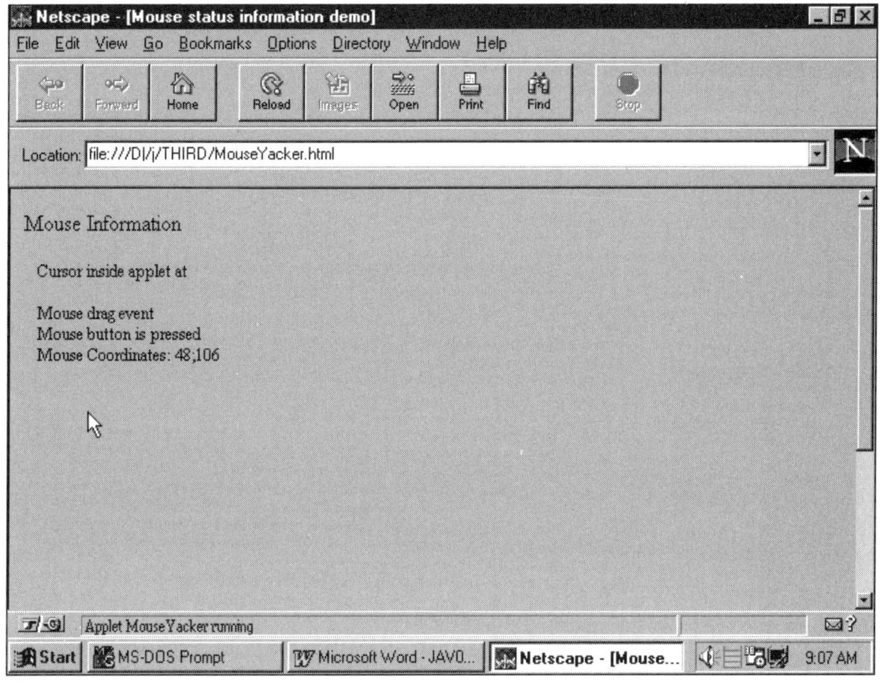

Figure 8-3: The MouseYacker sample applet.

Tying It All Together

So now you've seen the standard methods used to gain access to keyboard and mouse events. The last sample code I would like to present shows you how to access both the keyboard and the mouse. It is a simple painting applet that lets the user draw one of three shapes: lines, circles, or rectangles. The user selects the current shape by pressing keyboard keys. The user then uses the mouse to draw the endpoints of the shape.

Now don't hold your breath for too long and don't throw away your Adobe Illustrator. This applet won't make you want to trash your current animation packages, but it does include some of the topics we have covered in this chapter and shows you some of the power available with Java. Listing 8-7 contains the code for the PainterApplet.java, and Listing 8-8 contains the PainterApplet.html Web page (see Figure 8-4).

Listing 8-7 PainterApplet.java

```
/*
 *  PainterApplet.java - Work with keyboard & Mouse input
 *
 *  Creating Cool Web Applets with Java
 *  By: Paul J. Perry,  Publisher: IDG Books
 *
 */

import java.applet.*;
import java.awt.Graphics;
import java.awt.Event;
import java.awt.Point;
import java.awt.Frame;

public class PainterApplet extends java.applet.Applet
{
   // Data members
   int currentShape;   // Current drawing tool
   int width;
   int height;
   Point startPoint   = new Point(0, 0);
   Point endPoint     = new Point(0, 0);
   Point currentPoint = new Point(0, 0);

   // Shapes
   int LINE = 1;
   int CIRCLE = 2;
   int RECTANGLE = 3;

   // Initialization
   public void init()
   {
      currentShape = LINE;
   }

   // absolute value of a number
   int abs(int a)
   {
      return (a < 0) ? -a : a;
   }

   public boolean mouseDrag(Event evt, int x, int y)
```

```
{
    currentPoint.x = x;
    currentPoint.y = y;
    repaint();

    return true;
}

public boolean mouseDown(Event evt, int x, int y)
{
    startPoint.x = x;
    startPoint.y = y;

    return true;
}

public boolean mouseUp(Event evt, int x, int y)
{
    endPoint.x = x;
    endPoint.y = y;
    width = abs(endPoint.x - startPoint.x);
    height = abs(endPoint.y - startPoint.y);

    repaint();
    return true;
}

public boolean keyDown(Event evt, int key)
{
    if (key == 'l')
       currentShape = LINE;
   else
    if (key == 'c')
       currentShape = CIRCLE;
    else
    if (key == 'r')
       currentShape = RECTANGLE;

   return true;
}

public void paint(Graphics g)
{
    if (currentShape == RECTANGLE)
       g.fillRect(startPoint.x, startPoint.y, width, height);
    else
```

(continued)

Listing 8-7 ***(continued)***

```
        if (currentShape == LINE)
          g.drawLine(startPoint.x, startPoint.y,
                  endPoint.x, endPoint.y);
        else
        if (currentShape == CIRCLE)
          g.fillOval(startPoint.x, startPoint.y, width, height);

        // Always display mouse location in upper left-hand corner
       g.drawString("X: "+currentPoint.x+" Y: "
                  +currentPoint.y, 10, 10);

    }
  }
```

Listing 8-8 **PainterApplet.html Web page**

```
<HTML>
<!- PainterApplet.html ->
<HEAD>
   <TITLE>User Interactivity Demo</TITLE>
</HEAD>
<BODY>
Painter applet.  Make sure applet has focus and then press
'l', 'c', or 'r' to draw lines, circles, or rectangles.<P><P>
<APPLET CODE="PainterApplet.class" WIDTH="400" HEIGHT="400">
This Web page requires a <B>Java</B>-enabled Web Browser.
</APPLET>
</BODY>
</HTML>
```

I've written this applet in such a way that it does not keep track of the objects that have been drawn. In other words, the applet window area refreshes before a new object is drawn, thereby erasing any previously drawn objects. To display multiple shapes, the program would need to create an array of shapes, and within the `paint()` method, display every shape that has kept drawn.

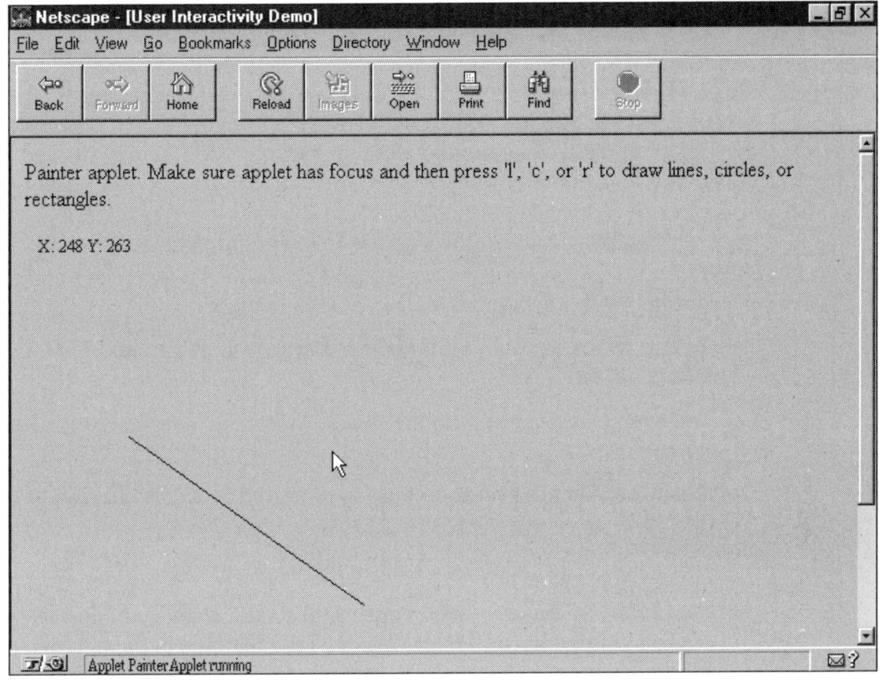

Figure 8-4: The PainterApplet sample code.

Quick Overview

This chapter covered interactivity through the most basic means: the keyboard and the mouse. You learned how to respond to events from both of these input devices. You also saw several pieces of sample code that, if studied, will help improve your understanding of Java programming.

In particular, this chapter covered the following topics:

- How to catch keyboard events in a Java applets.
- How to check for keyboard modifier keys, such as Ctrl and Shift, using the `Event` object.
- The events associated with the mouse button include `mouseUp()` and `mouseDown()`.
- Mouse movement events include `mouseMove()` and `mouseDrag()`.

Here is a brief overview of what is to come...

- Chapter 9, "Enhancing Web Pages with Java," shows you how to create the coolest Web pages around by using all the features of Java to extend your Web page.
- Chapter 10, "Network Communications," shows you how to transfer data over the Internet using your Java applet.
- Chapter 11, "User Interface Controls," shows you how to work with Java windows and how to use all those fancy controls, like buttons and list boxes, that are associated with fancy graphical operating systems.
- Chapter 12, "Windows and Dialog Boxes," provides valuable information about creating Java applets that create separate windows and dialog boxes that are separate from the basic Web page.

Enhancing Web Pages with Java

In This Chapter

Sample applets that you can use in your own Web page.

Examples of using the available applets.

A cross reference for each applet that provides a list of related applets of interest.

This chapter shows you some of the ready-made Java applets that will spruce up your Web page. All of them come as part of the Java Developers Kit, so you have immediate access to them. They are also perfect examples of object-oriented computing because they provide specific functionality in a small package (just like what Java applets should do).

Overview

Up to this point, you have learned most of the syntax required to program in Java. In fact, you have seen plenty of what Java can do: accessing images and sound, displaying text and graphics, and working with user input. Most of the examples in this book have been specific code samples to teach a topic. However, you haven't seen many examples of larger-scale applets. This chapter is for you because not only are all these Java classes provided with the Java Developers Kit, but you will also find full source code.

You can use the applets in this chapter as is, or you can examine the source code to learn how certain effects are created and extend the applets yourself. Although I mainly intend you to use this chapter as a learning tool, you will also find it useful as a reference.

I've arranged the applets in alphabetical order. Each applet includes a description along with remarks about using it, a list of the parameters that are passed to the applet from the HTML source code, an example of accessing the applet, and references to related applets. To use the example, you should copy the given HTML file into the appropriate directory in the JDK. For example, if you installed the JDK in the root of your C: drive, you will find these example applets under the c:\java\demo*.* subdirectory.

Animator

The Animator applet (see Figure 9-1) was designed to display a sequence of images, thereby creating the illusion of moving images. You can use any types of images that are stored as a bitmap in the .GIF file format. You can flick a switch that will play the images in a loop, thereby creating continuous animation. Besides allowing you to specify each frame in the animation, the class will play audio at the same time, and you can specify if the user should be allowed to stop the animation by clicking on it. This is probably one of the most used Java applets on the Web, and if you have been reading from the beginning to the end of this book, you learned a bit about it in Chapter 6.

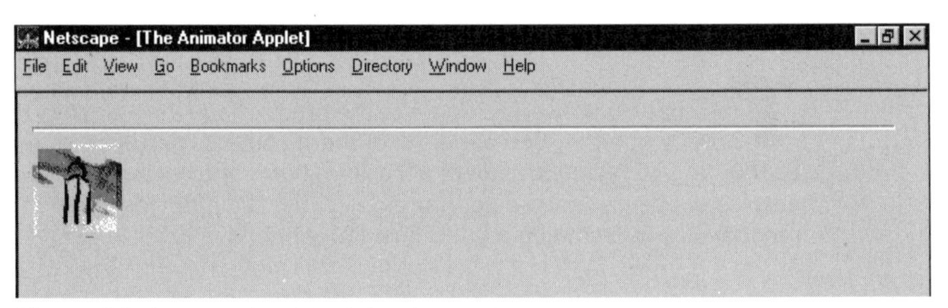

Figure 9-1: An example of the Animation applet.

Parameters

`IMAGESOURCE` — Contains the URL of the directory containing the frames or images of the animation. The naming convention is simply `T1.GIF`, `T2.GIF`, ... `Tx.GIF`, where *x* is the final frame of the animation.

`STARTUP` — Contains the URL of an image that is displayed while loading the frames of the animation. Using this parameter allows the user to view something while the individual animation frames are being loaded.

BACKGROUND	Contains the URL of an image that is displayed in the background of the animation.
STARTIMAGE	Provides the index of the first frame in the animation. Although this will usually be 1, you can use this parameter to tell the applet to start animation at a different frame.
ENDIMAGE	Provides the integer of the index for the last frame in the animation.
PAUSE	Specifies the time (in milliseconds) to pause between each frame. This will be used for every frame in the animation. If you wish to use a variable length of time between each frame, use the PAUSES parameter.
PAUSES	Defines a list of pauses in milliseconds. This allows you to specify a different pause for each frame in the animation. Each number is separated by the | character. For example: 100|50|300.
REPEAT	Set to either true or false to indicate if the animation should repeat in a loop. The default for this option is true.
POSITIONS	Specifies the coordinates in which to display each animation frame. This lets you move the animation around a Web page. Each pair of coordinates is separated by the | character.
IMAGES	Provides the index of each image in the animation sequence. This allows you to repeat frames of the animation. For certain animations, this improves performance because you won't have to load as many image files over the Internet. Each number is separated by a | character. For example, 1|2|3|4|2|1 will display the first four frames, followed by the second frame and the first frame.
SOUNDSOURCE	Contains the URL of a directory containing an audio file. This is only the directory. The next parameter provides the actual filename.
SOUNDTRACK	Contains the URL of an audio clip that is played repeatedly in the background.
SOUNDS	Contains a list of URLs of audio clips that are played for each individual frame. As usual, the list is separated by the | character.

Example

```
<HTML>
<! AnimatorDemo.html ->
<HEAD>
   <TITLE>The Animator Applet</TITLE>
</HEAD>
<BODY>
<HR>

<APPLET CODE=Animator.class WIDTH=200 HEIGHT=200>
<PARAM NAME=imagesource VALUE="images/SimpleAnimation">
<PARAM NAME=endimage VALUE=2>
<PARAM NAME=soundsource VALUE="audio">
<PARAM NAME=soundtrack VALUE=spacemusic.au>
<PARAM NAME=sounds
VALUE="1.au|2.au|3.au|4.au|5.au|6.au|7.au|8.au|9.au|0.au">
<PARAM NAME=pause VALUE=200>
This Web page requires a <B>Java</B>-enabled Web Browser.
</APPLET>
<HR>
<HR>
<A HREF="Animator.java">The source.</A>
</BODY>
</HTML>
```

See also

BlinkingText, NervousText, and ScrollingImages

ArcTest

The ArcTest applet (see Figure 9-2) is an interactive test of the `drawArc()` and `fillArc()` methods found in the `Graphics` object. You are more likely to use this applet to experiment with displaying graphics rather than incorporate it directly into your Web pages. The applet displays a grid, along with a superimposed image of an arc. You choose the beginning and ending coordinates (between 0 and 360 degrees) of the arc. You then click on a button to either draw or fill the arc.

Parameters

None.

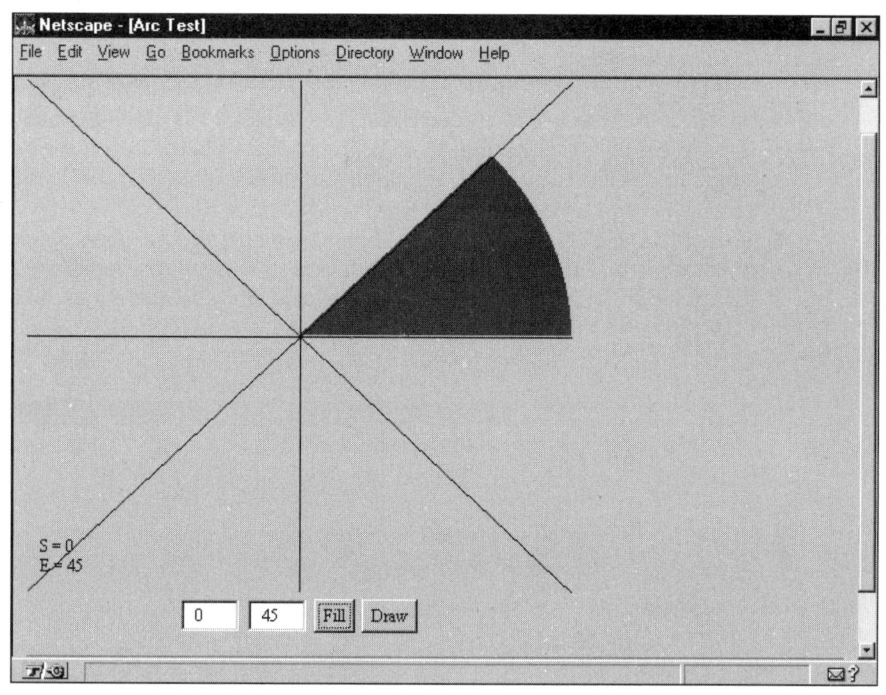

Figure 9-2: The ArcTestDemo applet.

Example

```
<HTML>
<!- ArcTestDemo.html ->
<HEAD>
   <TITLE>ArcTest Demo</TITLE>
</HEAD>
<BODY>
<HR>
<APPLET CODE=ArcTest.class WIDTH=400 HEIGHT=400>
This Web page requires a <B>Java</B>-enabled Web Browser.
</APPLET>
<HR>
<A HREF="ArcTest.java">The source.</A>
</BODY>
</HTML>
```

See also

CardTest, DitherTest, DrawTest, GraphicsTest, and ImageTest

BarChart

The BarChart applet (see Figure 9-3) displays a horizontal or vertical bar chart based on the parameters you pass to the applet. Provisions are included to specify the title, the number of columns (or bars) in the chart, the scale in which to draw the bar chart, and information about each individual bar.

To use this applet, you must first specify the title, the number of columns, the orientation, and the scale of the chart. You then need to specify the information for each bar, including the bar style (solid or striped), the actual integer value of the bar, the text label, and the color of the bar.

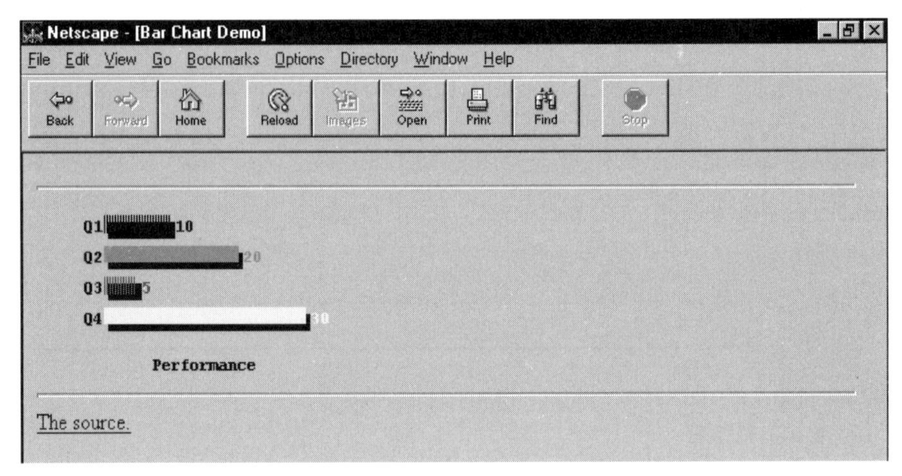

Figure 9-3: The BarChartDemo Web page.

Parameters

`Cx_STYLE`	Defines the appearance of the bar, which is either `"solid"` or `"striped"`.
`Cx_VALUE`	Contains a numeric value of the bar.
`Cx_LABEL`	Contains the label used on the specific bar.
`Cx_COLOR`	Specifies the color of the bar, which is either `"green"`, `"blue"`, `"pink"`, `"orange"`, `"magenta"`, `"cyan"`, `"white"`, `"yellow"`, `"gray"`, or `"darkgray"`.
`COLUMNS`	Specifies the number of columns in the bar chart.
`ORIENTATION`	Defines the position of the bar chart. Can be either `"horizontal"` or `"vertical"`.

SCALE	Specifies the number of pixels per unit in the bar chart.
TITLE	Indicates the title of the bar chart that is displayed below the chart.

Example

```
<HTML>
<!- BarChartDemo.html ->
<HEAD>
   <TITLE>Bar Chart Demo</TITLE>
</HEAD>
<BODY>
<HR>
<APPLET CODE="Chart.class" WIDTH=251 HEIGHT=125>
<PARAM NAME=c2_color VALUE="green">
<PARAM NAME=c2_label VALUE="Q2">
<PARAM NAME=c1_style VALUE="striped">
<PARAM NAME=c4 VALUE="30">
<PARAM NAME=c3 VALUE="5">
<PARAM NAME=c2 VALUE="20">
<PARAM NAME=c4_color VALUE="yellow">
<PARAM NAME=c1 VALUE="10">
<PARAM NAME=c4_label VALUE="Q4">
<PARAM NAME=title VALUE="Performance">
<PARAM NAME=c3_style VALUE="striped">
<PARAM NAME=columns VALUE="4">
<PARAM NAME=c1_color VALUE="blue">
<PARAM NAME=c1_label VALUE="Q1">
<PARAM NAME=c3_color VALUE="magenta">
<PARAM NAME=c3_label VALUE="Q3">
<PARAM NAME=c2_style VALUE="solid">
<PARAM NAME=orientation VALUE="horizontal">
<PARAM NAME=c4_style VALUE="solid">
<PARAM NAME=scale VALUE="5">
This Web page requires a <B>Java</B>-enabled Web Browser.
</APPLET>
<HR>
<A HREF="Chart.java">The source.</A>
</BODY>
</HTML>
```

See also

MoleculeViewer, SimpleGraph, and Spreadsheet

BlinkingText

The BlinkingText applet (see Figure 9-4) is a fun and entertaining piece of code that will display a paragraph of text that lets you supply and randomly hide (or blink) words in multiple colors.

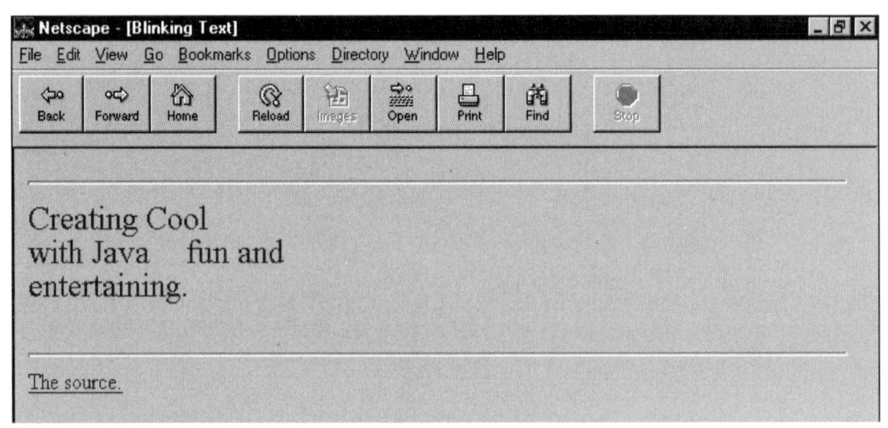

Figure 9-4: The BlinkingText Demonstration Web page. (It's blinking the words "Web Applets" and "is" in the text.)

Parameters

LBL	Contains the text to display.
SPEED	Determines the speed at which to display the text. You must pass a numerical value between 1 and 10 that is the number of times per second that the text blinks.

Example

```
<HTML>
<! BlinkingTextDemo.html ->
<HEAD>
   <TITLE>Blinking Text</TITLE>
</HEAD>
<BODY>
<HR>
<APPLET CODE="Blink.class" WIDTH=300 HEIGHT=100>
<PARAM NAME=lbl value="Creating Cool Web Applets with Java is fun
and entertaining.">
<PARAM NAME=speed value="4">
```

```
This Web page requires a <B>Java</B>-enabled Web Browser.
</APPLET>
<HR>
<A HREF="Blink.java">The source.</A>
</BODY>
</HTML>
```

See also

Animator, ImageMap, NervousText, ScrollingImages, and TumblingDuke

BouncingHeads

The BouncingHeads applet (see Figure 9-5) does just as its name implies. It takes a series of images and displays them as a series of bouncing or moving images. You can replace the images for those of your own head or maybe those of your favorite cartoon character. To use your own graphics images, you must replace the files T1.GIF through T8.GIF with your unique images.

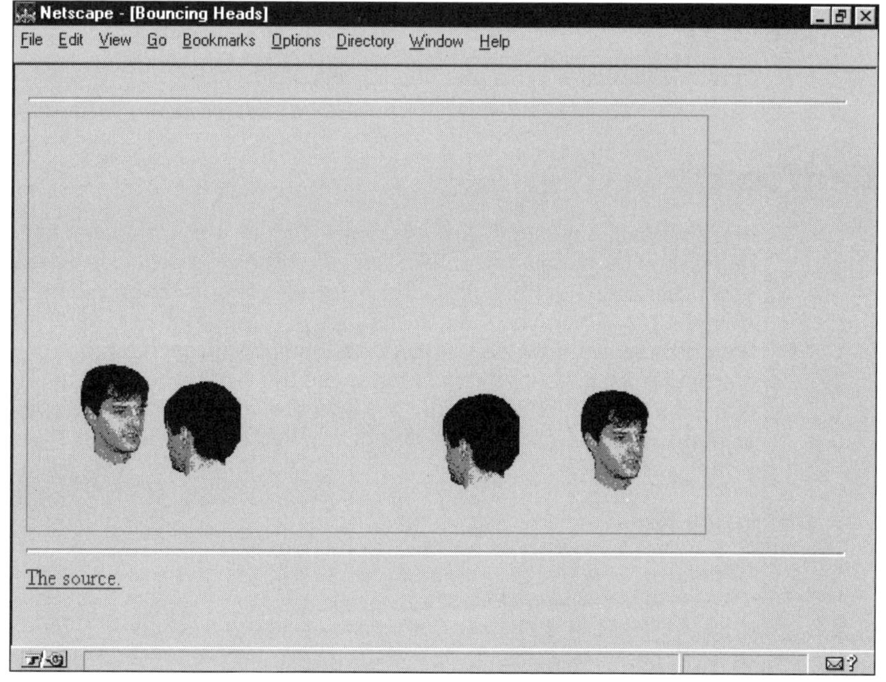

Figure 9-5: The BouncingHeads applet.

Parameters

None.

Example

```
<HTML>
<! BouncingHeadsDemo.html ->
<HEAD>
   <TITLE>Bouncing Heads</TITLE>
</HEAD>
<BODY>
<HR>
<APPLET CODE=BounceItem.class WIDTH=500 HEIGHT=300>
This Web page requires a <B>Java</B>-enabled Web Browser.
</APPLET>
<HR>
<A HREF="BounceItem.java">The source.</A>
</BODY>
</HTML>
```

See also

MoleculeViewer, WireFrame, and UnderConstruction

CardTest

You'll probably use the CardTest applet (Figure 9-6) for educational purposes rather than for building cool Web pages. This applet provides a means for experimenting with the built-in frame layout controls that are part of Java (see Chapter 11). When you view this applet, you will see two rows of buttons in the Web browser window. As you click on the buttons, each button (or card) rearranges itself, as if you had rearranged the size of the window. The purpose of the demonstration is to show you how to rearrange interface objects (such as buttons), depending on the size of the Web browser window.

Parameters

None.

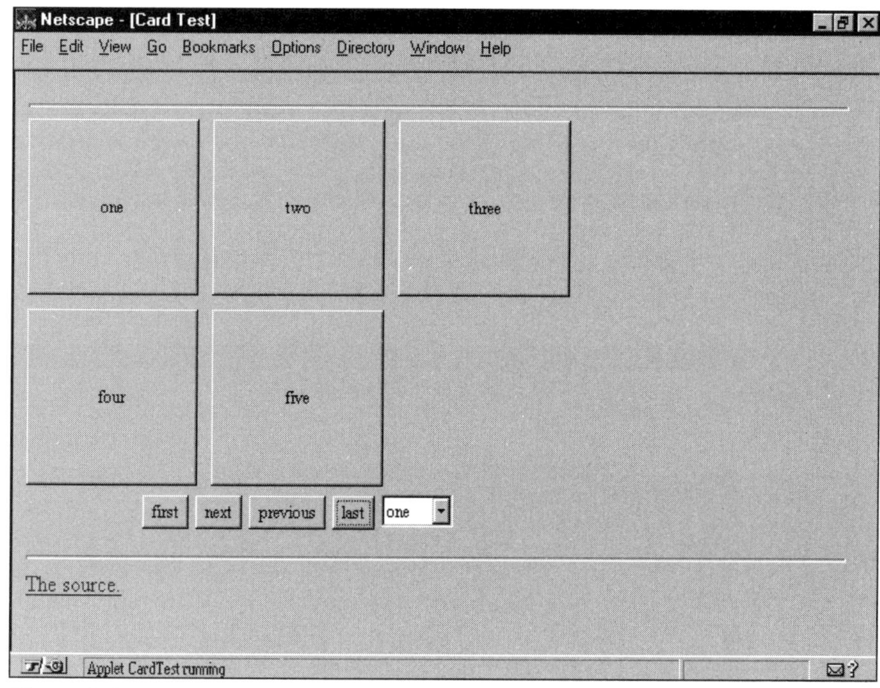

Figure 9-6: The CardTest applet.

Example

```
<HTML>
<!- CardTestDemo.html ->
<HEAD>
   <TITLE>Card Test</TITLE>
</HEAD>
<BODY>
<HR>
<APPLET CODE=CardTest.class WIDTH=400 HEIGHT=300>
This Web page requires a <B>Java</B>-enabled Web Browser.
</APPLET>
<HR>
<A HREF="CardTest.java">The source.</A>
</BODY>
</HTML>
```

See also

ArcTest, DitherTest, DrawTest, GraphicsTest, and ImageTest

DitherTest

The DitherTest applet (Figure 9-7) provides a good example for displaying RGB color values in your applets. It lets you specify the horizontal and vertical colors to use for a color chart (through button controls) and then draws the color chart with the appropriate colors. If the system executing the applet cannot display true color images, the color displayed will appear as close as possible to the intended color (something called *dithering*). This is important for applets that work on the Web because you could have a broad variety of users with many different types of computers viewing your Web page.

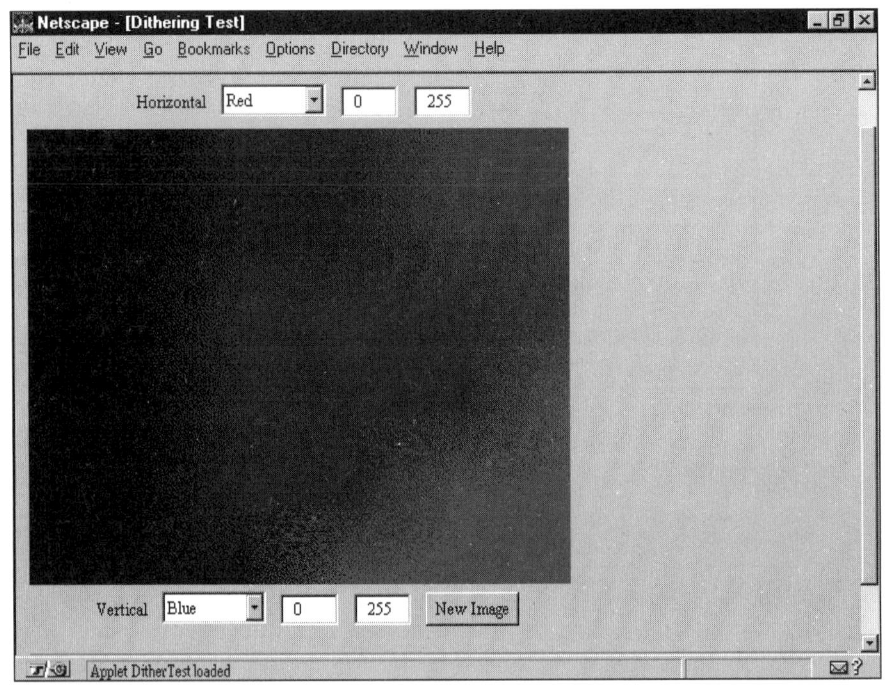

Figure 9-7: The DitherTestDemo Web page.

Parameters

None.

Example

```
<HTML>
<!- DitherTestDemo.html ->
<HEAD>
   <TITLE>Dithering Test</TITLE>
</HEAD>
```

```
<BODY>
<HR>
<APPLET CODE=DitherTest.class WIDTH=400 HEIGHT=400>
This Web page requires a <B>Java</B>-enabled Web Browser.
</APPLET>
<HR>
<A HREF="DitherTest.java">The source.</A>
</BODY>
</HTML>
```

See also

ArcTest, CardTest, DrawTest, GraphicsTest, and ImageTest

DrawTest

The DrawTest applet (Figure 9-8) is a small paint application that lets the user employ the Web page as a virtual painting canvas. With this applet, you can use on-screen controls to specify the color (red, green, blue, gray, yellow, or black) and whether to draw lines or points. You saw one example of a painter applet in Chapter 8. This is another example you might want to study more closely.

Parameters

None.

Example

```
<HTML>
<!- DrawTestDemo.html ->
<HEAD>
   <TITLE>Draw Test</TITLE>
</HEAD>
<BODY>
<HR>
<APPLET CODE=DrawTest.class WIDTH=400 HEIGHT=400>
This Web page requires a <B>Java</B>-enabled Web Browser.
</APPLET>
<HR>
<A HREF="DrawTest.java">The source.</A>
</BODY>
</HTML>
```

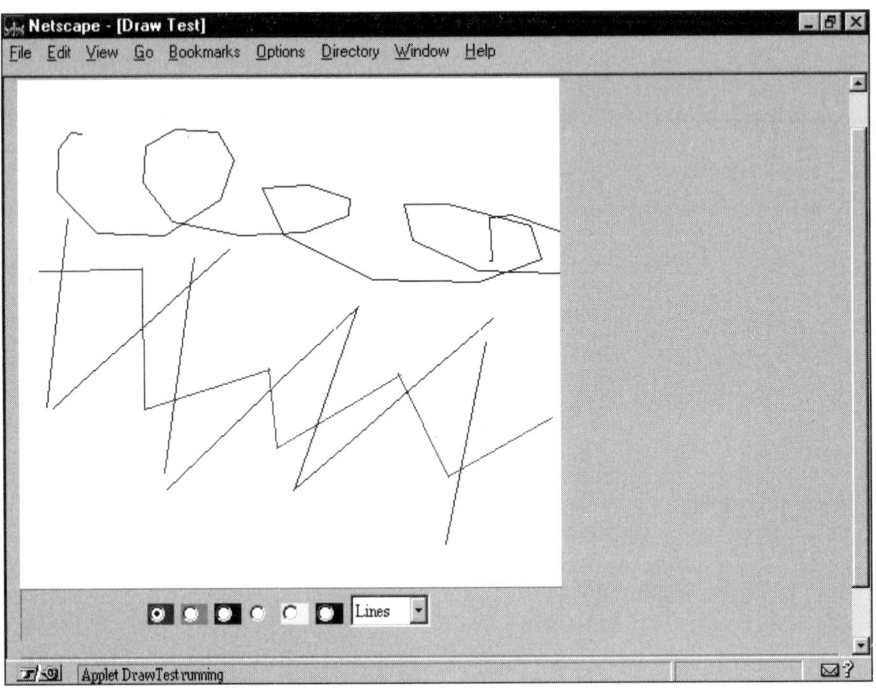

Figure 9-8: The DrawTestDemo Web page.

See also

ArcTest, DitherTest, GraphicsTest, and ImageTest

Fractal

The Fractal applet (class name `CLSFractal.class`) displays a fractal image (Figure 9-9). It starts with a straight line and continuously bends it into multiple angles and finally into a full fractal image. Many parameters are provided for customizing the final display.

Parameters

`AXIOM`	Specifies the acceptance value.
`BORDER`	Designates the width of the border.
`DELAY`	Specifies how often to update the fractal image (in milliseconds).
`INCREMENTAL`	Specifies if the image should be updated incrementally, set to either `"true"` or `"false"`.

LEVEL	Indicates the number of fractal levels to display.
NORMALIZESCALE	Specifies if the fractal scale should be normalized, set to either "true" or "false".
PREDx	Indicates the predicate level.
ROTANGLE	Designates the rotation angle.
STARTANGLE	Indicates the starting angle.

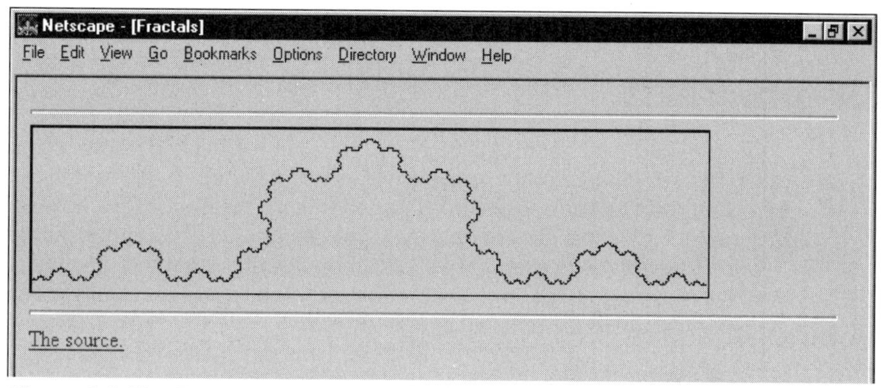

Figure 9-9: The FractalDemo Web page.

Example

```
<HTML>
<!- FractalDemo.html ->
<HEAD>
   <TITLE>Fractals</TITLE>
</HEAD>
<BODY>
<HR>
<APPLET CODE="CLSFractal.class" WIDTH=500 HEIGHT=120>
<PARAM NAME=level VALUE="5">
<PARAM NAME=rotangle VALUE="45">
<PARAM NAME=succ1 VALUE="F-F++F-F">
<PARAM NAME=delay VALUE="1000">
<PARAM NAME=axiom VALUE="F">
<PARAM NAME=normalizescale VALUE="true">
<PARAM NAME=incremental VALUE="true">
<PARAM NAME=pred1 VALUE="F">
<PARAM NAME=border VALUE="2">
<PARAM NAME=startangle VALUE="0">
This Web page requires a <B>Java</B>-enabled Web Browser.
```

```
</APPLET>
<HR>
<A HREF="CLSFractal.java">The source.</A>
</BODY>
</HTML>
```

See also

MoleculeViewer and WireFrame

GraphicsTest

If you liked ArcTest and DitherTest, you will really like GraphicsTest (Figure 9-10), which is another applet that you might want to use for learning purposes rather than to add to your Web page. This applet shows you how some of the graphics object methods operate in a Web applet. This applet includes controls at the top of the applet that let you choose which shape to display (either `Arc`, `Oval`, `Polygon`, `Rect`, or `RoundRect`). It then displays a visually pleasing image of the requested shape in multiple colors.

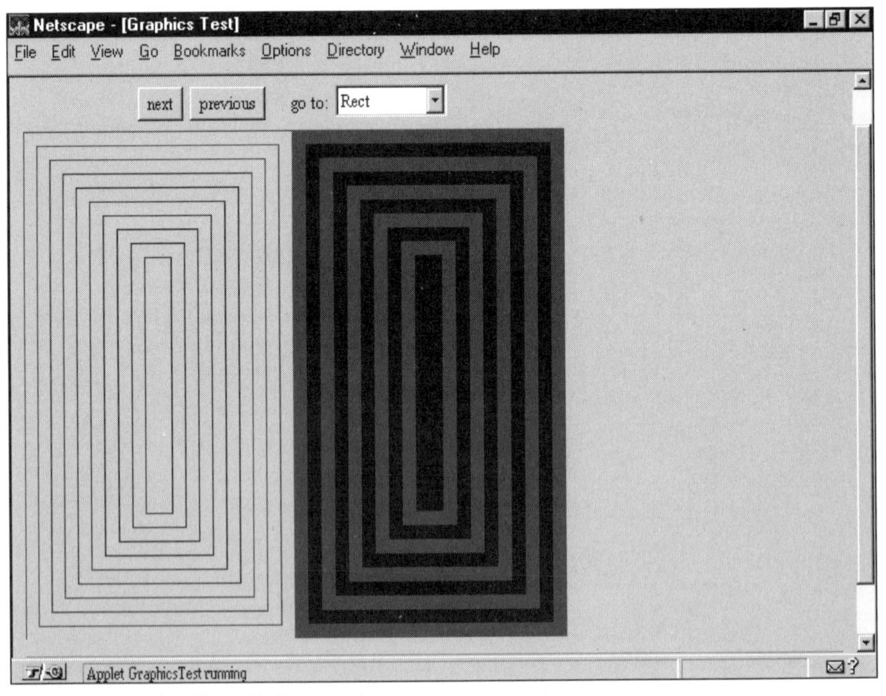

Figure 9-10: The GraphicsTest applet.

Parameters

None.

Example

```
<HTML>
<!- GraphicsTestDemo.html ->
<HEAD>
   <TITLE>Graphics Test</TITLE>
</HEAD>
<BODY>
<HR>
<APPLET CODE=GraphicsTest.class WIDTH=400 HEIGHT=400>
This Web page requires a <B>Java</B>-enabled Web Browser.
</APPLET>
<HR>
<A HREF="GraphicsTest.java">The source.</A>
</BODY>
</HTML>
```

See also

ArcTest, DitherTest, DrawTest, and ImageTest

GraphLayout

The GraphLayout applet (Figure 9-11) provides a visually appealing display, consisting of a group of nodes that move in real-time. Through parameters, you can define which nodes are used and the optimal length of the edges between them. While the applet is running, the user can click on each node and move it around the page. This applet provides a good example of displaying graphics and demonstrating interactivity through the mouse.

Parameters

`CENTER`	Specifies the center node of the graph. This node is displayed in red and is fixed to the center of the applet.
`EDGES`	Defines the edges of the graph. The format of this parameter consists of a comma-separated list of edges between nodes. The nodes are created as they're needed. Each edge is defined as a pair of nodes in the form of `"from-to"`. You can also specify the desired length of an edge as follows: `"from-to/length"`.

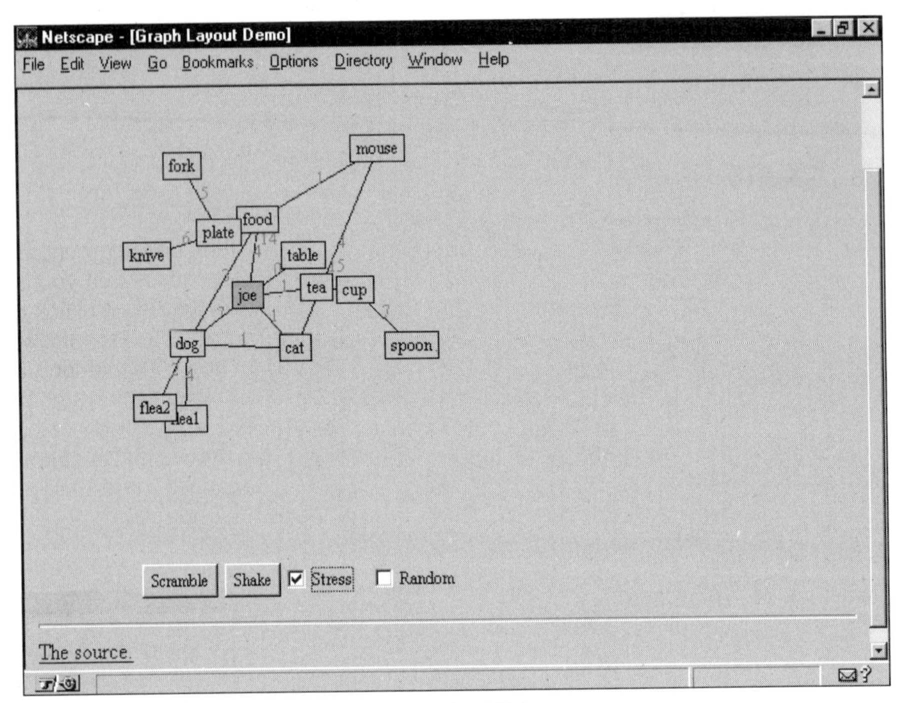

Figure 9-11: The GraphLayout demonstration Web page.

Example

```
<HTML>
<!- GraphLayoutDemo.html ->
<HEAD>
   <TITLE>Graph Layout Demo</TITLE>
</HEAD>
<BODY>
<HR>
<APPLET CODE="Graph.class" WIDTH=400 HEIGHT=400>
<PARAM NAME=edges VALUE="joe-food,joe-dog,joe-tea,joe-cat,joe-
table,table-plate/50,plate-food/30,food-mouse/100,food-dog/
100,mouse-cat/150,table-cup/30,cup-tea/30,dog-cat/80,cup-spoon/
50,plate-fork,dog-flea1,dog-flea2,flea1-flea2/20,plate-knive">
<PARAM NAME=center VALUE="joe">
This Web page requires a <B>Java</B>-enabled Web Browser.
</APPLET>
<HR>
<A HREF="Graph.java">The source.</A>
</BODY>
</HTML>
```

See also

CardTest and MoleculeViewer

ImageMap

The ImageMap applet (Figure 9-12) provides client-side segmented hypergraphic support for Web pages. What that means is that you can display a graphics image within your Web page and allow the user to click on an active area within the image (you can have as many as you like) to take a unique action. The action can be displaying a new Web page, highlighting a part of the image, playing an audio file, or displaying a message in the status bar.

The active areas of the image are defined as parameters to the applet. The ImageMap applet goes way beyond image maps in standard Web pages because the user can do more than just link to a unique spot.

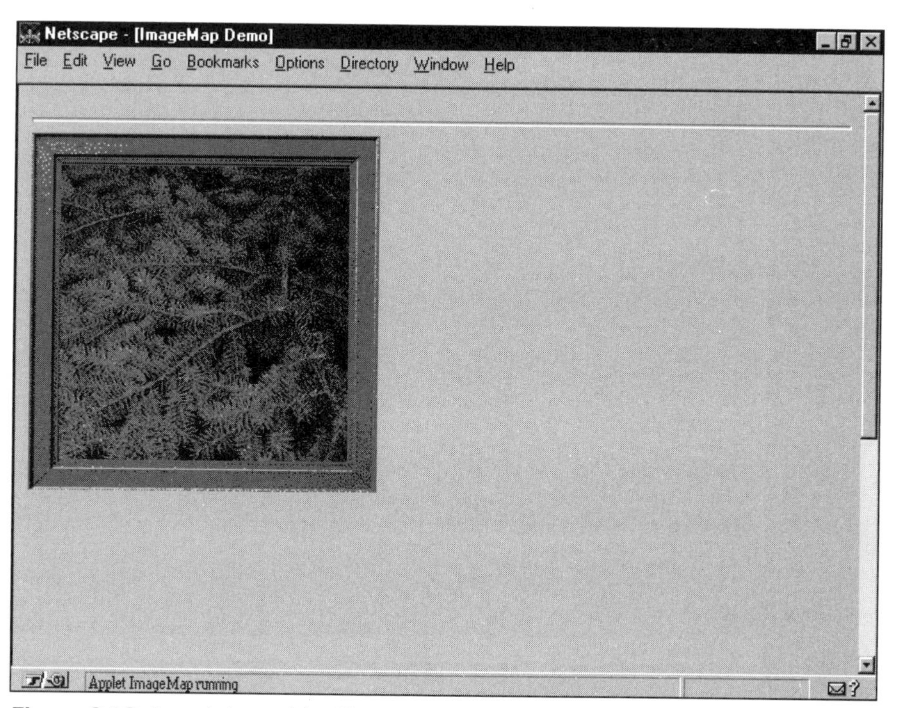

Figure 9-12: Sample ImageMap Web page.

Parameters

AREA*x*	Specifies an active area of the image, where *x* is the area number. Each applet can have one or more of these areas. Each area has the following format: *Action, x, y, width, height, arguments.* where Action is one of the names described in Table 9-1. The *x*, *y*, *width*, and *height* values define the coordinates of the area, and *arguments* is optional arguments required by some of the *Action* parameters.
HIGHLIGHT	Designates the type of highlighting that should be applied. Use either "brighter*x*" or "darker*x*", where *x* is the percentage change you want.
IMG	Contains the URL of the background image.
STARTSOUND	Contains the URL of an audio file (in .AU format) that is played as soon as the applet starts.

Table 9-1 ImageMap Action Names

Name	Description
SoundArea	Plays an audio clip. The argument is an audio filename.
NameArea	Shows text in the Web browser status bar. The argument is the displayed text.
HRefButtonArea	Goes to a new Web address. The argument is a URL.
RoundHrefButtonArea	Goes to a new Web address. The argument is a URL.
HighlightArea	Highlights the area when the mouse enters it.
ClickArea	Displays the coordinates when the user clicks in this area.

Example

```
<HTML>
<!- ImageMapDemo.html ->
<HEAD>
   <TITLE>ImageMap Demo</TITLE>
</HEAD>
<BODY>
<HR>
<APPLET CODE="ImageMap.class" WIDTH="600" HEIGHT="600">
```

```
<PARAM NAME="img" VALUE="forest.gif">
<PARAM NAME="highlight" VALUE="brighter30">
<PARAM NAME="startsound" VALUE="joy.au">
<PARAM NAME="Area1" VALUE="ClickArea, 0, 0, 125, 125">
<PARAM NAME="Area2" VALUE="SoundArea, 125, 0, 125, 125, gong.au">
<PARAM NAME="Area3" VALUE="NameArea, 125, 125, 125, 125, User
String">
<PARAM NAME="Area4" VALUE="HighlightArea, 0, 125, 125, 125">
This Web page requires a <B>Java</B>-enabled Web Browser.
</APPLET>
<HR>
<A HREF="ImageMap.java">The source.</A>
</BODY>
</HTML>
```

See also

Animator, NervousText, and ScrollingImages

ImageTest

ImageTest (Figure 9-13) is a visually appealing applet that lets you display images at different areas within an applet. It also demonstrates basic interactivity with the keyboard.

Parameters

None.

Example

```
<HTML>
<!- ImageTestDemo.html ->
<HEAD>
   <TITLE>Image Test</TITLE>
</HEAD>
<BODY>
<HR>
<APPLET CODE=ImageTest.class WIDTH=600 HEIGHT=300>
This Web page requires a <B>Java</B>-enabled Web Browser.
</APPLET>
<HR>
<A HREF="ImageTest.java">The source.</A>
</BODY>
</HTML>
```

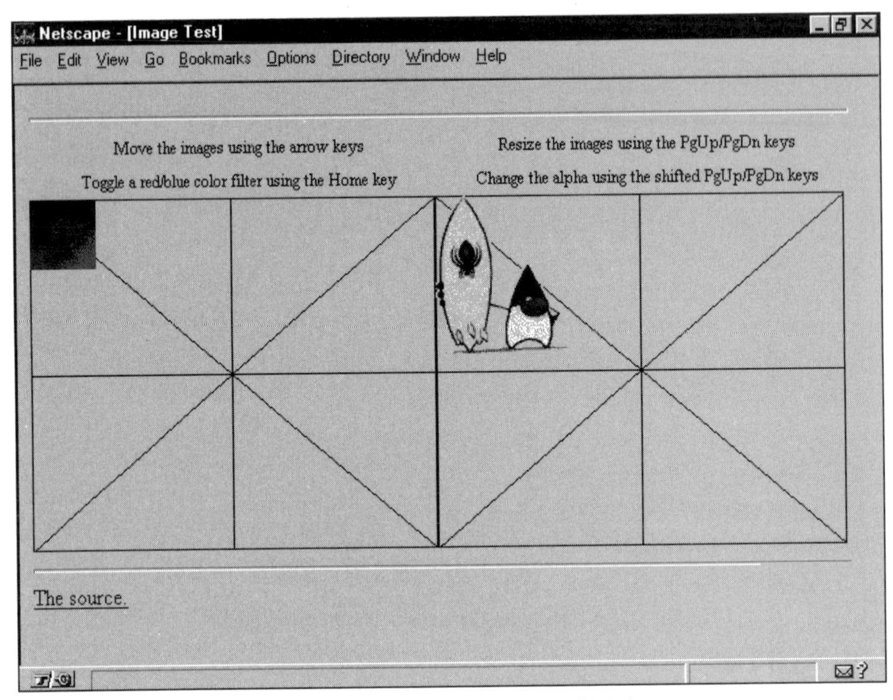

Figure 9-13: The ImageTestDemo Web page. Surf's up, Duke!

See also

ArcTest, CardTest, DitherTest, DrawTest, and GraphicsTest

JumpingBox

You can think of the JumpingBox applet (class name `MouseTrack.class`) as a dexterity building game (Figure 9-14), as well as an example of how to access mouse button presses in a Java applet. When the Web page displays, a box moves around the Web page and the user is supposed to click on it. Various sound files are played depending on how close the user comes to hitting the box.

Parameters

None.

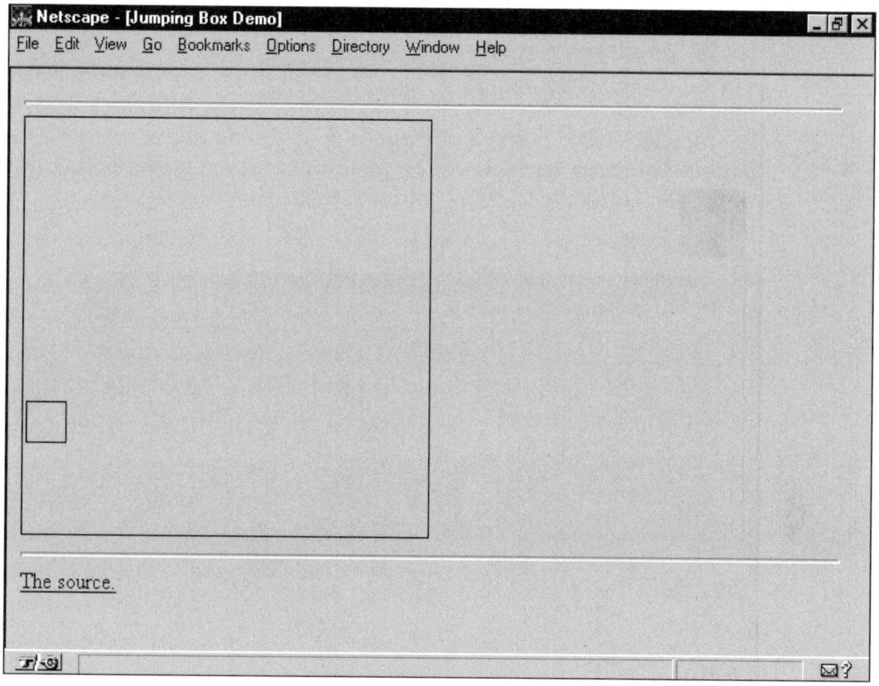

Netscape - [Jumping Box Demo]
File Edit View Go Bookmarks Options Directory Window Help

The source.

Figure 9-14: The JumpingBox demonstration Web page.

Example

```
<HTML>
<!- JumpingBoxDemo.html ->
<HEAD>
   <TITLE>Jumping Box Demo</TITLE>
</HEAD>
<BODY>
<HR>
<APPLET CODE=MouseTrack.class WIDTH=300 HEIGHT=300>
This Web page requires a <B>Java</B>-enabled Web Browser.
</APPLET>
<HR>
<A HREF="MouseTrack.java">The source.</A>
</BODY>
</HTML>
```

See also

TicTacToe

MoleculeViewer

The MoleculeViewer applet (Figure 9-15) is an educational applet that displays the chemical representation of a molecule. The user can rotate the image with the mouse. This is a very good applet for learning about molecular science because not only can you view a three-dimensional representation of the molecule, but you can also "grab-on" to it and rotate the image.

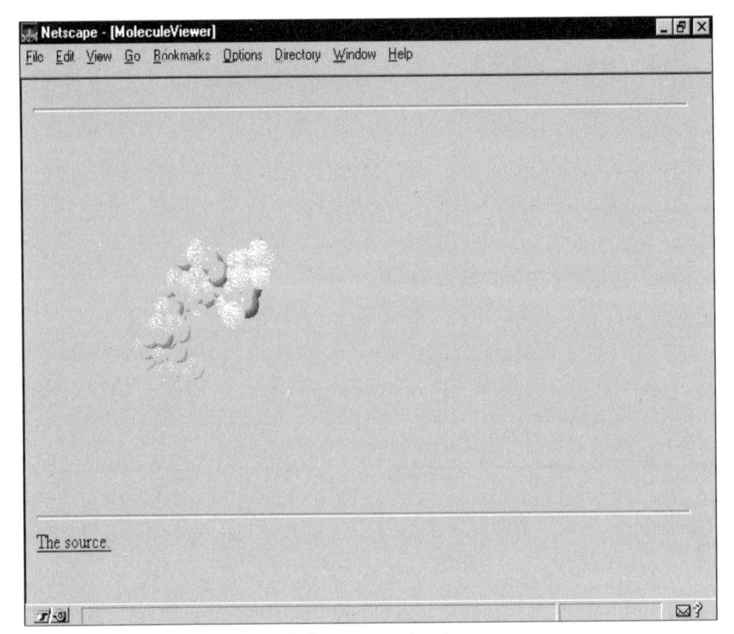

Figure 9-15: The MoleculeViewer applet demo.

Parameters

`MODEL`	The URL of a file containing the description of a molecule. The format of this file is one atom description per line, with each atom having the form: *`Element x y z`* where *`Element`* can be one of `C` (carbon), `H` (hydrogen), `NA` (sodium), and `O` (oxygen). The *x*, *y*, and *z* coordinates range from –1.0 to 1.0, but by modifying the scale, you can adjust these values.
`SCALE`	Specifies an optional scale factor. This lets you scale the display of the molecule by a certain factor. Acceptable values are in the range of 0.5 to 4.0.

Example

```
<HTML>
<!- MoleculeViewerDemo.html ->
<HEAD>
   <TITLE>MoleculeViewer</TITLE>
</HEAD>
<BODY>
<HR>
<APPLET CODE=XYZApp.class WIDTH=300 HEIGHT=300>
<PARAM NAME=model value=models/HyaluronicAcid.xyz>
This Web page requires a <B>Java</B>-enabled Web Browser.
</APPLET>
<HR>
<A HREF="XYZApp.java">The source.</A>
</BODY>
</HTML>
```

What follows is a partial example of the referenced molecule file:

```
C 2.239 -2.685 1.669
C 2.855 -3.796 2.510
C 1.869 -4.276 3.564
C 1.354 -3.098 4.381
.
.
.
NA .954 .446 10.965
NA .446 -.954 19.450
NA -.954 -.446 27.935
```

See also

Fractal, GraphLayout, and WireFrame

NervousText

The NervousText applet (Figure 9-16) is a nifty little applet that displays a line of text and randomly moves the letters around. The effect is actually quite simple, but the result is what attracts people's attention. When using this applet, you must make sure that the width of the applet is large enough to fit the entire applet.

If you drink too much coffee, you might want to avoid this applet.

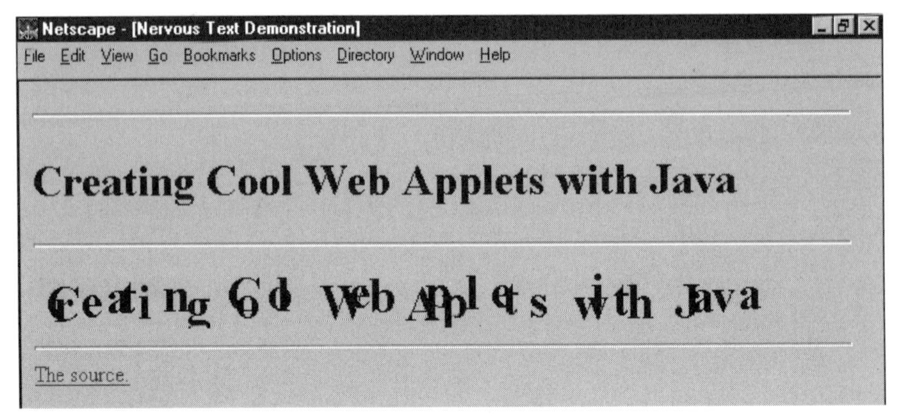

Figure 9-16: NervousText demonstration.

Parameters

TEXT	Specifies the text displayed in the applet. The applet can display only one line of text.

Example

```
<HTML>
<!- NervousTextDemo.html ->
<HEAD>
   <TITLE>Nervous Text Demonstration</TITLE>
</HEAD>
<BODY>
<HR>
<H1>Creating Cool Web Applets with Java</H1>
<HR>
<APPLET CODE="NervousText.class" WIDTH=600 HEIGHT=50>
<PARAM NAME=text VALUE="Creating Cool Web Applets with Java">
This Web page requires a <B>Java</B>-enabled Web Browser.
</APPLET>
<HR>
<A HREF="NervousText.java">The source.</A>
</BODY>
</HTML>
```

See also

Animator, BlinkingText, and ScrollingImages

ScrollingImages

This great little applet takes a series of graphical images as parameters and displays them in a scrolling fashion (see Figure 9-17). The example that follows references some of the images that are supplied with the JDK, that of the people who worked on the Java project at Sun. However, I must admit, I think I have seen one of these people on national television before.

Figure 9-17: *ScrollingImages demo.*

Parameters

`IMG`	Designates a directory, specifying where the series of images with the name `T1.GIF`, `T2.GIF`, `...Tx.GIF` are located, where *x* refers to the last image in the series.
`SPEED`	Specifies the relative speed of the scrolling images. The integer is the number of times per second that the images will be scrolled.
`DIR`	Indicates the direction (in pixels) that the image will be scrolled in each frame. Use a number from 1 to 10 to scroll right, and a number from –10 to –1 to scroll left.
`NIMGS`	Defines the number of images to be displayed.

Example

```
<HTML>
<!- ScollingImageDemo.html ->
<HEAD>
   <TITLE>Scrolling Image Demo</TITLE>
</HEAD>
<BODY>
<HR>
<APPLET CODE="ImageTape.class" WIDTH=550 HEIGHT=50>
```

```
<PARAM NAME=speed VALUE="4">
<PARAM NAME=img VALUE="images/team">
<PARAM NAME=dir VALUE="4">
<PARAM NAME=nimgs VALUE="15">
This Web page requires a <B>Java</B>-enabled Web Browser.
</APPLET>
<HR>
<A HREF="ImageTape.java">The source.</A>
</BODY>
</HTML>
```

See also

Animator, BlinkingText, and NervousText

SimpleGraph

The SimpleGraph applet (Figure 9-18) draws a simple line graph of a sine wave. It does not provide any way of customizing this wave.

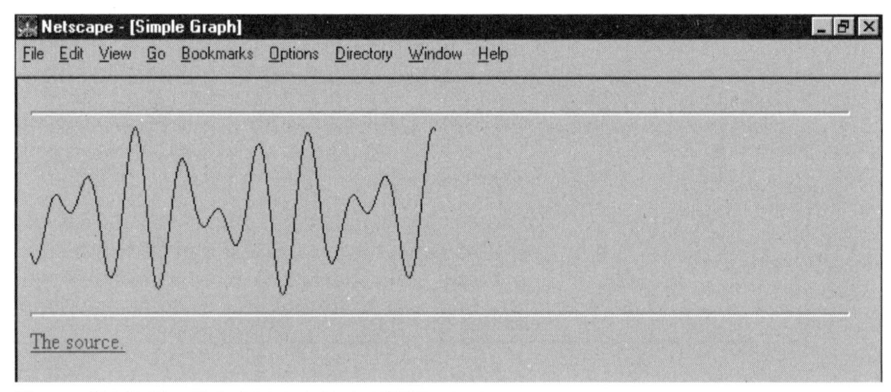

Figure 9-18: The SimpleGraphDemo Web page.

Parameters

None.

Example

```
<HTML>
<!- SimpleGraphDemo.html ->
<HEAD>
   <TITLE>Simple Graph</TITLE>
</HEAD>
<BODY>
<HR>
<APPLET CODE=GraphApplet.class WIDTH=300 HEIGHT=120>
This Web page requires a <B>Java</B>-enabled Web Browser.
</APPLET>
<HR>
<A HREF="GraphApplet.java">The source.</A>
</BODY>
</HTML>
```

See also

MoleculeViewer and WireFrame

SpreadSheet

Don't get rid of your Microsoft Excel or Lotus 1-2-3 spreadsheets quite yet, but this sample applet does allow you to include a simple spreadsheet in your Web page, which the user can browse and view the results of different calculations (Figure 9-19).

A cell can have either a string label, a numeric value, or a formula. To include a label, precede the cell contents with an `l`. For numeric values, precede the cell contents with a `v`. Finally, for formulas, precede the cell content with an (you guessed it!) `f`. Formulas are limited to the four basic mathematical functions (+, –, *, /).

Parameters

`COLUMNS`	Specifies the number of columns in the spreadsheet.
`TITLE`	Indicates the title for the spreadsheet.
`ROWS`	Specifies the number of rows in the spreadsheet.
`A1...Z99`	Each individual cell in the spreadsheet. You specify each cell by specifying a column (a letter from A to Z) and a row (a number between 1 and the number of rows).

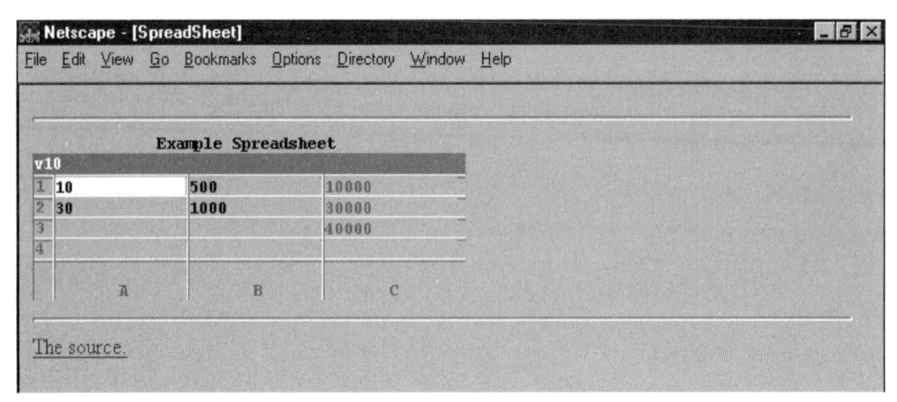

Figure 9-19: The sample SpreadSheet Demo Web page.

Example

```
<HTML>
<!- SpreadSheetDemo.html ->
<HEAD>
   <TITLE>SpreadSheet</TITLE>
</HEAD>
<BODY>
<HR>
<APPLET CODE="SpreadSheet.class" WIDTH=320 HEIGHT=120>
<PARAM NAME=title VALUE="Example Spreadsheet">
<PARAM NAME=rows VALUE="4">
<PARAM NAME=columns VALUE="3">
<PARAM NAME=a1 VALUE="v10">
<PARAM NAME=a2 VALUE="v30">
<PARAM NAME=b1 VALUE="v500">
<PARAM NAME=b2 VALUE="v1000">
<PARAM NAME=c1 VALUE="fA1*B2">
<PARAM NAME=c2 VALUE="fA2*B2">
<PARAM NAME=c3 VALUE="fC1+C2">
This Web page requires a <B>Java</B>-enabled Web Browser.
</APPLET>
<HR>
<A HREF="SpreadSheet.java">The source.</A>
</BODY>
</HTML>
```

See also

BarChart and GraphLayout

TicTacToe

The age-old game of tic-tac-toe has been brought to your Web page (Figure 9-20). If you examine the source code, you will see an example of working with the mouse and basic problem solving. The user always makes the first move by clicking on a blank square.

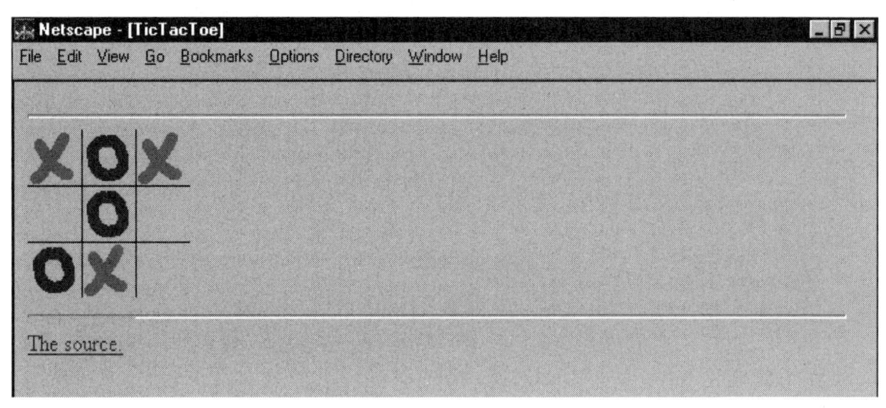

Figure 9-20: A sample tic-tac-toe applet.

Parameters

None.

Example

```
<HTML>
<!- TicTacToeDemo.html ->
<HEAD>
   <TITLE>TicTacToe</TITLE>
</HEAD>
<BODY>
<HR>
<APPLET CODE=TicTacToe.class WIDTH=120 HEIGHT=120>
This Web page requires a <B>Java</B>-enabled Web Browser.
</APPLET>
<HR>
<A HREF="TicTacToe.java">The source.</A>
</BODY>
</HTML>
```

See also

TumblingDuke and UnderConstruction

TumblingDuke

Duke is our old friend, the Java mascot. In this applet, Duke tumbles across the screen in a series of back-bending flips (Figure 9-21). The animation actually consists of 17 frames, numbered T1.GIF through 17.GIF. You could replace the graphics images with your own images, but you might find the general purpose Animator applet more suitable for the task.

Parameters

MAXWIDTH	Specifies the width of the widest image in the animation.
NIMGS	Specifies the number of images in the animation.
OFFSET	Designates the horizontal offset between the last and the first frame.
IMG	Defines the URL address of the directory containing the animation frames.

Example

```
<HTML>
<!- TumblingDukeDemo.html ->
<HEAD>
   <TITLE>Tumbling Duke</TITLE>
</HEAD>
<BODY>
<HR>
<APPLET CODE="TumbleItem.class" WIDTH=600 HEIGHT=95>
<PARAM NAME=maxwidth VALUE="120">
<PARAM NAME=nimgs VALUE="16">
<PARAM NAME=offset VALUE="-57">
<PARAM NAME=img VALUE="images/tumble">
This Web page requires a <B>Java</B>-enabled Web Browser.
</APPLET>
<HR>
<A HREF="TumbleItem.java">The source.</A>
</BODY>
</HTML>
```

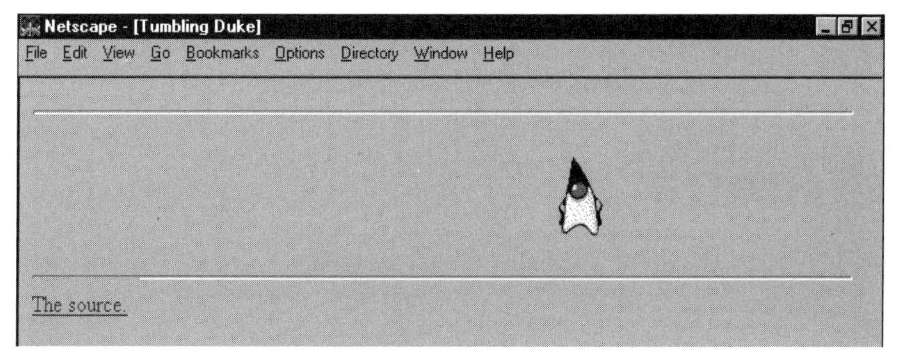

Figure 9-21: The TumblingDukeDemo.

See also

Animator, BlinkingText, and ImageMap

UnderConstruction

Another applet featuring the Java mascot, Duke. This one shows an example of him powering away at a jackhammer (Figure 9-22). You'll want to use this when you're putting the finishing touches on your Web page.

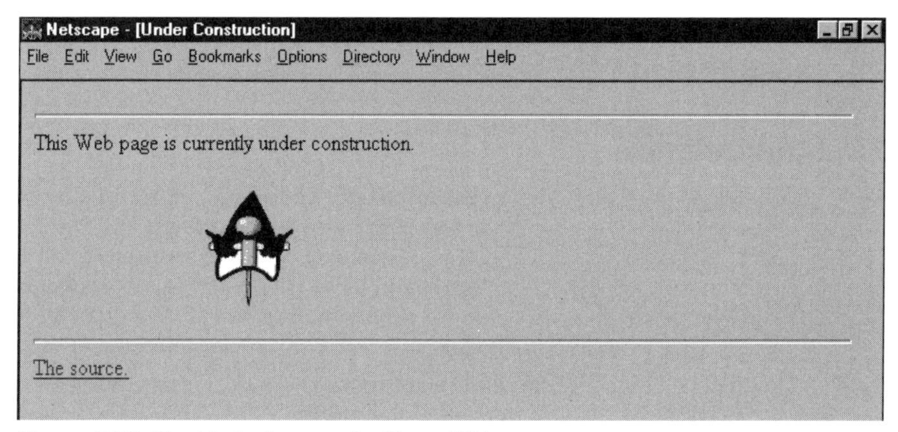

Figure 9-22: The UnderConstructionDemo Web page.

Parameters

None.

Example

```
<HTML>
<!- UnderConstructionDemo.html ->
<HEAD>
   <TITLE>Under Construction</TITLE>
</HEAD>
<BODY>
<HR>
This Web page is currently under construction. <P>
<APPLET CODE="JackhammerDuke.class" WIDTH=300 HEIGHT=100>
This Web page requires a <B>Java</B>-enabled Web Browser.
</APPLET>
<HR>
<A HREF="JackhammerDuke.java">The source.</A>
</BODY>
</HTML>
```

See also

TicTacToe and TumblingDuke

WireFrame

The WireFrame applet (Figure 9-23) displays a wire frame model. The user can rotate the model to any desired angle. The model that is displayed is specified as an external file.

Parameters

`MODEL`	Contains the URL address of a file containing the description of the wire frame model. The format used by the file is the WaveFront .OBJ format. Each line defines a coordinate. Lines that begin with the letter *v* define x-, y-, and z-coordinates. Lines starting with an *f* or *l* define an edge or a set of edges. See the example that follows.
`SCALE`	Designates an optional value that controls the overall scaling of the model. Values should be between .5 and 4.

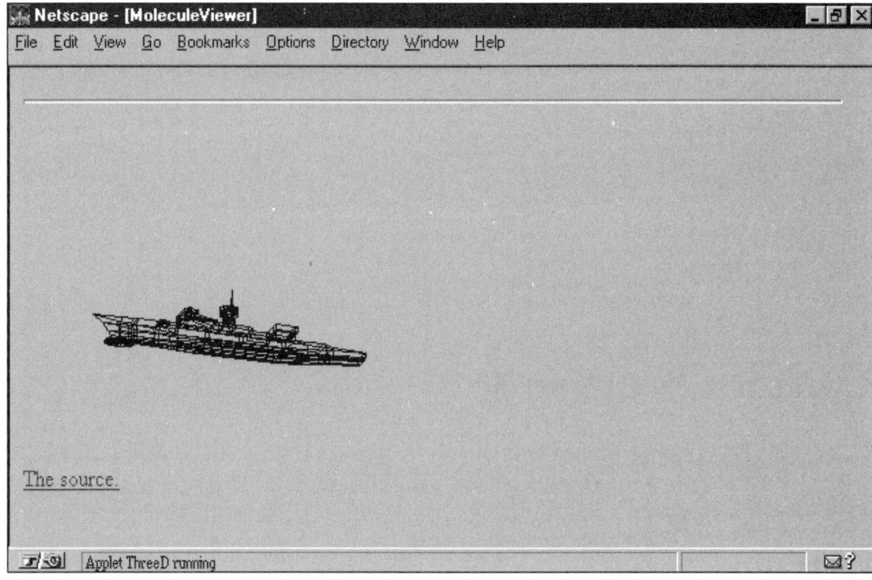

Figure 9-23: Sample WireFrame model.

Example

```
<HTML>
<!- WireFrameDemo.html ->
<HEAD>
   <TITLE>MoleculeViewer</TITLE>
</HEAD>
<BODY>
<HR>
<APPLET CODE=ThreeD.class WIDTH=300 HEIGHT=300>
<PARAM NAME=model VALUE=models/knoxS.obj>
This Web page requires a <B>Java</B>-enabled Web Browser.
</APPLET>
<HR>
<A HREF="ThreeD.java">The source.</A>
</BODY>
</HTML>
```

Here is a short example OBJ file:

```
v 0 0 0
v 1 0 0
v 1 1 0
.
.
```

```
.
1 1 5
1 2 6
1 3 7
1 4 8
```

See also

GraphLayout and MoleculeViewer

Quick Overview

This chapter examined the Java applets that come with the Java Developers Kit. You were able to obtain a good overview for some of the ready-made classes that you can use in your own Web pages. It also provides a source for you to learn about creating your own Web applets.

In particular, this chapter covered the following topics:

- A description of each applet.
- The parameters used by each applet.
- References to other related applets of interest.

Here is a brief overview of what is to come . . .

- Chapter 10, "Network Communications," shows you how to transfer data over the Internet using your Java applet.
- Chapter 11, "User Interface Controls," shows you how to work with Java Windows and find out how to use all those fancy controls, like buttons and list boxes that are associated with fancy graphical operating systems.
- Chapter 12, "Windows and Dialog Boxes," provides valuable information about creating Java applets that create separate windows and dialog boxes that are separate from the basic Web page.

Network Communications

10

In This Chapter

What exceptions are and how they can be helpful when writing network-enabled applets.

How to display a new Web page in the current Web browser window.

How to connect to your Web site and download information.

For a long time, Sun Microsystems has used the marketing theme "The network is the computer." This statement perplexed many computer professionals, who laughed it off as marketing hype. With the incredible growth of the Internet (which is the network of all networks), there is a chance that people at Sun's marketing department really knew what they were talking about — either that or they made a good guess. Either way, when Sun was developing the Java language, the company took the focus of network communications seriously because the Java language has built-in support for accessing data across networks. This chapter examines how you can make these network connections in your applets.

Error Handling

Before discussing network communications, you need to learn about another important topic: error handling. When connecting to networks, a program must be able to detect if that data connection was established. If an error condition results, the program must be able to carry out its task or exit gracefully. You are about to learn about a fantastic error reporting facility that is built into Java.

About error handling

Computer programmers have had to be concerned with checking for errors for as long as computers have been around. A programmer must consider three types of error conditions: those caused by the user (such as incorrect input or files that were once available and no longer are), those caused by the system (low memory), and those caused by the program (trying to access an out-of-bounds array or an invalid memory region).

Programs handle error conditions in different ways. The simplest and best method to handle errors is to display an error message and let the user correct the condition. The worst way of handling errors is for the operating system to catch it and cause a general protection fault, which aborts the program.

As an example, suppose you have a program that loads a file from a disk, and that file has mysteriously been deleted. The program must handle this situation appropriately. Many times, the function used to open the file will return an error code, which your code must check for and respond appropriately.

Suppose for a moment the example of a standard procedural programming language, like C. The `fopen()` function opens a disk file and returns a pointer to a variable type known as `FILE`. Later, in all your file input or output functions, you must use the variable to access the file contents. Take a look at the following sample of C code, which uses regular error handling:

```
FILE *f;

// Attempt to open filename "fname.txt" for read access
f = fopen("fname.txt", "r");
if (f==NULL)
{
   // Error state
   printf("File open error occurred.");
}
else
{
   // Do file I/O here
   //
   // When done, close file
   fclose(f);
}
```

This example is meant to illustrate error handling conditions. The main aspect to notice is that several extra lines of code are dedicated solely to error checking. This leads to somewhat cumbersome code because if you want to write a well-mannered program, your program must constantly be checking for return codes.

Furthermore, different functions report errors in different manners. One function might return a NULL value, whereas another function might return an error code. Still another might return a -1 value. In other words, when using the C programming language, error handling is inconsistent.

You are probably figuring that there must be a better way of checking for errors — and there is. Computer scientists have started to find easier ways of handling errors. Error handling has become more important with the widespread use of computers. Several years ago, if the computer you were using caused an error, you would just restart it and continue your task. However, with the proliferation of computers in almost every area of our lives, shrugging off computer faults and just restarting the computer is not good enough. This is especially true when doing real-life tasks.

Of course, computer errors still happen. Remember how you felt the last time your spreadsheet or word processor program suddenly caused a fatal error that caused the program to abort, thereby swallowing a couple of hours of work? I can tell you (because it just happened to me with an unnamed Windows word processor) that it never feels good to have to redo work that you've already done once. However, as a side benefit, you are actually reading the second draft of this chapter, so it should be better than the first.

Few people believe that computer errors will cease to occur. As a result, programmers have developed more advanced methods of dealing with these error conditions. Just think, wouldn't it be nice to write code with the assumption that no errors would ever occur? At the same time, the code would handle errors on its own. You can achieve this through a mechanism known as *exception handling,* which is built into the Java programming language.

About exception handling

Exception handling provides a clean way for a Java method to abort whatever it is doing and signal that something went wrong. Default error handling prints an error message in the Java console and terminates the applet, but in your code, you can handle these error conditions in a different manner.

An exception has two parts: signaling an exception and setting up an exception handler. To signal an exception, you use the `try` keyword. To set up an exception handler, you use the `catch` keyword. To tell the system that an error has occurred, you use the `throw` keyword. Here is a Java example:

```
FileInputStream fis;

try
{
```

(continued)

```
      // Attempt to open filename "fname.txt"
      fis = new FileInputStream("fname.txt");
   }
   catch (FileNotFoundException e)
   {
      // Error condition
      System.out.println(""File open error occurred.");
   }

   /*************************************/
   // This class is already implemented for you.  You don't
   //  need to write it yourself, this is only a demonstration.
   class FileInputStream
   {
      // Constructor
      FileInputStream(String s)
      {
         if (fileNotAvailable())
            throw new FileNotFoundException();
         else
            // open file and continue
      }
   }
```

The statement inside the braces of the `try` block is written as if no errors happen. If an error occurs inside the `try` block of code, the statements in the `catch` block execute. Notice that the only code executed in the `try` block is that of creating an instance of the `FileInputStream` class.

If the `FileInputStream` class causes an error, it needs some way of signaling an error state, which would execute the code in the catch block of code.

In Java, a class signals an error (such as file not being found) by throwing an exception, which is carried out through the `throw` keyword. When the class throws an exception, control returns to the `catch` block of code. Do you get it? The error condition throws an exception, and the error recover catches the error. This results in a very consistent way of handling errors.

Notice that when an exception is signaled, the `catch` block of code always handles it. You can have more than one `catch` keyword for every `try` block, where each catch statement can handle a certain kind of exception. For example:

```
FileInputStream fis;

try
{
   // Attempt to open filename "fname.txt"
   fis = new FileInputStream("fname.txt");
}
catch (FileNotFoundException e)
{
   // Error condition
   System.out.println(""File open error occurred.");
}
catch (InterruptedException e)
{
   // Handle exception
}
catch (RunTimeException e)
{
   // Handle exception
}
```

Table 10-1 lists many of the different types of exceptions that are already part of the Java class library. Obviously, each exception is valid only in certain situations. Furthermore, you can write your own exceptions by inheriting from the generic `Exception` class.

Table 10-1 Run-Time Exceptions in Java

Exception Name	Description
`ArithmeticException`	Integer division by zero.
`ArrayIndexOutOfBoundsException`	An invalid array index has been used.
`ArrayStoreException`	The wrong type of object has been stored in an array.
`ClassCastException`	An invalid cast has occurred.
`ClassNotFoundException`	The class could not be found.
`CloneNotSupportedException`	The object cannot be cloned.
`Exception`	A generic exception.
`FileNotFound`	The file was not available.
`IllegalAccessException`	The particular method could not be found.

(continued)

Table 10-1 ***(continued)***

Exception Name	Description
`IllegalArgumentException`	An illegal argument has been passed to a method.
`IllegalMonitorStateException`	An illegal monitor operation has occurred.
`IndexOutOfBoundsException`	The index value is out of bounds.
`InstantiationException`	Cannot instantiate an abstract class.
`NegativeArraySizeException`	The array size cannot be negative.
`NoSuchMethodException`	The method could not be found.
`NullPointerException`	An attempt to access a null object or array.
`NumberFormatException`	An invalid number format occurred.
`RuntimeException`	A run-time error has occurred.
`SecurityException`	Security has been violated.
`StringIndexOutOfBoundsException`	The string index is out of range.

Suppose you absolutely must perform a certain action, no matter what happens. It might be to free some external resource or close a file. Java has made provisions for this. You use the `finally` keyword to specify a block of statements that will execute no matter what. Here is an example:

```
int x;

try
{
   x = 25 / 0;
}
finally
{
   System.out.print("It is poor programming practice  ");
   System.out.println("to divide integer numbers by zero");

   // Any other kind of cleanup goes here
}
```

In many cases, you will combine all three keywords so that the system will try to execute a piece of code, catch an exception, and then force the block of code denoted by the `finally` keyword to execute. Here is a generic example of using the `try...catch...finally` set of keywords:

```
try
{
   // Try this block of code.
}
catch (Exception e)
{
   // Catch errors.  Error condition.  Handle error.
}
finally
{
   // Code which is executed no matter what happens.
}
```

Once you start using exception handling in your code, you will find it a superior way of handling error conditions.

The way you format your source code has little to do with the final operation of the applet. I like to start curly braces on a new line. Many people like to make their code more compact and will combine curly braces on the same line as some Java keywords.

Displaying a New Web Page

The most basic network operation a Java applet might wish to carry out is replacing the current Web page with a different one. An applet can display a new Web page at spaced intervals of time to create a slide show effect.

The uniform resource locator class

To link to a new Web page, the applet must supply a uniform resource locator (URL) address that tells the Web browser what page to retrieve and display. Java provides a URL class that stores this information for you. Several overloaded constructors are available so that you can provide URL information with great versatility. The easiest is to supply just a string with the appropriate address:

```
URL url = null;
url = new URL("http:\\www.idgbooks.com\index.html");
```

Notice that pre-initializing the URL object to `null` is a good idea. The compiler seems to require that URL objects be assigned to the `null` value when they are declared. Another method to create a URL object is to specify each component of the URL (the protocol, host name, and filename) separately. Here is an example:

```
URL url = null;
url = new URL("http", "www.idgbooks.com", "index.html");
```

If you want to retrieve a file from your own Web page, an alternative method is to call the `getDocumentBase()` method to retrieve the base Web address and then specify the HTML file as a separate parameter, like this:

```
is = new URL(getDocumentBase(), "index.html")
```

Finally, the URL class even allows you to choose different transfer protocols. You can choose between hypertext transfer protocol (http), ftp (file transfer protocol), gopher (a menu system), and file (a local disk file). Here is an example of an ftp request:

```
URL url = null;
url = new URL("ftp", "idgbooks.com", "coolstuff.zip");
```

This will cause the Web browser to download a file named coolstuff.zip from the ftp site named idgbooks.com. For those Internet junkies who know about TCP/IP and port address, you can use the most verbose form of the URL constructor, which lets you specify a port address (the Web always uses port 80). It looks like this:

```
URL url = null;
url = new URL("http", "www.idgbooks.com", 80, "main.html");
```

Now your applet has an object of type `URL` that indicates exactly what Web page to display. The next step is to get an applet context and then make a request to the Web browser to display a new Web page.

Getting the applet context

Once an applet has a URL address, it can create an applet context by calling the `getAppletContext()` method. With the applet context, the applet can finally call the `showDocument()` method, which takes a URL address and will display the new Web page. Here is an example:

```
URL url = null;
AppletContext ac;

url = new URL("http://www.idgbooks.com/index.com");
ac = GetAppletContext();
ac.showDocument(url);
```

You are not totally done yet, however. Remember what you learned about error handling? Now is the perfect time to make use of the exception handling information that you learned about earlier. After all, the URL address you specify may possibly be in an incorrect format. This could especially be true if the information was passed to your applet from a user. Here is code that links to a new Web page and supports exception handling:

```
URL url = null;

try
{
   url = new URL("http://www.idgbooks.com/index.html");
}
catch (MalformedURLException e)
{
   System.out.println("Bad URL address: " + url);
}
getAppletContext().showDocument(url);
```

Notice that the code was shortened by combining some of the lines of variable declaration with variable instantiation. This piece of code makes sure that the URL address supplied is in the correct format. If it is not, the system prints an error message on the Java Console.

Sample code

OK. It's time for some real code. Listing 10-1 is a sample program (see Figure 10-1) called ClickLink.java, which displays an image that appears like a user interface button (it is actually a three-dimensional rectangle) and waits for the user to click on it. When the user does so, the applet displays a new Web page. All the parameters come from the HTML file (see Table 10-2), so you can use it in as many Web pages as you like.

Listing 10-1 ClickLink.java Sample Code

```
/*
 *  ClickLink.java - Clickable hyperlink implementation
 *
 *  Creating Cool Web Applets with Java
 *  By: Paul J. Perry,  Publisher: IDG Books
 *
 *  HTML Parameters:
```

(continued)

Listing 10-1 *(continued)*

```
 *   Target - Target file to display.  Assumes base address.
 *   Text   - Text to display.
 *   Width  - Width of button image.
 *   Height - Height of button image.
 */

import java.applet.*;
import java.awt.*;
import java.net.*;

public class ClickLink extends java.applet.Applet
{
   // Data members
   int width;
   int height;
   boolean selected = false;

   // Initialization
   public void init()
   {
       // Set size of "click" area in applet
       String s = getParameter("Width");
       width = Integer.parseInt(s);
       s = getParameter("Height");
       height = Integer.parseInt(s);

       resize(width, height);
   }

   void linkNewDestination()
   {
       URL homePage = null;

      try
      {
         homePage = new URL(getDocumentBase(),
                   getParameter("Target"));
       }
      catch (MalformedURLException e)
      {
         System.out.println("Bad URL address: " +
                         getParameter("target"));
      }

      getAppletContext().showDocument(homePage);
```

```
    }

    // Mouse down event
    public boolean mouseDown(Event evt, int x, int y)
    {
        selected = true;
        repaint();
        return true;
    }

    // Mouse up event
    public boolean mouseUp(Event evt, int x, int y)
    {
        selected = false;
        repaint();
        linkNewDestination();
        return true;
    }

    // Display the information
    public void paint(Graphics g)
    {
        // Decide which color to display
        if (selected)
        {
            g.setColor(Color.gray);
        }
        else
        {
            g.setColor(Color.lightGray);
        }
        // Draw 3D rectangle
        g.fill3DRect(0, 0, width, height, true);
        // Display centered text
        g.setColor(Color.black);
        String str = getParameter("Text");
        FontMetrics fm = g.getFontMetrics();
        int w = fm.stringWidth(str);
        int h = fm.getHeight();
        Dimension r = size();
        g.drawString(str, (r.width-w)/2,
                     (r.height-h)/2);
    }
}
```

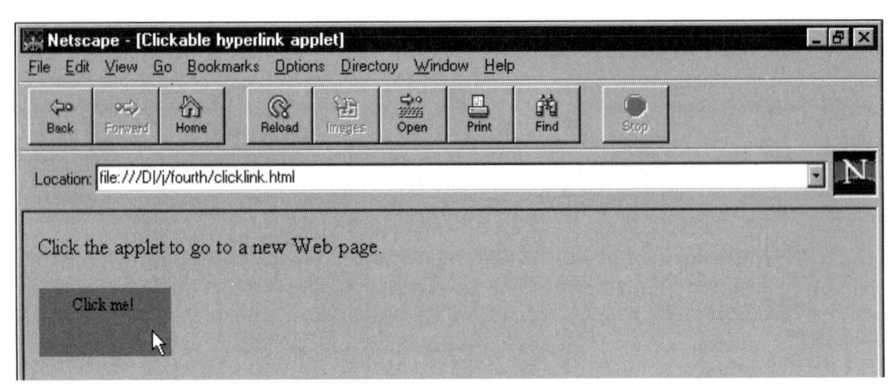

Figure 10-1: The ClickLink Web page demonstration.

Table 10-2 ClickLink.class Parameters

Parameter	Description
`Target`	The target file to display
`Text`	The text to display
`Width`	The width of the button image
`Height`	The height of the button image

Listing 10-2 is the ClickLink.html Web page, and Listing 10-3 is the ClickLink2.html Web page. Each of these pages is alternatively displayed as the user clicks on the button located in each page.

Listing 10-2 ClickLink.html Web Page

```
<HTML>
<!- ClickLink.html ->
<HEAD>
   <TITLE>Clickable hyperlink applet</TITLE>
</HEAD>
<BODY>
Click the applet to go to a new Web page.<P><P>
<APPLET CODE="ClickLink.class" WIDTH="100" HEIGHT="50">
 <PARAM NAME="Width"   VALUE="100">
 <PARAM NAME="Height"  VALUE="50">
 <PARAM NAME="Text"     VALUE="Click me!">
 <PARAM NAME="Target"  VALUE="clicklink2.html">
This Web page requires a <B>Java</B>-enabled Web Browser.
</APPLET>
</BODY>
</HTML>
```

Listing 10-3 ClickLink2.html Web Page

```
<HTML>
<!- ClickLink2.html ->
<HEAD>
   <TITLE>Clickable hyperlink applet</TITLE>
</HEAD>
<BODY>
<H1>Click the applet to go to a new Web page.</H1><P><P>
<APPLET CODE="ClickLink.class" WIDTH="100" HEIGHT="50">
 <PARAM NAME="Width"   VALUE="100">
 <PARAM NAME="Height"  VALUE="50">
 <PARAM NAME="Text"     VALUE="Click me!">
 <PARAM NAME="Target"  VALUE="clicklink.html">
This Web page requires a <B>Java</B>-enabled Web Browser.
</APPLET>
</BODY>
</HTML>
```

Because you have come this far, the operation of the program should be pretty simple. In the `init()` method, the code obtains the width and height parameters from the HTML file using the `getParameter()` method. The `paint()` method is called to display the text and rectangle.

Initially, the variable name selected is set to false. When the user clicks over the applet with the mouse, the `mouseDown()` method is called, which sets the selected variable to true and also instructs the applet to repaint itself. When the rectangle is displayed this time, it will have a dark gray color. When the user releases the mouse button, the `mouseUp()` method is called, which redraws the applet area and calls the `linkNewDestination()` method, which in turn calls the `showDocument()` method to tell the Web browser to display a new Web page that was passed into the applet from the HTML file.

Opening Files at Your Web Site

Rather than just telling the Web browser to display a new Web page, you might actually want to access the contents of a file and use it as data for something the applet is doing. For example, one of the sample applets (called WireFrame) that comes with the Java Development Kit displays wire frame three-dimensional images. It actually obtains the data for the images from a data file on the Web server.

For security reasons, you can access data files only on the Web server where the Java applet originated.

The URL class has a method that returns an object of type `InputStream`. Here is an example of opening a stream:

```
// Data objects
URL                  url = null;
InputStream          is;
DataInputStream      dis;
BufferedInputStream  bis;
String               txt;

// Get a URL address
try
{
   url = new URL("http://www.idgbooks.com/index.html");
}
catch (MalformedURLException e)
{
   System.out.println("Bad URL address: " + url);
}

// Open that file for input, and access it
try
{
   is = url.openStream();
   bis = new BufferedInputStream(is);
   dis = new DataInputStream(bis);

   while ((txt = dis.readLine()) != null)
   {
       System.out.println(txt);
   }
}
catch (IOException e)
{
   System.out.println("File open error: " + e.getMessage());
}
```

A lot appears to be happening here, but when you distill the code to its essentials, you will realize that this is not difficult. The first part of the code creates a URL address. Next, the program calls the `openStream()` method, which is the URL class to return an object of type `InputStream`. Next, the code passes the object of type `InputStream` to the `BufferedInputStream` constructor. This object in turn is passed to the `DataInputStream()` constructor. You are now at the point where the applet can start to read data.

The code sets up a `while` loop that uses the `readLine()` method to read every line of the file. It then displays the file contents in the Java Console. As you can see, the code has full exception handling.

Your program might use the separate file as a data file and parse information out of it, much like the WireFrame viewer.

As an example, the sample applet retrieves a text file from the Web server and displays the contents of that file in the applet screen area (see Figure 10-2). Listing 10-4 is the ViewFile.java sample source code, and Listing 10-5 is the ViewFile.html Web page that you will need to use to view the Web page. Listing 10-6 contains the ViewFile.txt sample text file, which the ViewFile applet accesses.

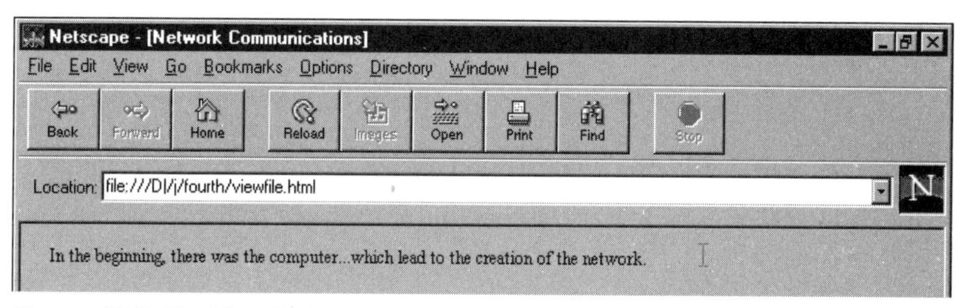

Figure 10-2: The ViewFile.java applet.

Listing 10-4 ViewFile.java Sample Source Code

```
/*
 *  ViewFile.java - Downloads text file over the
 *   network.
 *
 *  Creating Cool Web Applets with Java
 *  By: Paul J. Perry,  Publisher: IDG Books
 *
 */

import java.applet.*;
import java.awt.*;
import java.net.*;
import java.io.*;

public class ViewFile extends java.applet.Applet
{
   // Data objects
   URL                  url = null;
   InputStream          is;
   DataInputStream      dis;
```

(continued)

Listing 10-4 *(continued)*

```
    BufferedInputStream  bis;
    String               txt;
    StringBuffer         buf;

    // Initialization
    public void init()
    {
       // Get a URL address
       try
       {
          url = new URL(getDocumentBase(), "ViewFile.txt");
       }
       catch (MalformedURLException e)
       {
          System.out.println("Bad URL address: " + url);
       }

        // Create string buffer to store text read from file
        buf = new StringBuffer();

       // Open file for input, and read it into txt string
       try
       {
          is = url.openStream();
          bis = new BufferedInputStream(is);
          dis = new DataInputStream(bis);

          while ((txt = dis.readLine()) != null)
                buf.append(txt);
       }
       catch (IOException e)
       {
          System.out.println("File open error: " + e.getMessage());
       }
        finally
        {
           repaint();
        }
    }
    // This is where the graphics processing is done.
    public void paint(Graphics g)
    {
       g.drawString(buf.toString(), 10, 10);
    }
}
```

Listing 10-5 **ViewFile.html Web Page**

```
<HTML>
<!- ViewFile.html ->
<HEAD>
   <TITLE> Network Communications</TITLE>
</HEAD>
<BODY>
<APPLET CODE="ViewFile.class" WIDTH="450" HEIGHT="200">
This Web page requires a <B>Java</B>-enabled Web Browser.
</APPLET>
</BODY>
</HTML>
```

Listing 10-6 **ViewFile.txt Text File**

```
In the beginning, there was the computer...
which led to the creation of the network.
```

Communicating with Sockets

Sockets might sound like a forbidding term. Some people think of electrical sockets. I think of socket wrenches. However, the type of communication that you can accomplish with either of these sockets is limited. Network sockets are what make Internet networking possible. They allow a program to set up a conversation between two computers.

When you write to a socket, the data you send automatically appears at the other end of the socket. The other end might be another process running on the same machine, or it could be a computer that is halfway around the world. Sockets are two-way communication channels between two points.

Because of security restrictions, Java applets can only open sockets that connect back to the Web site from where the applet originated.

Under UNIX, sockets appear as disk files. Under Windows, programmers rely on WinSockets. However, with Java, built-in functionality for accessing data with sockets is already available. In fact, a class (called appropriately enough, `Socket`) is already available that makes accessing another computer easy.

You can find the Socket class support in Java in the java.net package, so any program that has socket access must use the appropriate import statement, as follows:

```
import java.net.*;
```

A socket connection has two sides: the server and the client. A server creates a socket and listens for a connection. Sockets use an address and a port number to form a unique connection. The server usually has a well-known port number and name. Clients can use the servers address and port number to connect. When a client makes a connection, the system assigns a private socket for the connection so that the server can continue to listen for other client requests.

Client socket connections

The Socket class provides a client socket implementation, similar to that used in UNIX sockets and WinSock. To open a new connection, you create an instance of the Socket class. You must specify the host name and the port number. For example:

```
Socket s;
s = new Socket("idgbooks.com", 80);
```

This specifies a host name of idgbooks.com and connects on port number 80. Once you have created a connection, you can read or write from that socket by creating input or output streams. Here is an example of opening a socket for reading:

```
DataInputStream      dis;
BufferedInputStream  bis;
InputStream          is;
String               s;

is = s.getInputStream();
bis = new BufferedInputStream(is);
dis = new DataInputStream(bis);

// Read line
s = dis.readLine();
```

Here is an example of writing to a socket:

```
DataOutputStream      dos;
BufferedOutputStream  bos;
```

```
OutputStream          os;
String                s;

os = s.getOutputStream();
bos = new BufferedOutputStream(os);
dos = new DataOutputStream(bos);

dos.WriteChars(s)
```

When you are done with the socket, you should close it with the `close()` method, as follows:

```
s.close();
```

Server socket connections

Server sockets are similar, but a server socket implementation must listen for data requests from the TCP port. When a client socket tries to connect to that port, the `accept()` method forms a connection from that client.

To create a server socket, you must instantiate the `ServerSocket` class. Here is an example:

```
ServerSocket ss = new ServerSocket(10);

// When ready to make a connection
ss.accept();
```

This listens for data requests from the specified port (10 in this case). When the program is ready to listen to a specific client request, you use the `accept()` method. Just like for a client socket connection, when the connection is done, you should call the `close()` method to end the socket connection.

By using a combination of server and client sockets, you can create true client-server programs. The TCP/IP and the entire Internet are based on socket connections. Obviously, sockets are more involved than the introduction I've given you. If the standard functions for accessing data at your Web site are not enough, you should be able to do what you want using the socket support in Java.

Quick Overview

This chapter took a look at network communications. You started out learning about error handling and Java exceptions. The chapter continued to teach you about the URL class and how to display a new Web page within the browser. You then moved to retrieving a file over network using input and output classes.

In particular, this chapter covered the following topics:

- Exception handling provides a consistent method of handling errors in a Java applet.
- The URL class allows a program to store a Web address. You can use the `showDocument()` method of the `AppletContext` class to display a new Web page.
- A Web applet can open a data file with the `openStream()` method of the URL class. In turn, it can be passed to a new `BufferedInputStream` class, which in turn can be passed to a `DataInputStream` class to allow for file input and output.
- Sockets provide a way for opening up a communication channel between a server and a client. Java provides the `Socket` and `ServerSocket` classes for carrying out these communications.

Here is a brief overview of what is to come...

- Chapter 11, "User Interface Controls," shows you how to work with Java windows and find out how to use all those fancy controls, like buttons and list boxes that are associated with fancy graphical operating systems.
- Chapter 12, "Windows and Dialog Boxes," provides valuable information about creating Java applets that create windows and dialog boxes that are separate from those created by the Web page.

User Interface Controls

In This Chapter

An overview of the controls that compose the Abstract Windowing Toolkit.

What layout managers are and how to specify the position of controls within a Java applet.

How to create and process the standard Java controls.

The difference with controlling the enhanced Java controls.

How to control the status line in a Web browser.

This chapter looks at creating a consistent user interface with Java applets. In some ways, the user interface is the most important part of a program. A computer program is meant to accomplish something. If a user can't make use of the program's features because the interface is complicated or unclear, the program is rendered completely useless. This is true even if the program has some of the most advanced internal algorithms ever devised. This fact turns the user interface into a key component of the final product, and this is why we learn how to use Java's built-in user interface system in this chapter.

About User Interface Controls

No doubt computer user interfaces have come a long way in the last five or ten years. No longer are users required to type long, confusing command lines. For the most part, users don't have to relearn a new way of interacting with an application in order to get up to speed with a new piece of software. If you know how to use one application, you are already halfway up to speed when it comes to using another application based on the same user interface.

Far and away, the graphical user interface (GUI) is responsible for this ease of use. The GUI first became a commercial reality with the Apple Macintosh computer and now has become a standard part of almost every computer sold, compliments to Microsoft Windows. Even UNIX-based computers, which have had a reputation as having the most confusing command lines, have had a windowing environment (usually X Windows) for many years. Unfortunately, writing a program is different for each of these environments.

Therefore, you should not be surprised to know that a newly developed programming language like Java has built-in support for creating graphical user interface controls. Because Java is a cross-platform language, the user interface is also cross-platform. The GUI support in Java is not so much in the language as in the classes that come with it. In fact, the applets you have developed have all been based on the `Applet` class, which is part of the windowing class that we examine in this chapter. Much of the support for loading images and displaying them, as well as playing audio files and drawing lines, is part of the windowing class, too.

Java calls its windowing classes the Abstract Windowing Toolkit, or AWT for short (early documents call it "Another Window Toolkit," but when Java became so popular, the developers changed the name). By creating applets based on these classes, your code will execute on any of the platforms supported by Java-enhanced Web browsers and still maintain a consistent and familiar user interface.

Working with Controls

The AWT library contains routines for creating separate windows and dialog boxes (as we'll see in Chapter 12). Before you can start creating these windows and dialog boxes, however, you need to learn how to work with the basic components of the user interface. You will be able to make good use of this knowledge because you can embed these basic components directly into a Java applet without having to create separate windows.

A complete user interface combines multiple components or controls to work in unison, which allows the user to enter information that your applet then processes. The AWT contains support for the following (see Figure 11-1) built-in components, or controls:

- **Labels** provide a way to display text that doesn't change.
- **Buttons** trigger an immediate action when the user "presses" (or clicks) on them.

- **Checkboxes** allow the user to toggle an option on or off.
- **Radio buttons** allow the user to select one option from a group of options.
- **Choice items** use little screen space and are a way to let the user select one option from a large group of options.
- **Text fields** enable the user to enter a single line of text.
- **List items** provide another way for the user to select one option from a large group of options.
- **Scrollbars** enable you to prompt the user for linear values and come in two types: horizontal and vertical.
- **Text areas** provide a way for the user to enter multiple lines of text.

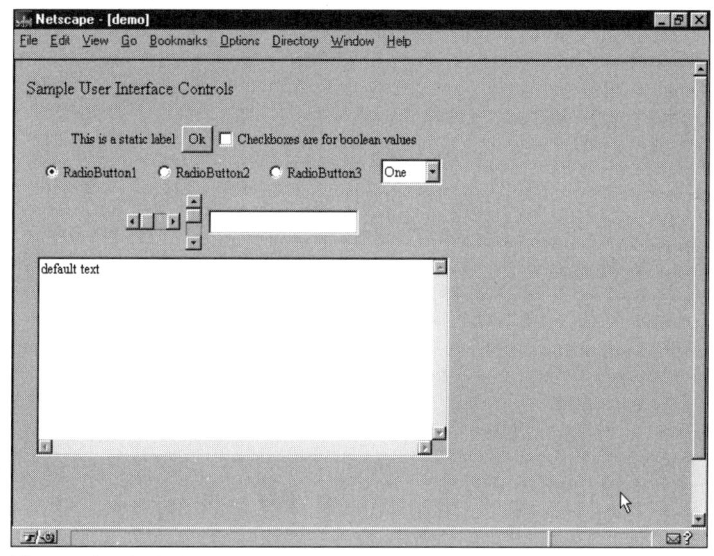

Figure 11-1: Built-in Abstract Window Toolkit (AWT) controls.

Each control interacts with the user in a different manner. As you can see, some obtain text input from the user. Others trigger an immediate action or query the user for a boolean value. The controls are the building blocks for the user interface of your applet. To create your user interface, you add a combination of controls to an applet.

First, you have to decide which controls to use. You have to think about the type of information your program needs and then use the controls that work most appropriately with that data. After learning how the controls work and how they are designed to interact with the user, the decision as to which controls to use will come with experience.

The first six controls (labels, buttons, checkboxes, radio buttons, choice items, and text fields) are considered the standard controls, while the last three (list items, scrollbars, and text areas) are considered enhanced controls. The big difference between standard and enhanced controls, as you will see in detail, is how a program detects user interaction. You begin with the standard controls, and once you have a good understanding of how they work, you will move on to the enhanced controls.

Creating controls

Each control has an associated class. To create a control, you must instantiate the class, which provides all the behavior for the control. Once you have an instance of the control class, you must make the applet aware of the control, which you do with the `add()` method. The label is the simplest of all the controls. Here is an example of creating a label control:

```
Label l;
l = new Label("This is a static label");
add(l);
```

Although you are going to examine how to create and manipulate each type of control in great detail, this example gives you an idea for how it is done. The code passes the text to be displayed in the label as a parameter to the `Label()` class constructor. The last line shows the use of the `add()` method to associate the control with the applet. Before going into more detail about working with controls, you need to take a look at how an applet controls the placement of these user interface controls.

Understanding Layout Managers

When writing Java applets, you must remember that you cannot target your applet to any specific platform: you cannot assume that your target user will be running Microsoft Windows, Apple Mac OS, Sun Solaris, LINUX, or any other system that supports Java. Furthermore, you cannot assume anything about the size of the computer screen where your applet will be running. This is especially true when creating applets. Remember, Java applets run inside the main Window of the Web browser. The user could be running on a very large screen but confine the Web browser to a small area of that, and your applet would still not have the space it might require. Luckily, Web browsers allow the user to simulate a larger viewing area through the use of scrollbars. If part of the Web page is out of view, the user can move it into view using the scrollbars and continue to interact with it.

When laying out the controls, you have a couple of choices, all based on layout managers. Remember, you specify the width and height of your Java applet as parameters to the <APPLET> tag in the HTML file, but your applet isn't stuck with these sizes and can change its size with the `resize()` method. Part of designing the user interface is deciding where controls will appear within its screen space. Java's use of the layout manager helps you decide how the user interface will appear to the user.

Choosing control locations

Most development systems rely on hard-coded values to determine where user interface controls appear within a page, but the Java developers considered this too restrictive. Furthermore, if an applet were to run on multiple platforms, how could you ever hard-code a specific offset? The Java developers came up with a system that relies on layout managers. The appearance of controls inside a Web applet is based on two things: the order in which controls are added to an applet and the layout manager that is currently active.

The layout manager determines how controls appear in a Java applet without having to specify hard-coded coordinate values. You can choose a different layout manager to have controls be laid out differently.

The following list provides an overview of the standard layout managers:

- `FlowLayout`. The default layout manager. All user interface controls are added one at a time, from left to right. If a component does not fit on a row, it's wrapped onto the next row.
- `Grid`. You partition the applet window area into a grid of columns and rows. Each user interface control is placed in a cell within the grid, going from left to right and top to bottom. This layout manager provides fairly precise control over where the user interface components will appear within the Applet.
- `Border`. The applet window area is divided into geographic sections: north, east, south, west, and center. You indicate the placement of user interface controls when you add them to the applet. Each control is laid out with as much space as it needs. The component in the center (if any) occupies the space that is left over.
- `Card`. Used to make better use of screen space, you use this layout manager to choose a series of controls to display at different times. When you add controls to the card layout, they are not all displayed at once. Methods select which named card will be displayed. You'll use this layout manager when creating more complex user interfaces.
- `GridBagLayout`. This is the most advanced layout manager and allows an applet to put weights on each control within the applet. If the applet is resized, the controls with the highest weight occupy more of the screen area.

Besides using these predefined layout managers, Java provides you with the flexibility to create your own. You really don't need to go to all the trouble, however, because the layout managers provided are more than enough. In fact, you probably don't need to know about all the layout managers here because one or two of them are all you will probably need, but let's take a closer look at each of them anyway.

FlowLayout

The `FlowLayout` layout manager is the most basic of layouts. It is also the default, so if you don't specify any other layout manager, this is the one the system will automatically use. With this layout manager, whenever new controls are added to an applet, they are added from left to right and top to bottom (see Figure 11-2). If a control does not fit at the end of a row, it is merely wrapped to the next row. Each control only takes the amount of space it requires. As a result, if a control needs more space, it receives more; as a corollary, if the control needs less space, it will receive less.

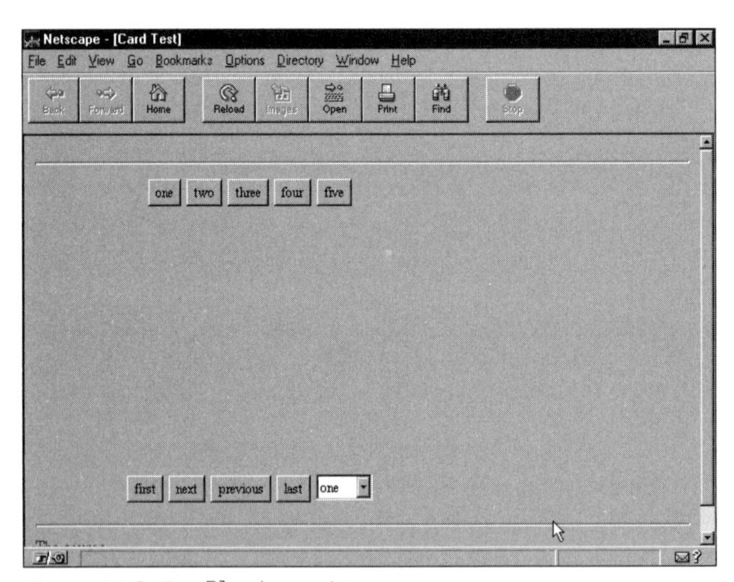

Figure 11-2: The `FlowLayout` layout manager.

You can specify the alignment of the controls in a row. By default, each row is center-aligned, but you can also use left- or right-alignment options.

To create a basic flow layout with a centered alignment, use the following notation:

```
public void init()
{
   setLayout(new FlowLayout(FlowLayout.CENTER));
}
```

The layout manager is commonly specified in the `init()` method because this code will execute only once, at the time the applet is initialized. You specify the alignment as the first parameter to the `FlowLayout()` constructor. You have the choice of `FlowLayout.CENTER`, `FlowLayout.LEFT`, and `FlowLayout.RIGHT`.

You can also specify the number of pixels that should be left between controls. This is referred to as the *gap area* in the Java language documentation. For example:

```
public void init()
{
   setLayout(new FlowLayout(FlowLayout.LEFT, 5, 5));
}
```

This creates a flow layout with left-alignment and a gap of 5 pixels for both horizontal and vertical spacing. The horizontal and vertical gap values are optional. If you don't specify them, the system uses the default value of 3 pixels.

Grid

The `Grid` layout manager splits the applet area up into a grid of columns and rows. As you add a control to the applet, `Grid` places it in a grid cell. The system always starts at the top-left corner and moves from left to right, and top to bottom (see Figure 11-3).

When you create a grid layout, you must specify the number of rows and columns. Java will evenly divide the applet screen area into the number of rows and columns you specify. An example follows:

```
public void init()
{
   setLayout(new GridLayout(4, 4));
}
```

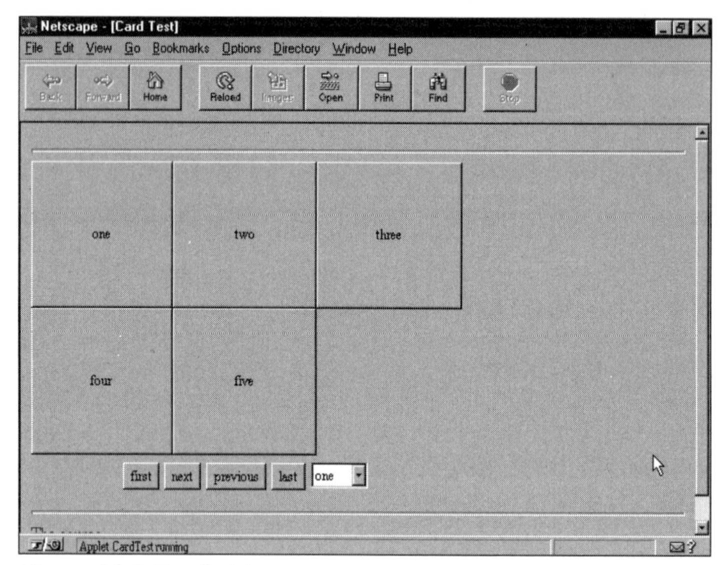

Figure 11-3: The `Grid` layout manager.

Here, the first parameter to the `Gridlayout()` constructor is the number of rows and the second parameter is the number of columns. If you don't like the default spacing of a 3-pixel gap around each control, you can change it, as follows:

```
public void init()
{
   setLayout(new GridLayout(4, 4, 10, 10));
}
```

This forces a 10-pixel gap around each control.

Border

`Border` layouts are a bit peculiar because this layout manager divides the applet screen area into geographic locations: north, south, west, east, and one extra location called center (see Figure 11-4). As a result, an applet based on the border layout can only hold five user interface controls.

To create a border layout, use the following code:

```
public void init()
{
   setLayout(new BorderLayout());
}
```

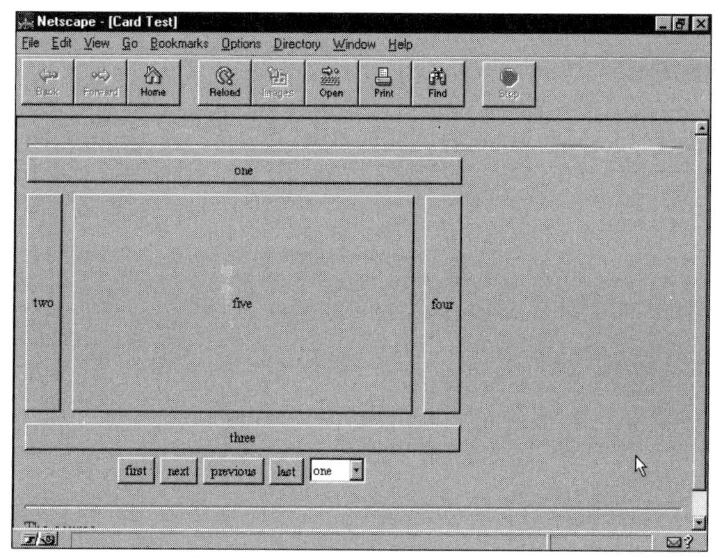

Figure 11-4: The Border layout manager.

The `BorderLayout()` constructor takes no parameters and is easy to use. If you want to specify the grid space, you can do that, too. Here is the format:

```
public void init()
{
   setLayout(new BorderLayout(8, 8));
}
```

This specifies an 8-pixel gap size. When you add controls to the applet, you must specify where the controls appear by providing the location to the `add()` method. The first parameter to the `add()` method takes a string describing the location where that control should appear. Here is an example:

```
public void init()
{
   Label l = new Label("This is a static label");

   add("North", l);
   add("South", l);
   add("East", l);
   add("West", l);
   add("Center", l);
}
```

If you use one of this form to add controls with the other layout managers, the location argument is ignored because it's not used.

Card

The `Card` layout is best used when you have a screen area that should contain different user interface controls at different times. Usually, when you use the card layout, you will create several different panels. You then have multiple panels, and you use the card layout manager to choose which panel should be displayed. With this layout, you can use screen space more efficiently. If you have used the new tabbed dialog boxes (sometimes called property sheets) in Windows 95, you can imagine how the Card layout manager works.

Here is an example of how to create a Card layout manager:

```
public void init()
{
    setLayout(new CardLayout());
}
```

To make real use of the `Card` layout manager, you should know about panels: a *panel* is a way to group controls within an area of an existing window. By creating multiple panels, each with unique controls, you can use the card layout manager to control which panel should be visible.

Each Java applet has a panel that fits inside the screen area of the entire applet. Therefore, you are using panels whether you know it or not. However, multiple panels seem to crop up mostly in standalone Java applications and are not used as frequently with Java applets.

GridBagLayout

The `GridBagLayout` layout manager is the most sophisticated, flexible layout manager provided by Java. It aligns components vertically and horizontally without requiring that the components be the same size (see Figure 11-5).

Each `GridBagLayout` uses a rectangular grid of cells, with each component occupying one or more cells (called its *display area*). Each control managed by a `GridBagLayout` is associated with a `GridBagConstraints` class that specifies how the component is laid out in its display area. The way a `GridBagLayout` places a set of components depends on each component's `GridBagConstraints` and the minimum size and the preferred size of the component's container.

To use a `GridBagLayout` effectively, you must customize one or more `GridBagConstraints` classes. The number of `GridBagConstraints` data members is plentiful. The `gridx` and `gridy` data members specify the cell at the top-left of the display area. The `gridwidth` and `gridheight` members specify the number of cells in a row and column. The `weightx` and `weighty` members determine how to distribute space within the applet. Unless you specify a

weight for at least one component in a row (`weightx`) and column (`weighty`), each component clumps together in the center of its container. This is because when the weight is zero (the default), the `GridBagLayout` puts any extra space between its grid of cells and the edges of the container. The `fill` data member determines whether (and how) to resize the component. Valid values are `GridBagConstraint.NONE` (the default), `GridBagConstraint.HORIZONTAL` (make the component wide enough to fill its display area horizontally, but don't change the height), `GridBagConstraint.VERTICAL` (make the component tall enough to fill the display area vertically, but don't change its width), and `GridBagConstraint.BOTH` (make the component fill its display area entirely).

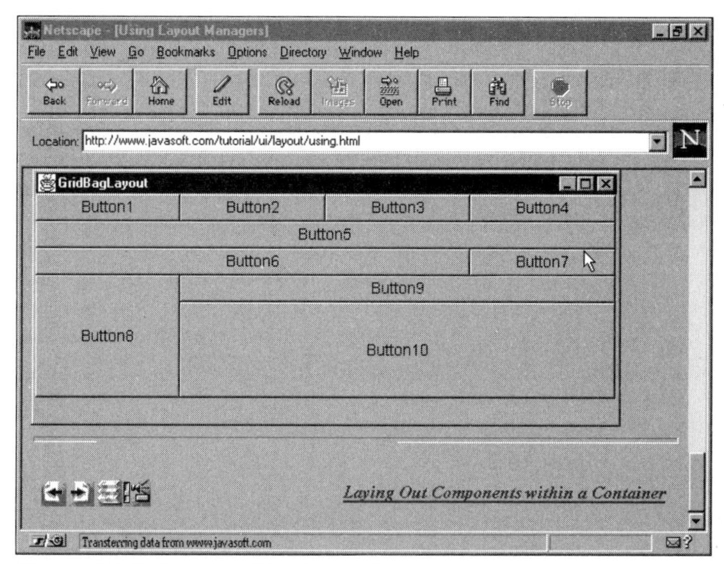

Figure 11-5: The `GridBagLayout` layout manager.

To use a layout based on the `GridBagLayout` layout manager, you must first select it as the current layout manager (using the `setLayout()` method). You then must create a `GridBagConstraints()` object for each control within the applet. After that, you must specify the constraint information. Here is an example:

```
public void init()
{
   // Create GridBagLayout object, and select layout manager
   GridBagLayout gridbag = new GridBagLayout();
   setLayout(gridbag);

   // Create instance of GridBagConstraints to specify informa-
tion
```

```
    //  about each control in the applet.
    GridBagConstraints c = new GridBagConstraints();
    c.fill = GridBagConstraints.BOTH;
    c.weightx = 1.0;
}
```

As you can see, the `GridBagLayout` layout manager has much information you can specify as to laying out controls. If you are creating an applet that requires this functionality, you should check the Java language documentation for greater detail.

Working with Standard Controls

The development environments for many mature Windows programming languages like Visual Basic, Delphi Developer, Paradox for Windows, and Microsoft Access provide tools that allow the programmer to drag and drop controls onto a form visually (hence the name). Java development is not quite to this point yet (although it is coming soon). The procedure used to create applets that include user interface controls requires you to add code that creates an instance of the control class. You then add the control class to the applet. To do anything with the control, you add code that processes the events generated.

Adding label controls

The simplest type of control is a *label*. Labels are descriptive lines of text that provide comments about other user interface controls. The label fields are static text, in that they usually don't change. You use labels in an applet to help the user know how the applet is used and how to make selections within the user interface. You have the choice of creating centered, left-aligned, or right-aligned labels.

To create a label, use one of the following syntax:

```
public void init()
{
    Label lbl;
    lbl = new Label("Label text");
    add(lbl);
}
```

You can shorten the code necessary as follows:

```
public void init()
{
    Label lbl = new Label("Label text");
    add(lbl);
}
```

For controls like `Label`, which don't require an object instance variable around, you can create the control and add it to the applet in a single line of code, as follows:

```
public void init()
{
    add(new Label("Label text"));
}
```

Whichever method you choose is really up to you. One final parameter to the `Label` class constructor that you can specify is label alignment, which is specified as the last parameter. Here is an example:

```
public void init()
{
    add(new Label("Label text", alignment));
}
```

Here, the alignment option is either `Label.LEFT`, `Label.CENTER`, or `Label.RIGHT`. The default is `Label.LEFT`. The font used by the label is the same overall font used for the rest of the text in the applet. (See the discussion of the `setFont()` method in Chapter 6.)

Using buttons

You use a *button* in any situation where you would like the user to trigger an immediate action. Code to create a new button and add it to the user interface looks like this:

```
public void init()
{
    Button but;
    but = new Button("OK");
    add(but);
}
```

This creates a new user interface button from the `Button` object with the text *OK*. The label is important because later, when you go to detect the press of a button, each button is identified by its label text.

In Windows, you commonly see buttons labeled *OK* and *Cancel* in every dialog box. This is less common with a Java applet because you usually have no need to continue or abort an operation because the results won't cause any system changes on your computer. However, the label you use points the user to what the action of the button will trigger.

Using checkboxes

Checkboxes enable the user to toggle boolean items on or off. You wouldn't use the checkbox control to query the user for any information other than yes/no or on/off pieces of data. You create checkboxes with the `Checkbox` class. The following example shows how it's done:

```
public void init()
{
   Checkbox chk;
   chk = new Checkbox("Checkboxes are for boolean values");
   add(chk);
}
```

This code creates a new checkbox that is unselected (unchecked). Sometimes you may want the checkbox already selected. To do so, simply add another parameter to the `Checkbox()` constructor, as follows:

```
public void init()
{
   Checkbox chk;
   chk = new Checkbox("Checkboxes are for boolean values",
                      null, true);
   add(chk);
}
```

The last parameter to the `Checkbox()` constructor is a boolean value that specifies whether the checkbox is selected. You pass either `true` or `false`. You must pass the `null` value as the second parameter, which acts as a placeholder for data that is used later for other uses of the `Checkbox` class.

Using radio buttons

Radio buttons are similar in appearance to checkboxes (in fact, radio buttons use much of the same code designed for checkboxes), but radio buttons help a user choose a single item from a group of items. You can select only one item at a time from a group of radio buttons, and the user changes a selection by choosing a different radio button. In most browsers, the selected button contains a black circle.

Radio buttons receive their name from the buttons in older car radios. On those radios, you could press only one button to choose a station because you can only tune your radio to one station at a time. Those radios were common before digital stereos became popular, but car stereos with digital display use the same concept.

Radio buttons are actually based on checkboxes. The first thing you must do is create an instance of the `CheckboxGroup` class, as follows:

```
public void init()
{
   CheckboxGroup cbg;
   cbg = new CheckboxGroup();
}
```

The `CheckboxGroup` class lets you define each of the radio buttons inside the group. You create and add individual radio buttons using the `CheckboxGroup` object as the second argument to our friend, the `Checkbox()`. You also specify whether each checkbox is selected. Only one radio button in a series can be selected. Here is what the code looks like:

```
public void init()
{
   CheckboxGroup cbg;
   cbg = new CheckboxGroup();

   // Create a group of radio buttons and add to applet
   add(new Checkbox("RadioButton1", cbg, true));
   add(new Checkbox("RadioButton2", cbg, false));
   add(new Checkbox("RadioButton3", cbg, false));
}
```

You will notice that the Java developers put the `Checkbox()` class on double duty because it is used with regular checkboxes and also radio buttons. Don't let this confuse you, though. The code may look similar, but the functionality between the controls is vastly different.

Using choice items

Windows users sometimes refer to a *choice item* as a *pulldown list box*. It enables you to select one item from a group of menu items. You can only see one selection at a time, but when you click on the down arrow button to the right of the control, the menu drops down so you can see a larger selection of menu items. Choice items are similar to radio buttons in that they allow the user to select one option from a group of several options. Choice items use less screen space than radio buttons and are better if you have more than three or four options.

You implement choice items as part of the `Choice` class. You must create an instance of this class and then add each menu item to the list. What follows is an example of creating a choice list:

```
public void init()
{
    // Instance of Choice class
    Choice ch;

    // Create choice menu item
    Choice ch = new Choice();

    // Add menu items to choice list
    ch.addItem("One");
    ch.addItem("Two");
    ch.addItem("Three");
    ch.addItem("Four");

    // Add choice item to applet
    add(ch);
}
```

This process creates an instance of the `Choice` class, adds four menu items to it, and adds the control to the applet. Once you create a choice menu, even if you have already added it to the applet, you can continue to add items by using the `addItem()` method.

Using text fields

Text fields enable you to prompt the user for a single line of textual data. You can use several different forms to obtain text from the user, depending on the amount and type of text that you want the user to enter. The minimum code required for a text field is as follows:

```
public void init()
{
```

```
    TextField tf;
    tf = new TextField(20);
    add(tf);
}
```

Here, the single parameter to the `TextField()` constructor specifies the width of the text field. You can use another form in which you can specify default text, as follows:

```
public void init()
{
    TextField tf;
    tf = new TextField("default text", 20);
    add(tf);
}
```

This time, the first parameter to the `TextField()` constructor specifies the default text to appear in the text field.

With computers, security is always an important issue. You can create text fields that will mask what the user types (sometimes called a *password text field*). Instead of making the actual text appear, a character, usually an asterisk, is displayed in place of each character the user types. You use the same format as we have already seen, but you must specify an echo character. Here is an example:

```
public void init()
{
    TextField tf;
    tf = new TextField("default text", 20);
    tf.setEchoCharacter('*');
    add(tf);
}
```

This example calls the `setEchoCharacter()` method of the `TextField` class to choose which character will be displayed as the user enters data.

Handling Standard Control Actions

You have seen how to select a layout manager that will display controls in your Web page. After that, you saw how to create each of the standard controls. Most often, you carry this out with the `init()` method because you want the controls to appear when the applet first begins. The final step of implementing a user interface is to detect when the user has interacted with, or selected, a control.

Checking for user interface control actions is a form of event management. This makes sense because, when a user clicks on a button or types text into a text field, an event occurs. To check for any user interface action with the standard controls, you must define an `action()` method, which looks like this:

```
public boolean action(Event evt, Object arg)
{
   // Processing of user interface control events is done here
}
```

The `action()` method is passed two parameters. The first is of type `Event`. You test this variable with the type of user interface control you have in your applet. This lets you know which control generated the event. The second parameter is of type `Object` (a generic class), and it provides extra information related to each control. Often, you will need to cast this generic class to the class related to the control that you are processing.

Let's learn how you find out which control is generating the action. Because the first parameter, of type `Event`, contains a data member called `target` (which specifies the class of the control creating the action), you can compare this value with the actual control user name. Here is an example:

```
public boolean action(Event evt, Object arg)
   {
      if (evt.target instanceof Button)
         // Button control pressed.  Do something.
      else
      if (evt.target instanceof Checkbox)
         // Checkbox control selected. Do something.
      else
      if (evt.target instanceof Choice)
         // Choice menu control selected.  Do something.
      else
      if (evt.target instanceof TextField)
         // Text field control entered.  Do something.

       return true;
   }
```

The `instanceof` operator compares the `Event` type with each user interface control class type. Your program can either process the action directly within this method or can call another method to carry out the processing.

Because each user interface control has a different way of interacting with the user, each one also has unique information passed to the `action()` method. Here is an overview:

- **Labels** don't generate any event, therefore no information is passed to the `action()` method.
- **Buttons** cause the object parameter to contain the button label text.
- **Checkboxes** pass the boolean state as the object parameter.
- **Radio buttons** pass the state of the radio button (remember radio buttons are actually a group of checkbox controls, tied together with the `CheckBoxGroup` class) to the object parameter.
- **Choice items** pass the string of the selected item as the object parameter.
- **Text fields** create an action when the user presses the Return key inside the text field. The text that the user types is passed as the `Object` parameter.

This gives you an idea of the type of unique information passed as the `Object` parameter. It allows your program to react appropriately, depending on which action was generated.

You might be wondering how a program discriminates between multiple controls of the same type. The answer is that you must check for the label associated with the control creating the event. For example, the `Button` control passes the label of the button generating the event as the `Object` parameter. Therefore, you can test this value and find out which button control caused the event.

An applet sample

Listing 11-1 is a sample program that creates and displays all the standard controls in a Java applet. Listing 11-2 provides the Web page that uses the applet. The applet shows you how control events work by sending information to the Java Console. Every time an action occurs, the Java Console displays which control caused it and the extra parameter information passed to the applet (see Figure 11-6).

Listing 11-1 StandardControlsDemo.java Sample Code

```
/*
 *  StandardControlsDemo.java - Demonstration of
 *   the standard user interface controls.
 *
 *  Creating Cool Web Applets with Java
 *  By: Paul J. Perry,  Publisher: IDG Books
 *
 */

import java.applet.*;
```

(continued)

Listing 11-1 ***(continued)***

```
import java.awt.*;

public class StandardControlsDemo extends java.applet.Applet
{
   // Data members
   Label lbl;
   Button but;
   Checkbox chk;
   Checkbox rb1, rb2, rb3;
   CheckboxGroup cbg;
   Choice ch;
   TextField tf;

   // Initialization
   public void init()
   {
      // Set layout manager
      setLayout(new FlowLayout(FlowLayout.LEFT));

      // Create label and add it to applet
      lbl = new Label("This is a static label");
      add(lbl);

      // Create button and add it to applet
      but = new Button("Ok");
      add(but);

      // Create new checkbox and add it to applet
      chk = new Checkbox("Checkboxes are for boolean values");
      add(chk);

      // Create a group of radio buttons and add to applet
      cbg = new CheckboxGroup();
    rb1 = new Checkbox("RadioButton1", cbg, true);
    rb2 = new Checkbox("RadioButton2", cbg, false);
    rb3 = new Checkbox("RadioButton3", cbg, false);
      add(rb1);
      add(rb2);
      add(rb3);

      // Create choice menu items and add to applet
      Choice ch = new Choice();
      ch.addItem("One");
```

```
        ch.addItem("Two");
        ch.addItem("Three");
        ch.addItem("Four");
        add(ch);

        // Create text field and add to applet
       tf = new TextField(20);
       add(tf);
    }

    public boolean action(Event evt, Object arg)
    {
        if (evt.target instanceof Button)
        {
            System.out.print("Button control pressed.  Argu-
ment=");
            System.out.println(arg);
        }
        else
        if (evt.target instanceof Checkbox)
        {
            System.out.print("Checkbox toggled.  Label=");
            // Get label of checkbox and display it
            String x = ((Checkbox)evt.target).getLabel();
            System.out.print(x);
            // Display argument (true or false)
          System.out.print(" Argument=");
            System.out.println(arg);
        }
        else
        if (evt.target instanceof Choice)
        {
            System.out.print("Choice box selected.  Argument=");
            System.out.println(arg);
       }
       else
       if (evt.target instanceof TextField)
        {
            System.out.print("Textfield action.  Argument=");
            System.out.println(arg);
        }
        return true;
    }

}
```

Listing 11-2 StandardControlsDemo.html Web Page

```
<HTML>
<!- StandardControlsDemo.html ->
<HEAD>
   <TITLE>Java Standard User Interface Controls</TITLE>
</HEAD>
<BODY>
To see control actions, open Java Console.<P>
Sample User Interface Controls:<P><P>
<APPLET CODE="StandardControlsDemo.class" WIDTH="400"
HEIGHT="400">
This Web page requires a <B>Java</B>-enabled Web Browser.
</APPLET>
</BODY>
</HTML>
```

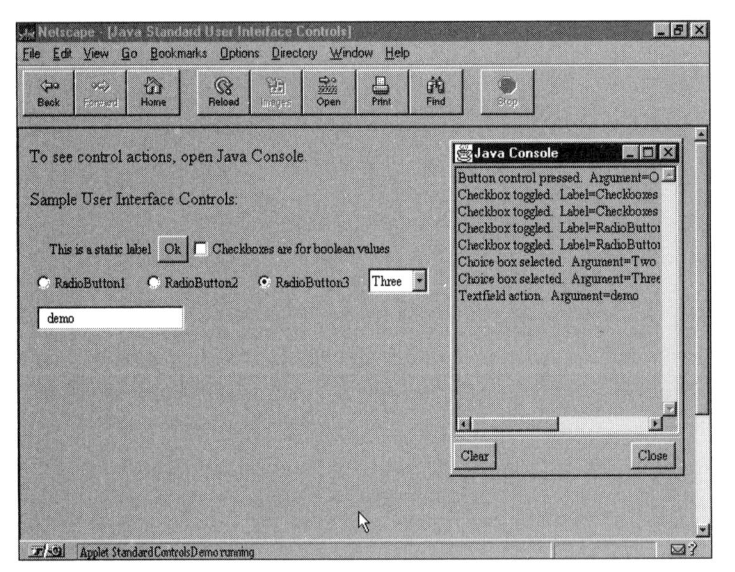

Figure 11-6: The StandardControlsDemo sample applet in action.

Working with Enhanced Controls

You will want to examine three enhanced controls. Although you have probably seen all these controls before, the only reason we refer to them as *enhanced controls* is because their actions are processed differently than the standard

controls. This probably stems from the fact that these controls are a bit more complex, cause more than just the trigger of an event (like a button), and provide more control over event information than standard controls.

List items

Windows users commonly refer to *list items* as *list boxes*. You can control the number of items that appear in the list item, and you can also let the user select multiple items. A list item is functionally similar to the choice menu that we have already examined, but list items have more flexibility and provide added features.

To create a list item, you really only use two steps. First, you create an instance of the `List` class. Second, you add the items in the list using the `addItem()` method. Here is an example of creating a basic list:

```
public void init()
{
   List lst;
   lst = new List();
}
```

That's pretty simple, but you can provide more information that provides a better control. Here is another form:

```
public void init()
{
   List lst;
   lst = new List(5, false);
}
```

In the first parameter, you specify the number of lines visible, and the second parameter indicates whether this list enables multiple selections. The `false` value allows only a single item to be selected. Passing `true` permits the selection of multiple items.

So, now that you have the list created, you need to add items and then add the entire control to the applet. Here is an example:

```
public void init()
{
   // Create list item
   List lst;
   lst = new List(6, false);

   // Add menu items
```

```
    lst.addItem("January");
    lst.addItem("February");
    lst.addItem("March");
    lst.addItem("April");
    lst.addItem("May");
    lst.addItem("June");
    lst.addItem("July");
    lst.addItem("August");
    lst.addItem("September");
    lst.addItem("October");
    lst.addItem("November");
    lst.addItem("December");

    // Add list item menu to applet
    add(lst);
}
```

You can see that although list items are referred to as enhanced controls, they are not much harder to work with than standard controls.

Scrollbar controls

Scrollbar controls allow the user to select a linear value. Although scrollbars are commonly used as a component in other controls (like list items and text areas), you can also create them separately and let the user easily select numeric values between a minimum and a maximum value. Scrollbars come in two types: vertical and horizontal.

In interacting with the scrollbar, the user can click on either of the arrows at the far ends of the control to increment or decrement the numeric value. The user can also click on the scrollbar *thumb*, which is the rectangular region inside the scrollbar, and drag it to select a specific value. Finally, the user can click directly in the scrollbar area and increment the scrollbar by a specified amount.

You create a scrollbar using the `Scrollbar` class. By passing the appropriate values, you control the minimum and maximum value of the scrollbar, the orientation (vertical or horizontal), and the overall size.

The simplest method to create a scrollbar is to pass no parameters, as follows:

```
public void init()
{
    Scrollbar sb;
    sb = new Scrollbar();
    add(sb);
}
```

This creates a vertical scrollbar with minimum and maximum values of 0. Luckily, you can specify this information when you first create the scrollbar. Here is an example:

```
public void init()
{
   Scrollbar sb;
   sb = new Scrollbar(Scrollbar.HORIZONTAL, 1, 5, 1, 10);
   add(sb);
}
```

The first parameter is the orientation of the scrollbar. Use either of the constants `Scrollbar.HORIZONTAL` or `Scrollbar.VERTICAL`. The second parameter is the initial value of the scrollbar, which must be a value between the minimum and maximum scrollbar values. The third parameter is the size of the scrollbar thumb. Usually, a larger thumb size indicates that the user can view a larger amount of the scrollbar's information. The last two parameters are the minimum and maximum values for the scrollbar.

Text areas

Text areas are similar to text fields, but they provide much more functionality for handling larger amounts of text. You can give text areas width and height values, and they will automatically provide a scrollbar to help the user navigate through the text. Here is an example:

```
public void init()
{
   TextArea ta;
   sb = new TextArea("Default text", 5, 10);
   add(sb);
}
```

The first parameter to the `TextArea()` constructor allows you to specify default text. This text will appear inside the text area control when you first create it. The user can edit or delete the text. If you don't have a need to display default text, you don't need to pass information as this parameter: you can pass a null string (`""`). The second parameter is the number of rows in the text area, and the third parameter is the number of columns in the text area.

Handling Enhanced Control Events

To handle enhanced control events, you must override the `handleEvent()` method. You can intercept a specific event by testing for the event's identifier. You use the same technique that you used earlier, where the `instanceof` operator compared the target event object with the type of controls contained in the applet. Here's an example:

```
public boolean handleEvent(Event evt)
   {
        if (evt.target instanceof List)
        {
        // List item event occurred
        }
        else
        if (evt.target instanceof Scrollbar)
        {
        // Scrollbar event occurred
        }
        else
        if (evt.target instanceof TextArea)
        {
        // TextArea event occurred
        }

        return true;
   }
```

Unlike the `action()` method, the `handleEvent()` does not pass any extra parameters about the control. However, because the target member of the `Event` class literally provides a pointer to the class instance, the applet can call methods associated with each control to query the system for more information. For example:

```
public boolean handleEvent(Event evt)
{
   if (evt.target instanceof List)
   {
      System.out.print("List Item event occurred.
                        Selected item=");
      String s = ((List)evt.target).getSelectedItem();
      System.out.println(s);
   }
}
```

This checks for the action of a `List Item` control. If the control was selected, the code calls the `getSelectedItem()` method. It does this by casting the `evt.target` member to a `List` class and then in turn calling the `getSelectedItem()` method. All this data is returned as a string value and then displayed in the Java console.

A sample applet

Listing 11-3 contains the EnhancedControlsDemo.java sample code (see Figure 11-7), which makes use of the enhanced user interface controls. Similar to the earlier sample applet, this code sends its output to the Java Console. This code also uses some of the methods associated with each control to obtain the information your code might need to know about each control. Listing 11-4 contains the EnhancedControlsDemo.html Web page, required to view the applet inside Netscape Navigator.

Listing 11-3 EnhancedControlsDemo.java Sample Source Code

```
/*
 *  EnhancedControlsDemo.java - Demonstration of
 *   the enhanced user interface controls.
 *
 *  Creating Cool Web Applets with Java
 *  By: Paul J. Perry,  Publisher: IDG Books
 *
 */

import java.applet.*;
import java.awt.*;

public class EnhancedControlsDemo extends java.applet.Applet
{
   // Data members
   List lst;
   TextArea ta;
   Scrollbar hsb, vsb;

   // Initialization
   public void init()
   {
       // Set layout manager
       setLayout(new FlowLayout(FlowLayout.LEFT));

      // Create List controls and add to applet
       lst = new List();
       lst.addItem("January");
```

(continued)

Listing 11-3 *(continued)*

```
        lst.addItem("February");
        lst.addItem("March");
        lst.addItem("April");
        lst.addItem("May");
        lst.addItem("June");
        lst.addItem("July");
        lst.addItem("August");
        lst.addItem("September");
        lst.addItem("October");
        lst.addItem("November");
        lst.addItem("December");

      add(lst);


        // Create scrollbars (vertical and horizontal) and
        //  add to applet
        hsb = new Scrollbar(Scrollbar.HORIZONTAL, 1, 0, 1, 100);
        add(hsb);
        vsb = new Scrollbar(Scrollbar.VERTICAL, 1, 0, 1, 100);
        add(vsb);

      // Create new text area and add it to applet
        ta = new TextArea("default text", 10, 60);
        add(ta);
   }


   public boolean handleEvent(Event evt)
   {
        if (evt.target instanceof List)
        {
          System.out.print("List Item event occurred. Selected
item=");
            String s = ((List)evt.target).getSelectedItem();
           System.out.println(s);
        }
        else
        if (evt.target instanceof Scrollbar)
        {
          System.out.print("Scrollbar event occurred.  Value=");
            int i = ((Scrollbar)evt.target).getValue();
            System.out.println(i);
        }
        else
        if (evt.target instanceof TextArea)
        {
```

```
        System.out.print("TextArea event occurred.  Text=");
          String s = ((TextArea)evt.target).getText();
          System.out.println(s);
        }

        return true;
    }

}
```

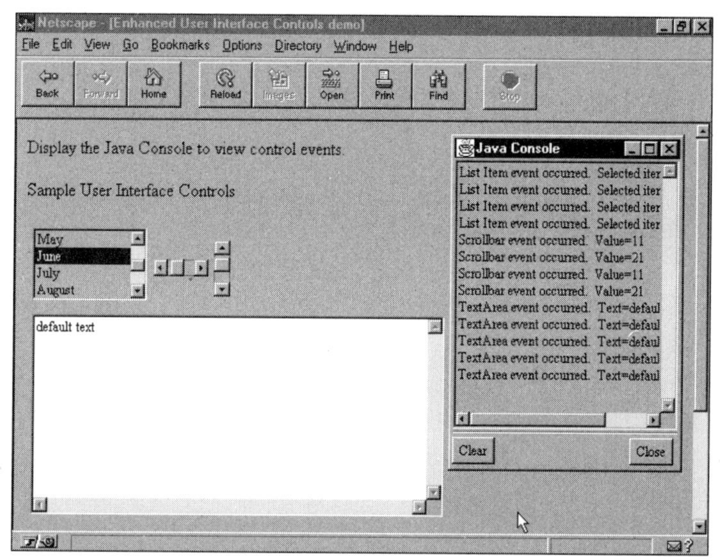

Figure 11-7: The EnhancedControlsDemo sample applet in action.

Listing 11-4 EnhancedControlsDemo.html Web Page

```
<HTML>
<!- EnhancedControlsDemo.html ->
<HEAD>
   <TITLE>Enhanced User Interface Controls demo</TITLE>
</HEAD>
<BODY>
Display the Java Console to view control events.<P>
Sample User Interface Controls<P><P>
<APPLET CODE="EnhancedControlsDemo.class" WIDTH="400"
HEIGHT="400">
This Web page requires a <B>Java</B>-enabled Web Browser.
</APPLET>
</BODY>
</HTML>
```

Controlling the Status Line

One part of the user interface that we haven't had a chance to discuss is the *status line* (see Figure 11-8). Sometimes called a *status bar,* the status line appears horizontally at the bottom of the Web browser window and contains a line of text with prompt or status information. These days, most commercial programs contain status bars. They have become a standard part of even the simplest graphical user interface. Luckily, the Java developers decided that an applet should have a way of controlling the status line.

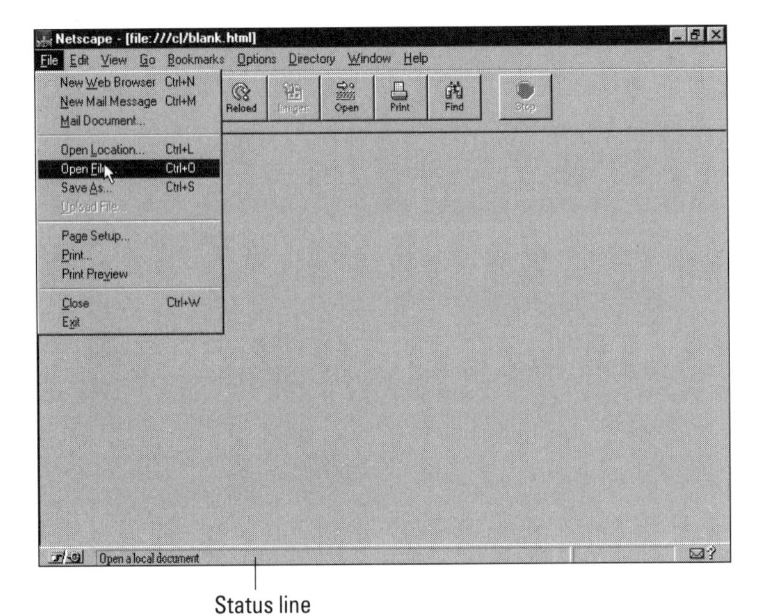

Figure 11-8: The status line in Netscape Navigator.

Although Java applets don't have their own status line, most Web browsers do. The developers of the Java windowing system thought it might be nice to provide a way for a Java applet to display information in the status line. Doing this is easy. You just need to call the `showStatus()` method, as follows:

```
showStatus("My Java applet is cooler than your Java applet!");
```

Here, you pass a single string to the `showStatus()` method that is what's displayed in the Web browser status line. The method is declared to return a void value. The text you display will appear in the status line until either your applet displays a new message or the Web browser does.

Although Netscape Navigator allows a Java applet to display text in the status line, the Java documentation says that you should not count on this taking place. Some browsers may choose not to provide this functionality. In which case, your applet would have no way of knowing that the text was not displayed. As a result, it may be a good idea to use the status line only as a place to display backup or supplemental messages. You shouldn't rely on the status line as the main method of communicating to the user.

A sample applet

The last program of this chapter makes use of what you just learned about the status line and builds upon everything you have learned in this book so far. Although not a long piece of code, the sample applet creates a user interface button that is displayed inside the Web applet. When the user clicks on the button, a message appears in the Web browser status line (see Figure 11-9).

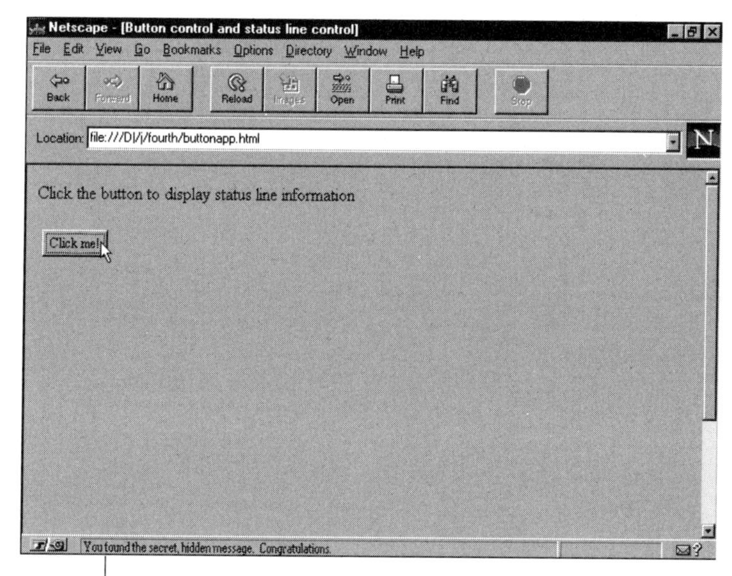

Figure 11-9: The ButtonApp applet in action.

The code works by accessing information from the HTML file, as parameters to the applet. Therefore, you can use this applet in numerous Web pages. Table 11-1 shows the parameters that you can pass.

Table 11-1 Parameters for the ButtonApp Applet

Parameter	Meaning
ButtonWidth	Specifies the width of the button
ButtonHeight	Specifies the height of the button
Text	Specifies the text to be displayed inside the button
Message	Specifies the message to be displayed in the status line control

Most of the processing occurs inside the `init()` method. The parameters are accessed from the HTML file, and the button is created and added to the applet. The `action()` method takes care of responding to the press of the button and displays the appropriate message in the status line.

Listing 11-5 contains the ButtonApp.java source code. Listing 11-6 contains the ButtonApp.html Web page that shows how to use the applet.

Listing 11-5 The ButtonApp.java Source Code

```
/*
 *  ButtonApp.java - Create user interface button
 *
 *  Creating Cool Web Applets with Java
 *  By: Paul J. Perry,  Publisher: IDG Books
 *
 *  HTML Parameters:
 *   ButtonWidth  - Width of the button.
 *   ButtonHeight - Height of the button.
 *   Text         - Text to be displayed in button.
 *   Message      - Message to display on status line.
 *
 */

import java.lang.*;
import java.applet.*;
import java.awt.*;

public class ButtonApp extends java.applet.Applet
{
   // Data members
   Button b;  // Button control
   int bw;       // Button width
   int bh;    // Button height
   String msg;

   // Initialization
```

```
    public void init()
    {
        // Set layout manager
        setLayout(new FlowLayout(FlowLayout.LEFT));

        // Set size of applet
        String s = getParameter("ButtonWidth");
        bw = Integer.parseInt(s);
        s = getParameter("ButtonHeight");
        bh = Integer.parseInt(s);
        resize(bw, bh);

       // Create new button, the size of the applet
       b = new Button(getParameter("Text"));
        add(b);
    }

    public boolean action(Event evt, Object arg)
    {
       if (evt.target instanceof Button)
        {
           showStatus(getParameter("Message"));
        }

        return true;
    }
}
```

Listing 11-6 The ButtonApp.html Web Page

```
<HTML>
<!- ButtonApp.html ->
<HEAD>
   <TITLE>Button control and status line control</TITLE>
</HEAD>
<BODY>
Click the button to display status line information<P><P>
<APPLET CODE="ButtonApp.class" WIDTH="400" HEIGHT="400">
 <PARAM NAME="ButtonWidth"   VALUE=100>
 <PARAM NAME="ButtonHeight"  VALUE=50>
 <PARAM NAME="Text"          VALUE="Click me!">
 <PARAM NAME="Message"       VALUE="You found the secret, hidden
message.  Congratulations.">
This Web page requires a <B>Java</B>-enabled Web Browser.
</APPLET>
</BODY>
</HTML>
```

Hopefully, you will find this a useful (and educational) program that you can make use of in many of your own Web pages.

Quick Overview

This chapter presented what you need to know to work with user interface controls. You learned about the controls that come with Java: both standard and enhanced controls. You saw how to create each type of control and how to respond to their actions and events.

In particular, this chapter covered the following topics:

- The controls available in Java include: labels, buttons, checkboxes, radio buttons, choice items, text fields, list items, scrollbars, and text areas. These compose the basic components of how a user interacts with the computer.
- A layout manager controls how controls appear with a Web page. Standard layout managers include: `FlowLayout`, `Grid`, `Border`, `Card`, and `GridBagLayout`. The most commonly used layout manager (and the default) is the `FlowLayout`.
- Standard control events are processed with an `action()` method. In this method, the code can check which type of control action occurred and the current state of the control.
- Enhanced control events are processed in the `handleEvent()` method, which allows your code to check which type of control event occurred. You can use control methods to find out the exact state of each control.
- You control the status line of a Web browser through the `showStatus()` method.

Here is a brief overview of what is to come...

- Chapter 12, "Windows and Dialog Boxes," provides valuable information about creating Java applets that create separate windows and dialog boxes separate from the basic Web page.

Windows and Dialog Boxes

In This Chapter

What the `Frame` class is and how to implement a frame class in your applet to create independent and separate windows.

What main menu bars are and how to add one to your window.

The difference between a frame window and a dialog box.

How to implement your own platform-independent dialog boxes.

The final step in creating complete user interfaces with Java's Abstract Window Toolkit is to know how to create windows and dialog boxes that are separate and independent from the Web browser's main window. This chapter teaches you how to create your own windows and how to add main menu items to these windows. You will also learn about the different types of dialog boxes available and how to make them a part of your user interface.

Working with Frames

The `Frame` class lets you create windows that are independent of the main Web browser window (see Figure 12-1). Frames are easy to create because they are based on objects. All you have to do is create an object that is responsible for controlling the separate window. Of course, the AWT contains a class that you can inherit from to make the entire process easier.

Before showing you the code for creating your own frames, you should become familiar with some security issues. In particular, you should notice at the bottom of Figure 12-1 a long stripe (it *is* yellow, but you can't tell that from a black-and-white figure) with the words *Untrusted Java Applet Window*. This message will appear on every separate Window that you create with a Java applet. It is one of the security measures that the Java developers added to the windowing class. These developers wanted the user to know that the window or dialog box was not part of the Web browser or any local program and that it was created by an applet that was most likely downloaded over the Internet. They wanted to prevent people from writing applets that created familiar looking dialog boxes. It would prevent an applet from creating a dialog box that looked like a system dialog box requesting a password or a Quicken dialog box that might query for financial information. A user might probably not think twice when seeing one of these familiar looking dialog boxes. The result might be some malicious applet that could innocently query for all kinds of confidential information.

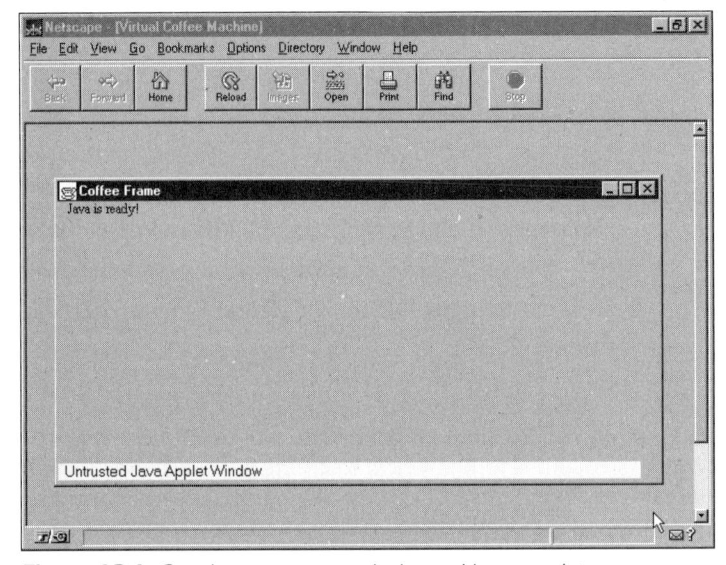

Figure 12-1: Creating a separate window with an applet.

Now, whether everybody is absent-minded enough to enter this type of information while they are running their Web browser is up for debate. However, you can see that the Java developers were serious about adding security measures to the language.

Creating the frames

Separate windows are associated with a Java class called frames. You create an instance of the `Frame` class by passing a string that is used as the text in the window title bar. Here is sample code:

```
public void init()
{
   Frame f;
```

```
    f = new Frame("Title bar Text");
    f.show();
}
```

When you initially create a frame, it is hidden, hence the call to the method to make it visible. You can use both `show()` and `hide()` to control the display of the window. The previous code will create a `Frame` window and allow the user to interact with it. This frame window won't be too useful, though, because the frame window is using the default behavior provided by the system. Other than the custom title bar text that you supply, you cannot display your own text inside the window.

In order to display text in the window, you create a class that inherits from the `Frame` class and includes appropriate methods for displaying your unique text. For example:

```
class CustomFrame extends Frame
{
    // Constructor
    CustomFrame(String title)
    {
        super(title);
    }
    public void paint(Graphics g)
    {
        g.drawString("Java is Cool!", 10, 10);
    }
}
```

This code is a simple instance of creating a custom class, called `CustomFrame`, which inherits from the `Frame` class. Notice that you must create your own constructor (which has the same name as the class name). The constructor in the previous example does nothing more than pass the title string on to the constructor for the frame class using the keyword `super`. You could also add initialization code to the constructor. The `CustomFrame` class here also implements its own `paint()` method. This allows it to display custom information inside the window.

So now you have a `Frame` class that will actually do something. To use it in your code, you would include code that looks like this:

```
public void init()
{
    CustomFrame frm;
    frm = new CustomFrame("Title bar Text");
    frm.show();
}
```

This is the same thing we used with the `Frame` class, but it uses our own `CustomFrame` class instead. You can see that this code creates an instance of the `CustomFrame` class (instead of the `Frame` class) and then calls the `show()` method to make the window appear.

If you want to add controls to frame windows, the default layout for windows is `BorderLayout` (as you learned about in Chapter 11). You add controls the same way you do for applets.

Listing 12-1 contains the source code for SeparateWindowDemo.java, which is code that shows how to create a separate window (see Figure 12-2). Listing 12-2 for SeparateWindowDemo.html is the Web page to display the applet.

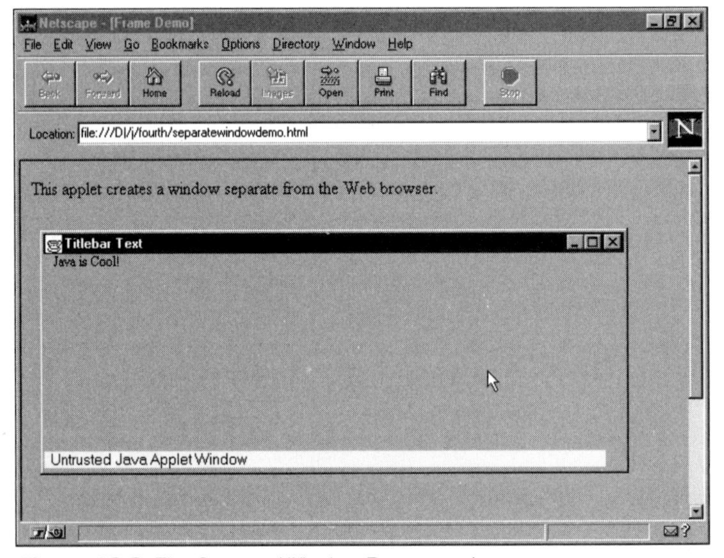

Figure 12-2: The SeparateWindowDemo applet.

Listing 12-1 SeparateWindowDemo.java Sample Code

```
/*
 *  SeparateWindowDemo.java - Creates window which is
 *   independent of the Web browser window.
 *
 *  Creating Cool Web Applets with Java
 *  By: Paul J. Perry,  Publisher: IDG Books
 *
 */

import java.applet.*;
import java.awt.*;
```

```
/***************************************************/
public class SeparateWindowDemo extends java.applet.Applet
{
   // Data members
   CustomFrame frm;

   // Initialization
   public void init()
   {
       frm = new CustomFrame("Title bar Text");
       frm.show();
   }
}

/***************************************************/
class CustomFrame extends Frame
{
   // Constructor
   CustomFrame(String title)
   {
      super(title);
   }

   public void paint(Graphics g)
   {
       // This displays text in the separate window
      g.drawString("Java is Cool!", 10, 10);
   }

}
```

Listing 12-2 SeparateWindowDemo.html Web Page

```
<HTML>
<!- SeparateWindowDemo.html ->
<HEAD>
   <TITLE>Frame Demo</TITLE>
</HEAD>
<BODY>
This applet creates a window separate from the Web browser.<P><P>
<APPLET CODE="SeparateWindowDemo.class" WIDTH="400" HEIGHT="400">
This Web page requires a <B>Java</B>-enabled Web Browser.
</APPLET>
</BODY>
</HTML>
```

Menus and Menu Bars

Most Windows programs use menus as the key method to receive commands from the user. A menu belonging to a specified window is displayed immediately under the title bar. The menu bar is usually referred to as the program's *main menu*. Most top-level windows, like the kind you just created with the `Frame` class, have main menus. Of course, Java provides a way to add main menus to your frame windows.

Adding main-menu support to your program comes in several steps. Here is an overview:

1. Create a `MenuBar` class to tell the frame that a main menu is associated with it.
2. Create `Menu` classes for each menu group your main menu will have. Common examples of menu groups include "File," "Edit," and "Window."
3. Add menu items to each menu group. A common example for the File menu group would be "Open," "New," and "Save."
4. Process menu actions so that an event occurs when the user selects a menu item.

Creating a `MenuBar` for a frame window is easy: you just create a new instance of the `MenuBar` class and associate it with the frame. Here is an example:

```
CustomFrame(String title)
{
   . . .

   // Data member
   MenuBar mb;

   // Create new MenuBar
   mb = new MenuBar();

   // Associate menu bar with frame
   setMenuBar(mb);

   . . .
}
```

This code won't affect the frame window because no menus or menu items are attached to the menu bar. Usually, you wait until you have created all the menu groups and menu items before you call the `setMenuBar()` method. Let's look at this further.

Creating menus

Common menu groups include "File," "Edit," "View," and "Window." The Menu class creates a menu group. You must specify the title of the menu to the Menu( ) constructor as you create the menu. Here is an example:

```
CustomFrame(String title)
{
   . . .
   // Data member
   Menu m;

      // Create menu
      m = new Menu("&File");

   . . .
}
```

Notice the use of the ampersand (&), which makes the next letter a *quick key*. A quick key lets the user access a menu item with the keyboard. For example, in the previous example, when the user is selecting the menu, he or she can go directly to that menu by typing the F key rather than navigating solely with the mouse or arrow keys. Because this is a top-level menu, the user can use the Alt+F key combination to display the menu. A menu group without any menu items is almost useless. In order to really make use of menus, you must add menu items to a menu group. Let's look at that next.

Creating menu items

You must create an instance of the MenuItem class for each menu item that appears under a top-level menu group. For example, if the menu group is "File," common menu items are "Open," "New," and "Save." The MenuItem class provides support for creating new menu items. To create a regular menu item and add it to a menu, use the following code:

```
CustomFrame(String title)
{
   . . .

   // Data members
   MenuItem mi;
   Menu m;

   // Create menu with one menu item
   m = new Menu("&File");
   mi = new MenuItem("&Open");
```

(continued)

```
    m.add(mi);

    . . .
}
```

Here, the string parameter to the `MenuItem()` constructor is the text of the menu item. Again, you are free to use the ampersand character (&) to specify a quick key (although it's not required).

You can add several types of menu items to a menu. You just saw the most common type of menu item. Another common menu item type is called a *separator bar*. A separator bar does not have any functionality in itself and is used entirely for aesthetics. The separator bar makes it easier to understand how a program works by grouping related menu items within a menu. To create a separator bar, just create a regular menu item, but instead of passing the text for the menu item, pass the minus sign (-). Here is an example of creating a separator bar:

```
CustomFrame(String title)
{
    . . .

    // Data members
    MenuItem mi;
    Menu m;

    // Create menu with one menu item, a separator bar
    m = new Menu("&File");
    mi = new MenuItem("-");
    m.add(mi);

    . . .
}
```

Separator menu items don't provide any way to check when they have been selected. This backs up the claim that separator bars have no real purpose, other than for looks.

Submenu items

You might like to get fancy with creating your menu items and submenus. You can do this simply by creating a new instance of the `Menu` class and adding it to a previously created menu item. For example:

```
CustomFrame(String title)
```

```
{
    . . .

    // Data members
    MenuItem mi;
    Menu m;

    // Create regular menu and menu item
    m = new Menu("&File");
    mi = new MenuItem("&Open");
    m.add(mi);

    // Create sub-menu
    Menu sm = new Menu("Sub-menu");
    m.add(sm);

    // Add sub-menu items to sub-menu
    sm.add(new MenuItem("Item 1"));
    sm.add(new MenuItem("Item 2"));
    sm.add(new MenuItem("Item 3"));

    . . .
}
```

The key to remember when working with submenus (and all menus, for that matter) is that adding menu items is hierarchical: you must first create the menu bar, the menu, and each menu item. If you would like to add submenus, you can easily add another layer of menus, but it must be in the correct order.

Checkbox menu items

A checkbox menu item is one that a user can toggle on and off. Similar to the checkbox control that we learned about in Chapter 11, the checkbox menu item is a boolean value that is toggled between selected or deselected when the user selects it. You create checkbox menu items just like you would regular menu items. Here is some sample code to show how this works:

```
CustomFrame(String title)
{
    . . .

    // Data member
    CheckboxMenuItem cbmi;
    Menu m;

    // Create menu
    m = new Menu("&File");
```

```
    // Create checkbox menu and add it to menu
    cbmi = new CheckboxMenuItem("Boldface");
    m.add(cbmi);

    . . .
}
```

You can see that creating a checkbox menu item is just as easy as creating a regular menu item.

Detecting menu action

After adding all these fancy menus to a program, you need to detect that the user has selected one of the menu items. You do this through our old friend the `action()` method. In this method, you receive two parameters: an `Event` object and an object class. The code can test the event to make sure it is an instance of the type of menu you want the user to respond to and then take appropriate action. Here is an example:

```
public boolean action(Event evt, Object arg)
{
    if (evt.target instanceof MenuItem)
    {
        String txt = (String)arg;

        if (txt.equals("&Open"))
        {
            // Process menu item
        }
        else
        if (txt.equals("&Save"))
        {
            // Process menu item
        }
        else
        if (txt.equals("&New"))
        {
            // Process menu item
        }

        //
        //  etc.
        //
    }
        return true;
}
```

Notice that this code first checks to see whether the event is of the `MenuItem` type. If you use `CheckboxmenuItems` in your code, you will need to check for that event object type. Inside the processing, the `Object` parameter is cast to a string. The code then uses the `equals()` method of the string class to compare the menu text of the event that occurred with several menu texts that were added to the frame window. If the text is the same, an appropriate action would occur. Notice that if you use the ampersand character (`&`) to denote quick keys, you must include it in the string you test.

Sample code

The sample code contains a frame window that has a main menu (see Figure 12-3) and processes the menu item commands. Every time the user makes a menu selection, the applet displays new text inside its main window area. Listing 12-3 is the MenuDemo.java source code, and Listing 12-4 contains the MenuDemo.html Web page. You will want to examine the sample listing to see an example of how menus are created and how their events are processed.

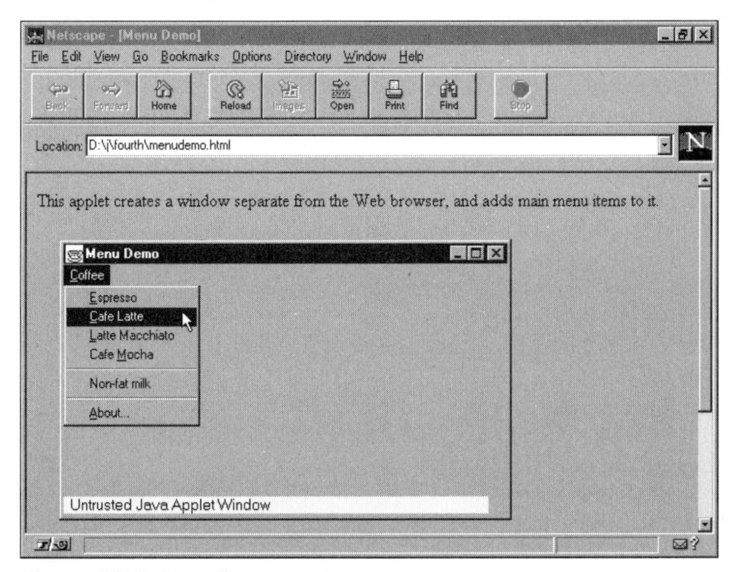

Figure 12-3: MenuDemo applet.

Listing 12-3 MenuDemo.java Sample Source Code

```
/*
 *  MenuDemo.java - Creates main menu in Java windows.
 *
 *  Creating Cool Web Applets with Java
```

(continued)

Listing 12-3 *(continued)*

```
*  By: Paul J. Perry,  Publisher: IDG Books
 *
 */

import java.applet.*;
import java.awt.*;

/**************************************************/
public class MenuDemo extends java.applet.Applet
{
   // Data members
   CustomFrame frm;

   // Initialization
   public void init()
   {
       frm = new CustomFrame("Menu Demo");
       frm.show();
   }
}

/**************************************************/
class CustomFrame extends Frame
{
   // Data members
   MenuBar mb;
   Menu m;
   MenuItem mi1, mi2, mi3, mi4, mi5, mi6, mi7;
   CheckboxMenuItem cbmi;
   String msg;

   // Constructor
   CustomFrame(String title)
   {
      super(title);

       // Create menu bar
       mb = new MenuBar();

       // Create menu
       m = new Menu("&Coffee");

       // Create menu items
       mi1 = new MenuItem("&Espresso");
       mi2 = new MenuItem("&Cafe Latte");
       mi3 = new MenuItem("&Latte Macchiato");
       mi4 = new MenuItem("Cafe &Mocha");
```

```
        mi5 = new MenuItem("-");
        mi6 = new MenuItem("-");
        mi7 = new MenuItem("&About...");

        // Create checkbox menu item
        cbmi = new CheckboxMenuItem("Non-fat milk");

        // Add Menu items to menu
        m.add(mi1);
        m.add(mi2);
        m.add(mi3);
        m.add(mi4);
        m.add(mi5);
        m.add(cbmi);     // Checkbox menu item
        m.add(mi6);
        m.add(mi7);

        // Add Menu to Menubar
        mb.add(m);

        // Associate menu to Frame
        setMenuBar(mb);

       // Set initial message
       msg = "Choose a menu item";

    }

    public void paint(Graphics g)
    {
        // This displays text in the separate window
       g.drawString(msg, 10, 100);
    }

    public boolean action(Event evt, Object arg)
    {
        if (evt.target instanceof MenuItem)
        {
           String txt = (String)arg;

            if (txt.equals("&Espresso"))
               msg = "Your Espresso order is coming up...";
            else
            if (txt.equals("&Cafe Latte"))
               msg = "Your Cafe Latte is coming up...";
            else
            if (txt.equals("&Latte Macchiato"))
               msg = "Your Latte Macchiato is coming up...";
```

(continued)

Listing 12-3 *(continued)*

```
            else
            if (txt.equals("Cafe &Mocha"))
               msg = "Your Cafe Mocha is coming up...";
            else
            if (txt.equals("&About..."))
               msg = "MenuDemo.class, written by Mr. Coffee";
          }
          repaint();
       return true;
    }
 }
```

Listing 12-4 MenuDemo.html Web Page

```
<HTML>
<!- MenuDemo.html ->
<HEAD>
   <TITLE>Menu Demo</TITLE>
</HEAD>
<BODY>
This applet creates a window separate from the Web browser,
and adds main menu items to it.<P><P>
<APPLET CODE="MenuDemo.class" WIDTH="400" HEIGHT="400">
This Web page requires a <B>Java</B>-enabled Web Browser.
</APPLET>
</BODY>
</HTML>
```

Working with Dialog Boxes

Dialog boxes provide the user with a convenient way to enter data. Although they are functionally similar to frame windows, dialog boxes are designed to hold user interface controls. Dialog boxes are used both to request information from the user and provide information to the user.

You will find that dialog boxes created with Java contain the same warning message, "Untrusted Java AppletWindow" as frame windows, for the same reason of security.

You can classify dialog boxes in two categories: modeless or modal. *Modeless* dialog boxes allow the user to switch between dialog boxes and other open windows that are available for an applet. *Modal dialog boxes* don't enable the user to utilize the dialog box's parent frame when it is active.

In order to create a dialog box, you must attach it to a frame window. If you don't think your applet needs the frame window for user interface, you can always create it and never show it. As a result, you can create the dialog box, but you don't have to be concerned with too many open windows for the user.

While I was working with Java dialog boxes, I found that no matter whether I specified a modal or modeless dialog box, the dialog box was always created as modeless.

When you create a dialog box, you really need to know about two parameters. The first is a boolean value specifying whether the dialog box is modal or modeless. The other parameter is the text to use in the title bar of the dialog box. This is pretty easy, huh? Here is the prototype for the `Dialog()` constructor:

```
Dialog(Frame f, String title, bool modal);
```

Notice that you must pass a parent window frame as the first parameter. This means that you must always have a frame window available when you create dialog boxes. The second parameter is the text to be displayed in the dialog box title bar. The last parameter specifies `true` for modal dialog boxes and `false` for modeless dialog boxes. Here is an example of creating a dialog box:

```
public void init()
{
   // Data members
   Frame f;
   Dialog d;
   Button b;

   // Create frame window, which is required to create dialog box
   f = new Frame("frame window");

   // Create modeless dialog box
   d = new Dialog(f, "Title Text", false);

   // Add user interface controls to dialog box
   b = new Button("1");
   d.add(b);
   // etc.

   // Make dialog box appear
   d.show();
}
```

You can see that the process creates a frame window (which is never displayed), creates the dialog box, adds controls to the dialog box, and makes the dialog box appear using the `show()` method.

To respond to the user interface controls, add an `action()` method just like you have seen previously in this chapter for working with menu items. You carry out the same routine of checking for the instance of the specified control and then take an action based on that. Here is an example:

```
public boolean action(Event evt, Object arg)
{
   if (evt.target instanceof Button)
   {
      // Button pressed.  Take action.
   }
   else
   if (evt.target instanceof Choice)
   {
      // Choice menu selected.  Take action.
   }

   // etc.

   return true;
}
```

In your own program, you can either handle the event directly in the `action()` method, or if you have substantial processing, you might decide to call a separate method. By calling another method, the code is simplified somewhat because you won't have a large amount of code in one method, and it is spread out functionally.

Java dialog boxes

As you examine the Java dialog box documentation, you might find reference to a special type of a dialog box called a `FileDialog`. This is a standard file open/save dialog box that enables the user to access the computer's file system and choose a filename. This type of dialog box is not discussed here for two reasons.

First, for Java applets, security is a big issue. The Java developers don't want an applet to be able to read and write information on a local computer. At the very least, creating an external file becomes a burden to the user, and at the worst, the file could be some type of virus that could cause harm to the computer system. However, you can still use `FileDialog` with standalone Java applications.

The second reason for not discussing `FileDialog` is that Netscape Navigator does not implement it. Even if you try to use it, Navigator will provide a warning message that the `FileDialog` is not implemented.

Sample dialog box

The sample code creates a dialog box (see Figure 12-4) with a numbered grid, from 1 to 9 (similar to a tic-tac-toe board). As you click on each button, the title bar text is replaced with the label of the button you clicked. Although not breathtaking by any means, the code does provide you with an example of creating your own dialog box that responds to button presses. Listing 12-5 contains the DialogBoxDemo.java source code. Listing 12-6 contains the DialogBoxDemo.html Web page.

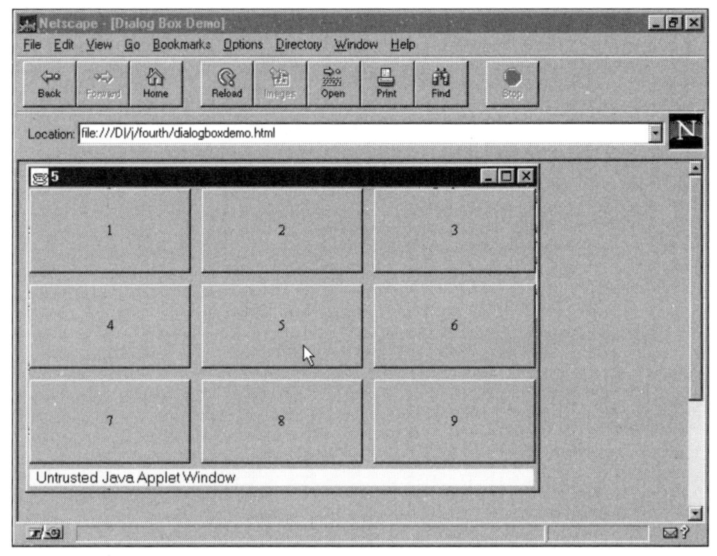

Figure 12-4: DialogBoxDemo applet.

Listing 12-5 DialogBoxDemo.java Source Code

```
/*
 *  DialogBoxDemo.java - Create a dialog box.
 *
 *  Creating Cool Web Applets with Java
 *  By: Paul J. Perry,  Publisher: IDG Books
 *
 */

import java.applet.*;
import java.awt.*;

/****************************************************/
```

(continued)

Listing 12-5 *(continued)*

```
public class DialogBoxDemo extends java.applet.Applet
{
   // Data members
   Frame f;
   NineSquaresDialog d;
   Button b1, b2, b3, b4, b5, b6, b7, b8, b9;

   // Initialization
   public void init()
   {
       // Create frame
       f = new Frame("frame window");

       // Create dialog box
       d = new NineSquaresDialog(f, true);

       // Set layout manager for dialog box
       d.setLayout(new GridLayout(3, 3, 10, 10));

       // Don't allow user to resize the dialog box
       d.setResizable(false);

       // Create buttons
       b1 = new Button("1");
       b2 = new Button("2");
       b3 = new Button("3");
       b4 = new Button("4");
       b5 = new Button("5");
       b6 = new Button("6");
       b7 = new Button("7");
       b8 = new Button("8");
       b9 = new Button("9");

       // Add buttons to dialog box
       d.add(b1);
       d.add(b2);
       d.add(b3);
       d.add(b4);
       d.add(b5);
       d.add(b6);
       d.add(b7);
       d.add(b8);
       d.add(b9);

       d.show();
   }
```

```
}

/***************************************************/
class NineSquaresDialog extends Dialog
{
   NineSquaresDialog(Frame f, boolean b)
   {
       // Call parent constructor
      super(f, b);
   }

   public boolean action(Event evt, Object arg)
   {
       // Check for button presses
       if (evt.target instanceof Button)
       {
          String s = (String)arg;
           System.out.println(s);
           // Change dialog box title to button pressed
           setTitle(s);
       }
      return true;
   }


}
```

Listing 12-6 DialogBoxDemo.html Web Page

```
<HTML>
<!- DialogBoxDemo.html ->
<HEAD>
   <TITLE>Dialog Box Demo</TITLE>
</HEAD>
<BODY>
This applet creates a dialog box.<P><P>
<APPLET CODE="DialogBoxDemo.class" WIDTH="400" HEIGHT="400">
This Web page requires a <B>Java</B>-enabled Web Browser.
</APPLET>
</BODY>
</HTML>
```

A sample applet

For your coding enjoyment, I put one final applet together. It combines several of the user interface topics that we have discussed in this chapter. With a programming language with a name like Java, the most appropriate applet to leave you with is a virtual coffee machine (see Figure 12-5). The applet creates a dialog box that lets the user choose what kind of coffee he or she would like, using user interface controls to allow for options such as regular or nonfat milk. I've even included an option to create extra hot coffee. Obviously, the applet can't really brew a cup of coffee (after all, the Java language hasn't yet been ported to your coffee machine). In the meantime, it provides a good learning experience. The dialog box that is displayed uses many of the controls we have discussed, including labels, buttons, list items, checkboxes, radio buttons, and scrollbars. When the user clicks on the "Place order" button, a new frame window appears that tells the user that the Java is ready.

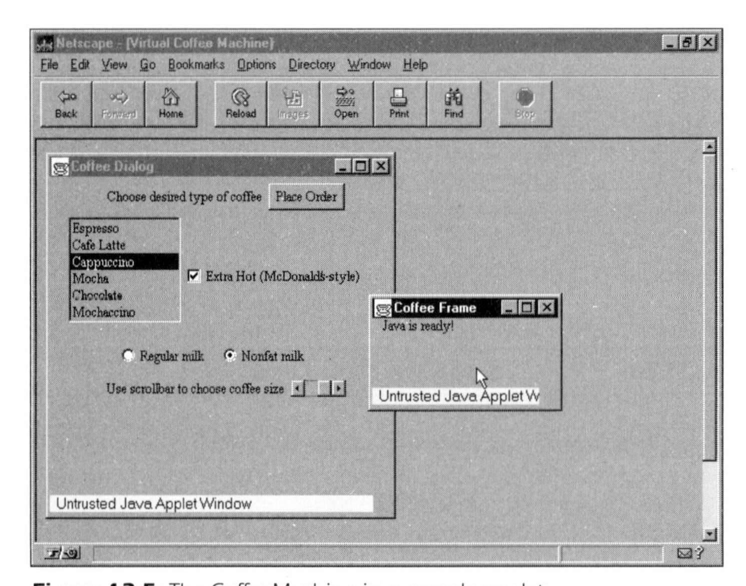

Figure 12-5: The CoffeeMachine.java sample applet.

Listing 12-7 contains the CoffeeMachine.java sample source code, and Listing 12-8 contains the CoffeeMachine.html Web page, which you will need in order to view the applet. By the way, this is the last coffee cliché you will see in this book. However, since you have reached the end of the book, you probably already knew that. Enjoy.

Listing 12-7 CoffeeMachine.java Sample Source Code

```
/*
 *  CoffeeMachine.java - Sample user interface code
 *
 *  Creating Cool Web Applets with Java
 *  By: Paul J. Perry,  Publisher: IDG Books
 *
 */

import java.applet.*;
import java.awt.*;

public class CoffeeMachine extends java.applet.Applet
{
   // Data members
   Frame    frm;
   CoffeeDialog   dlg;

   Label          lbl;
   Button         but;
   List           lst;
   Checkbox       cb;
   CheckboxGroup  cbg;
   Scrollbar      hsb;

   // Initialization
   public void init()
   {
       // Create frame window, which is always hidden,
       //  but required to create a dialog box.
      frm = new Frame("Coffee Shop");

       // Create dialog box
      dlg = new CoffeeDialog(frm, "Coffee Dialog", false);

       // Create label control
       lbl = new Label("Choose desired type of coffee");
       dlg.add(lbl);

       // Create button control
       but = new Button("Place Order");
       dlg.add(but);

      // List item control
       lst = new List(6, false);
       lst.addItem("Espresso");
       lst.addItem("Cafe Latte");
```

(continued)

Listing 12-7 *(continued)*

```
        lst.addItem("Cappuccino");
        lst.addItem("Mocha");
        lst.addItem("Chocolate");
        lst.addItem("Mochaccino");
        dlg.add(lst);

        // Checkbox control
        cb = new Checkbox("Extra Hot (McDonalds style)");
        dlg.add(cb);

        // Radio Control
        cbg = new CheckboxGroup();
        dlg.add(new Checkbox("Regular milk", cbg, true));
        dlg.add(new Checkbox("Nonfat milk", cbg, false));

        // Scrollbar control, along with descriptive text
        dlg.add(new Label("Use scrollbar to choose coffee size"));
        hsb = new Scrollbar(Scrollbar.HORIZONTAL, 100, 5, 1, 100);
        dlg.add(hsb);

        // Display dialog box
        dlg.show();
    }

}

/*****************************************************/
class CoffeeFrame extends Frame
{
   // Data members

   // Constructor
   CoffeeFrame(String title)
   {
       // Call parent constructor
      super(title);
   }

   // Display text
   public void paint(Graphics g)
   {
      g.drawString("Java is ready!", 10, 10);
   }
}

/*****************************************************/
class CoffeeDialog extends Dialog
```

```
{
   // Data Members
   CoffeeFrame cf;

   // Class constructor
   CoffeeDialog(Frame f, String s, boolean b)
   {
       // Call parent constructor
      super(f, s, b);

       // Set grid layout manager
       setLayout(new FlowLayout());

       // Create Result frame
       cf = new CoffeeFrame("Coffee Frame");
   }

   // Process dialog box controls
   public boolean action(Event evt, Object arg)
   {
       if (evt.target instanceof Button)
           MakeCoffee(evt, arg);

      return true;
   }

   void MakeCoffee(Event evt, Object arg)
   {
       cf.show();

   }
}
```

Listing 12-8 CoffeeMachine.html Web Page

```
<HTML>
<!- CoffeeMachine.html ->
<HEAD>
   <TITLE>Virtual Coffee Machine</TITLE>
</HEAD>
<BODY>
<APPLET CODE="CoffeeMachine.class" WIDTH="400" HEIGHT="400">
This Web page requires a <B>Java</B>-enabled Web Browser.
</APPLET>
</BODY>
</HTML>
```

Quick Overview

Well, you have made it to the end of this book. Obviously you realize that you have learned a lot of information about creating cool Web applets with Java. You have learned how to mark up text with HTML, how to write small applets using Java, and how to integrate multimedia elements like text, audio, and graphics into them. You have also learned how to access data over the Internet and how to make use of Abstract Window Toolkit, which comes with Java.

In particular, this chapter covered the following topics:

- Frame windows are separate from the main Web browser window. You create a frame window by extending the `Frame` class.
- Main menus are a part of almost all top-level windows. As a result, Java frame windows have a way to add menus and menu items.
- Dialog boxes are designed to contain user interface controls and provide a way to obtain input from the user, while also allowing a method to present information to the user.

Here is a brief overview of what is to come...

If you have made it to this point, I do believe that you are dedicated to learning about Java. Because the language is still young and constantly growing, you will want to seek help in other places. What follows is information about extra information in this book that will point you to locations where you can keep most up-to-date about Java.

- Appendix A, "HTML Quick Reference," provides a quick reference guide to the hypertext markup language.
- Appendix B, "Java Language Reference," provides a quick reference guide to the Java programming language.
- Appendix C, "Java Resources," provides places to look for additional information and assistance with Java programming.
- Appendix D, "Glossary," provides a reference to the vocabulary used in this book.

HTML Quick Reference

HTML tags are not case-sensitive. The tag `<TITLE>` is the same as `<title>`.

Structural tags

`<HTML> ... </HTML>`	Delimits the beginning and end of the document
`<HEAD> ... </HEAD>`	Delimits the beginning and end of the document header
`<TITLE> ... </TITLE>`	Page title
`<BODY> ... </BODY>`	Delimits the beginning and end of the document body
`<! ... ->`	Embedded comments

Paragraph formatting

`<P>`	Paragraph marker
`<H1> ... </H1>`	Heading level 1
`<H2> ... </H2>`	Heading level 2
`<H3> ... </H3>`	Heading level 3
`<H4> ... </H4>`	Heading level 4
`<H5> ... </H5>`	Heading level 5
`<H6> ... </H6>`	Heading level 6
`<PRE> ... </PRE>`	Pre-formatted text
`<PRE WIDTH="80"> ... </PRE>`	Pre-formatted text of specified width
`<HR>`	Displays the horizontal line the width of the browser window
` `	Forces a line break, but uses no extra spaces

Character formatting

<B> ... </B>	Boldface text
<I> ... </I>	Italic text

Logical text formatting

<ADDRESS> ... </ADDRESS>	Displays address information. Usually italics.
<BLOCKQUOTE> ... </BLOCKQUOTE>	Indents text to separate from surrounding text.
<CITE> ... </CITE>	Used for citations (titles of books, films, and so forth). Usually italics.
<CODE> ... </CODE>	Used for snippets of computer code. Usually a fixed-width font.
<DFN> ... </DFN>	Used for words being defined. Usually italics.
<EM> ... </EM>	Used for emphasis. Usually italics.
<KDB> ... </KDB>	Used for keyboard entry. Usually bold fixed-width font.
<SAMP> ... </SAMP>	Used for computer status messages. Usually a fixed-width font.
<STRONG> ... </STRONG>	Used for strong emphasis. Usually boldface.
<VAR> ... </VAR>	Used for variable text. Usually italics.

Hypertext links

<A HREF="target URL"> HotSpot text</A>	Hypertext link to another server page
<A NAME=targetname> HotSpot text</A>	Specifies hypertext target name
<A HREF="#targetname> target location text</A>	Hyperlink target location
<A HREF="target URL#targetname">HotSpot text</A>	Hyperlink to a named location in a target URL

Lists

<UL> ... </UL>	Unordered (bulleted) lists
<OL> ... </OL>	Ordered (numbered) lists
<MENU> ... </MENU>	Menu lists
<DIR> ... </DIR>	Directory (horizontal) lists
<DL> ... </DL>	Glossary (definition) lists
<DT>	Definition text (for glossary lists)
<DD>	Definition description (for glossary lists)

In-line images and sound

<IMG SRC="fname.gif">	Inserts a graphics image file
<IMG ALIGN=top SRC=Image_URL>	Inserts a graphics image and aligns text with the top
<IMG ALIGN=middle SRC=Image_URL>	Inserts a graphics image and aligns text with the center of the image
<IMG SRC = "fname.gif" ALT = "text">	Inserts a graphic image. If not using GUI, uses "display text".
<A HREF = "file://fname.mov">HotSpot text</A>	Links to an external image (movie, sound, and so on)

Extended characters

Code	Description	Character
Á	Uppercase A with acute accent	Á
Â	Uppercase A with circumflex	Â
Æ	Uppercase AE diphthong	Æ
À	Uppercase A with grave accent	À
Ã	Uppercase A with tilde	Ã
Ä	Uppercase A with umlaut	Ä
Ç	Uppercase C with cedilla	Ç
É	Uppercase E with acute accent	É
Ê	Uppercase E with circumflex	Ê
È	Uppercase E with grave accent	È
Ë	Uppercase E with umlaut	Ë

(continued)

Code	Description	Character
í	Uppercase I with acute accent	Í
î	Uppercase I with circumflex	Î
ì	Uppercase I with grave accent	Ì
ï	Uppercase I with umlaut	Ï
Ñ	Uppercase N with tilde	Ñ
Ó	Uppercase O with acute accent	Ó
Ô	Uppercase O with circumflex	Ô
Ò	Uppercase O with grave accent	Ò
Õ	Uppercase O with a tilde	Õ
Ö	Uppercase O with umlaut	Ö
Ú	Uppercase U with acute accent	Ú
Û	Uppercase U with circumflex	Û
Ù	Uppercase U with grave accent	Ù
Ü	Uppercase U with umlaut	Ü
Ý	Uppercase Y with acute accent	Ý

Escape sequences

Command	Description	Character
<	Less than	<
>	Greater than	>
&	Ampersand	&
"	Double quote	"
	Non-breaking space	' '

Embedding a Java applet

To add a Java applet to your Web page, you must use the <APPLET> tag. The tag has a specific format as well as a number of different parameters.

General format

```
<APPLET CODE="ClassName.class" WIDTH="x" HEIGHT="y">
<PARAM NAME="parameter name" VALUE="parameter value">
This text is displayed on non Java-enabled browsers.
</APPLET>
```

You must specify the class name with the same case as its filename. The WIDTH and HEIGHT parameters let you specify the size of the area where the applet has access. You specify the area in pixels. In the <APPLET> tag, you can use any number of <PARAM> tags to pass information (or parameters) to the applet.

Any text that appears between the beginning and ending <APPLET> tags is not displayed by Java-enabled browsers, but any browser that is not Java-enabled displays it.

Optional parameters

ALT="Text"	Specifies alternate text for text-only Web browsers to display.
CODEBASE="http://www.myurl.com/directory"	Provides a path to a directory containing class files.
NAME="Text"	Assigns a symbolic name to an applet. Other applets on the same page can use the name.
ALIGN="Position"	You can position a Java applet just like you position an image in a Web page. You can choose one of: LEFT, RIGHT, TOP, MIDDLE, BOTTOM, TEXTTOP, BASELINE, MIDDLE, or ABSBOTTOM. If you use the LEFT or RIGHT alignment options, the text in the Web page will flow around the space assigned to the applet.
VSPACE="size"	Used only when ALIGN="LEFT" or ALIGN="RIGHT" and allows you to specify the vertical space around the applet. This allows you to specify the amount of whitespace around the applet.
HSPACE="size"	Used only when ALIGN="LEFT" or ALIGN="RIGHT" to specify the horizontal space around the applet. Allows you to specify the amount of whitespace around the applet.

In most instances, you don't need to use all the parameters.

Netscape enhanced tags

<table>
<tr><td><Body bgcolor="FFFFFF" text="000000"></td><td>Specifies background and foreground color of the Web page</td></tr>
<tr><td><hr size=xx, width=xx align = "left"|"right" |"center"></td><td>Specifies width, height, and alignment for horizontal bars</td></tr>
<tr><td><blink> … </blink></td><td>Displays blinking text</td></tr>
<tr><td><center>… </center></td><td>Centers text</td></tr>
</table>

Netscape tables

<TABLE border=1 CELLSPACING=5 cellpadding=5>	Specify table
<CAPTION ALIGN=TOP>Title</CAPTION>	Specify table caption
<TR>	Table row begin
<TD>row 1 item</TD>	Table cell
<TH>row 1 item</TH>	Table heading item
<TH>row 1 item</TH>	Table heading item
<TH>row 1 item</TH>	Table heading item
</TR>	Table row end
<TR>	Next table row begin
<TH>row 2 item </TH>	Table heading item
<TD>row 2 item</TD>	Table cell
<TD>row 2 item </TD>	Table cell
<TD>row 2 item </TD>	Table cell
</TR>	Table row end
</TABLE>	End of table

Netscape font specification

<BASEFONT>	Uses the default font
<BASEFONT SIZE=x>	Specifies the size of the font, a value between 1 and 7
<FONT SIZE=x>	Changes the size of the font
<FONT SIZE=+2>	Modifies the font in relation to its current size

Java Language Reference

In This Chapter

How to access Internet electronic mail over commercial network computers.

Electronic mail is important when you are working with the Web. To contact other people who are in charge of home pages (Web Masters), you often need to contact them through e-mail. This appendix shows how to access Internet e-mail through several other services. You'll learn how to send and receive e-mail from CompuServe, Prodigy, and AOL and use standard Internet e-mail tools such as Eudora.

General Applet Construction

A minimal Java Applet has the following construction:

```
/*
 *  MinimalJavaApplet.java - Sample Template
 *
 *  Creating Cool Web Applets with Java
 *  By: Paul J. Perry,  Publisher: IDG Books
 *
 */

import java.applet.*;
import java.awt.Graphics;

public class MinimalApplet extends java.applet.Applet
{
   public void init()
   {
      // Always called first time applet is executed.
   }
```

```
   public void start()
   {
      // Called after init() and also whenever Web page is
revisited.
   }
   public void stop()
   {
      // Called when Web page that contains this applet disap-
pears.
   }
   public void destroy()
   {
      // Called when applet is being purged from memory.
   }
   // This is where the graphics processing is done.
   public void paint(Graphics g)
   {
      g.drawString("Java is Cool!", 10, 10);
   }
}
```

Data types

Type	Description
`boolean`	Either true or false
`byte`	Eight-bit integer
`char`	Character (‘ ’)
`double`	64-bit double precision floating point
`float`	32-bit single precision floating point
`int`	32-bit integer
`long`	64-bit integer
`short`	16-bit integer
`String`	String Object (“ ”)

Character formatting sequences

Sequence	Description
`\n`	Line feed
`\t`	Horizontal tab
`\b`	Backspace
`\r`	Carriage return
`\f`	Form feed

\\	Backslash
\'	Single quotation mark
\"	Double quotation mark
\uxxxx	Unicode character

Relational operators

Operator	Description
<	Less than
>	Greater than
<=	Less than or equal to
>=	Greater than or equal to
==	Equal to
!=	Not equal to

Unary operators

Operator	Description
~	Unary negation
++	Increment by one
--	Decrement by one

Mathematical operators

Operator	Description
+	Addition
-	Subtraction
*	Multiplication
/	Division

Conditional statements

A simple `if` statement

```
if (booleanTest)
   callfunction();
```

A multiline `if` statement

```
if (booleanTest)
{
   callFunction();
   callAnotherFunction();
   // etc.
}
```

The `if...else` statement

```
if (booleanTest)
{
   // Value is true.
}
else
{
    //  Value is false.
}
```

The `while` statement

```
while (booleanTest)
   statement;
```

The `do...while` loop

```
do
{
   // do something
}
while (booleanTest);
```

The `switch` statement

```
switch(expression)
{
   case FirstCase :
      // First set of statements
      break;

   case SecondCase :
      // Second set of statements
      break;
```

```
   case ThirdCase :
      // Third set of statements
      break;
.
.
.

   default :
      // Default statement
      break;
}
```

Program control statements

```
for (initialization; condition; increment)
   statement;
```

Defining classes

The basic structure of defining a class is as follows:

```
Scope class ClassName [extends class]
{
   // Class implementation
}
```

When declaring the scope of the class, you have several options to control how other classes can access this class:

- `public`. The class can be used by code outside of the file. Only one class in a file may have this scope. The file must be named with the class name followed by the four-letter .java extension.
- `private`. The class can only be used within a file.
- `abstract`. The class cannot be used by itself and must be subclassed.
- `final`. The class cannot be used by a subclass.
- `synchronizable`. Instances of this class can be made arguments.

If you don't use a scope modifier, the class is only accessible within the current file.

Defining methods

A *method* is the code that acts on data inside a class and is always declared inside the class declaration. A method has the following syntax:

```
Scope ReturnType MethodName(arguments)
{
    // Method implementation
}
```

The scope allows the programmer to control access to methods and can be one of the following:

- `public`. The method is accessible by any system object.
- `protected`. The method is only accessible by subclasses and the class in which it is declared.
- `private`. The method is accessible only within current class.
- `final`. The method cannot be overridden by any subclass.
- `static`. The method is shared by all instances of the class.

If a method is not given a scope, it is only accessible within the scope of the current file. You can also use these scope operators when declaring variables.

Exception handling

An exception has two parts: signaling an exception and setting up an exception handler. To signal an exception, use the `try` keyword. To set up an exception handler, you use the `catch` keyword. You use the `finally` keyword to specify a block of statements that will execute no matter what. To tell the system that an error has occurred, use the `throw` keyword.

```
try
{
    // Try this block of code.
}
catch (Exception e)
{
    // Catch errors.  Error condition.  Handle error.
}
finally
{
    // Code which is executed no matter what happens.
}
```

Java Resources

This appendix is a place for you to learn where to go to find out more about Java. Java is a new language, and much new information is constantly being made available. Because the language is still in its infancy, so much is happening, and unless you keep an eye open, you'll find it hard to keep up-to-date with the latest news. The resources found in this appendix will keep you abreast of all the happenings of Java. However, remember that new sites are always appearing so make sure you always keep your eyes open for cool new Java resources.

The Java home page

Located at http://www.javasoft.com, this home page has the most current version of the Java Developers Kit for multiple platforms, documentation, and the HotJava browser. This is also the official site where Java is being developed, so it provides information about what's happening with Java. You will want to visit this site regularly.

The Java newsgroup

Another great source of information is the Java newsgroup (comp.lang.java). Just like most newsgroups these days, you may find a lot of noise on this page, but you will also find plenty of good information. If you have questions, this is a good place to post them, and other experienced users can respond to them.

The Java Developer page

The Java Developer page (http://www.digitalfocus.com/digitalfocus/faq/index.html) is a Web site maintained by the folks at Digital Focus. It provides a good Q&A section on developing for Java and also provides links to the newest applets that are being developed.

The Symantec home page

Symantec (http://www.symantec.com) already has a beta version of a Java development tool called Espresso. It is an add-on to the company's C++ compiler, and the patch is available free of charge from the Symantec Web site. Some say that the company is working on Java development tools for both Windows and the Macintosh. You might want to keep tuned into this page for more information on Java development tools.

The Borland home page

The exciting news is that Borland (http://www.borland.com) is working on a Java Development tool as well, called Latté. Not much is known about it, but if it is anything like the tools this company has developed for Pascal, it should be a great hit. This is the site that will keep you tuned into these developments.

The Netscape home page

Of course, we can't forget the Netscape home page, http://www.netscape.com. Being the number one browser, you definitely want to keep your eyes peeled as to when new releases become available, as well as other news that might be of interest.

The *JavaWorld* home page

JavaWorld magazine (http://www.javaworld.com) strives to be the authoritative Java information source. Each issue gives expert opinions, news, and reviews about Java-specific products, applets, and real-world examples of Java in action.

Symbols

& (ampersand), 85, 305, 306, 309
* (asterisk), 102, 103, 114–115, 140
\ (backslash), 123, 331
: (colon), 22, 134
{} (curly brackets), 116, 128, 133
$ (dollar sign), 120
" (double quotes), 85, 122–123, 136–137, 331
... (ellipsis), 42
! (exclamation point), 323
/ (forward slash), 22, 67, 114, 140
> (greater-than sign), 67, 84–85, 104
< (less-than sign), 67, 84–85, 104
- (minus sign), 85, 121, 306
' ' (non-breaking space), 85
() (parentheses), 132
% (percent sign), 76
+ (plus sign), 85, 121
# (pound sign), 94
; (semicolon), 132–133, 139
' (single quotes), 123, 331
[] (square brackets), 168
_ (underscore character), 120
32-bit programming, 38
3DO, Inc., 17

<A> (anchor) tag, 93–95, 97–99, 324–325
Á, 86, 325
abort action, when downloading, 45, 59
About the Internet option, 58
About Netscape, 56
About Plug-ins, 56
ABSBOTTOM option, 112
accept() method, 263
Access, 276
Â, 86, 325
action() method, 282–283, 290, 296, 308, 314
Add Bookmark, 51, 59
addItem() method, 280
addition operator, 132, 331
add() method, 268, 273
addPoint() method, 160
<ADDRESS> (address information) tag, 82, 324
Adobe Illustrator, 203
Æ, 86, 325
À, 86, 325
AIFF format, 98–99
aliases, creating, 51
alignment. *See also* ALIGN parameter
  of applets, 112, 327
  of caption text, 81
  of horizontal rules, 77
  of images, 96
  of user interface controls, 270–271, 277
ALIGN parameter, 76, 81, 96, 112, 327. *See also* alignment
alphabetic object types, 122–123
Alt key
  Alt+F4 (Abort), 59
  modifier keys and, 189, 190
ALT parameter, 111, 327
Amiga, 23
&, 85, 326
ampersand (&), 85, 305, 306, 309
Andreessen, Marc, 19
AnimateDemo.html, 172–173
animation
  basic description of, 167–170
  creating, two basic steps for, 168
  multithreaded code and, 169–170
  in the Rolling Stones Web site, 30–31
  sound and, 171–172
Animator applet, 171–172, 210–211
Animator class, 172–173
AOL (America Online), 34, 63, 65
<APP> (applet tag), 113
Apple. *See also* Macintosh
  AIFF format, 98–99
  Newton PDA, 16
  the Unicode character set and, 122

applet(s)
alignment of, 112, 327
creating, three steps involved in, 109–113
definition of, 14, 109
events, introduction to, 125–128
file types, 110
general construction of, example of, 329–330
passing parameters to, 134–138
<APPLET> (applet) tag, 110–113, 127, 269, 326–327
Applet class, 146, 266
applications, definition of, 109
Arabic numbers, 66
ArcTest applet, 212–213
ArithmeticException exception, 249
array declarations, 125
ArrayIndexOutOfBoundsException exception, 249
ArrayStoreException exception, 249
ASCII (American Standard Code for Information Interchange), 20, 62, 67, 147, 189–190
asterisk (*), 102, 103, 114–115, 140
Ã, 86, 325
audio
animation and, 171–172
file formats, 98–99, 175–177
helper applications and, 25, 176
HTML tags for, 98–99, 176
objects, working with, 176–179
playing, 179–185
sampling, 175
working with, overview of, 175–186
AudioClip class, 177–178
AudioClip object, 177–179, 191
AUDIO.WAV, 98
AU format, 98–99, 176, 177
Ä, 86, 325
autoflowing, definition of, 73
Auto Load Images, 53
AUTO value, 103
awt class, 163
AWT (Abstract Windowing Toolkit), 266–268
creating dialog boxes with, 299, 312–321
creating windows with, 299–303
frames and, 299–303
keyboard support, 188–194
mouse support, 194–207

B

<B> (boldface) tag, 83, 324
Back button, 44, 50
background(s)
color, 70–71, 95, 98, 155–156, 164–165
specifying, with the drawImage() method, 164–165
wallpaper, 97–98
BACKGROUND parameter, 171
backslash (\), 123, 331
backspace character, 123, 330
backward compatibility, 17, 27. *See also* compatibility
banners, 99
BarChart applet, 214–215
<BASEFONT> (font size) tag, 85, 328
BASELINE option, 112
BASIC, 27, 108
BGCOLOR parameter, 70–71, 95
binary files
compiling source code into, 118–119, 138–139
file extension for, 110, 138
bin subdirectory, 118
bitmaps, used as backgrounds, 97–98. *See also* graphics; images
<BLINK> (blinking text) tag, 84, 328
BlinkingText applet, 216–217
<BLOCKQUOTE> (indent quote) tag, 82, 324
BMW Web site, 5, 7
<BODY> (body) tag, 70–71, 73, 95, 97–98, 100, 323, 328
boldface font, 66, 77, 83–84
<B> (boldface) tag and, 83, 324
BOLD attribute and, 148
bookmarks, 38, 50–53, 59
Bookmarks menu, 42, 51, 59
boolean data type, 120–121, 283, 330
checkbox menu items and, 307
graphics and, 156, 160
if...else statements and, 128–130
modifier keys and, 190
borders, 81, 97, 103, 269, 272–273
BorderLayout() constructor, 273
BORDER parameter, 81
Borland, 5, 34, 336
BOTTOM option, 96, 112
BouncingHeads applet, 217–218

 (line break) tag, 74–75, 323
brackets
 {} (curly brackets), 116, 128, 133
 [] (square brackets), 168
brighter() method, 154
broken key icon, 47, 57
browsers. *See also* Netscape Navigator browser
 autoflowing and, 73
 basic description of, 11
 history of, 13–14
 HotJava, 17–18, 110, 113
 Internet Explorer, 11, 63–64
 Mosaic, 11, 13–14, 19, 37, 52, 69
 Spry Mosaic, 11
 text-only browsers, 96, 111
 viewing source code with, 67–68
 WebRunner, 17
BufferedInputStream constructor, 258
bulleted (unordered) lists, 63, 87–89, 325
ButtonApp.html, 296, 297
ButtonApp.java, 296–297
ButtonHeight parameter, 296
buttons, adding, 266–268, 277–278, 283
ButtonWidth parameter, 296
byte code verification systems, 27–28
byte data type, 120, 330
bytesWidth() method, 149–150

C (programming language), 10, 113, 246, 247
 the #include directive and, 115
 OOP and, 108
C++ (programming language), 10, 26–28, 34, 123
 for loops in, 130, 131
 graphics and, 163
 Java object libraries and, 108
Calendar applet, 32–33
Canada, 9
CAPTION tag, 81, 328
Card layout manager, 269, 274
CardTest applet, 218–220
carriage return character, 122–123, 330
case keyword, 134
case-sensitivity, 23, 111
 HTML tags and, 67
 the Java compiler and, 119, 139
catch keyword, 247, 250–251, 334
Ç, 86, 325
CELLPADDING parameter, 81
CELLSPACING parameter, 81
<CENTER> (center text) tag, 85, 328
CENTER keyword, 77
CERN (European Laboratory for Particle Physics), 12
character formatting, 66, 83–86, 324. *See also* fonts
char data type, 330
charsWidth() method, 149–150
Checkbox class, 278
Checkbox() constructor, 278–279
checkboxes, 267–268, 278–279, 283, 307–308
CheckboxGroup class, 279
Choice class, 280
choice items, 267–268, 280, 283
circles/circular shapes, 160–161, 203–207
<CITE> (citation) tag, 82, 324
citizens band (CB) radio, 9
Clark, Jim, 19
class(es). *See also* specific classes
 basic description of, 9, 108–109
 defining, 114–116, 123–124, 333–334
 files, converting, into source code, 141–142
 imports, specifying, 114–115
 inheritance, 28, 109
 MFC (Microsoft Foundation Classes), 108
 names, 116, 120
 program documentation and, 140
 scope of, 124, 333
 standard, list of, 115
ClassCastException exception, 249
class keyword, 115–116
ClassNotFoundException exception, 249
CLASSPATH variable, 139
clearRect() function, 155–156
ClickLink.class parameters, 256
ClickLink.html, 256–257
ClickLink2.html, 257
ClickLink.java, 253–256
clipboard, 59
CloneNotSupportedException exception, 249
close() method, 263
Close Window, 59
CNN Web site, 5–6
<CODE> (computer code) tag, 82, 324
CODEBASE parameter, 111

CODE parameter, 111
Codewright, 109
CoffeeMachine.html, 318, 321
CoffeeMachine.java, 318–321
colon (:), 22, 134
color
 of backgrounds, 70–71, 95, 98, 155–156
 the Color object and, 153–154
 hexadecimal values for, 71
 HSB color scheme, 154
 of hyperlinks, 95
 of lines, 155
 returning brighter/darker versions of, 154
 RGB color scheme, 71, 95, 154
 of squares and rectangles, 155–158
 working with multiple, 153–154
column(s)
 displaying multiple, 102
 labels, 82
command line, 118, 139, 141–142, 266
comments, 71–72, 114, 140
commercials, background music in, 179
Commodore, 23
Compaq Web site, 5
compatibility, 17, 23, 27, 65, 266
compilers. *See also* compiling
 case-sensitivity and, 119, 139
 default statements and, 134
 import commands and, 115
 platform independence and, 26
compiling, 109–110. *See also* compilers
 comments and, 114
 errors, 132
 source code into binary class files, 118–119, 138–139
compression, 66
constructors
 basic description of, 117
 BorderLayout(), 273
 BufferedInputStream, 258
 Checkbox(), 278–279
 DataInputStream(), 258
 Dialog(), 213
 FlowLayout(), 271
 GridLayout(), 272
 Label(), 268
 Menu(), 305
 MenuItem(), 306
 TextArea(), 289
 TextField(), 281
consumer electronics, 14–17, 33–34, 109. *See also* television
context-sensitivity, 42
control flow statements, 128–134
Control Panel, 40
coolstuff.zip, 252
copying
 bookmarks/hot lists, 52
 and pasting, in Netscape, 42, 59
copyright notices, 100
Courier font, 78, 148
Creative Labs, 175
credit card numbers, transmitting, 57
cross-platform compatibility, 23, 266. *See also* compatibility
Ctrl key, modifier keys and, 189. *See also* Ctrl key combinations
Ctrl key combinations
 Ctrl+< (Go Back), 59
 Ctrl+> (Go Forward), 59
 Ctrl+A (Select All), 59
 Ctrl+B (View Bookmarks), 59
 Ctrl+C (Copy to clipboard), 59
 Ctrl+D (Add Bookmark), 51, 59
 Ctrl+D (Down Arrow), 194
 Ctrl+F (Find Character String)), 59
 Ctrl+H (View History List), 50, 59
 Ctrl+I (Load Images), 59
 Ctrl+L (Open Location), 48, 59
 Ctrl+M (New Mail Message), 59
 Ctrl+N (New Web Browser), 41, 59
 Ctrl+O (Open File), 48, 59
 Ctrl+R (Reload), 59
 Ctrl+S (Save As), 48, 59
 Ctrl+V (Paste from clipboard), 59
 Ctrl+W (Close Window), 59
 Ctrl+X (Cut to clipboard), 59
 Ctrl+Z (Undo), 59
curly braces ({}), 116, 128, 133
CustomFrame class, 301, 302
Cut to clipboard (command), 59

D

darker() method, 154
data compression, 66
DataInputStream() constructor, 258
data types, 26–27, 120–121, 330
<DD> (glossary definition) tag, 91, 325

debugging, 139. *See also* errors
decimal numbers, 121
decrement operator, 131, 331
default statements, 134
deleting bookmarks, 52
Delphi, 34, 276
Delphi Developer, 276
demographics, 9
destroy() method, 127, 179
developer tool kits, 29–30. *See also* JDK (Java Development Kit)
<DFN> (defined word) tag, 83, 324
DialogBoxDemo.html, 315, 317
DialogBoxDemo.java, 315–317
dialog boxes, 312–321
  modal/modeless, 312–313
  standard open/save, 314
  tabbed, 274
Dialog() constructor, 313
Dialog font, 148
DialogInput, 148
Digital Focus, 336
digital video. *See* video
Dimension object, 150
<DIR> (directory list) tag, 87, 90–91, 325
Director (Macromedia), 20
directories
  class file, providing paths to, 111
  containing Java development tools, at the Java Web site, 118
  specifying, for Netscape installation, 39, 40
directory bars, 38, 40, 46
directory buttons, 42
directory lists, 87, 90–91, 325
Directory menu, 40, 42, 46, 58
display area, definition of, 274
DisplayColor.html, 158
DisplayColor.java, 157–158
distribution, software, 24, 28–29
DitherTest applet, 220–221
division operator, 132, 331
<DL> (glossary list) tag, 87, 91–92, 325
DLLs (Dynamic Link Libraries), 105
do...while statements, 132–133, 332
documentation, program. *See* Java documentation tool
Document Encoding option, 53
Document Info window, 48
Document Source, 48, 68
Dolby Labs, 16
dollar sign ($), 120
DOS (Disk Operating System), 1, 23, 67, 118
double data type, 120–121, 330
double quotes ("), 85, 122–123, 136–137, 331
down arrow key, 59, 191, 194
downloading
  aborting, 45, 59
  displaying the progress of, with the status bar, 41, 46–47
Down radio button, 45
drawArc() method, 161
drawImage() method, 164, 165
drawLine() method, 155
drawPolygon() method, 158–159
drawRect() method, 155
drawString() method, 116, 128, 145–147
DrawTest applet, 221–222
<DT> (definition text) tag, 325
Duke (Java Mascot), 25, 240–241

É, 86, 325
Ê, 86, 325
Edit menu, 42
educational applications, 29, 30–31
È, 86, 325
ellipsis (...), 42
<EM> (emphasis) tag, 83, 324
e-mail, 47, 53–55, 95, 134, 329–334
ENDIMAGE parameter, 171
End key, 191
EnhancedControlsDemo.html, 291, 293
EnhancedControlsDemo.java, 291–293
envelope icon, 47
equals() method, 309
error(s). *See also* debugging
  compiling, 132
  handling, 245–247
  resulting from misplaced semicolons, 132
Escape key (Abort), 59
escape sequences, 85, 326
Espresso, 143, 336
Ë, 86, 325
Event class, 190, 195
Event object, 199
Event parameter, 282
events, introduction to, 125–128
Exception (generic) exception, 249
exception handling, 247–251, 334

exclamation point (!), 323
exiting Netscape, 42, 59
extended characters, 86, 325–326
extends keyword, 116

F3 (Exit), 59
false keyword, 120
FedEx Web site, 14–15
file access restrictions, 27–28
FileDialog dialog boxes, 314
file extensions
 character limit for, 110
 .class, 110, 111, 118
 .gif, 168
 .HTM, 67
 .HTML, 67, 110
 .java, 110
 .WAV, 98
FileInputStream class, 248
File menu, 39, 41–42, 45, 48
 File⇨Open File, 119
 File⇨Print, 50
filenames, long, 67, 110
FileNotFound exception, 249
fillPolygon() method, 159–160
fillRect() method, 156
finally keyword, 250–251, 334
final methods, 124, 334
financial transactions, security for, 28, 57
Find Again, 59
Find button, 44, 45
Find Character String, 59
Find dialog box, 45
FirstPerson, Inc., 17
float data type, 120–121, 330
FlowLayout() constructor, 271
Flowlayout layout manager, 269, 270–271
font(s), 78–86. *See also* character formatting
 Netscape settings for, 54, 328
 specifying, with Java, 147–152
Font getFont() method, 149
FontMetric objects, 148–149
Font object, 147–148
footers, 99
fopen(), 246
foreign languages, 86, 122, 325–326
for loops, 130–132
form feed character, 123, 330
FORTRAN, 10, 108
Forward button, 44, 50
forward slash (/), 22, 67, 114, 140
Fractal applet, 222–224
frames, 99–103, 299–303
 animating, steps for, 167–170
 dialog boxes and, 313–314
<FRAME> (frame) tag, 100–102, 103
Frame class, 299–302
frameholders, 100
<FRAMESET> (frameset) tag, 100–102
Frequently Asked Questions option, 56, 57
FTP (File Transfer Protocol), 21, 28, 38
function calls, testing for values/results from, 129–130
function keys, 59, 191

games, 17, 26, 28–29, 32
garbage collection, 27
General Preferences dialog box, 53, 54–55
General Preferences menu item, 44
getAppletContext() method, 252–253
getAudioClip() method, 177, 181
getBlue() method, 154
getBoundingBox() method, 160
getCodeBase() method, 138
getColor() method, 154
getDescent() method, 149
getDocument() method, 252
getDocumentBase method, 137–138, 164, 177–178
getFont() method, 148
getHeight() method, 149–150
getHSBColor() method, 154
getImage() method, 164, 165, 168
getLeading() method, 149
getMaxAdvance() method, 149
getMaxAscent() method, 149
getMaxDescent() method, 149
getParameter() method, 137, 257
getSelectedItem() method, 291
getWidths() method, 149
GIF (Graphics Interchange Format), 96, 168
glossary (definition) lists, 87, 91–92, 325
Go Back, 59
Go button, 50
Go Forward, 59
Go menu, 42

Gosling, James, 15–16
Goto Bookmark option, 51
graphics. *See also* backgrounds; images; shapes
  displaying, overview of, 155–161
  file types, list of, 165
  HTML tags for, 96–98, 165
  interactivity and, 203–207
Graphics class, 146–148
Graphics object, 116, 153, 155–161, 164
GraphicsTest applet, 224–225
GraphLayout applet, 225–227
greater-than sign (>), 67, 84–85, 104
Green team, 15–17
GridBagConstraints class, 274–275
GridBagLayout layout manager, 269, 274–275
GridLayout() constructor, 272
Grid layout manager, 269, 271–272
grids, 269, 271–272, 274–275
>, 85, 326
GUI (graphical user interface), 23, 266

<H1...H6> (heading) tags, 77–78, 323
Handbook button, 46
Handbook option, 46, 56, 57
handleEvent() method, 290–293
Hangman game (Hang Duke), 31
<HEAD> (header) tag, 69–70, 73, 323
headings, 77–78, 323
HEIGHT parameter, 111, 256, 327
Hello World program, 113–119
help, 42, 46, 56–58
helper applications, 25, 176
HEP (High Energy Physics), 12
hexadecimal values, 71, 121
Hewlett-Packard Web site, 5
hide(), 301
history lists, 50–51
Home button, 44
Home key, 191
Home option, 44, 58
horizontal rules, 75–77, 323
horizontal tab character, 123, 330
HotDog, 105
HotJava browser, 17–18, 110, 113
hotlists. *See* bookmarks
HoTMetaL, 105
hotspots, 83–85. *See also* hypertext
How to Create Web Services option, 56, 57
How to Get Support option, 56, 57
How to Give Feedback option, 56, 57
HPSPACE parameter, 112
<HR> (horizontal rule) tag, 75–77, 323
HSB color scheme, 154
HSBtoRGB() method, 154
HSPACE parameter, 327
HTML (hypertext markup language), 10, 20. *See also* HTML tags (listed by name)
  advantages/disadvantages of, 65–66
  asset integration commands, 67, 95–104
  authoring tools, 104–105
  basic description of, 61–106
  character formatting tags, 66, 83–86, 324
  file formats, 67, 110, 140–141
  files, applets and, passing data between, 134–138
  files, loading/saving, 47–49
  hypertext link tags, 67, 93–95, 324
  list specification tags, 67, 87–92, 325
  logical text formatting tags, 82–83, 324
  multimedia and, 95–105
  paragraph formatting tags, 66, 73–82, 323
  purpose of, 63–65
  quick reference, 323–328
  source code, viewing, 48, 67–68
  structural commands, 66, 68–72, 323
  templates, 72, 105
  versions of, 62, 79
HTML tags (listed by name). *See also* HTML (hypertext markup language)
  <A> (anchor) tag, 93–95, 97–99, 324–325
  <ADDRESS> (address information) tag, 82, 324
  <APP> (applet tag), 113
  <APPLET> (applet) tag, 110–113, 127, 269, 326–327
  <B> (boldface) tag, 83, 324
  <BASEFONT> (font size) tag, 85, 328
  <BLINK> (blinking text) tag, 84, 328
  <BLOCKQUOTE> (indent quote) tag, 82, 324
  <BODY> (body) tag, 70–71, 73, 95, 97–98, 100, 323, 328

 (line break) tag, 74–75, 323
  <CENTER> (center text) tag, 85, 328
  <CITE> (citation) tag, 82, 324

(continued)

HTML tags (listed by name) *(continued)*
<CODE> (computer code) tag, 82, 324
<DD> (glossary definition) tag, 91, 325
<DFN> (defined word) tag, 83, 324
<DIR> (directory list) tag, 87, 90–91, 325
<DL> (glossary list) tag, 87, 91–92, 325
<DT> (definition text) tag, 325
<EM> (emphasis) tag, 83, 324
<FRAME> (frame) tag, 100–102, 103
<FRAMESET> (frameset) tag, 100–102
<H1...H6> (heading) tags, 77–78, 323
<HEAD> (header) tag, 69–70, 73, 323
<HR> (horizontal rule) tag, 75–77, 323
<HTML> tag, 67, 68–69, 73, 323
<I> (italics) tag, 83, 324
<IMG> (image) tag, 96–97, 165, 325
<KDB> (keyboard entry) tag, 83, 324
<LI> (list item) tag, 87, 88–89
<MENU> (menu list) tag, 87, 90–91, 325
<NOBR> (NO BReak) tag, 75
<OL> (ordered list) tag, 87, 89–90, 325
<P> (paragraph) tag, 73–74, 323
<PARAM> (parameter information) tag, 111, 136, 327
<PRE> (pre-formatted text) tag, 78–82, 323
<SAMP> (strong emphasis) tag, 83, 324
<TABLE> (table definition) tag, 79–82, 328
<TD> (table data) tag, 82
<TH> (table header) tag, 82
<TITLE> (title) tag, 69, 73
<TR> (row definition) tag, 80, 82
<UL> (unordered list) tag, 87–89, 325
<VAR> (variable information) tag, 83, 324
<WBR> (Word BReak) tag, 75
HTTP (hypertext transfer protocol), 12, 70, 96
software distribution and, 28
URL formats and, 21–22
hyperlink(s). *See also* hypertext
color of, 95
definition of, 93
frames and, 103–104
hypertext, 83–85. *See also* hyperlinks
basic description of, 11–12
link tags, 67, 93–95, 324
as the main method of interactivity, before Java, 25

I

<I> (italics) tag, 83, 324
í, 86, 326
î, 86, 326
IBM (International Business Machines), 5, 34, 62, 84
icon(s)
adding, to Windows 95 desktops, 51
Netscape program, 39, 40
IDG Books
end-user license agreement, 357–360
Web site, 22
IEEE (Institute of Electrical and Electronic Engineers), 26–27, 121
if...else statements, 128–129, 133, 332
if statements, 128–129, 133, 331–332
ì, 86, 326
IllegalAccessException exception, 249
IllegalArgumentException exception, 250
IllegalMonitorException exception, 250
Illustrator, 203
image(s). *See also* backgrounds; graphics; shapes
drawing, overview of, 163–167
HTML tags for, 96–98, 165–167, 325
loading, with Netscape, 38, 44–45, 59
updating, with Netscape, 20
width/height specifications for, 97, 165
ImageApplet.html, 166–167
ImageApplet.java, 166
Image class, 163, 168–169
ImageMap applet, 227–229
imagemaps, 97–98, 227–229
Image object, 177
ImageObserver object, 164
Images button, 44
IMAGESOURCE parameter, 171
IMAGES parameter, 172
ImageTest applet, 229–230
<IMG> (image) tag, 96–97, 165, 325
img.gif, 165
Import Bookmarks button, 52
importing
bookmarks, 52
classes, 114–115
import keyword, 114–115
Impressionist paint application, 33–34
#include directive, 115
income levels, for World Wide Web users, 9
increment operator, 131, 331
index.html, 22
IndexOutOfBoundsException exception, 250
inheritance, 28, 109
init() method, 127, 137, 179, 181, 257, 271, 281, 296

InputStream object type, 258
inside() method, 160
installation
  JDK, 118
  Netscape, 39–40
  routines, the advantages of Java and, 24, 28
  sound card, 175
instanceof operator, 282, 290
InstantiationException exception, 250
int data type, 120–121, 330
interactivity, 24–25
  adding, overview of, 187–208
  the keyboard and, 188–194
  the mouse and, 194–207
internationalization, 122–123
Internet
  access agents, 29, 32–33
  basic description of, 11
  connections, Netscape settings for, 54–55
  the development of Java for, 10
  directories/white pages, 58
  technical details on, 20–23
Internet Assistant, 105
Internet Directory option, 58
Internet Explorer browser, 11, 63–64
Internet Search option, 58
Internet Shortcut option, 51
Internet White Pages option, 58
italics, 66, 82–83
  <I> (italics) tag and, 83, 324
  ITALIC attribute and, 148
ï, 86, 326

java.applet class, 115
Java applet viewer (JDK), 138, 140
java.awt class, 115
Java compiler, 118–119, 138–139
Java Clouds, 166–167
Java Console, 30, 127–128, 253, 259, 283–286
Java dissassembler, 138, 141–142
Java documentation tool, 138, 140–141
Java interpreter, 138, 139–140
java.io class, 115
java.lang class, 115
java.net class, 115
JavaScript, 20
java.util class, 115
Java Web site, 10, 118, 335–336
JDK (Java Development Kit), 118, 209–210, 335
  basic description of, 138–142
  future development tools and, 142–144
Joy, Bill, 17
JPEG (Joint Photographic Experts Group) format, 96
JumpingBox applet, 230–231

<KDB> (keyboard entry) tag, 83, 324
Kernighan, Brian, 113, 119
keyboard. *See also* keyboard shortcuts
  entry tag (<KDB> tag), 83, 324
  events, 188–189
  extended characters and, 86
  interactivity and, 188–194
  modifier keys, 189–190
  and the PainterApplet example, 203–207
  special keys, 190–191
  viewing Web pages with, 42
keyboard shortcuts. *See also* keyboard shortcuts (listed by name)
  assigning, for menus, 305
  Netscape, list of, 58–59
keyboard shortcuts (listed by name). *See also* keyboard shortcuts
  Alt+F4 (Abort), 59
  Ctrl+< (Go Back), 59
  Ctrl+> (Go Forward), 59
  Ctrl+A (Select All), 59
  Ctrl+B (View Bookmarks), 59
  Ctrl+C (Copy to clipboard), 59
  Ctrl+D (Add Bookmark), 51, 59
  Ctrl+D (Down Arrow), 194
  Ctrl+F (Find Character String)), 59
  Ctrl+H (View History List), 50, 59
  Ctrl+I (Load Images), 59
  Ctrl+L (Open Location), 48, 59
  Ctrl+M (New Mail Message), 59
  Ctrl+N (New Web Browser), 41, 59
  Ctrl+O (Open File), 48, 59
  Ctrl+R (Reload), 59
  Ctrl+S (Save As), 48, 59
  Ctrl+V (Paste from clipboard), 59
  Ctrl+W (Close Window), 59
  Ctrl+X (Cut to clipboard), 59
  Ctrl+Z (Undo), 59

KeyboardYacker.html, 190, 193–194
KeyboardYacker.java, 190–193
KeyDown() method, 188–189
key icon, 47, 57
KeyUp() method, 189

Label() constructor, 268
labels, 82, 266–268, 276–277, 283
languages, foreign, 86, 122, 325–326
layout manager, 268–272, 281
left arrow key, 191
LEFT keyword, 77
LEFT option, 112
length() method, 137
less-than sign (<), 67, 84–85, 104
<LI> (list item) tag, 87, 88–89
libraries, 27–28, 105, 108
licensing
  agreement, IDG end-user, 357–360
  of Java, 19, 34
line(s)
  breaks, 74–75, 323
  continuation characters, 122–123, 330
  displaying, 155
  drawing, 203–207
  feed character, 122–123, 330
linkNewDestination() method, 257
links. *See* hyperlinks
list(s), 66–67, 87–92
  bulleted (unordered) lists, 63, 87–89, 325
  directory lists, 87, 90–91, 325
  glossary (definition) lists, 87, 91–92, 325
  items, the AWT and, 267–268, 287–288
  menu lists, 87, 90–91, 325
  numbered lists, 66, 87, 89–90
  ordered lists, 87, 89–90, 325
List class, 287
literal strings, passing, 116
LiveWire, 20
location box, 40, 42, 46–47
logical text formatting tags, 82–83, 324
Logitech mouse, 195
logos, 47, 56
long data type, 120–121, 330
loop() method, 178
loops, 130–132, 178, 259
<, 85, 326

Macintosh, 13, 19, 26, 38, 266
  audio format (AIFF), 98–99
  cross-platform compatibility and, 23
  mouse input and, 194
  platform independence and, 26
Macromedia Director, 20
Mail and News Preferences dialog box, 53, 54–55
main window, in Netscape, 40–47
malloc function, 27
MARGINHEIGHT parameter, 103
margins, inside frames, 103
MARGINWIDTH parameter, 103
mathematical operators, 131–132, 331
Media Player, 99
memory
  allocating, for arrays, 125
  caching applets in, 127
  efficient usage of, the advantages of Netscape and, 38
  garbage collection and, 27
  the init() method and, 179
  the preview area and, 41
  security and, 27
  sound files and, 179, 181
menu(s). *See also* specific menus
  actions, detecting, 308–309
  bars, 40, 42–43, 304–312
  commands displayed in gray, 42
  creating, 304–312
  lists, 87, 90–91, 325
<MENU> (menu list) tag, 87, 90–91, 325
MenuBar class, 304
Menu class, 305, 306–307
Menu() constructor, 305
MenuDemo.html, 309, 312
MenuDemo.java, 309–312
MenuItem() class, 305
MenuItem() constructor, 306
Message parameter, 296
Meta keys, 190
methods. *See also* constructors; methods (listed by name)
  available in the FontMetric object, 149–150
  basic description of, 116–118, 124
  creating multiple, 118
  scope of, 124, 334

methods (listed by name). *See also* methods
accept(), 263
action(), 282–283, 290, 296, 308, 314
addItem(), 280
add(), 268, 273
addPoint(), 160
brighter(), 154
bytesWidth(), 149–150
charsWidth(), 149–150
close(), 263
darker(), 154
destroy(), 127, 179
drawArc(), 161
drawImage(), 164, 165
drawLine(), 155
drawPolygon(), 158–159
drawRect(), 155
drawString(), 116, 128, 145–147
equals(), 309
fillPolygon(), 159–160
fillRect(), 156
finals, 124, 334
Font getFont(), 149
getAppletContext(), 252–253
getAudioClip(), 177, 181
getBlue(), 154
getBoundingBox(), 160
getCodeBase(), 138
getColor(), 154
getDescent(), 149
getDocument(), 252
getDocumentBase, 137–138, 164, 177–178
getFont(), 148
getHeight(), 149–150
getHSBColor(), 154
getImage(), 164, 165, 168
getLeading(), 149
getMaxAdvance(), 149
getMaxAscent(), 149
getMaxDescent(), 149
getParameter(), 137, 257
getSelectedItem(), 291
getWidths(), 149
handleEvent(), 290–293
HSBtoRGB(), 154
init(), 127, 137, 179, 181, 257, 271, 281, 296
inside(), 160
KeyDown(), 188–189
KeyUp(), 189
length(), 137
linkNewDestination(), 257
loop(), 178
mouseDown(), 195, 199–200, 257
mouseEnter(), 199
mouseExit(), 199
mouseMove(), 198–199
mouseUp(), 195, 257
nestInt(), 182
openStream(), 258
paint(), 116, 146, 170, 206, 257, 301
play(), 178
readLine(), 259
repaint(), 170
resize(), 127, 137, 269
RGBtoHSB(), 154
run(), 169–170
setColor(), 153
setEchoCharacter(), 281
setFont(), 148
setLayout(), 275
setMenuBar(), 304
setSeed(), 182
showDocument(), 252–253, 257
show(), 301–302, 313
showStats(), 294
size(), 150
sleep(), 170
start(), 127, 170, 179, 181
stop(), 127, 170, 178, 181
StringtoString(), 149
stringWidth(), 149–150
MFC (Microsoft Foundation Classes), 108
MGM United Artists Web site, 5, 7
Microsoft. *See also* specific software
licensing of Java to, 34
Setup, 39
Web site, 5, 105
microwave ovens, 109
MIDDLE option, 96, 112
MinimalApplet.html, 112–113
MinimalApplet2.html, 126–127, 142
MinimalApplet.java, 113–119
MinimalApplet2.java, 125–126, 142
MINIMAL.HTM, 72
MiniSig.html, 135–136
minus sign (-), 85, 121, 306
Mitsubishi Electronics, 33–34
modifier keys, 189–190

MoleculeViewer applet, 232–233
monitors, monochrome, 84
monospace font, 78
Mosaic browser, 11, 13–14, 19, 37, 52, 69
mouse, 187, 194–207
dragging, 199–203
movement events, 198–199
and the PainterApplet example, 203–207
mouseDown() event, 195, 200
mouseDown() method, 195, 199–200, 257
MouseDroppings.html, 196, 197–198
MouseDroppings.java, 196–197
mouseEnter() method, 199
mouseExit() method, 199
mouseMove() event, 200
mouseMove() method, 198–199
mouseUp() event, 200
mouseUp() method, 195, 257
MouseYacker.html, 200, 202–203
MouseYacker.java, 200–202
MPEG (Motion Picture Experts Group), 99
MS-DOS, 67. *See also* DOS (Disk Operating System)
multimedia, definition of, 24. *See also* interactivity
multiple inheritance, 28. *See also* inheritance
multiplication operator, 132, 331
multithreading operating systems, 26

name(s)
class, 116, 120
frame, 103, 168
methods with identical, creating, 118
symbolic, for applets, 111
variable, in arrays, 125
NAME parameter, 103, 111, 327
native file formats, 63
navigating
enhancing, with frames, 100
with Go menu commands, 43
with the vertical scrollbar, 42
Navigator Gold, 38
 , 85, 326
NCSA (National Center for Supercomputing Applications)
Mosaic, 13–14, 19, 37, 52
Web site, 13
negation operator, 131, 331
NegativeArraySizeException exception, 250
NervousTest applet, 233–234
nesting
comments, 72
multiple frames, 102
nestInt() method, 182
Net Directory button, 46
Netscape Communications Corporation, 19, 37
sale of Web server software by, 38
Web site, 58, 336
Netscape Galleria, 58
Netscape Navigator browser, 11, 29–30, 291, 295, 314
advantages of, 37–38
the <APPLET> tag and, 110
basic description of, 19–20, 37–60
frames and, 99–100
getting the latest version of, 38
header information and, 69
installation of, 39–40
keyboard shortcuts, 58–59
loading/saving HTML files with, 47–49
logo, 47, 56
modifying preferences with, 54–55
program icon, 39, 40
program options, 47–52
registration, 38, 56–57
setting options with, 53–55
-specific HTML tags, 62, 69–70, 75–76, 85, 88–89, 95, 97, 328
starting, 40
support for table definitions, 79
testing applets with, 119
top-line display, 42–44
viewing HTML source code with, 67–68
Netscape Navigator Gold, 38
Net Search button, 46
networking
displaying new Web pages and, 251–257
error handling and, 245–247
exception handling and, 247–251
opening files at your Web site and, 257–261
overview of, 245–264
sockets and, 261–263
Network Preferences dialog box, 53, 54–55
new keyword, 125
New Mail Message, 59
new() operator, 182
newsgroups, 21, 38, 335

<i>Newsweek</i>, 9
NeXT, 13, 23
<NOBR> (NO BReak) tag, 75
non-breaking spaces, 85
NORESIZE parameter, 103
NOSHADE parameter, 76
NoSuchMethodException exception, 250
Notepad, 109
Ñ, 86, 326
NullPointerException exception, 250
NumberFormatException exception, 250
numbers
  Arabic, 66
  credit card, transmitting, 57
  decimal, 121
  hexadecimal, 71, 121
  numbered lists, 66, 87, 89–90
  numerical object types, 120–121
  octal, 121
  pseudo-random, 181–182
NumbPoints parameter, 159

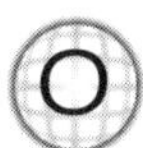

Ó, 86, 326
Oak operating system, 16, 17
object(s). *See also* OOP (object-oriented programming)
  alphabetic, 122–123
  definition of, 9, 108
  numerical, 120–121
  types, 120–123
Object class, 109
Object Pascal, 108
Object parameter, 282, 283, 309
Ô, 86, 326
octal numbers, 121
Ò, 86, 326
<OL> (ordered list) tag, 87, 89–90, 325
On Security option, 56, 57
OOP (object-oriented programming), 10, 28. *See also* objects
  animation and, 170–173
  import commands and, 114–115
  overview of, 107–144
Open button, 44–45
Open dialog box, 48
opening files, 74, 119
  in Netscape, 48, 59
  at your Web site, 257–261
Open Location, 44–45, 48, 59
Open Location dialog box, 44–45
openStream() method, 258
operator(s)
  addition, 132, 331
  decrement, 131, 331
  division, 132, 331
  increment, 131, 331
  instanceof, 282, 290
  mathematical, 131–132, 331
  multiplication, 132, 331
  negation, 131, 331
  new(), 182
  overloading, definition of, 118
  relational, 128, 331
  subtraction, 132, 331
  unary, 131, 331
Options menu, 42, 44, 53–54, 127
ordered (numbered) lists, 66, 87, 89–90
Õ, 86, 326
Ö, 86, 326

<P> (paragraph) tag, 73–74, 323
PageMaker, 61, 147
paint() method, 116, 146, 170, 206, 257, 301
PainterApplet.html, 203, 206
PainterApplet.java, 203–206
paper envelope icon, 47
Paradox for Windows, 276
paragraph formatting tags, 73–75, 323
<PARAM> (parameter information) tag, 111, 136, 327
parameters, passing, to an applet, 134–138
parentheses, 132
Pascal, 26, 163
password text fields, 281
Paste from clipboard (command), 59
PAUSE parameter, 171
PAUSES parameter, 171
PCM (pulse code modulation), 175
<i>PC Magazine</i>, 16
PDAs (personal digital assistants), 16, 109
percent sign (%), 76
PgDown key, 42, 59, 191
PgUp key, 42, 59, 191
pixel(s), 102, 155, 199, 273
  specifying applet size in, 111
  specifying horizontal rule width in, 76–77

PLAIN attribute, 148
platform independence, 23–24, 26–27
play() method, 178
PlaySound.html, 180–181
PlaySound.java, 179–180
Playstation, 188
plug-ins, support for, 20
plus sign (+), 85, 121
Point class, 196
Polygon class, 159–160
polygons, 158–160
POSITIONS parameter, 171
Postscript, 61
pound sign (#), 94
POV (persistence of vision), 167
<PRE> (pre-formatted text) tag, 78–82, 323
Premia Systems, 109
preview area, in Netscape, 40–42
Print button, 44–45
Print dialog box, 50
printing
  with Netscape, 42, 45, 50
  previewing before, 45
private methods, 124, 334
Prodigy, 34
productivity tools, basic description of, 29, 33
program control statements, 333
Program Manager, 39, 40
progress bar. *See* status bar
Properties... option, 51
property sheets, 274
protected methods, 124, 334
protocols, 11–12, 21–23
  FTP (File Transfer Protocol), 21, 28, 38
  HTTP (hypertext transfer protocol), 12, 21–22, 28, 70, 96
  information about, in the Document Info window, 48
  TCP/IP (Transmission Control Protocol/ Internet Protocol), 21, 23, 28, 40, 252, 263
public functions, 116
public key encryption, 28
public keyword, 116
public methods, 124, 334
pulldown list boxes, 280

quick keys, 305
QuickTime for Windows (QTW), 99
", 85, 326
quotes
  " (double quotes), 85, 122–123, 136–137, 331
  ' (single quotes), 123, 331

radio, citizens band (CB), 9
radio buttons, 267–268, 279–280, 283
Random class, 182
RandomSound.html, 182, 185
RandomSound.java, 183–184
readLine() method, 259
readme.txt, 38
rectangles, 155–158, 203–207
registration, Netscape, 38, 56–57
relational operators, 128, 331
Release Notes, 56, 57
Reload action, 44, 59
repaint() method, 170
REPEAT parameter, 171
resize() method, 127, 137, 269
resizing. *See* sizing
RGBtoHSB() method, 154
RGB values, 71, 95, 154
Right arrow key, 191
RIGHT keyword, 77
RIGHT option, 112
Ritchie, Dennis, 113, 119
Rolling Stones Web site, 8, 31
Roman numerals, 66, 90
rows, 82, 102, 270–272, 328
Run dialog box, 39
run() method, 169–170
run-time class verification, 27–28
RuntimeException exception, 250

<SAMP> (strong emphasis) tag, 83, 324
Saturn game, 188
Sausage Systems Web site, 105
saving
  files with Netscape, 42, 47–49, 59
  Netscape settings, 53
scrollbar, 42, 103, 267–268, 288–289
Scrollbar class, 288
ScrollingImages applet, 235–236
SCROLLING parameter, 103

security, 24, 27–28, 38
  for financial transactions, 28, 57
  the key icon and, 47, 57
  Netscape and, 47, 48, 53–54, 56–57
  sockets and, 261
SecurityException exception, 250
Security Preferences dialog box, 53, 54, 56
Sega, 188
Select All, 59
self-extracting files, 38
semicolon (;), 132–133, 139
SeparateWindowDemo.html, 302, 303
SeparateWindowDemo.java, 302–303
separator bars, 306
ServerSocket class, 263
setColor() method, 153
setEchoCharacter() method, 281
setFont() method, 148
setLayout() method, 275
setMenuBar() method, 304
setSeed() method, 182
set-top boxes, 14–17, 29, 109
setup. *See also* installation
  Netscape, 39–40
  printer, in Netscape, 50
Setup (Microsoft), 39
SGML (Standard Generalized Markup Language), 62, 105
Shakespeare Web site, 8
shapes
  circles/circular shapes, 160–161, 203–207
  polygons, 158–160
  rectangles, 155–158, 203–207
  squares, 155–158
  triangles, 159
Shift key, 189
ShockWave (Macromedia), 20
short data type, 120–121, 330
Show Directory Buttons, 53
showDocument() method, 252–253, 257
Show Java Console, 53, 127
Show Location, 53
show() method, 301–302, 313
showStats() method, 294
Show Toolbar, 53
signatures, 134–138
Silicon Graphics, 19
SimpleGraph applet, 236–237
single inheritance, 28. *See also* inheritance
single quotes ('), 123, 331
size() method, 150
SIZE parameter, 76, 77
sizing
  applets, 127, 137, 269
  frames, 102–3
  images, 97
  windows, 48
slashes
  \ (backslash), 123, 331
  / (forward slash), 22, 67, 114, 140
sleep() method, 170
Smalltalk, 108
SND format, 98–99
Socket class, 262
sockets, 261–263
Softquad Systems, 105
Software button, 46
software distribution, 24, 28–29
Software option, 56, 57
Solaris, 18–19, 26
Sonic Foundry, 176
Sony, 188
sound
  animation and, 171–172
  file formats, 98–99, 175–177
  helper applications and, 25, 176
  HTML tags for, 98–99, 176
  objects, working with, 176–179
  playing, 179–185
  sampling, 175
  working with, overview of, 175–186
Sound Blaster sound cards, 175
Sound Forge for Windows, 176
SOUNDSOURCE parameter, 172
SOUNDS parameter, 172
SOUNDTRACK parameter, 172
source code
  file extensions for, 110
  using pre-formatted text for, 78–82
  viewing HTML, with browsers, 67–68
SPARC platforms, 18
SpreadSheet applet, 237–238
Spry Mosaic browser, 11
square brackets ([]), 168
Square class, 117
squares, 155–158. *See also* rectangles
SRC parameter, 96, 103
StandardControlsDemo.html, 286
StandardControlsDemo.java, 283–285
Stanford University, 15

Star Seven (*7), 16
STARTIMAGE parameter, 171
starting Netscape, 40
start() method, 127, 170, 179, 181
STARTUP parameter, 171
static methods, 124, 334
status bar, 38, 294
status line, 294–298
Stop button, 44, 45
stop() method, 127, 170, 178, 181
String class, 123
StringIndexOutOfBoundsException
exception, 250
StringtoString() method, 149
stringWidth() method, 149–150
structural commands, 66, 68–72, 323
subclasses, definition of, 109
subtraction operator, 132, 331
Sun Microsystems, 14–18, 245
AU format, 98–99, 176, 177
licensing of Java by, 19, 34
Web site, 5
superclasses, definition of, 109
super keyword, 301
switches, command line, 139
switch statements, 133–134, 332–333
Switzerland, 12
Symantec Corporation, 5, 34, 142–143, 335
Symantec Web site, 5, 142–143, 335
symbols
& (ampersand), 85, 305, 306, 309
* (asterisk), 102, 103, 114–115, 140
\ (backslash), 123, 331
: (colon), 22, 134
{} (curly brackets), 116, 128, 133
$ (dollar sign), 120
" (double quotes), 85, 122–123, 136–137, 331
... (ellipsis), 42
! (exclamation point), 323
/ (forward slash), 22, 67, 114, 140
> (greater-than sign), 67, 84–85, 104
< (less-than sign), 67, 84–85, 104
- (minus sign), 85, 121, 306
' ' (non-breaking space), 85
() (parentheses), 132
% (percent sign), 76
+ (plus sign), 85, 121
# (pound sign), 94
; (semicolon), 132–133, 139
' (single quotes), 123, 331
[] (square brackets), 168
_ (underscore character), 120
system-independence, 65

tab character, 122–123, 330
table of contents, 100
<TABLE> (table definition) tag, 79–82, 328
tags (listed by name)
<A> (anchor) tag, 93–95, 97–99, 324–325
<ADDRESS> (address information) tag, 82, 324
<APP> (applet tag), 113
<APPLET> (applet) tag, 110–113, 127, 269, 326–327
<B> (boldface) tag, 83, 324
<BASEFONT> (font size) tag, 85, 328
<BLINK> (blinking text) tag, 84, 328
<BLOCKQUOTE> (indent quote) tag, 82, 324
<BODY> (body) tag, 70–71, 73, 95, 97–98, 100, 323, 328

 (line break) tag, 74–75, 323
<CENTER> (center text) tag, 85, 328
<CITE> (citation) tag, 82, 324
<CODE> (computer code) tag, 82, 324
<DD> (glossary definition) tag, 91, 325
<DFN> (defined word) tag, 83, 324
<DIR> (directory list) tag, 87, 90–91, 325
<DL> (glossary list) tag, 87, 91–92, 325
<DT> (definition text) tag, 325
<EM> (emphasis) tag, 83, 324
<FRAME> (frame) tag, 100–102, 103
<FRAMESET> (frameset) tag, 100–102
<H1...H6> (heading) tags, 77–78, 323
<HEAD> (header) tag, 69–70, 73, 323
<HR> (horizontal rule) tag, 75–77, 323
<HTML> tag, 67, 68–69, 73, 323
<I> (italics) tag, 83, 324
<IMG> (image) tag, 96–97, 165, 325
<KDB> (keyboard entry) tag, 83, 324
<LI> (list item) tag, 87, 88–89
<MENU> (menu list) tag, 87, 90–91, 325
<NOBR> (NO BReak) tag, 75
<OL> (ordered list) tag, 87, 89–90, 325
<P> (paragraph) tag, 73–74, 323
<PARAM> (parameter information) tag, 111, 136, 327
<PRE> (pre-formatted text) tag, 78–82, 323
<SAMP> (strong emphasis) tag, 83, 324
<TABLE> (table definition) tag, 79–82, 328

<TD> (table data) tag, 82
<TH> (table header) tag, 82
<TITLE> (title) tag, 69, 73
<TR> (row definition) tag, 80, 82
<UL> (unordered list) tag, 87–89, 325
<VAR> (variable information) tag, 83, 324
<WBR> (Word BReak) tag, 75
target data member, 282
target parameter, 256
TCP/IP (Transmission Control Protocol/ Internet Protocol), 28, 252, 263
basic description of, 21
cross-platform compatibility and, 23
drivers, enabling, 40
<TD> (table data) tag, 82
Technical Excellence award, 16
technical support, accessing, 57
television
commercials, background music in, 179
frame rates used by, 167
set-top boxes, 14–17, 29, 109
templates
classes as, 108
HTML, 72, 105
TestApp class, 141
TestFont.html, 152
TestFont.java, 150–151
testing, 109–110, 119
font displays, 150–152
for values/results from function calls, 129–130
variables, in switch statements, 134
Web pages with the appletviewer tool, 139
text, 70–71, 95, 98. *See also* fonts
areas, 267–268, 289
blinking, 84, 216–217, 328
caption, 81
centering, 85
color of, 71
displaying, overview of, 145–154
fields, 267–268, 280–281, 283
formatting, with spaces, 73
-only browsers, 96, 111
word wrap and, 79
TextArea() constructor, 289
TextField() constructor, 281
TEXT parameter, 70–71, 95, 98, 256, 296
TEXTTOP option, 112
<TH> (table header) tag, 82
thread(s)
definition of, 169
multithreaded code and, 169–170
Thread class, 169–170
throw keyword, 248, 334
Tic-tac-toe game, 31, 239–240
time out, definition of, 44
Time-Warner, 17
<TITLE> (title) tag, 69, 73
toolbar, 38, 40, 42, 44–45, 54
TOP option, 112
<TR> (row definition) tag, 80, 82
triangles, displaying, 159
true keyword, 120
try keyword, 247–248, 250–251, 334
TumblingDuke applet, 240–241
Turtle Beach, 175
txt variable, 137
TYPE parameter, 89

Ú, 86, 326
Û, 86, 326
Ù, 86, 326
<UL> (unordered list) tag, 87–89, 325
unary operators, 131, 331
UnderConstruction applet, 241–242
underlining, 84
underscore character (_), 120
Undo action, 59
Unicode character set, 122–123, 330
UNIX, 13, 190, 261–262, 266
Netscape and, 38
platform independence and, 26–27
sound formats and, 99, 176
URL formats and, 23
up arrow key, 59, 191
Up radio button, 45
URLs (Uniform Resource Locators). *See also* bookmarks; history lists
URL class
basic description of, 21–23
checking, 47
entering new, using the Open button, 44–45
using frames to specify, 103
host names in, 21–22, 262
hyperlink formatting tags and, 93–95
for image files, 96
in the Netscape location box, 40, 45–47
sockets and, 262
of Web pages, returning, 137–138, 164, 177–178, 252
URL class, 138, 251–252, 258

Usenet newsgroups, 21. *See also* newsgroups
user interface controls, 265–298
  choosing locations for, 269–276
  enhanced control events and, 290–293
  enhanced controls, 286–289
  layout managers and, 268–276
  sample applets for, 283–286
  standard controls, 276–281
  the status line and, 294–298
Ü, 86, 326

<VAR> (variable information) tag, 83, 324
VCRs (video-cassette recorders), 33
video, 187–188. *See also* animation; interactivity
  file formats, 99–100
  helper applications and, 25
  HTML tags for, 99–104
VIDEO.AVI, 99
Video for Windows (VfW), 99
ViewFile.html, 259, 261
ViewFile.java, 259–261
ViewFile.txt, 259, 261
viewing
  bookmarks, 59
  digital video, 99–104
  history lists, 59
  HTML source code, 48, 67–68
  image layout, 48
  next/previous line, 59
  next/previous page, 42, 59
  Web pages, with the Netscape preview area, 40–42
View menu, 42, 48–49, 68
viruses, 27
Visual Basic, 10, 29, 276
VRML (Virtual Reality Modeling Language), 20
VSPACE parameter, 112, 327

wallpaper, 97–98. *See also* backgrounds
Wall Street Journal Web site, 5–6
warning messages, turning off, 139
WAV format, 176
<WBR> (Word BReak) tag, 75
Web browsers. *See also* Netscape Navigator browser
  autoflowing and, 73
  basic description of, 11
  history of, 13–14
  HotJava, 17–18, 110, 113
  Internet Explorer, 11, 63–64
  Mosaic, 11, 13–14, 19, 37, 52, 69
  Spry Mosaic, 11
  text-only browsers, 96, 111
  viewing source code with, 67–68
  WebRunner, 17
Web pages
  applets you can use in, examples of, 209–244
  displaying new, networking and, 251–257
  loading, aborting, 45, 59
  returning URLs of, 137–138, 164, 177–178, 252
  saving, 48, 59
  viewing, 40–42
WebRunner browser, 17
Web servers, basic description of, 11
Web sites
  BMW Web site, 5, 7
  Borland Web site, 5, 336
  CERN Web site, 12
  CNN Web site, 5–6
  Compaq Web site, 5
  FedEx Web site, 14–15
  Hewlett-Packard Web site, 5
  IBM Web site, 5
  IDG Books Web site, 22
  Java Web site, 10, 118, 335–336
  MGM United Artists Web site, 5, 7
  Microsoft Web site, 5, 105
  NCSA Web site, 13
  Netscape Web site, 58, 336
  Rolling Stones Web site, 8, 31
  Sausage Systems Web site, 105
  Shakespeare Web site, 8
  Sun Microsystems Web site, 5
  Symantec Web site, 5, 142–143, 335
  Wall Street Journal Web site, 5–6
What's Cool option, 43, 46, 58
What's New option, 43, 46, 58
while keyword, 132–133
while loops, 132, 259
while statements, 132–133, 332
whitespace, 78, 81. *See* pre-formatted text
WIDTH parameter, 76–77, 79, 111, 256, 327
Window menu, 41–42, 50

windows. *See also* frames
  creating, with the AWT, 299–303
  resizing, 48
Windows (Microsoft), 13, 23, 99, 108. *See also* Windows 3.*x*; Windows 95; Windows NT
  native file format, 63
  Netscape and, 19, 38, 40, 51
  sound and, 175–176
Windows 3.*x*, 19, 26, 38
Windows 95, 18, 21, 26, 64
  Internet Shortcut icons, 51
  long-filename support, 67, 110
  Netscape and, 19, 38, 40, 51
Windows NT, 18, 23, 26
  long-filename support, 67, 110
  Netscape and, 19, 38, 40
  TCP/IP and, 21
Windows Sockets (WinSock), 21, 262
WireFrame, 242–244, 257
Word for Windows, 105
WordPerfect, 63
WordStar, 194
word wrap, 79
World Wide Web. *See also* Web browsers; Web pages
  access agents, 29, 32–33
  basic description of, 11–12
  demographics, 9
  history of, 12–14

Xerox, 122
X Windows, 266

Ý, 86, 326

ZapfDingBats font, 148

IDG BOOKS WORLDWIDE, INC. END-USER LICENSE AGREEMENT

Read This. You should carefully read these terms and conditions before opening the software packet(s) included with this book ("Book"). This is a license agreement ("Agreement") between you and IDG Books Worldwide, Inc. ("IDGB"). By opening the accompanying software packet(s), you acknowledge that you have read and accept the following terms and conditions. If you do not agree and do not want to be bound by such terms and conditions, promptly return the Book and the unopened software packet(s) to the place you obtained them for a full refund.

License Grant. IDGB grants to you (either an individual or entity) a nonexclusive license to use one copy of the enclosed software program(s) (collectively, the "Software") solely for your own personal or business purposes on a single computer (whether a standard computer or a workstation component of a multiuser network). The Software is in use on a computer when it is loaded into temporary memory (i.e., RAM) or installed into permanent memory (e.g., hard disk, CD-ROM, or other storage device). IDGB reserves all rights not expressly granted herein.

Ownership. IDGB is the owner of all right, title, and interest, including copyright, in and to the compilation of the Software recorded on the disk(s)/CD-ROM. Copyright to the individual programs on the disk(s)/CD-ROM is owned by the author or other authorized copyright owner of each program. Ownership of the Software and all proprietary rights relating thereto remain with IDGB and its licensors.

Restrictions on Use and Transfer.

You may only (i) make one copy of the Software for backup or archival purposes, or (ii) transfer the Software to a single hard disk, provided that you keep the original for backup or archival purposes. You may not (i) rent or lease the Software, (ii) copy or reproduce the Software through a LAN or other network system or through any computer subscriber system or bulletin-board system, or (iii) modify, adapt, or create derivative works based on the Software.

You may not reverse engineer, decompile, or disassemble the Software. You may transfer the Software and user documentation on a permanent basis, provided that the transferee agrees to accept the terms and conditions of this Agreement and you retain no copies. If the Software is an update or has been updated, any transfer must include the most recent update and all prior versions.

Restrictions on Use of Individual Programs. You must follow the individual requirements and restrictions detailed for each individual program. These limitations are contained in the individual license agreements recorded on the disk(s)/CD-ROM. These restrictions include a requirement that after using the program for the period of time specified in its text, the user must pay a registration fee or discontinue use. By opening the Software packet(s), you will be agreeing to abide by the licenses and restrictions for these individual programs. None of the material on this disk(s) or listed in this Book may ever be distributed, in original or modified form, for commercial purposes.

Limited Warranty.

IDGB warrants that the Software and disk(s)/CD-ROM are free from defects in materials and workmanship under normal use for a period of sixty (60) days from the date of purchase of this Book. If IDGB receives notification within the warranty period of defects in materials or workmanship, IDGB will replace the defective disk(s)/CD-ROM.

IDGB AND THE AUTHOR OF THE BOOK DISCLAIM ALL OTHER WARRANTIES, EXPRESS OR IMPLIED, INCLUDING WITHOUT LIMITATION IMPLIED WARRANTIES OF MERCHANTABILITY AND FITNESS FOR A PARTICULAR PURPOSE, WITH RESPECT TO THE SOFTWARE, THE PROGRAMS, THE SOURCE CODE CONTAINED THEREIN, AND/OR THE TECHNIQUES DESCRIBED IN THIS BOOK. IDGB DOES NOT WARRANT THAT THE FUNCTIONS CONTAINED IN THE SOFTWARE WILL MEET YOUR REQUIREMENTS OR THAT THE OPERATION OF THE SOFTWARE WILL BE ERROR FREE.

This limited warranty gives you specific legal rights, and you may have other rights which vary from jurisdiction to jurisdiction.

Remedies.

IDGB's entire liability and your exclusive remedy for defects in materials and workmanship shall be limited to replacement of the Software, which is returned to IDGB at the address set forth below with a copy of your receipt. This Limited Warranty is void if failure of the Software has resulted from accident, abuse, or misapplication. Any replacement Software will be warranted for the remainder of the original warranty period or thirty (30) days, whichever is longer.

In no event shall IDGB or the author be liable for any damages whatsoever (including without limitation damages for loss of business profits, business interruption, loss of business information, or any other pecuniary loss) arising out of the use of or inability to use the Book or the Software, even if IDGB has been advised of the possibility of such damages.

Because some jurisdictions do not allow the exclusion or limitation of liability for consequential or incidental damages, the above limitation or exclusion may not apply to you.

U.S. Government Restricted Rights. Use, duplication, or disclosure of the Software by the U.S. Government is subject to restrictions stated in paragraph (c) (1) (ii) of the Rights in Technical Data and Computer Software clause of DFARS 252.227-7013, and in subparagraphs (a) through (d) of the Commercial Computer—Restricted Rights clause at FAR 52.227-19, and in similar clauses in the NASA FAR supplement, when applicable.

General. This Agreement constitutes the entire understanding of the parties, and revokes and supersedes all prior agreements, oral or written, between them and may not be modified or amended except in writing signed by both parties hereto which specifically refers to this Agreement. This Agreement shall take precedence over any other documents that may be in conflict herewith. If any one or more provisions contained in this Agreement are held by any court or tribunal to be invalid, illegal, or otherwise unenforceable, each and every other provision shall remain in full force and effect.

Installation instructions

1. This CD-ROM is AutoPlay-enabled. When you insert it into the CD-ROM drive on your computer running Windows 95, a startup application will begin. It is meant as a shell and a starting point that will make it easier to access the software on the CD. You can access all components on the CD without this program.

2. The Java Developers Kit (JDK) is provided compliments of Sun Microsystems. The latest information about Java can be found at Sun's Web site, http://www.javasoft.com. The filename on the CD-ROM is JDK-1_~1 EXE. If you don't use the START application, you should rename it to JDK-1_0_1-WIN32-X86.EXE on your hard disk.

3. A sample issue of *JavaWorld* has been included on the CD-ROM. Because the files included with *JavaWorld* use long filenames, and CD-ROMs do not support long filenames, the sample issue of *JavaWorld* is in ZIP format, and it must be uncompressed on your hard drive.

   Obviously this can take up quite a bit of hard disk space. If you prefer to access JavaWorld directly, visit their Web site at http://www.javaworld.com.

4. The sample source code is included in the BOOKDISC subdirectory. Again, because CD-ROMs do not support long filenames, a batch file named LFN.BAT is included, which you can use to rename the files once they have been copied to your hard drive.

5. Thank you for the purchase of this book. We hope you enjoy it.

IDG BOOKS WORLDWIDE REGISTRATION CARD

RETURN THIS
REGISTRATION CARD
FOR FREE CATALOG

Title of this book: Creating Cool™ Web Applets with Java®

My overall rating of this book: ❑ Very good [1] ❑ Good [2] ❑ Satisfactory [3] ❑ Fair [4] ❑ Poor [5]

How I first heard about this book:

❑ Found in bookstore; name: [6] ________ ❑ Book review: [7] ________

❑ Advertisement: [8] ________ ❑ Catalog: [9] ________

❑ Word of mouth; heard about book from friend, co-worker, etc.: [10] ________ ❑ Other: [11] ________

What I liked most about this book: ________

What I would change, add, delete, etc., in future editions of this book: ________

Other comments: ________

Number of computer books I purchase in a year: ❑ 1 [12] ❑ 2-5 [13] ❑ 6-10 [14] ❑ More than 10 [15]

I would characterize my computer skills as: ❑ Beginner [16] ❑ Intermediate [17] ❑ Advanced [18] ❑ Professional [19]

I use ❑ DOS [20] ❑ Windows [21] ❑ OS/2 [22] ❑ Unix [23] ❑ Macintosh [24] ❑ Other: [25] ________ (please specify)

I would be interested in new books on the following subjects:
(please check all that apply, and use the spaces provided to identify specific software)

❑ Word processing: [26] ________ ❑ Spreadsheets: [27] ________

❑ Data bases: [28] ________ ❑ Desktop publishing: [29] ________

❑ File Utilities: [30] ________ ❑ Money management: [31] ________

❑ Networking: [32] ________ ❑ Programming languages: [33] ________

❑ Other: [34] ________

I use a PC at (please check all that apply): ❑ home [35] ❑ work [36] ❑ school [37] ❑ other: [38] ________

The disks I prefer to use are ❑ 5.25 [39] ❑ 3.5 [40] ❑ other: [41] ________

I have a CD ROM: ❑ yes [42] ❑ no [43]

I plan to buy or upgrade computer hardware this year: ❑ yes [44] ❑ no [45]

I plan to buy or upgrade computer software this year: ❑ yes [46] ❑ no [47]

Name: ________ Business title: [48] ________ Type of Business: [49] ________

Address (❑ home [50] ❑ work [51]/Company name: ________)

Street/Suite# ________

City [52]/State [53]/Zipcode [54]: ________ Country [55] ________

❑ **I liked this book!** You may quote me by name in future IDG Books Worldwide promotional materials.

My daytime phone number is ________

IDG BOOKS
THE WORLD OF COMPUTER KNOWLEDGE

Please keep me informed about IDG's World of Computer Knowledge. Send me the latest IDG Books catalog.

NO POSTAGE
NECESSARY
IF MAILED
IN THE
UNITED STATES

BUSINESS REPLY MAIL

FIRST CLASS MAIL PERMIT NO. 2605 FOSTER CITY, CALIFORNIA

IDG Books Worldwide
919 E Hillsdale Blvd, STE 400
Foster City, CA 94404-9691